T*SQ Transgender Studies Quarterly

Volume 4 ★ Numbers 3–4 ★ November 2017

Transpsychoanalytics

Edited by Sheila L. Cavanagh

T0335291

STATEMENTS

REPORT

General Editors' Introduction

SUSAN STRYKER and PAISLEY CURRAH

Transgender studies has, generally speaking, paid more attention (albeit critical attention) to sexological than psychoanalytic schools of thought. Pioneering, openly homosexual sexologist Magnus Hirschfeld—founder of the Scientific Humanitarian Committee in 1897 that sought to secure the rights of sexual minorities, author of the early and influential casebook *Die Transvestiten* (1910), and instrumentally useful medical ally for trans people seeking access to genital surgery, hormone therapy, name change, and legal recognition of their self-understood gender identity—is accorded the status of sympathetic fellow traveler in trans circles. Sigmund Freud? Not so much. This is a shame, because psychoanalysis offers exciting—and underdeveloped—potentials for trans studies.

Hirschfeld had actually been a founding member in 1908 of Berlin's Psychoanalytic Association, but he broke with psychoanalysis in 1911 after a very public three-way spat between him, Freud and Carl Jung. Much of the difficulty between these three "Einsteins of sex" was personal (some of it revolving around homosexuality and homophobia), but it also involved genuine differences in theoretical and practical understandings of the roots and motivations of human sexuality. Hirschfeld tended toward a biologistic concept of sexuality, while the Freudians and others who retained a psychoanalytic perspective moved toward theories of unconscious drives and identifications whose structures and processes needed to be understood through language, history, culture, and embodied phenomenological experience, and these were incapable of being explained by biology alone.

Psychoanalysis ranks alongside Darwinian theories of evolution and Marxian critiques of political economy as a foundational framework for modern Western secular thought, whether or not one embraces those rubrics in any formal or orthodox fashion. While psychiatric power as a social institution has been resisted on many fronts, structuralist, poststructuralist, postcolonial, antiracist,

TSQ: Transgender Studies Quarterly ★ Volume 4, Numbers 3–4 ★ November 2017 **323**
DOI 10.1215/23289252-4189856 © 2017 Duke University Press

feminist, and queer versions of psychoanalytic theory have nevertheless offered trenchant critiques of the dominant forms of heteropatriarchal and heterosexist culture. The contribution of psychoanalysis to the investigation of trans topics has been more limited, however, owing no doubt to a long history of interpreting transgender phenomena as psychopathological, despite the affinity trans cultural studies might be expected to have with psychoanalytic theory's attunement to the cultural domain.

And yet, as Sheila Cavanagh and the contributors to this remarkable collection of articles, essays, reports, and reviews make abundantly clear, psychoanalytic perspectives are not intrinsically hostile to transgender modes of being in the world. They can offer critical insight into the viability of a transgender sense of self and help to ameliorate individual psychical suffering. Admittedly, opening psychoanalytic theory up in ways that make it useful for living a transgender life requires a bit of revisionism, but what makes the works selected, edited, and contextualized by Cavanagh for this issue of *TSQ: Transgender Studies Quarterly* so exciting is that they advance that revisionist project quite powerfully, along numerous lines.

Just as significant, however, if not more so, than the demonstrable usefulness of psychoanalysis for insight into transgender existence, is the usefulness of transgender and transsexual ways of being for revitalizing psychoanalysis itself. What Cavanagh calls "transpsychoanalytics" offers a powerful intervention into conventional psychoanalytic theory. As several of the contributors to this issue point out, confronting the quotidian existence of trans people who are no more or less neurotic or psychotic than cisgender people, and just as mentally healthy, necessitates a profound reevaluation of core psychoanalytic concepts and interpretive traditions, including the concept of sex itself. In the oft-quoted aphorism of Lacanian analyst Patricia Gherovici, "Psychoanalysis needs a sex change." The work in this issue of *TSQ*, as well as the contributors' work elsewhere, along with the work of many other trans-affirming clinicians and theorists, is making that psychoanalytic sex change a reality.

Psychoanalytic theory is not everyone's cup of tea. Its foundational assumptions are not universally embraced, and it deploys a specialist vocabulary that some don't have the patience or the inclination to learn. But psychoanalysis nevertheless remains one of the most powerful heuristics available for interpreting, understanding, and living with the affective dimensions of our individual and collective lives, and of the creative and artistic works that impart such meaning to those lives. The capacity of transgender insight to transform the theory and practice of psychoanalysis is one of the surest signs yet that transgender studies, its methods abstracted from living trans lives, has become a vital interdisciplinary undertaking for making and remaking our contemporary social worlds.

Susan Stryker is associate professor of gender and women's studies and director of the Institute for LGBT Studies at the University of Arizona and general coeditor of *TSQ: Transgender Studies Quarterly*.

Paisley Currah is professor of political science and women's and gender studies at Brooklyn College and the Graduate Center of the City University of New York and general coeditor of *TSQ: Transgender Studies Quarterly*.

Transpsychoanalytics

SHEILA L. CAVANAGH

Psychoanalysis needs a sex change.
—Patricia Gherovici, *Please Select Your Gender*

It could be argued that analytic discourse is inherently transsexual.
—Oren Gozlan, *Transsexuality and the Art of Transitioning: A Lacanian Approach*

This issue of *TSQ: Transgender Studies Quarterly* profiles the transgender turn in psychoanalytic theory, and the development of what I refer to as "trans-psychoanalytics." This transition has not been easy because psychoanalytic theorists and analysts have often represented trans* subjectivity and gender variance as pathological. Sigmund Freud's early writing on the "masculinity complex" and "penis envy," for example, have been used to render female masculinities (Halberstam 1998) deviant. Jacques Lacan's writing on "transsexualist jouissance" has been used to substantiate claims of trans* mental illness, and contemporary Lacanian psychoanalysts over rely on Catherine Millot's (1989) *Horsexe*, a book that establishes a metonymic link between trans* feminine subjects and psychosis (Adams 2013; Chiland 2009; Morel 2011; and Shepherdson 2000). This Lacanian tendency to reduce trans* subjectivity to psychosis is evident in most other psychoanalytic paradigms as well, including Freudian, object relations, relational, Kleinian, and feminist psychoanalytic theory (Caldwell and Keshavan 1991; and Siomopoulos 1974).[1] Despite a great deal of sophisticated psychoanalytic theorizing on psychical life, there has been a dearth of nonpathologizing psychoanalytic writing on trans* subjectivity informed by clinical practice and cultural critique.

This is beginning to change. Original critiques of psychoanalysis by trans* scholars have led to important reassemblages of core psychoanalytic ideas. Moreover, they have challenged understandings of transsexuals as overinvested in

TSQ: Transgender Studies Quarterly ★ Volume 4, Numbers 3–4 ★ November 2017 **326**
DOI 10.1215/23289252-4189865 © 2017 Duke University Press

normative gender binaries (and thus dupes of gender) and as unable to accept the aporias of sexual difference. Jay Prosser (1998a) and Gayle Salamon (2004) were among the first trans* studies scholars to use Freud's writing on the bodily ego to understand trans* embodiments of sex. In Lacanian psychoanalysis, Shanna Carlson (2010), Sheila Cavanagh (2016b and 2016c), Patricia Gherovici (2010), Oren Gozlan (2014), and Patricia Elliot (2001) have not only critiqued the reduction of trans* to pathology but also effectively used psychoanalytic theories to advance a nonpathologizing understanding of trans* identification. In so doing, they have developed new understandings of trans* embodiment, desire, and *jouissance*. Among clinical psychoanalysts of the relational school, who are well represented in the special issue of *Psychoanalytic Dialogues* on "Transgender Subjectivities" guest edited by Virginia Goldner (2011), there is a concerted effort to "distinguish 'psychodynamic' suffering from the trans-phobic 'cultural' suffering caused by stigma, fear and hatred" (154). Adrienne Harris, in her book *Gender as Soft Assembly* (2012), invites us to focus on gender as process as opposed to structure. Her objective is to consider what trans* offers to psychoanalytic thought in terms of "being" and "meaning." Avgi Saketopoulou (2011 and 2014) has written insightfully about "gender trauma" in work with trans* clients. Alessandra Lemma (2013) stresses the role of mirroring and the importance of "being seen" (277) for her trans* clients. Like most relational clinicians critical of transphobia, Lemma considers the impact of transphobia and the importance of "witnessing" transsexualities (in the plural). Compelling work in trans* studies is also happening in feminist psychoanalytic theory influenced by the formative writings of Helene Cixous, Bracha L. Ettinger, Luce Irigaray, Julia Kristeva, and Monique Wittig, among others (Cavanagh 2016b and 2016c; and Salamon 2004). Although trans* studies often ignores feminist psychoanalytic theories understood (often with just cause) to be essentialist and transphobic, multiple more-progressive readings are possible when the feminine is approached as a sexual position, as opposed to a natal female corporeal "truth" fixed by gender or biology.

On Not Treating People like Shit

To exhibit and circumscribe the turn toward a transpsychoanalytics, this issue profiles a range of innovative works that refuse to pathologize trans* subjectivity. Each author psychoanalytically engages the beauty, complexity, and viability of trans* lives. These paradigm-shifting works invite us to understand transsubjectivities as creative ways of being in relation to unconscious sexual difference. They also push psychoanalysis beyond a normative Oedipal and cisgender conceptual frame. To use a term suggested by Franz Kaltenbeck (1992), transsexuality can supply a *belvédère* for the clinic: an open psychical architecture or vantage point that offers a "beautiful view" from which to consider the life of the subject.

In other words, trans∗ subjectivity can tell us something about what Lacanians call "the real"—the unsymbolizable domain of sexual difference. But as the rich assortment of articles and statements included in this issue demonstrate, transpsychoanalytics is not beholden to any one psychoanalytic paradigm or theorist. The strength of transpsychoanalytics is that it cuts across paradigmatic borders and is, unabashedly, hybrid and trans-generative in its reading of desire and subjectivity.

What unites the transpsychoanalytic writings in this collection is a willingness to value trans∗ experience and make it central to the analysis. In so doing, each contributor is committed to expanding the boundaries of existing psychoanalytic concepts and theories guiding clinical work. At the same time, the contributors shift our understandings of what counts as "trans∗ studies" toward greater inclusion of psychoanalytic perspectives on desire, sexuality, embodiment, and subjectivity. For trans∗ studies readers new to psychoanalysis, it may take time to accept the critique of identity built into the psychoanalytic premise. Gender identity—all gender identities—in psychoanalytic terms are defenses against difference as well as a way to frame our desire.

Let us take Lacan's approach as an example. There is no one-to-one correspondence between gender identity, sexual orientation, and sexuated positions in his model. The manifest distinctions between gender identity and sex morphology central to trans∗ studies and feminist theories are radically undone in the Lacanian approach. Moreover, what the English-speaking world calls gender identity is ill equipped to manage what Lacan calls the aporia of sexual difference. More than a few trans∗ analysands have been troubled by their analyst's disinterest in gender identity. Sometimes this is because analysts are resistant to the specific identifications of trans∗ clients, but it is also, for the psychoanalytic clinician, because identity is inherently defensive. While many transpeople are accustomed to having their genders invalidated in social circuits (and this is, of course, a problem in need of redress), there is an equally significant problem to be addressed with respect to the function of *all* gender identifications as defenses against difference. Identities unify ambiguity in normalizing ways, order and regulate the drives, and attempt to protect the subject from anxiety. They inevitably fail. It may seem paradoxical to note that "failure is the measure of recognition" (Butler 2006, x), but let us consider that it is where (and when) we, as subjects, escape the norm that we can be apprehended in our uniqueness.

In Lacanian terms, gender helps us to negotiate a larger problem we have with the real of sexual difference, but it is incorrect to conclude that transgender is thus a way to override sexual difference, as some Lacanians, following Millot (1989), have done. The most recent example is in Slavoj Žižek's controversial talk at the London School of Economics in 2016 (Coffman 2012; Gossett 2016). Contra

Žižek, trans* subjectivity is a viable way to negotiate the impasse of sexual difference. As feminist psychoanalytic theorist Jacqueline Rose (2016) writes in "Who Do You Think You Are?," the "bar of sexual difference is ruthless but that doesn't mean that those who believe they subscribe to its law [i.e., nontrans* subjects] have any more idea of what is going on beneath the surface than the one who submits less willingly [i.e., trans* subjects]" (8). While none of us can evade the question of unconscious sexual difference, it is trans* experience that enables us to think in more profound ways about what that sexual difference consists of. Che Gossett (2016), for example, in their critique of Žižek in the *Los Angeles Review of Books*, reads systems of racialization as structured, in part, through recourse to sexual difference and argues that "Žižek ignores the fact that we can't think the gender binary outside of the context of racial slavery and colonialism within which it was forged. Žižek also leaves unthought the entire scope of trans* studies in general and trans* of color critique in particular."

The pretense of cis-normativity and the concordant presumption of trans-pathology are not only erroneous but, in my view, defenses, used by nontrans-people, against the very difference Žižek, as a Lacanian, understands to be the bedrock of subjectivity. Public discourse surrounding transsexuality is "stalled," as one contributor to this special issue punningly points out, in the toilet. But this inability to think about sexual difference in other ways, in trans* sex specific ways, is psychically invested and bound to painful repetition.[2] This is why psychoanalysis—the famous "talking cure" (Breuer and Freud [1895] 1995) whereby messy, unconscious material can be subject to analysis—is so important. The proverbial "shit" that happens in everyday life must be worked through if it is to become a fertile ground for change.

Psychoanalysts have a lot to say about how shit functions in psychic life. British object relations theory, shaped by the formative work of Sándor Ferencz (1873–1933), Melanie Klein (1882–1960), and Donald Winnicott (1896–1971), among others, is about nothing if not how we come to treat others like shit. Klein, for example, in 1946, theorized "projective identification" as an unconscious psychical process through which we split off a part of our selves and project it onto another person. Projective identification is an object relations defense whereby good and bad objects, feelings, desires, fantasies, etc., are put upon another person. But more than this, projective identification occurs when the subject at whom a projection is directed comes to identify with the affective material projected by another person (Klein 1946).

That projective "disowning" can be understood in terms of abjection, a discarding and devaluing of what one wishes to divorce from the self in order to produce subjective coherence and "purity." In her work on the sociopsychic life of gender, Judith Butler notes that abjection "designates a degraded or cast out status within the terms of sociability" (1993: 242n2). She also explains that through "social abjection, people constituted as Other, or as different, are literally banished to 'zones of inhabitability'" (Butler 1990: 243). Writing about masculinities in literature, Calvin Thomas (2008) contends that "abjection assuages, discharges, or 'gets rid' of a subject's own 'god-awful feeling' of scatontological anxiety by punitively projecting that affect onto a degraded 'other' who is forced to assume the fecal position" (147). The analytic of abjection put forward by Julia Kristeva (1982), which leads her to characterize human excrement as the "most striking example of the interference of the organic with the social" (75), is especially apropos of current public discourse on the presence of transgender people in public toilets. I have used Kristeva's notion of abjection in *Queering Bathrooms* (2010) to understand how the difficulties people have with gender, sexuality, and the body become displaced onto LGBTQ people in public toilets. Identity-based borders, like public toilets, are frantic zones of aggressive projection whereby one person's disavowed difficulties with gender get projected onto others, often in aggressive ways.

Countering transphobia is shitty work, and transpsychoanalytics prompts us to turn the analytic gaze to those institutions, modalities of thought, and actors who, consciously and unconsciously, treat trans* people like shit. The contributors to this issue mine a new transpsychoanalytic field, thereby turning this experiential shit into analytic gold. This is epistemological work of broad relevance to the psychoanalytic project. In what follows, I review the scholarship that undergirds the new transpsychoanalytic approach before offering capsule summaries of the articles included in this issue. Like all reviews, it is selective, and I focus primarily on Lacanian scholarship that intersects with, and seriously engages, trans* cultural studies. This is in part because it is primarily Lacanian-inspired theorists who are now engaging trans* studies in new and progressive ways. It is also because Virginia Goldner (2011) has already admirably showcased relational psychoanalysts who are also doing trans-positive work in clinical settings.

Literature Review

Jay Prosser

Although trans* studies scholarship and psychoanalysis proceed along different theoretical tracks and, perhaps understandably, have different conceptual projects and political agendas, there are significant areas of crossing that are productive points of dialogic entry. One of the first and most important examples of trans* studies engagements with psychoanalysis is to be found in Jay Prosser's (1998a) early work on transsexual embodiment, *Second Skins: The Body Narratives of Transsexuality*. He is, to the best of my knowledge, the first scholar to bring the budding field of trans* cultural studies into conversation with psychoanalysis. Prosser engages important psychoanalytic insights having to do with the bodily ego as theorized by Freud, the mirror-stage as theorized by Lacan, and the skin-ego as theorized by Didier Anzieu. He anticipated the Lacanian concept of the sinthome (one's idiosyncratic manner of identifying with one's psychical symptom, and thus coming to enjoy unconscious life), which Lacan developed in a seminar translated into English only in 2016, by making the materiality of the body, and trans* sex materiality in particular, central to his analysis of transsexual autobiographical narratives and photographic images. He did much to delineate trans* studies as a field of research distinct from queer theory. Prosser is especially critical of the way "transsexuality" figures as a trope in queer writings on gender without due attention to trans* embodiment and corporeality. Prosser thus offers an important critique of queer theory in general, and of Judith Butler's (1990) writing on gender performativity in particular. Notably, Prosser wrote that the "transsexual reveals queer theory's own limits" (6). As Prosser observes, in "transsexuality sex *returns*, the queer repressed, to unsettle its theory of gender performativity" (Prosser 1998a: 27).

Prosser is also critical of the sociocultural constructionist approach. Too often, this approach asks how transsexuality is constructed by way of medicine, technology, and gender role socialization without due attention to the agency of transsexual subjects. He contends that, owing, in part, to the disproportionate focus on the body as an effect of discourse, the "transsexual is read as either a literalization of discourse—in particular the discourse of gender and sexuality—or its deliteralization" (13). As such, transsexuals are, in queer theoretical circles, too often "condemned for reinscribing as referential the primary categories of ontology and the natural that poststructuralism seeks to deconstruct" (13). Prosser is right to be critical of the way transsexuals have been positioned as dupes of gender in some strands of queer, feminist, and psychoanalytic theory. Transpeople are often accused of taking the body "too" seriously or, alternatively, using the body to illustrate the instability of the flesh by transitioning.[3] Either option puts transpeople in an untenable position. Prosser's intention is to carve out a "living space" for transpeople that lies between reinscription (where transpeople are presumed to reify gender polarities) and subversion (where transpeople are presumed to exceed gender polarities). To do so, Prosser finds it necessary to challenge the reduction of bodily materiality, on the one hand, to discourse (Michel Foucault) and, on the other hand, to the play of the signifier (Jacques Lacan). For Prosser, bodily materiality in Foucault, Butler, Lacan, Jacques Derrida, and the other poststructuralists never refers to the flesh (13). He is deeply critical of what he views as a "deliteralization of sex" in Judith Butler's oeuvre, and while he duly notes that his own work in trans* studies is enabled by

Butler's scholarship, perhaps the strongest and most sustained area of critique in *Second Skins* is to be found in his reading of her books *Gender Trouble* and *Bodies That Matter.*

Prosser makes much of the Butlerian distinction between gender as "on," as opposed to "in," the body. In Butler's account, through phantasy we acquire a sex, but this sex is, as the theory goes, gender all along. Turning to Freud, Prosser argues that Butler's analysis depends upon an understanding of the body as a psychical projection that has no "material" weight. He contends that Butler misreads Freud's original notes on the bodily ego, in which Freud wrote that "the ego is first and foremost a bodily ego; it is not merely a surface entity, but is itself the projection of a surface" (Prosser 1998a: 19–20). As Prosser notes, Butler reads the "it" as body rather than as ego. Freud's objective, according to Prosser, was precisely the opposite: to better understand the "bodily origins of the ego, the conception of the ego as product of the body not the body as product of the ego" (41).

Prosser insists that Freud's conception of the bodily ego was an attempt to "materialize the psyche," not to "dematerialize the body" (42). The privileging of surfaces in Butler's account of gender performativity converts what Prosser calls "corporeal interiority" into fantasy. To remedy Butler's error, Prosser sets off in search of what he calls "material reality," a "literality and referentiality" (58) central to the sexed body that he believes queer theory obfuscates. In pursuit of this quest, he turns his attention to theorizing the skin and the flesh of the body through Didier Anzieu's ([1985] 1989) conceptualization of the skin-ego. Anzieu was a Parisian psychoanalyst and philosopher who wrote extensively about Freudian self-analysis, projection, and group psychoanalysis and, after breaking off his own analysis with Lacan, became a staunch critic of Lacanian psychoanalysis. Anzieu took issue with the privileged position Lacan assigned to the signifier relative to sensory and phenomenological systems.

Prosser's engagement with the skin-ego is curious, if not paradoxical, because it returns our attention to the body's surface, and he is at pains to theorize the transsexual trajectory as being authorized by something other than the body's surface as he claims that queer poststructuralists, following Butler, have done. Unfortunately, Prosser does not fully engage the psychic apparatus central to Freud's conceptualization of the bodily ego. He treats the bodily ego as a tool for stressing the significance of materiality while, ultimately, extracting it from phantasy, desire, and the unconscious processes Freud saw as central to it. There is nothing "un-phantasmatic" about the bodily ego, as Prosser would have it be (1998a: 44). For Freud, the bodily ego is a mental projection of a surface and, as such, involves a narcissistic investment in the self as coherent. This coherence is not biologically determined. It is a psychical process. Butler is, in my reading, not wrong to say that Freud's bodily ego anticipates Jacques Lacan's later work on the mirror-stage. Prosser is right to note that for Lacan the "body is the ego's mis-recognition" (42) in the mirror, but he misleads us when he writes that for Freud "the body is the site of the ego's conception" (42). Prosser's (1998a) focus on the skin does not enable him to explain why the transsexual body feels false, hollow, or empty, or why there is a sex specificity to this feeling of bodily alienation. He does offer interesting elaborations of how one can fail to take ownership of the skin, of psychodermatology, bodily agnosia, depersonalization, bodily modification practices, somatic memory, the "missing limb" phenomenon discussed by Oliver Sacks, and other related topics. But Prosser is not able to explain how the specificity of the skin is linked to the specific question of trans* sex embodiment.

Nevertheless, what *Second Skins* offers to a transpsychoanalytics is of utmost importance. Prosser asks us to consider, along with Anzieu, that tactility, the felt sense of the body's contours, as opposed to visuality, how the body looks, plays an important role in sexed embodiment. By asking queer theorists to consider what *is* that part of the body that is not "gender all along" (77), he, and the field of trans* studies more generally, is asking a vital question. Prosser prompts psychoanalysts to account for what might cause a subject to disidentify with a sex assigned at birth. Additionally, Prosser's formulation of fantasies specific to trans* subjects is compelling. The fantasy of "recovering" through sex reassignment surgery (SRS) a body that should have been there all along resonates for many transpeople. Prosser writes affirmatively and engagingly about surgery as a bodily rite, about transsexual desire for coherence (203), about the importance of feeling "at home." In reading transsexuality through narrative and maintaining that the transsexual body is made possible through the narrativization of the transitions of sex (5), Prosser has done much to underscore the importance of trans* experience to the psychoanalytic clinic and to theories of gender, sex, and embodiment more generally.

Gayle Salamon

In her article "The Bodily Ego and the Contested Domain of the Material," Gayle Salamon (2004) offers an impressive review of selected psychoanalytic, queer, and phenomenological approaches to materiality. She is guided by the question: "How does the body manifest a sex?" (95). Like Prosser, Salamon returns to Freud's *Three Essays* ([1905] 1975) to mine psychoanalytic theories of materiality, but she does so with greater attention to the interplay between the body, its visual representation, and discourse. It is this focus on the visual realm of fantasy, as well as Maurice Merleau-Ponty's theorization of the phenomenology of perception (1962), that Salamon finds most helpful for theorizing trans* embodiment. She is more sympathetic than Prosser to Butler's (1993) reading of sex morphology, the imaginary, and erotogenicity through Freud and Lacan. Unlike Prosser, Salamon explains that the Freudian bodily ego is a projection of a surface that must involve the operation of fantasy.

What Salamon finds useful in Freud's writing on sexuality is the fact that the sex of the body does not determine sexual identification. While Freud was committed to developing a universal theory of sexual difference, he could not do it because the so-called "fact" of biology was, for him, muddied by an ever-present awareness of "hermaphroditism, both psychologically and biologically" (Salamon 2004: 102). Far from regarding hermaphroditism as "abnormal," Freud read it as an indicator of a universal inclination toward bisexuality. This universal bisexuality was, for Freud, following Wilhelm Fleiss (1858–1928), a part of the human condition. From this premise he reasoned that masculinity and femininity cannot be assured by biology. While contemporary readers view hermaphroditism as an intersex condition, it was also, for Freud, a form of sexual inversion.[4]

Like Prosser, Salamon stresses that Freud's concept of the bodily ego is of particular use in thinking transgenderism because it shows that the body of which one has a "felt sense" is not necessarily contiguous with the physical body as it is perceived from the outside, including the relationship between sex identity and genitalia (2004: 96). This is the crucial insight that anchors Salamon's archeological mapping of the psychoanalytic terrain to pinpoint ideas relevant to the materialization of the body. She is particularly interested in the way the erotogenic zones Freud discusses in *Three Essays* confound any stable sense of bodily unity. While Prosser persuasively argues that discourse does not enable us to understand the bodily significance of the ego (and is thus invested in theorizing materiality apart from discourse), Salamon is interested in how, precisely, discourse enables us to "assume a body" that is neither biologically given nor static. Bodies, rather, are characterized by their lability, as opposed to their fixity, in her account. As such, Salamon believes that Prosser's search for a materially grounded body image is a diversion from the more important question having to do with how the body image "allows for a resignification of materiality itself" (117). Salamon concludes that Prosser's commitment to a materialist approach does not enable him to fully actualize psychoanalytic insight relating to gender and sexual difference. She is right to note that we cannot found subjectivity on a "bodily materiality that is ostensibly nondiscursive" and that insofar as Prosser does so, he impossibly "places the subject in a 'domain of radical alterity'" (119) or, in Lacanian terms, the real.

Salamon (2004) finds it necessary to engage Lacanian theory but does so alongside other, more phenomenologically engaged theorists such as Merleau-Ponty and Paul Schilder (1886–1940), a Viennese psychoanalyst and student of Freud. Schilder's *The Image and Appearance of the Human Body* (1950) is, in my view, one of the most understudied texts in body studies, with great resources for trans* studies. It offers a theoretically robust engagement with questions of embodiment linked to, among myriad other topics, depersonalization, transposition, disassociation, psychosomatic integrity, hysteria, psychosomatic symptoms, neurasthenia, pain and masochism, phantom limbs, hypochondria, narcissism, agnosia, and the phenomenology of perception—even erthrophobia (fear of blushing). Schilder's position is that psychoanalysis has "neglected the structure of the schema of the body" (201). He demonstrates that "every desire and libidinous tendency immediately changes the structure of the image of the body and gets its real meaning out of this change in the postural model of the body" (201). More specifically, Schilder argues that we have access to our bodies through what he calls a "body image." This image is a psychically invested internal representation of the body; it is not singular but multiple, and it must be reinforced. This reinforcement comes by way of touch, erotogenicity, affect, and visual and sensory perception. More significantly, when the body image changes, what counts as the materiality of the body concordantly changes with it. Schilder's observations that the "body is certainly not only where the borderline of the body and its clothes are" (211) is certainly consistent with trans* scholarly observations about embodiment.

Although Salamon productively draws upon Schilder's work to underscore the lability of the body, its operation of memory, its sensory systems, nerve impulses, fantasies, and so forth, she is ultimately unsatisfied and suggests that the body image cannot be the only way we attain a sense of materiality. Referring directly to Schilder's discussion of kinesthetic and tactile impressions, Salamon writes, "Without the libidinal investment that can only be routed to the body through the mediating effect of the body image, the stuff of the body is reduced to 'vague material' without shape or form" (112). This critique of Schilder is not entirely accurate. Schilder's reference to "vague material" is specific to a larger discussion about a particular patient he treated who was experiencing psychosomatic symptoms that led the patient to feeling his body outside its material contours. Schilder uses this example not only to illustrate how we "overrate the cohesion of the body" (Schilder 1950: 165) but also to explicate what he actually calls a "*queer* exteriorization of feeling which made him [the patient] feel that parts of his own body were lying in the street" (166; emphasis added). Where Salamon could have made a more significant critique of Schilder of relevance to trans* studies is with the doctor's relative neglect of Freud's writing on sexual difference.

There is little attention in Schilder's work to what Freud calls "sexual difference" except when he discusses patients who, by contemporary standards, would count as transsexual! In Schilder's discussion of the "sociology" of the "body image," he attends to one patient in particular who "plays the part of a woman" (1950: 234). Although Schilder doesn't name this patient "transsexual" (or even "sexual invert"), it is clear from the case description that his "male" client is dealing with a postural model of the body complicated by what Schilder calls a "feminine situation." Far from pathologizing his patient, Schilder uses this case study to illuminate the psychosociality of the bodily image. He writes, "No better instance could be given of the fact that in an individual's own postural image many postural images of others are melted together" (234). The melding together of the various postural images of others occurs, Schilder writes, "under the influence of an erotic need" (234). To his credit, Schilder does not use his patient to illustrate pathology or deviant psychosexual development. It is, rather, an indication of the extent to which body image is shaped by identificatory circuits, projection, and object relations involving the body images of others.

Certainly, Schilder's observation that some people with a "queer feeling" relative to the body image avoid mirrors precisely because the images reflected in the looking glass are at odds with the body image is fertile ground for trans* scholarly investigation. Although Schilder adheres rigidly to the Oedipal complex developed by Freud along with a somewhat negative view of "sado-masochistic tendencies," which, in his view, lead to a "dismembering of the whole body" (299), his writing on the lability of the body is instructive for Salamon's interest in materialization and, ultimately, for trans* studies. Salamon's engagement with Schilder enables new trajectories in psychoanalysis, and her article is one of the most important writings on how the body materializes a sex in the trans* cultural studies literature.

Patricia Elliot

Canadian psychoanalytic feminist Patricia Elliot (2001) also offers a serious engagement with and critique of *Second Skins* from a Lacanian perspective. While many cisgender feminist scholarly responses to transgender studies had up to this point been dismissive, patronizing, and aggressive (Garber 1992; Hausman 1995; Jeffreys 1997; Raymond 1980), Elliot and Katrina Roen's (1998) thoughtful reading of transgender studies was a welcome change. Although not a clinician, Elliot insightfully identifies important and urgent questions having to do with Lacanian psychoanalytic theory and analytic practice concerning trans* subjectivities. Following the early work of Biddy Martin (1994), who critiques a queer theoretical reduction of sex and gender to discourse, Elliot and Roen (1998) convincingly argue, along with Martin, that the interplay between the body and psyche must not be ignored. That is, we must seriously contend with the psyche if we are going to understand the deep personal investments we have in gender, sex, and embodiment.

Elliot writes, "Because Prosser offers the most sophisticated transsexual theory of embodiment to date . . . I draw on psychoanalytic insights to argue both with and against Prosser, to deepen the trauma theory he alludes to but does not develop, and to raise questions about the value of psychoanalytic contributions to transsexuality" (2001: 301). While acknowledging Prosser's important contributions to transgender studies, particularly in bringing psychoanalysis to bear on questions relating to gender, embodiment, and sex, Elliot is ultimately concerned, like Salamon, that Prosser approaches the body too literally. As Elliot notes, Prosser does not engage the more useful aspects of Lacanian scholarship having to do with the desiring subject, the other, and the phallic signifier.

For Elliot, Lacan's analytic of sexuation provides a way to understand the interplay between the body image (a function of the imaginary), the phallus (as signifier), and the desire of the other. A sexual position is, for Lacan, a relation to loss: "This marking of the body is not based on the existence of two natural anatomical sexes but is the result of two responses to phallic loss" (Elliot and Roen 1998: 245). While we are not wrong to call Lacan's model phallocentric, there must be an understanding of what he means by the phallic signifier. The Lacanian phallus is not the penis. Nor is it a marker of cultural capital. It must also be stressed that the Lacanian phallus is fallible. It is fallible because it is a signifier of imprecise meaning. Lacan calls the phallus the fundamental signifier because it is the only one that has no actual referent. It is supposed to signify sexual difference, which is, for Lacan, real. The real is in excess of language. As such, the phallus will always fail and signification will be, forever, deferred. The Lacanian phallus is, for the late Parisian analyst, the universal signifier that anchors all relationships between the subject and all other signifiers. It is within this context that his often-cited refrain "there is no sexual relationship" must be understood. Lacan posits two universal sexual positions. One can be either "all" subject to the phallic premise as demarcated by the masculine position or "not-all" subject to the phallic premise as demarcated by the feminine position. This is not a cisgender binary formula but rather, in the Lacanian formulation, a problem of language and logic.[5]

It follows that what Prosser calls "transsexual skins" must be engaged at the level of the real, not at the level of a material truth (and certainly not from the perspective of gender identity). One of the benefits of Lacanian psychoanalysis, as Elliot sees it, is that it enables us to understand how desire is structured by a relation to the phallus (as signifier of loss). For Lacan, castration is not about the loss of a particular body part like the penis but a cut or limit imposed upon one's *jouissance* (a painful pleasure). There are two ways of dealing with this cut or loss of jouissance. We may either presume to be or to have the phallus. The feminine position is characterized by a wanting to be the signifier of the desire of the other.

The masculine position is characterized by the fantasy that one has, or can have, the phallus (or, rather, the thing lacking in the other). "Man" and "woman" are, for Lacan, signifiers and not referents with fixed meaning anchored in biology.

Given her Lacanian orientation to gender, sex, and embodiment, Elliot is well positioned to evaluate Prosser's use of Lacan in his discussion of transsexuality. She agrees with Prosser that one must assume a livable sex position. Elliot is correct to note a productive point of convergence between Lacanian theory and trans* writing on sex morphology and gender identity. The state of feeling neither one sex nor the other, then, implies that one has not adequately separated from the other. In this state, there is a lack of lack. Without a gap, the subject cannot establish a position in relation to the desire of the other. In this precarious state, it is not surprising that one's body should feel somewhat alien, not one's own, or simply "wrong" (Elliot 2001: 302). It must be stressed that Elliot takes this feeling of "wrongness" seriously. She agrees with Prosser when he writes that "sexed dislocation is uninhabitable" (quoted in Elliot 2001: 204). Arriving at a sexed positioning is a prerequisite for desire in the Lacanian frame. Lacanian analysis is thus designed to enable the play of desire, thereby supporting the mode of enjoyment by which the subject has come into being in relation to the desire of the other.

In her discussion of *Second Skins*, Elliot acknowledges the central importance of palliating the "state of alienation or exile" that Prosser describes. She endorses a trans-progressive health-care model that includes SRS. What Elliot adds to the contemporary Lacanian conversation is the observation that the postsurgical moment very often enables transpeople to "renounce previously held fantasies" (2001: 317) about an idealized sex position. In other words, the "outcome of surgery may well create conditions that enable subjects to achieve the sexed embodiment that is crucial to their existence as subjects" (318). Elliot's position is consistent with what trans* people have been saying for quite some time. Although the psychoanalytic and mental health literature has been slow to recognize the importance of access to medical interventions, this is beginning to change.[6]

Shanna T. Carlson

Another highly original and important work that brings together Lacanian psychoanalysis and gender studies is Shanna T. Carlson's "Transgender Subjectivity and the Logic of Sexual Difference" (2010). Like Elliot, Carlson believes that the scholarly and political concerns of both areas should be brought together "less fractiously, but no less queerly" (47). This may happen, Carlson suggests, "if contemporary psychoanalytic thinkers were willing to listen to their compatriots' desires and to redefine some of their more exclusionary 'shibboleths' [quoting

Tim Dean, *Beyond Sexuality*, 226], and if gender theorists were willing to reread psychoanalysis, again" (69). A critical rereading of Lacan's theory of sexuation along with the unique position of the hysteric is, as Carlson suggests, fruitful for trans* scholarly studies.

Like Salamon, Carlson directs our attention to Freud's theory of bisexuality, not as a sexual orientation but as "related to psychical hermaphroditism and/or physical hermaphroditism" (48). Although she introduces Freud mainly to contextualize Lacan's later work on sexual positions, Carlson is right to direct our attention to Freud's early formulation of bisexuality. The bisexual composition of the subject is central to Freud's writing on hysteria as evidenced in his discussion of Anna O. (Bertha Pappenheim [1859–1936]). Carlson thereby opens a conceptual route to reading hysteria alongside transgender, not as pathology but as a unique response to a lack in the other. This is not a lack or loss of a body part. It is, rather, a lack in being, which is, for Lacan, inescapable. More significantly, Carlson reminds us that Lacan understood the hysteric's position as epistemologically significant. The hysteric addresses the master from a position of lack where his discourse flounders. In other words, she assumes a position of agency, as speaking being, in the place of impasse. The hysteric is, as Carlson writes, preoccupied with the "question that discourse wishes to mask," and as such she is uniquely able "to 'do something' to the social tie" (2010: 66). We could say that the hysteric speaks from the margins in the terms of intersectional feminism (Prosser 1998a), but this would not capture the radical challenge the hysteric makes to the phallic premise (and thus to language and to the symbolic more generally). The hysteric seeks to expose the inability (impotence) of the phallic signifier to write woman through her very being. She knows that the phallic signifier can inscribe man but not woman, at least not entirely.

Carlson makes her most important contribution to trans* studies through her discussion of the feminine axis of difference and, also, through the distinction she makes between transgender and transsexual. Carlson understands the "feminine" as a position any gender might occupy (2010: 66). Carlson's reading of the feminine enables her to counter the charge that Lacanian psychoanalysis, as opposed to gender theory (as inspired by Judith Butler in particular), is more narrow and conservative in its approach to sexuality. Carlson explains that Lacan prompts us to engage substantive questions about being. When we begin with the Lacanian question of "being" our attention turns from gender identity to the question of unconscious sexual difference. Carlson contends, like Elliot, that gender identity is not reducible to the Lacanian notion of "sexual positioning." Carlson suggests that transgender, like hysteria, may be a feminine solution to the sexual impasse. "Transgender," for her, includes those who identify as bi-, a-, or nongender; gender fluid; and/or gender queer—while "transsexual," in her provisional definition, refers to those who identify as "man" or "woman." In other words, for Carlson, "transsexuality is not in and of itself any more extreme a type of symptom than is 'man' or 'woman'" (65), whereas transgender is a position that may come closest to embodying what Freud called an unconscious, though universal, bisexuality. This position would not be adopted as a "solutionless solution to the impasses of sexual difference, a sort of unconscious scene of undecideability [as Millot (1990) would have it], but an undecideability fundamentally shared by all human subjects, no matter their seeming gender" (65). But Carlson notes that there is a second way to read transgender in terms of the feminine position—"as an expression of the logic of sexual difference" (65).

Carlson equates this second solution with hysteria. Carlson is right to stress that the "hysteric tends to interrogate societal norms at large, oftentimes embodying a subversive attitude that arises in part from a profound suspicion that her own sexed and sexual body is incommensurate to cultural injunctions regarding gender identity" (66). The hysteric and those Carlson provisionally calls "transgender" are interested in what it means to "be" not wholly subject to the phallic premise. The hysteric's question leads us to consider what it means to be castrated and to suffer from a certain form of exclusion in the sociosymbolic. It is this capacity to speak from a liminal position that uniquely enables hysteria and transgender to "enact social transformation" (67). As such, both structures are uniquely positioned to generate new transpsychoanalytic insight relevant to the clinic.

Patricia Gherovici

Patricia Gherovici is one of the first Lacanian clinicians to directly challenge Millot's (1990) thesis that transsexuality indexes psychosis. As a practicing Lacanian analyst in Philadelphia who works extensively with Latinx trans* clients, Gherovici is well positioned to challenge the psychotic thesis with concrete clinical examples. Given her pivotal roles in Lacanian associations and psychoanalytic networks internationally, she has been able to inaugurate a significant shift in clinical thought about trans* subjectivity. In *Please Select Your Gender* (2010), Gherovici writes that "transsexualism is not necessarily or uniquely a psychotic phenomenon and that 'transgender' is not in itself a pathological category" (183). She invites Lacanian psychoanalysts to "analyse" and not "pathologize." She uses the Lacanian notion of the sinthome—a subject's unique manner of coming to identify with its psychical symptoms and thereby gaining the capacity to enjoy its unconscious life—as one way to read trans* narratives as fictions essential to life, as opposed to indicators of pathology.

To understand the specificity of transsexual suffering, Gherovici suggests that we examine the character of *jouissance*, which in turn requires us to examine the sinthome. In the case of "Henri," a transsexual woman Lacan treated between 1952 and 1954, Gherovici speculates that there may be a "demand for a cut in the real of the body that would subtract a privileged piece of flesh from the Other's jouissance" (159). The speculation that transsexuality may enable the subject to impose a limit to the other's *jouissance* is similarly exemplified in Gherovici's case study of a transsexual man, who told her that after his[7] bilateral double mastectomy he was able to feel as though his body had a limit. "Before, [he] felt [his] body to be boundless. The surgically found limit revealed a relationship to the body in which the imaginary was accessed through the Real" (160). Gherovici's argument that transsexuality should be understood as a sinthome offers a fundamental contribution to trans* studies and to psychoanalytic theory and practice alike.

Lacan's later writings on the sinthome, in a year-long seminar on James Joyce, represent a fundamental change in his thinking about psychoanalytic symptoms ([1975–76] 2016). Lacan considers Joyce to have staved off psychosis by writing, and he uses this insight into the author's career as "a man of letters" to develop a theory of the symptom (or *sinthome*, in an older French spelling) as a fourth ring that knots together the three Lacanian registers, the symbolic, the imaginary, and the real. The symptom is no longer understood as something needing to be cured but, rather, as something that must be seriously engaged and narrativized because it serves a vital palliative function. Catherine Millot (1990) was, as Gherovici points out, actually the first to recognize that the transsexual symptom serves a psychic function analogous to the role of writing for James Joyce. Rather than "curing" the symptom, the newer Lacanian approach invites us to engage its creative function and to understand it as an "art" that mitigates the nonexistent sexual relation. As Gherovici further explains, the "sinthome is a purified symptom" that "remains beyond symbolic representation and exists outside the unconscious structured as language" (231). It is "not trying to 'make up' for the disharmony between the sexes; it is a creation that 'makes do' around the disjunction" (185). Unlike the ego, which is troubled by difference and clings to identity as defense against difference, the sinthome creatively animates and enjoys difference: it puts difference into play as supplement.

In developing her analysis of transsexuality as sinthome, Gherovici explains that we first must be able to theorize both the real and the unconscious processes. This is where she identifies the limitations embedded in Judith Butler's theory of gender performativity and in queer theory more generally. In so doing she draws productive distinctions between queer theory and transgender cultural studies on the one hand and Lacanian psychoanalysis on the other. Grounding her analysis in Lacan's theory of sexuation, which proposes a nonbinary, asymmetrical positioning of "man" and "woman" as noncomplementary solutions to the impasse of sexual difference, Gherovici views unconscious sexual difference as a problem of the real that engages something beyond the signifier. Butler's focus on discourse follows Lacanian theory only to the extent that she works in postmodern terms with the symbolic (the register of language, signs, and symbols) and the imaginary (where gender identity coheres). Butler, in Gherovici's assessment, negates the register of the real (relating to *jouissance* and the desire of the other). "If gender construction is reduced to a speech act," Gherovici asks, "who is the subject speaking, and who constructs this subject?" (2010: 115). Butler and Lacan both agree that the subject is split by language, but Butler, unlike Lacan, assumes a preexisting sociohistorical subject that can respond to the call of the other. Lacanians, by contrast, adopt a more radical claim: the historical subject is a symptom of the real (Copjec 2015), and what counts as personal history is the effect of its unsymbolizable excess. In other words, history is not what happens to us, we are what happens to history. In other words, our own personal histories are products of an unavoidable excess linked to a real problem of being. What this means for our understanding of sexual difference is that we must engage the unique way the phallus fails us. Transsexuality is, for Gherovici, one way to inscribe a real problem with the phallus.

Gherovici's analysis is comparable to Carlson's with respect to the fact that both theorists adhere to a Lacanian notion of sexual difference fixed by a phallic premise. Both scholar-analysts also agree that while there are only two ways to situate oneself in Lacan's formulas, this does not preclude multiple gender identifications. There is, however, a difference with respect to how each views hysteria and its relation to trans* subjectivity. Gherovici notes that hysterics arrive at an "Oedipal crisis without being able to overcome it at the level of the Symbolic" (2010: 196). Contra Carlson, she maintains that "hysteric identifications are always partial, whereas the identification with the sinthome [for the transsexual] is total. . . . The sinthome produces a complete structural adequation that encompasses the whole body" (212). Gherovici draws thoughtfully upon Prosser (1998a) to suggest that there is, as evidenced in the case of transsexual autobiographies, a push to write that enables transsexuals to embody sexual difference. As such, Prosser's push to write transsexuality resonates with Gherovici's view that transsexuality functions as a sinthome. What is unique and important about Gherovici's engagement with trans* autobiographies is her use of the sinthome to think about what Prosser calls the transsexual trajectory: "I claim that an art similar to that of actual artists . . . can be found in transsexual artificiality" (Gherovici 2010: 153). While trans* studies is legitimately critical of this notion of "artificiality," especially when compared to a nontrans body that is thought to be "real," "natural," and "authentic," Gherovici is referring to a creative and artistic psychical assemblage that is not unique to trans* people.

Oren Gozlan

Gherovici establishes a foundation for Toronto-based psychoanalyst Oren Gozlan's (2014) analysis of what he calls the art and aesthetics of transitioning. Gozlan builds upon his previous work (2008, 2010, and 2011) to expand upon his reading of gender as narrative, through examples culled from clinical vignettes about postsurgical scars, artwork, and fiction. Gozlan, like Gherovici, suggests that psychoanalysis needs to transition its thinking about transsexuality. He finds clinicians too often unable to "play" with gender. As a result, transsexuality can evoke anxiety in analysts along with a clinical inability to deal with gender as enigma, metaphor, and stumbling block. Gozlan suggests that we read transsexuality as involving a struggle to symbolize gender but also as resistance to symbolization. He is also interested in the interiority of otherness, that is, in how the subject maps sexual difference internally, as well as between self-subject and others as objects. The analytic task, as Gozlan understands it, is not to "arrive" at gender certainty but to enable desire and analytic play.

Like Elliot and Gherovici, Gozlan is critical of psychoanalytic and medical attempts to pathologize and normalize transsexuality, and he demands instead that we read transsexualities in their specificities. Gozlan's interest in the aesthetic conflict of gender is heavily influenced by the Kleinian psychoanalyst Donald Meltzer (1822–1904), who viewed psychoanalysis as an art and aesthetics involving the making of symbols (Meltzer and Williams 2008). The maternal environment is central to Meltzer's theory of aesthetic conflict. For Meltzer, symbolization is enabled by the recognition of difference in the object relations between the infant and the mother, and the aesthetic is shaped by the ambivalence, loss, aggression, and desire in those object relations. To more fully elaborate the aesthetic conflict, Gozlan also draws upon the British object relations theorist and pediatrician Donald Winnicott (1896–1971). He understands gender as a "transitional object" in Winnicottian terms. Gozlan also reads Winnicott alongside Lacan and ultimately argues, like Elliot and Gherovici again, that sexual difference exceeds symbolic articulation. Insofar as gender identity is employed as a way to mediate this symbolic "excess," it will always be an incomplete identification.

In order to consider the imaginary axis of gender, Gozlan turns to the art of Anish Kapoor, a British sculptor born in Bombay, and Louise Bourgeois, a French-American sculptor. Through his reading of these artists, along with Jeffrey Eugenides's semiautobiographical novel *Middlesex* (2002) and Michel Foucault's historical writing on the French intersex schoolteacher Herculine Barbin (Barbin and Foucault 1980), Gozlan considers how transsexuality is a "placeholder for the incommensurability between gender and sexual difference" (2014: 7). Transsexuality represents an aesthetic crisis that reveals the inherent instability of gender. To better understand this instability, Gozlan asks us to challenge the psychoanalytic fantasy of "phallic monism," that is, that we are either castrated or not castrated. He argues that by returning to the Freudian premises that we are all polymorphously perverse, and that the unconscious knows no gender and is unfaithful to any one object, psychoanalysts will be better able to accept the radical heterogeneity of the drive (73).

To the extent that psychoanalysis has been unable to deal with transgender, it is entrapped in what Gozlan calls a "concrete encasement" (72). The rigidity in most psychoanalytic writing on transsexuality must itself be subject to analysis. Gozlan views transsexualities as viable psychical positions involving subjectifying transformations. Moreover, he suggests that transsexuality be understood not as a diagnostic category but as a "universal psychic position that allows sexuality to remain in a state of flux, always in transit" (21). He also asks us to read trans-sexuality more broadly as a metaphor for transitional experiences in the analytic encounter. Like Gherovici (2010), Gozlan views transsexuality as central to an elaboration of the sexual impasse originally theorized by Lacan, which is a universal enigma not particular to transsexuals: all identities, including transsexual identities, are structured like fictions that demand to be read and interpreted. Transitions, for all of us, are ongoing, forever in motion like all gendered becomings. Everyone can use the clinic to elaborate new ways of being in relation to gender. We never "arrive" at a fixed gender identity. The fantasy of a coherent match between the body and gender must always be traversed and worked upon aesthetically and psychically.

Unlike Gherovici (2010) and Carlson (2010), Gozlan is reluctant to embrace the hysteric as a model or way of thinking about trans-subjective experience. Referring back to Freud's formative writing on hysteria along with later work by Paul Verhaeghe (2009), Gozlan understands hysteria as a dual identification with the one and the other and, as such, an aggressive refusal to differentiate between passivity and activity. In Gozlan's reading, the hysteric's refusal to differentiate between gender positions is predicated upon a belief in the phallus not as symbol but as "truth," which inaugurates an endless (and fruitless) "search for a guarantor" (2014: 49) of phallic truth. In this respect, the hysteric becomes proximate to the Lacanian psychotic who searches for a perfect *jouissance*, or union with the other, which is, all Lacanian analysts would agree, impossible. A great deal of feminist psychoanalytic writing challenges the interpretation, which is not unique to Gozlan, of hysteria as a frenzied and delirious demand for a phallic guarantor (Dane 1994; Gallop 1982; Jacobus 1986; and Hunter 1983). Feminists often attribute pathological accounts of hysteria in the psychoanalytic literature to sexism, claiming that hysteria is a viable position to assume in relation to a (phallic) master. But it is certainly fair and reasonable to caution, as Gozlan does, that transsexuality is not reducible to hysteria as a clinical structure, Carlson's (2010) and Gherovici's (2010) productive deployments of hysteria to gain insight into transgender and transsexual experience notwithstanding.

Where Gozlan agrees with Gherovici (2010) is in approaching transsexuality as sinthome. In Gozlan's terms, we make a sinthome when we identify with our symptom and turn it into a fiction that enables us to "play" with its truth as untruth (on this point, see Hannah Wallerstein, this issue). While Lacanians following Millot (1990) accuse transsexuals of "acting out," Gozlan is in agreement with Gherovici, who reads transsexuality as a way to undertake what Lacan calls a "passage to the act." "Acting out" is understood by Lacan as a repetitive address to the other that does not enable change. By contrast, the "passage to the act" temporarily dissembles the subject so that they can alter their fundamental fantasy. By reconfiguring the fundamental fantasy (usually a fantasy of origin), the subject also reconfigures the sociosymbolic constellation. Such a passage is the ultimate goal and end of analysis.

In This Issue

Patricia Elliot and Lawrence Lyons subject Sheila Jeffrey's (2014) book titled *Gender Hurts: A Feminist Analysis of the Politics of Transgenderism* to psychosocial critique. Elliot and Lyons take us outside the clinic and into the sociopolitical and academic realm where they read transphobia as in need of psychoanalysis. Instead of countering the transphobic premises central to Jeffrey's text with attention to real-life evidence and examples culled from trans* experience, Elliot and Lyons adopt a new tack. They use Freudian and Lacanian insight about anxiety and shame to develop a "symptomatic reading of the text." In other words, they read the book as a symptom of a radical lesbian feminist (RLF) passion for ignorance. Lacan wrote about how we all, to varying degrees and in different ways, cultivate a desire not to know. Using the Lacanian category of the "unwoman" and the woman (who, for Lacan, does not exist), Elliot and Lyons argue that RLFs are threatened by the loss of an imaginary coherence and likeness among women as a social group. But more than this, RLFs are, through their transphobia, attempting to cover a latent anxiety about the instability and contingency of sexual difference to enable the community of women they imagine. Focusing on desire, the scopophilic drive, the uncanny, repression and aggression, Elliot and Lyons enable us to understand the tenacity and longevity of transphobia based as it is upon a fear of difference functioning at the level of the imaginary. They propose that transphobia be treated as a symptom and understood in psychosocial context.

Griffin Hansbury is a social worker and psychotherapist based in New York City who is well known for his book *The Nostalgist* (2012), about a man who poses as a woman's missing, grief-stricken boyfriend. In psychoanalytic circles, Hansbury has made significant clinical contributions to our understandings of trans* masculinities (2005) and to what he calls the "trans–trans analytic dyad" (2011). His analytic work is based in the relational and intersubjective models and is acutely focused on how transphobic countertransferences emerge in the analytic setting. Like Elliot and Lyons, Hansbury subjects transphobia to critical psychoanalysis. In "Unthinkable Anxieties: Reading Transphobic Counter-transferences in a Century of Psychoanalytic Writing," Hansbury offers a chronology of transphobic prejudice exhibited by analysts in their work with trans* clients. His examples begin with Freud's early writing on the German judge Daniel Paul Schreber and proceed to the American reception of Christine Jorgensen, Robert Stoller's Gender Identity Research Clinic at the University of California, Los Angeles, School of Medicine, and present-day French Lacanian analyst Collette Chiland, who is unapologetic in her position that gender-affirming surgeries are mutilations. Attending to Avgi Saketopoulou's writing on the interface between psyche, soma, and culture, Hansbury concurs that trans* patient issues often stem from the "unmentalized impact"[8] of being trans* as opposed to transsexuality itself. Their analytic work is undermined by the transphobic countertransferences of analysts who are reluctant to confront their own internalized fears of gender variance. We must, Hansbury concludes, move beyond the question of "why" trans, to a more analytically inclined question about "how" to mentalize ways of being trans*.

Hilary Offman's psychoanalytic scholarship and practice, like Hansbury's, is grounded in the relational school. In "The Queering of a Cisgender Psycho-analyst," she is concerned with being a "good enough trans-parental object." In keeping with the relational practice that calls for thoughtful reflection on the countertransference within the psychoanalytic dyad, Offman speaks candidly and honestly about her experience with gender-nonnormative clients. In so doing, she addresses many of the concerns outlined by Hansbury having to do with the negative countertransferences experienced by nontrans* analysts in their work with trans* clients. More significantly, she suggests that what counts as "trans-positivity" can sometimes undermine the important psychical process through which trans* clients work through the implications of the analyst's "imperfect attunement" to them. While respecting the usefulness of key terms and distinctions like *trans* and *cisgender*, she notes that the clinical situation demands attention to dynamics more complex than those encapsulated by such identitarian concepts. Provocatively, she writes about how she herself psychically "transitions" over the course of her analytic work with her trans* client Sam, and she characterizes her subjectively felt changes as "queer." Conversely, in order to understand another client, Patrick, whose gender does not map easily onto the cis/trans* binary, Offman had to discover the "queerness" latent in her own "cisgender" identity. She concludes that the "antinormative" thrust of trans-positive clinical work must be accompanied by an acknowledgment that what it means to be trans and cisgender is far from transparent and self-evident.

In "Putting the 'Trans' Back in 'Truth': A Psychoanalytic Take on Gender's Authenticity," Hannah Wallerstein offers a transpositive critique of two corollary claims: the naive transphobic claim that transpeople deliberately obscure a biological truth in pretending to be the opposite sex and queer postmodernism's claim that transpeople desire to achieve a "true" alignment of sex embodiment and gender. Wallerstein is, like most transpositive Lacanians, troubled by the reduction of trans* subjectivity to an impossible desire to eclipse representation and reality. She suggests that we move from understanding truth as a kind of correspondence toward truth as a kind of translational practice. This process of translation should be understood as a creative act that resonates with Lacanian writing on the *sinthome* (Gherovici 2010; Gozlan 2014; Cavanagh 2016c). Wallerstein writes that trans* subjectivity is not predicated upon a foreclosure of truth but, rather, on a creative use of truth. Wallerstein then engages with Freudian approaches to the question of truth, and with the work of British group psychodynamic theorist Wilfred Bion, to show how there is no objective truth, only subjective meaning that must be inhabited by the subject. This discussion then enables her to turn our attention to the intersubjective composition of truth for trans* subjects, and the ways in which transitioning can enable the subject to exist truthfully.

Jacob Breslow's article, "'There Is Nothing Missing in the Real': Trans Childhood and the Phantasmatic Body," begins with a case analysis of a Colorado elementary school administrator's decision to bar Coy Mathis, a six-year-old trans* girl, from using the "girl's" bathroom. While there has been a great deal of press coverage of the antitrans* laws in the United States that prohibit transpeople from using public bathrooms, changing rooms, and locker rooms that match their identity and appearance rather than their birth-assigned sex, Breslow offers a psychoanalytic take on the structure of that prohibition. Building upon the foundational work of Prosser and Salamon, Breslow underscores the role of phantasy in the ban and in its temporality. Drawing insightfully upon Freud's early writing on child psychosexual development and Lacan's later writing on the penis/phallus distinction, Breslow argues that transphobic exclusions, along with transpositive policies, depend upon and are structured by ambivalence about the political and psychic life of the child. Banning Coy from a sex-segregated school toilet because of what school administrators fantasize her future body has the capacity to become (that is, a man) is understood as a projective cisgender fantasy that assumes a particular anatomical mapping of sexual difference. The phantasmatic body of cisgender futurity, where we are all normatively sexually differentiated, is bound to be either missing something (the phallus) or, alternatively, having something incongruously and conspicuously present (the penis). But in the "real" of childhood, Breslow claims, nothing is missing. By analyzing narratives of childhood in relation to trans* autobiographies, and the critical role of mirror scenes in those autobiographies, Breslow troubles the presumption that children exist in some atemporal moment before sexual difference comes to matter. He also challenges the presumption of childhood "innocence" and "ignorance" in matters relating to gender and sexual difference.[9]

Oren Gozlan's essay, "Stalled on the Stall: Reflections on a Strained Discourse," also chronicles a problem of gender, time, and phantasy in the bathroom. He invites us to consider how the North American debate about public toilet accessibility is structured by, on the one hand, an unproductive tension between liberal rights-based rhetoric focusing upon equity, inclusion, and accommodation and, on the other hand, stereotypical images of transsexuals as predators, pedophiles, and monsters who pose a threat to nontrans women and children. This imagined threat is, for Gozlan, tied to a cisgender fantasy about the cohesive nature of gender and the associated projection of gender anxiety onto others. But the antithesis, Gozlan explains, is no better. Trans* activist discourse is steeped in a logic of certainty that demands a "right" to bathroom use, which is characterized by an unwillingness to assume a position of indifference to the other's tyrannical *jouissance*. Gozlan finds those who adopt the discourse of trans* rights to have internalized a passive position whereby it is the trans* subject who is victim and the nontrans* subject who is aggressor and thus aligned with parental authority. Psychoanalytically speaking, gender recognition in the stall is laced with unconscious desire and is not easily given. Both political positions refuse to engage the phantasy, play, and anxieties about gender that ground the psychic life of the bathroom. Gozlan is not opposed to public policy and universal rights but insists that they are not enough. As such, he offers a third position by advocating for the adoption of a "transsexual stance." A transsexual stance would, for him, refuse what is given to be true.

Chris Coffman is a scholar whose research focuses on feminist, queer, trans*, and psychoanalytic theory. In "Žižek's Antagonism and the Futures of Trans-Affirmative Lacanian Psychoanalysis," Coffman critiques the Slovenian Lacanian's controversial statements about trans* subjectivity. In a podcast interview by the London School of Economics and Political Science on April 20, 2016, Žižek flatly stated, "I don't believe in transgenderism." He refers to transgenderism and the "gender theory" he considers to have produced it as a "conspiracy" that aims to undermine sexual difference. He also characterizes transgender rights claims as an example of political correctness run amok. In previously published work, Coffman (2012) argues that Žižek's Lacanian account of sexual difference is heterosexist, and in this article she continues to call Žižek out for his heterosexism, his lack of engagement with trans★ psychoanalytic studies, and his transphobia. She also faults his embrace of these reactionary positions, which, in turn, prevent him from recognizing the utility of his scholarship for trans★ studies. Like other Lacanian-inspired theorists and practitioners in this collection, Coffman does not view Lacanian psychoanalysis as at odds with trans★ studies. She argues that by acting in the Lacanian "real," trans★ subjects actually traverse the fundamental fantasy of sexual difference. To illustrate the possibilities of this traversal, Coffman engages Susan Stryker's early writing on transsubjectivity to show how an act in the real, rooted in the imaginary, reconfigures the symbolic.

Jordan Osserman is a London-based psychoanalytic scholar interested in questions of sexual difference and leftist politics. Following Shanna Carlson's call in *TSQ* (2014: 171) to reengage the question of the Lacanian phallus along with its status as fundamental signifier for the subject's lack-in-being, Osserman explains how Lacanian writing on the phallus can help us understand felt discordances between sex embodiment and anatomy. Although Lacanians are quick to distinguish between the penis (as organ) and phallus (as signifier), Osserman wonders if there is not something lost in turning away from the anatomical coordinates of the sexed body. Like Prosser, he is interested in the materiality of the body. Unlike Prosser, Osserman finds Lacanian theory useful. In his contribution, "Is the Phallus Uncut? On the Role of Anatomy in Lacanian Subjectivization," Osserman discusses the now-famous case of David Reimer—a twin, born in Winnipeg in 1965, who lost his penis in a botched circumcision and was, under the guidance of psychologist John Money, raised by his parents as a girl. Osserman moves from the Reimer case to a discussion of circumcision, "intactivists" who organize against compulsory circumcision, and trans★ subjectivity. Noting that desire is at stake in foreskin restoration narratives as well as in narratives of trans★ subjectivity, Osserman shows how imaginary phallic morphology plays a pivotal but nondeterminative role in sexual positioning. For him, becoming a subject must involve attention to anatomy even if we do not know what a given organ might mean in advance.

Kate Foord is a practicing psychoanalyst and scholar based in Melbourne, Australia. Her article, "Queeranalyst," brings queer theory, trans★ studies, and Lacanian psychoanalysis together to engage gender and sexual difference in clinical practice. Foord argues that psychoanalysis must involve the deconstruction of gender, just as queerness demands a deconstruction of subjectivity. Subjectivity, Foord maintains, is an impasse founded upon a gap between ego-based identifications and difference, but in the queer clinic, analysts must resist the tendency to "suture" that gap and consider, at every stage, the importance of first untying and then reknotting gender for both the analyst and the analysand. Echoing Gherovici (2010), Foord also considers psychoanalysis to need a sex change, but she adds an important Lacanian nuance: that psychoanalysis cannot identify itself with any given gender. It must put gender into crisis if it is to be properly psychoanalytic, which it cannot be if the analyst is always already situated in the place of identity. The analyst must therefore resist the seductive push to paper over differences at the level of the imaginary, where questions of gender identity, embodiment, and body image reside. Foord's cautions and solicitations enable us to better understand the critical role of language and castration in sexual positioning. Moreover, she underscores the central importance, for the queer Lacanian clinic, of the dictum, "The analyst must be able to hear the saying of the analysand." It is that very "saying," as signifier, that makes any given client a unique subject.

In her contribution, "Depathologizing Trans: From Symptom to *Sinthome*," Patricia Gherovici expands and builds upon her revisionist Lacanian analysis of transgender, which argues persuasively against the misguided tendency in contemporary Lacanian practice to reduce trans* subjectivity to psychosis. By carefully focusing on the cases of "Henri," "Primeau," and Daniel Paul Schreber, Gherovici demonstrates that Lacan himself did not endorse the reduction of transsexuality to psychosis. Rather, Lacan made a fine-grained distinction in his clinical work between a psychopathological "transsexual delusion" and a nonpathological "demand for gender reassignment." His overriding concern was with the function of the phallic signifier and the desire of the other, and with the particular, "symptomatic" way in which a subject has come to enjoy the unconscious—a symptom not to be "cured" but encouraged. Using Lacan's later work on the *sinthome* (a person's symptomatic way of knotting together the registers of the symbolic, the imaginary, and the real), Gherovici reads transsexuality as a push to write the symptom, or in other words, as a creative way to narrate the sexual impasse. Reflecting on her earlier work in *Please Select Your Gender* (2010), Gherovici notes that she did not sufficiently address the questions of life and death central to transpeople in their transit from symptom to *sinthome*. Transsexuality, as she now sees, is a way to instate a border, a difference between life and death where being is ultimately at stake.

In "*Transessualità* Italian-Style or Mario Mieli's Practice of Love," Elena Dalla Torre introduces us to the "erotic communism" of the late Italian theorist and activist Mario Mieli (1952–83). As a specialist in Italian language and cultural history, Dalla Torre is well positioned to consider Mieli's radical philosophy in relation to contemporary American queer theory and transgender studies. Mieli was an important figure in the 1970s gay-communist Italian scene who authored a play as well as five books, including his revised dissertation *Elementi di critica omosessuale* (translated into English as *Homosexuality and Liberation: Elements of a Gay Critique*), the final chapter of which was widely circulated as the pamphlet

Towards a Gay Communism. Dalla Torre offers a careful reading of Mieli's life and work to insist that we consider his relevance to queer feminism and to transgender studies as well as communist thought and homosexual liberation. Mieli desired to be a woman and believed that all men must avow the "woman within." In so doing, men must embrace an inner transsexual consciousness otherwise stifled by what he called "educastration." Dalla Torre places Mieli's scholarship in conversation with Judith Butler, Teresa De Lauretis, Luce Irigaray, and Guy Hocquenghem to offer a powerful critique of what Jack Halberstam (2008) calls the antisocial turn in queer theories beholden to Lacan. Dalla Torre demonstrates how Meili's call to "liberate the anus" is not about a self-shattering *jouissance* associated with the writings of Leo Bersani (1987) but, rather, the making of trans* subjectivity. The sexual and communist ethics of alterity in Mieli's work is, as Torre demonstrates, revolutionary and trans-generative.

In "Transgender Subjectivity in Revolt: Kristevan Psychoanalysis and the Intimate Politics of Rebirth," Amy Ray Stewart uses Julia Kristeva's analytic of "intimate revolt" to think about the social and psychic politics of transsexual transitions. She finds the French feminist's work on "return, rupture, and rebirth" especially helpful for better understanding how those who are trans* and queer grapple with and ultimately reconfigure the logic of liminality. Stewart begins with the case study of Laura Jane Grace, the trans* leader of the punk band Against Me! who sets her birth certificate on fire in front of a packed concert hall while yelling, "Goodbye, gender!" Stewart reminds us that for Kristeva, the analytic space, like art and literature, enables us to uncover a "trans-symbolic *jouissance*." This trans-symbolic jouissance can enact intimate yet symbolic revolutions and give us another perspective on the political, which is not only about activism and lobbying for legal and policy change but also about transformation from within. Stewart is keenly aware of the administrative, sociopolitical, economic, and cultural barriers to enacting a life-sustaining intimate revolt for queer and trans* subjects. But following Kristeva, she makes the case that gender transitioning, whatever form it may take, is predicated upon an extraordinary capacity for renewal, reconfiguration, and regeneration at the level of subjectivity.

Simon van der Weele's "Mourning Moppa: Mourning without Loss in Jill Soloway's *Transparent*" asks how we might better understand losses experienced by intimate others when loved ones transition. He analyzes the character Josh Pfefferman in the Amazon Prime show *Transparent*. Pfefferman is melancholic and anxious about his former father Mort becoming his transgender mother Maura (Moppa). In his analysis, van der Weele engages Freud's formative essay "Mourning and Melancholia" (1917), Nicolas Abraham and Maria Torok's (1994) work on incorporation and introjection, Jacques Derrida's (1989) writing on loss and infidelity, and Judith Butler's writing on "coming undone" (2004). In doing so, he demonstrates how melancholia, as opposed to mourning, has been pathologized in psychoanalytic theorizing. In van der Weele's analysis, Josh mourns without loss. Although his parent has not died and is palpably present, albeit in her new gender identity, Josh nevertheless experiences intense grief. This grief is, in some way, ungrievable. There is an inability to grieve because the object-subject (Moppa) is not lost. Josh is thus confronted with the loss of a father image as opposed to the loss of a person as such. Van der Weele turns to Israeli feminist psychoanalytic scholar Bracha L. Ettinger to consider how a subject mourns without loss. Ettinger's writing on the matrixial borderspace, whereby we are all partial subjects tied to others in stringlike webs, gives van der Weele a way to understand the structure of Josh's melancholia. What matters from an Ettingerian perspective is "differentiation in co-emergence" whereby we are all partial subjects transconnected to others. Van der Weele's engagement with Ettinger's writing on the feminine is important for trans* studies because it enables us to understand how gender transitions touch and affect everyone in a given matrixial web.

Following the feature articles are a series of invited short statements by psychoanalysts and scholars who are uniquely positioned to comment on the state of psychoanalytic theorizing and clinical engagements with trans* studies. Shanna Carlson's article appears first and offers a Lacanian clinical take on transgender as it contributes to the social link. Trish Salah, author of *Wanting in Arabic* (2002) and *Lyric Sexology Vol. 1* (2014), gives us an orientation to her reading of Tiresias, a translike character and prophet in the Oedipal trilogy authored by Sophocles. She centers her Tiresian poetics in relation to Daniel Paul Schreber (the German court judge who experienced what Lacan calls a "push-to-Woman"), thus distinguishing it from my own Ettingerian (2006) read of the Theban prophet (Cavanagh 2016b). Abraham B. Weil, a scholar at the University of Arizona, brings Félix Guattari's notion of transversality to bear upon trans* studies. Weil undoes binary logics that reduce trans* ecologies to a singular axis of difference. Marco Posadas, a Toronto-based psychoanalyst, talks candidly about his psychoanalytic education in Mexico City, the International Psychoanalytic Association (IPA), and the state of a psychoanalytic discourse that pathologizes, erases, or precludes transpeople. Dina Al-Kassim offers an important discussion of Afsaneh Najmabadi's *Professing Selves: Transsexuality and Same-Sex Desire in Contemporary Iran*. Al-Kassim's focus on the Middle East introduces questions of political subjectivity and state power, placing trans* studies in dialogue with psychoanalysis and international studies.

Sheila L. Cavanagh is associate professor of sociology at York University.

Acknowledgments

I thank Caitlin Janzen for the editorial work she did on this special issue along with the orchestration of the reviews. I also thank Tracey Rapos for his support and inspiration along the way.

Notes

1. I was truly disappointed to hear Julia Kristeva echo the most objectionable element of Millot's thesis in *Horsexe* (1998) when she said at the "Symposium: On the Body in New York City" (2016) sponsored by the Association for Psychoanalytic Medicine (and I paraphrase because an accompanying text is not available for quotation) that "when the difference between men and women is erased lack no longer exists." Lack is, in Lacanian terms, what makes desire possible. Although to the best of my knowledge Kristeva does not refer to transsexuality in her presentation (mediated by Skype), she does refer to those who are "recomposed" and to the "fabrication of genders by overly sympathetic gynecologists and endocrinologists." Her worry, as a psychoanalyst, is with a lack of limit to fulfillment, "immediate gratification," and "absolute satisfaction."

2. As I write this introduction, US president Donald Trump is issuing executive orders that would not only curtail the rights and freedoms of trans* subjects (and a host of others, notably Muslims, refugees, gays, lesbians, and so forth) but their existence as socio-political subjects (bios). The politics of erasure, abjection, negation, and aggressive disassociation operative in the US political scene is not only real (in a geopolitical sense), but it touches upon what Lacan calls "the real" (which is in excess of the sociosymbolic). The Lacanian real concerns the question of being itself. Laverne Cox is right to say that the bathroom issue is about the rights of trans* people to exist. Take, for instance, the North Carolina ban that prohibits trans* people from using public toilets, locker rooms, and so forth, consistent with their gender identities. The prohibition is a repetition, in the present, of an older Jim Crow law employed in the Southern states; albeit a repetition with a difference (Cavanagh 2016a). The new iteration of the bathroom bill is, of course, dangerously real, but it is also reminiscent of an older, more deeply entrenched problem with the real of sexual difference. Let us remember that the real of sexual difference can also be articulated as a problem of racial difference as Kalapana Seshadri-Crooks (2000) illustrates in *Desiring Whiteness: A Lacanian Analysis of Race*.

3. This tendency to reduce transsexuality to a false literalization of the referent in some queer theoretical circles is, in my observation, also evident in some psychoanalytic writings, including those presented at conferences affiliated with the International Psychoanalytic Association, the World Association of Psychoanalysis, and those held by the New Lacanian School of Psychoanalysis (among others).

4. As Prosser (1998b) argues in his writing on sexology, it is a mistake to presume that the category of sexual inversion only, and always, refers to homosexuality. In point of fact, sexology's "most enduring category of this extensive field [of sexology] . . . [is] the dynamic of transgender, of gender identifications that cross ('trans') at angles to bodily sex" (116). Prosser explains how the reduction of sexual inversion to homosexuality in Freud's theories has sidelined trans* studies in psychoanalysis.

5. Lacan defines the signifier as that which has "meaning effect [*effet de signifié*] . . . [and urges us to remember that] between the signifier and meaning effect there is something barred that must be crossed over" (1975: 18). He also writes that a signifier is what

"represents a subject for another signifier" (1998: 207). For Lacan, there is something arbitrary about the signifier and more precisely the relation between the signifier and the signified: "The signified misses the referent. The joiner doesn't work" (1975: 20). To put this in another way, the signifier is radically unattached to its "meaning effect." It belongs, rather, to a discourse, "a mode of functioning or a utilization of language qua link" (30). Lacan's signifier is, as he says, "nothing but what can be defined as a difference from another signifier . . . [and, as such] is the introduction of difference . . . into the field" (142).

6.   There is no clinical evidence to suggest that SRS or hormone therapies are at odds with the psychoanalytic cure as theorized by Lacan. In fact, medically supported transitions may, in some cases, enable psychoanalytic work that was, prior to a medical transition, not possible (Suchet 2011). It must also be noted that researchers are increasingly documenting the positive effects of gender confirming surgeries (Ainsworth and Spiegel 2010), hormone-blocking protocols for trans* youth (Smith, van Goozen, and Cohen-Kettenis 2001), and hormone therapy. Medical intervention when desired by the patient can be psychologically beneficial and palliative, even salubrious. It must also be emphasized that "regret" in the case of sex reassignment surgeries is extremely low (Johansson et al. 2010; van de Grift et al. 2017; Ettner 2016; and Bockting 2014).

7.   I am using the pronoun *he* (as opposed to the *she* Gherovici uses) because I believe the client is a transsexual man.

8.   "Mentalization" refers to a process whereby subjects can become cognizant of their affective states. It is often used by attachment theorists to understand the impact of caregivers who do not provide an appropriate "holding" space for child development.

9.   For a discussion of trans* temporalities, see the special issue of *Somatechnics* (Fisher, Phillips, and Katri 2017).

References

Abraham, Nicolas, and Maria Torok. 1994. *The Shell and the Kernel: Renewals of Psychoanalysis.* Vol. 1. Chicago: University of Chicago Press.

Adams, Parveen. 2013. *The Emptiness of the Image: Psychoanalysis and Sexual Differences.* Abingdon, UK: Routledge.

Ainsworth, Tiffiny A., and Jeffrey H. Spiegel. 2010. "Quality of Life of Individuals with and without Facial Feminization Surgery or Gender Reassignment Surgery." *Quality of Life Research* 19, no. 7: 1019–24.

Anzieu, Didier. (1985) 1989. *The Skin Ego.* Translated by Chris Turner. New Haven, CT: Yale University Press.

Barbin, Herculine, and Michel Foucault. 1980. *Herculine Barbin: Being the Recently Discovered Memoirs of a Nineteenth-Century French Hermaphrodite.* New York: Pantheon.

Bersani, Leo. 1987. "Is the Rectum a Grave?" *October*, no. 43: 197–222.

Bockting, Walter. 2014. "The Impact of Stigma on Transgender Identity Development and Mental Health." In *Gender Dysphoria and Disorders of Sex Development*, edited by Baudewijntje P. C. Kreukels, Thomas D. Steensma, and Annelou L. C. de Vries, 319–30. Boston: Springer.

Brennan, Teresa. 2004. *The Transmission of Affect.* Ithaca, NY: Cornell University Press.

Breuer, Josef, and Sigmund Freud. (1895) 1995. *Studies on Hysteria.* Vol. 2 of *The Standard Edition of the Complete Psychological Works of Sigmund Freud.* London: Hogarth Press.

Butler, Judith. 1990. "Gender Trouble, Feminist Theory, and Psychoanalytic Discourse." In *Feminism/Postmodernism*, edited by Linda J. Nicholson, 324–39. New York: Routledge.

———. 1993. *Bodies That Matter: On the Discursive Limits of "Sex."* London: Routledge.

———. 2004. *Undoing Gender*. New York: Routledge.

———. 2006. Foreword to Ettinger 2006: vii–xii.

Caldwell, Cary, and Matcheri S. Keshavan. 1991. "Schizophrenia with Secondary Transsexualism." *Canadian Journal of Psychiatry* 36, no. 4: 300–301.

Carlson, Shanna T. 2010. "Transgender Subjectivity and the Logic of Sexual Difference." *differences* 21, no. 2: 46–72.

———. 2014. "Psychoanalytic." *TSQ* 1, nos. 1–2: 169–71.

Carroll, Richard A. 1999. "Outcomes of Treatment for Gender Dysphoria." *Journal of Sex Education and Therapy* 24, no. 3: 128–36.

Cavanagh, Sheila L. 2010. *Queering Bathrooms: Gender, Sexuality, and the Hygienic Imagination*. Toronto: University of Toronto Press.

———. 2016a. "Gender, Sexuality, and Race in the Lacanian Mirror: Urinary Segregation and the Bodily Ego." In *Psychoanalytic Geographies*, edited by Paul Kingsbury and Steve Pile, 323–38. Surrey, UK: Ashgate.

———. 2016b. "Tiresias and Psychoanalysis *after* Oedipus." *European Journal of Psychoanalysis*. www.journal-psychoanalysis.eu/tiresias-and-psychoanalysis-without-oedipus/.

———. 2016c. "Transsexuality as Sinthome: Bracha L. Ettinger and the Other (Feminine) Sexual Difference." *Studies in Gender and Sexuality* 17, no. 1: 27–44.

Chiland, Colette. 2009. "Some Thoughts on Transsexualism, Transvestism, Transgender and Identification." In *Transvestism, Transsexualism in the Psychoanalytic Dimension*, edited by Giovanna Ambrosio, 41–54. London: Karnac Books.

Coffman, Chris. 2012. "Queering Žižek." *Postmodern Culture* 23, no. 1. muse.jhu.edu/article/513308.

Cohen-Kettenis, Peggy T., and L. J. G. van Goozen. 1999. "Transsexualism: A Review of Etiology, Diagnosis, and Treatment." *Journal of Psychosomatic Research* 46, no. 4: 315–33.

Copjec, Joan. 2015. *Read My Desire: Lacan against the Historicists*. New York: Verso Books.

Dane, Gabrielle. 1994. "Hysteria as Feminist Protest: Dora, Cixous, Acker." *Women's Studies: An Interdisciplinary Journal* 23, no. 3: 231–55.

Derrida, Jacques. 1989. *Mémoires: For Paul de Man*. Rev. ed. New York: Columbia University Press.

Elliot, Patricia. 2001. "A Psychoanalytic Reading of Transsexual Embodiment." *Studies in Gender and Sexuality* 2, no. 4: 295–325.

Elliot, Patricia, and Katrina Roen. 1998. "Transgenderism and the Question of Embodiment: Promising Queer Politics?" *GLQ* 4, no. 2: 231–61.

Ettinger, Bracha L. 2006. *The Matrixial Borderspace*. Theory Out of Bounds 28. Minneapolis: University of Minnesota Press.

Ettner, Randi. 2016. "Surgical Treatments for the Transgender Population." In *Lesbian, Gay, Bisexual, and Transgender Healthcare*, edited by Kristen L. Eckstrand and Jesse M. Ehrenfeld, 363–75. Cham, Switzerland: Springer.

Eugenides, Jeffrey. 2002. *Middlesex: A Novel*. New York: Macmillan.

Fisher, Simon D. Elin, Rasheedah Phillips, and Ido H. Katri, eds. 2017. "Trans Temporalities." Special issue, *Somatechnics* 7, no. 1.

Freud, Sigmund. (1905) 1975. *Three Essays on the Theory of Sexuality*. Translated by James Strachey. New York: Basic Books.

Gallop, Jane. 1982. *The Daughter's Seduction: Feminism and Psychoanalysis*. Ithaca, NY: Cornell University Press.

Garber, Marjorie B. 1992. *Vested Interests: Transvestism and Cultural Anxiety*. New York: Routledge.

Gherovici, Patricia. 2010. *Please Select Your Gender: From the Invention of Hysteria to the Democratizing of Transgenderism*. London: Routledge.

Goldner, Virginia. 2011. "Transgender Subjectivities: Introduction to Papers by Goldner, Suchet, Saketopoulou, Hansbury, Salamon and Corbett, and Harris." *Psychoanalytic Dialogues* 21, no. 2: 153–58.

Gossett, Che. 2016. "Žižek's Trans/gender Trouble." *Los Angeles Review of Books*, September 13.

Gozlan, Oren. 2008. "The Accident of Gender." *Psychoanalytic Review* 95, no. 4: 541–70.

———. 2010. "The 'Real' Time of Gender." *European Journal of Psychoanalysis*, no. 30: 61–84.

———. 2011. "Transsexual Surgery: A Novel Reminder and a Navel Remainder." *International Forum of Psychoanalysis* 20, no. 1: 45–52.

———. 2014. *Transsexuality and the Art of Transitioning: A Lacanian approach*. London: Routledge.

Halberstam, Judith. 1998. *Female Masculinity*. Durham, NC: Duke University Press.

———. 2008. "The Anti-Social Turn in Queer Studies." *Graduate Journal of Social Science* 5, no. 2: 140–56.

Hansbury, Griffin. 2011. "King Kong and Goldilocks: Imagining Transmasculinities through the Trans-Trans Dyad." *Psychoanalytic Dialogues* 21, no. 2: 210–20.

———. 2012. *The Nostalgist*. Douglas, Isle of Man: MP Press.

———. 2005. "The Middle Men: An Introduction to the Transmasculine Identities." *Studies in Gender and Sexuality* 6, no. 3: 241–64.

Harris, Adrienne. 2012. *Gender as Soft Assembly*. New York: Routledge.

Hausman, Bernice L. 1995. *Changing Sex: Transsexualism, Technology, and the Idea of Gender*. Durham, NC: Duke University Press.

Hunter, Dianne. 1983. "Hysteria, Psychoanalysis, and Feminism: The Case of Anna O." *Feminist Studies* 9, no. 3: 465–88.

Jacobus, Mary. 1986. *Reading Woman: Essays in Feminist Criticism*. London: Taylor and Francis.

Jeffreys, Sheila. 1997. "Transgender Activism: A Lesbian Feminist Perspective." *Journal of Lesbian Studies* 1, nos. 3–4: 55–74.

Johansson, Annika, et al. 2010. "A Five-Year Follow-Up Study of Swedish Adults with Gender Identity Disorder." *Archives of Sexual Behavior* 39, no. 6: 1429–37.

Kaltenbeck, Franz. 1992. "Le 'pousse-à-la-femme,' un belvédère clinique." *La Lettre Mensuelle de L'École de la Cause Freudienne*, no. 112: 9–10.

Klein, Melanie. 1946. "Notes on Some Schizoid Mechanisms." *International Journal of Psycho-Analysis* 27: 99–110.

Kristeva, Julia. 1982. *Powers of Horror: An Essay on Abjection*. New York: Columbia University Press.

———. 2016. "Transformations of *Parentality*," translated by Edward Kenny. Paper presented at the symposium On the Body, Association for Psychoanalytic Medicine, New York, May 6–7.

Lacan, Jacques. 1975. *Le seminaire XX: Encore*. Paris: Seuil.

———. (1975–76) 2016. *The Sinthome*. Book 11 of *The Seminar of Jacques Lacan*, edited by Jacques-Alain Miller, translated by A. R. Price. Cambridge: Polity.

———. 1998. *The Four Fundamental Concepts of Psycho-Analysis*. Book 11 of *The Seminar of Jacques Lacan*, translated by Alan Sheridan. New York: Norton.

Lemma, Alessandra. 2013. "The Body One Has and the Body One Is: Understanding the Transsexual's Need to be Seen." *International Journal of Psychoanalysis* 94, no. 2: 277–92.

Martin, Biddy. 1994. "Sexualities without Genders and Other Queer Utopias." *diacritics* 24, nos. 2–3: 104–21.

Meltzer, Donald, and M. Harris Williams. 2008. *The Apprehension of Beauty: The Role of Aesthetic Conflict in Development, Art, and Violence*. London: Karnac Books.

Merleau-Ponty, Maurice. 1962. *Phenomenology of Perception*. London: Gallimard.

Millot, Catherine. 1989. *Horsexe: Essay on Transsexuality*. New York: Autonomedia.

Morel, Geneviève. 2011. *Sexual Ambiguities: Sexuation and Psychosis*. Translated by Lindsay Watson. London: Karnac Books.

Prosser, Jay. 1998a. *Second Skins: The Body Narratives of Transsexuality*. New York: Columbia University Press.

———. 1998b. "Transsexuals and the Transsexologists: Inversion and the Emergence of Transsexual Subjectivity." In *Sexology in Culture: Labelling Bodies and Desires*, edited by Lucy Bland and Laura Doan, 116–31. Cambridge: Polity.

Raymond, Janice G. 1980. *The Transsexual Empire*. London: Women's Press.

Rose, Jacqueline. 2016. "Who Do You Think You Are?" *London Review of Books*, May 5.

Saketopoulou, Avgi. 2011. "Minding the Gap: Intersections between Gender, Race, and Class in Work with Gender Variant Children." *Psychoanalytic Dialogues* 21, no. 2: 192–209.

———. 2014. "Mourning the Body as Bedrock: Developmental Considerations in Treating Transsexual Patients Analytically." *Journal of the American Psychoanalytic Association* 62, no. 5: 773–806.

Salamon, Gayle. 2004. "The Bodily Ego and the Contested Domain of the Material." *differences* 15, no. 3: 95–122.

Schilder, Paul. 1950. *The Image and Appearance of the Human Body*. New York: International Universities Press.

Seshadri-Crooks, Kalpana. 2000. *Desiring Whiteness: A Lacanian Analysis of Race*. London: Routledge.

Shepherdson, Charles. 2000. *Vital Signs: Nature, Culture, Psychoanalysis*. New York: Routledge.

Siomopoulos, V. 1974. "Transsexualism: Disorder of Gender Identity, Thought Disorder, or Both?" *Journal of the American Academy of Psychoanalysis* 2, no. 3: 201.

Smith, Yolanda L. S., Stephanie H. M. van Goozen, and Peggy T. Cohen-Kettenis. 2001. "Adolescents with Gender Identity Disorder Who Were Accepted or Rejected for Sex Reassignment Surgery: A Prospective Follow-Up Study." *Journal of the American Academy of Child and Adolescent Psychiatry* 40, no. 4: 472–81.

Suchet, Melanie. 2011. "Crossing Over." *Psychoanalytic Dialogues* 21, no. 2: 172–91.

Thomas, Calvin. 2008. *Masculinity, Psychoanalysis, Straight Queer Theory: Essays on Abjection in Literature, Mass Culture, and Film*. New York: Palgrave Macmillan.

van de Grift, Tim C., et al. 2017. "Surgical Satisfaction, Quality of Life, and Their Association after Gender Affirming Surgery: A Follow-up Study." *Journal of Sex and Marital Therapy*. E-pub ahead of print. doi.org/10.1080/0092623X.2017.1326190.

Verhaeghe, Paul. 2009. *New Studies of Old Villains. A Radical Reconsideration of the Oedipus Complex*. New York: Other.

Transphobia as Symptom

Fear of the "Unwoman"

PATRICIA ELLIOT and LAWRENCE LYONS

Abstract Although today most queer and feminist theorists advocate valuing transgender persons, radical lesbian feminist Sheila Jeffreys contests that position, reviving a much older debate that actively disparages transwomen. The authors' intervention in this debate is to investigate the meaning and function of transphobia in Jeffreys's text through employing the psychoanalytic method of a symptomatic reading. This psychoanalytic reading enables the authors to pose the following questions: What motivates the fear of transwomen that permeates this radical lesbian feminist discourse? Insofar as defenders of this discourse require sexual categories to be rooted in the body and inviolable, what happens when those sexual categories are transgressed? If anxiety produces transphobia, as the authors suggest, then what is needed to free oneself from the fears and the fantasies that underlie it?
Keywords transphobia, symptom, drive, anxiety, Sheila Jeffreys

With the publication of Sheila Jeffreys's *Gender Hurts: A Feminist Analysis of the Politics of Transgenderism* (2014), the thirty-year-old debate about whether feminists should embrace transwomen as women once again rears its ugly head. For most feminists today who support the personal and political struggles of transgender persons to live as women and men or to live as neither or both genders, the revival of this debate represents a wearisome refusal on the part of radical lesbian feminists (RLFs) to respect and value transpersons in general and transwomen in particular.[1] Revisiting this debate raises a question: Why does this form of transphobia persist? We offer a response to that question through promoting a deeper understanding of transphobia using psychoanalytic tools that inform a symptomatic reading of the text. Our methodological focus on the unconscious construction of transphobia as a symptom enables us to explore aspects of this phobia that often go unexplored in the field of trans studies. As will become clear, our symptomatic reading is one that grapples with the root of transphobia as it appears in Jeffreys's text, and it contributes to trans studies by exploring how transphobia works and why it is so difficult to eradicate.

TSQ: Transgender Studies Quarterly ★ Volume 4, Numbers 3–4 ★ November 2017
DOI 10.1215/23289252-4189874 © 2017 Duke University Press

In our view, Jeffreys's text lends itself well to a symptomatic reading. In reiterating the negative claims that transgendering causes nothing but harm, her text repeats earlier RLF views about trans—most notably those of Janice Raymond (1979), but also those of Jeffreys's (2003) previous work. Moreover, and contrary to what transwomen "have to say about their experiences of discrimination, humiliation, oppression, subordination, and subjection" (Becki Ross, quoted in Elliot 2010: 25), Jeffreys persists in positioning them as aggressors, while positioning nontrans women, children, and feminists as victims of transwomen. Indeed the RLF argument Jeffreys (2014) makes is that transgender—construed as the male fantasy of becoming woman—is a harmful practice that should not be supported by anyone, least of all by feminists. First, there is harm to the partners of transgender persons who are allegedly forced to support the transition, and whose sexual identities and communities are disrupted. Second, there is harm to those feminists whose critique of "gender" as a socially constructed form of dominance is threatened. Third, there is harm to transpersons themselves who rely on hormones and other "mutilating" (70) medical practices. Fourth, there is harm to children "diagnosed" as transgender whose nonconformist and otherwise queer behaviors are being targeted.[2] Finally, there is harm to women's rights in general, especially when exclusive nontrans or cisgender women's spaces are required to provide access to transwomen or to "male-bodied transgenders," as Jeffreys (8) calls them. Changing sex is not only negatively construed in this litany of harms; it is also regarded as impossible: male-to-female transgender persons allegedly remain male (or at least, nonwomen), and female-to-male transgender persons remain female (8).

Of course, one way to engage Jeffreys's text would be to critique her assumptions based on the multiple and complex counternarratives produced by trans writers and theorists.[3] But such an approach runs the risk of rehashing well-known critiques, while failing to explain why we are called upon to revisit this debate over the value of trans lives.[4] Instead, we believe that RLF interpretations of transgender exhibit what Jacques Lacan (1998: 121) called a "passion for ignorance," a desire to not know about this form of gender and the oppression experienced by transgender persons. This is why we propose a symptomatic reading of Jeffreys's text, a reading that enables us to pose some potentially more productive questions. Before setting out these questions, it is useful to clarify the meaning of a symptomatic reading.

A symptomatic reading is an immanent reading that does not appeal to an external criterion of judgment or a political critique but to the truth expressed in the text itself. This is not a truth that is consciously or intentionally expressed; a symptomatic reading strives to uncover a knowledge that doesn't know itself as such. It seeks the meaning of the text through an analysis of its major signifiers, repetitions, and fantasies, all of which point to the unconscious of the text. Like other formations of the unconscious such as dreams, parapraxes, and jokes, symptoms have a sense based on the logic of unconscious functioning and appear with a vividness that goes beyond typical representations of lived experience.

Beyond the psychosocial dynamic of exclusion of transwomen from the RLF community that we shall also address, our symptomatic reading analyzes the production of a symptom we will call "the unwoman" as the unconscious source of the phobic syndrome. We will also analyze the drives as represented in this construct by the text. Based on this psychoanalytic approach to transphobia, we pose the following questions: What personal or cultural fantasies underlie the accusations of harm that permeate this text? Insofar as transwomen become the phobic object here, what is it that needs to be avoided, and what is it that requires protection? What motivates the repetition, the recurring attack on transwomen? What fantasies are expressed in the scenarios Jeffreys describes to justify her adoption of a negative position? What representations of unconscious drives appear in the text, and what inherent contradictions do these indicate in the discourse or in the symbolic identity of the RLF perspective? This approach locates specific representatives of unconscious drives as they appear in the text not as an individual pathology but as the indication of a contradiction inherent in a text, in a perspective, in a discourse and symbolic identity, even in a politics.

Beyond the "truths" that Jeffreys promotes as unassailable—that sex is fixed and unalterable, that "gender identity" is simply a masculinist, hierarchical fiction, and that transgendering is delusional and harmful—our analysis reveals another sort of truth. For Lacan, truth is understood as that which motivates a person or a discourse and of which one is unaware. Following Slavoj Žižek's (1996) Lacanian analysis of anti-Semitism as a symptom of an unattainable fantasy of social purity that produces "the Jew" as its uncanny other, we read transphobia as a symptom of a similarly unattainable fantasy, one that produces the unwoman as its uncanny other.[5] The truth we encounter at this level of analysis concerns the fantasy of a politically unified and harmonious lesbian feminist community, an idealized community that is impossible given the inevitability of conflicting desires, and given that it is dependent for its very existence on the untenable belief that sex is fixed and does not change. We argue that what sets anxiety in motion here is the unmooring of symbolic categories of sex by those who cross boundaries and who represent what must be repressed if the RLF identity is to be maintained. Moreover, we analyze how the drives engaged through the text's fantasy scenarios indicate a threat to the structure of RLF identity itself, a threat that is signified by the recurrent textual emphasis on the disappearance of the lesbian subject, if not on the disappearance of the RLF political project itself.

As Žižek points out with respect to anti-Semitism, there is no point in mounting rational arguments against the racist whose phantasmatic constructions of the other are symptoms of an anxiety about which they are unaware and which therefore cannot be given credibility by the other (1996: 105–6). Likewise, the inadequacy of rational argument against the RLF discourse supports our preference for a symptomatic reading of Jeffreys's text in which the author is at pains to locate the force of danger in the transwoman instead of in her own projected fears as phobic subject.

We begin the first section with a psychosocial description of the RLF critique of the transgender project because this critique contributes to a general understanding of transphobia in the text. After addressing the psychoanalysis of phobia in the second section, we describe how phobia is revealed through an analysis of the symptom of unwoman and through an analysis of the drives as represented in two vivid scenarios. Going beyond the commonsense meaning of transphobia as a consciously adopted hatred that could easily be given up, we suggest that it is based on an unconscious anxiety about the disappearance of the structure of RLF subjectivity. In this regard, we offer some concluding observations about the knowledge produced by Jeffreys's text in particular and by the RLF discourse in general. These observations support an interpretation of the structure of the RLF discourse as one of Lacan's (2007) four fundamental discourses, as the discourse of hysteria that produces knowledge of which the subject remains unaware.

Against Transgender: Transphobia as Group Psychology

At the most basic level of the text, Jeffreys is at pains to demonstrate the evil effects of transgender "transmogrifications" (2014: 8) on women and children in general, and on lesbian partners of transpersons in particular. While the discourse of women as victims of men is a familiar one to readers of RLF politics, here the position of male dominance is extended to transgender persons, particularly to transwomen who are read as men regardless of their personal or legal status as women. Pronouns for transpersons in the book reflect Jeffreys's view of them as either "male-bodied transgenders" or "female-bodied transgenders" to emphasize the importance of their originally assigned sex, important because for her a "sex caste" (5) is a system that uses biological sex to subordinate and victimize women.

In sync with other RLF interpretations, Jeffreys's view is that gender is a concept devised by men to ensure male domination and the oppression of women (1). In the text, *gender* refers exclusively to this oppressive hierarchy, and *gender identity* refers to identification with its attendant, stereotypical "sex-roles" that trans people allegedly promote as natural (17).[6] Moreover, what Jeffreys (7) calls "transgender ideology" is defined as "men's views of what women are" (even when such views are supported by other feminists who are then considered duped by that ideology). As such, this ideology represents an attack on nontrans or cisgender women's knowledge and experience, particularly as this knowledge and experience have been conceived from the 1970s onward by RLFs such as Germaine Greer (1999), Janice Raymond (1979), and Robin Morgan (1978). Poststructuralist and queer feminists are criticized for their dissension from RLF perspectives and for participating in this male-driven transgender ideology. Although the former clearly share the goals of creating sexual equality and ending women's oppression, they do not agree with RLF views about the existence of a unified "women's knowledge and experience" or about the causes and solutions to complex and intersectional forms of oppression. The RLF disregard for differences among women, differences that introduce disturbances, disagreements, and other forms of inequality, therefore suggests that what is at stake is an imagined harmonious and egalitarian community of women. The exclusion of transwomen from the community of women on the grounds that they are really men seeking to invade women's spaces is one way to protect this fantasy.

As Sigmund Freud argues in chapter 5 of *Civilization and Its Discontents* (1985a), the general ambivalence of human relations is purged of its aggression and hatred by projecting them onto others. The unity of love and hate is broken in favor of love of the self-same and hatred of the excluded others. The solidity of the group depends on the clarity of this line of demarcation such that any transgression of this line represents a disturbing influence. From a psychosocial perspective, then, one can see how the transperson is taken to be a willful boundary crosser who transgresses the fixed and natural categories of sexual difference, categories that are required by the RLF community to secure its own boundaries.[7] The RLF discourse is directed against the tyranny of masculine power and is determined by the difference of this tyranny from the community of the feminine, defined in opposition to it. So the transperson, especially the transwoman, is seen to be a transgressive boundary crosser who undermines the clear boundaries marking the fixed categories of sex that are necessary for establishing the identity of the RLF community. Those who are not submitted to the symbolic categories of the social order are the source of fear, disgust, and rejection as they put the categories into question. Transwomen do not necessarily blur the lines of difference, but they do not submit to them despite their powerful valorization of the differences. What transgender persons therefore expose is the instability or contingency of sexual difference. They do this through refusing their assigned sex and by their practice of transition, which marks the difference in the body.

The transwoman is the particular target of rejection here, not just as another "male" to be excluded but as a sign of the limits of an exclusive sexed identity because transgendering itself creates an uncertainty around the idea of an essential and bodily sexual difference. This uncanny feeling of uncertainty creates a sense of loss of the bodily basis for sexual difference and identity. At a time when gender identity is regarded—either positively or negatively—as performative, as social construction, sexual identity must be rooted somewhere else: in a bodily difference taken to be given or natural. The trans project, however, makes the presumably natural unnatural, and the presumably essential merely contingent. As such, it undermines the RLF conviction that the body itself is a natural signifier of sexual identity, and so the certainty of sexual identity cannot be maintained. For the RLF, the failure to give sexual difference this certainty or, rather, the perception of its inherent uncertainty as provoked by the very existence of the transwoman threatens her own identity: it represents an existential crisis that must be repressed. The repression of this perception also serves to mask a contradiction in the RLF discourse that we address after describing one more reason for the exclusion of the border crosser.

From Jeffreys's perspective, the task of feminism is to "abolish" gender altogether, not to celebrate it through catering to the mistaken views of transgender, poststructuralist, queer, or other feminist theorists who are interpreted as collaborating with men in the oppression of women (2014: 43). Once we have liberated ourselves and our society from patriarchal gender constructs of masculinity and femininity, the rationale for transgendering will supposedly disappear because the idealization of femininity will no longer exist. To buttress her view of this claim, Jeffreys explicitly adopts (28–32) the hypotheses of Ray Blanchard (2005), Michael Bailey (2003), and Anne Lawrence (2008) that transwomen are either repressed homosexuals (those who transition in order to legitimize their choice of women partners) or "autogynephilic" (those who are in love with the image of themselves as women). She suggests that if transwomen properly addressed their homophobia and/or their idealization of femininity, they would no longer seek to identify as women.[8] In other words, if transwomen weren't pathologically disposed or driven by repressed desires, they would remain members of their assigned sex and not seek to cross its borders.

Our summary of psychosocial dynamics reveals that even at the level of the explicit arguments of the text there is a strong sense of anxiety, not only about potential harms to women or children but also about the meaning of the border-crossing transwoman. The generalized threat signaled by this textual generation of anxiety is bound up with the contradictory nature of the RLF discourse, a discourse that founds its identity on the sexual distinction as essential to its political project. The dominance of the male as the other to be rejected is phallic, an aspect of phallocracy. But if one's primary identity as female is based on this distinction, then one's identity is itself dependent on the phallic, the logic of the phallic differentiation of the world. The image of the "woman-identified" woman

(Rich 1980: 648), the woman who defines herself only in relation to women, is challenged by the figure of the male-identified woman, the woman who is the symptom of the phallocratic male.[9] The gains of the woman-identified woman, perhaps especially the lesbian woman, must be protected from the excluded male other. More urgently still, the RLF must be protected from the subversive return of female identification through the male gaze. But the need for identity in difference in which the difference is defined in relation to and in opposition to phallic identity poses a contradiction for this particular text as well as for the RLF discourse in general (in which the underlying relation to phallic identity must be repressed). It is a contradiction that keeps on generating symptoms! After outlining what constitutes a psychoanalytic approach to phobia, we will proceed to analyze the specific phobia of the text in which the internal enemy is the woman who is not a woman but the woman who carries the virus of the male gaze and who speaks with the persecutory voice of the other.

The Psychoanalysis of Phobia

While the psychosocial depiction of hatred provoked by the inside outsider contributes to our social and psychological understanding of the production of transphobia in which the transwoman is conceived as the hated and persecuting other, more work is needed to grasp the meaning of the phobia itself. *Phobia* is a term used by Freud (1977a) to analyze the workings of pathological processes in patients. We contend that an exploration of this theory as it applies to the text can bring one closer to an understanding of the issue of transphobia from a psychoanalytic perspective. The function of a phobic object is to specify and contain a generalized threat signaled by an unlimited affect of anxiety. The repression of the ideational representative of what might be an affectionate trend unbinds its libidinal energy, transforming it into anxiety. The resulting uncontrolled anxiety can be contained by being embodied in an object that can then be avoided by specific actions such as those of avoidance or exclusion. One could assume that the generalized anxiety of identity provoked by the construction of RLF identity, an identity that allows for none of the desired solidity of identity, would be embodied in the transwoman. For the RLF, it is the transwoman who brings the masculine essence and influence into the defined and defended lines of demarcation under the guise of being feminine. That is, the transwoman's identity represents and makes present a relation to masculinity that has been repressed in the construction of the RLF identity. As Freud describes it in the case history of Dora, the purpose of the phobia is "to safeguard her against any revival of the repressed perception" (1977b: 62). The presence of a phobia therefore indicates a repressed content, the uncovering of which would undo the phobia in the case of an analytic patient. In the case of the transphobic text, the phobia reveals a contradiction at the heart of RLF discourse in which the perception of one's identity as dependent on its masculine counterpart must be repressed.

In the case history of Little Hans, Freud (1977a: 267–77) determines that the generalized anxiety, an anxiety that is defended against by the phobia, results from the repression of the ideational representative of a libidinal trend. The repression entails a loss of meaning and the conversion of affect into anxiety, which is an affect that can't be identified or named and is experienced as overwhelming. Overwhelming anxiety can become the basis of conversion symptoms in hysteria or be left free to invade one's perception of the world. Another response is the phobic response, which consists of "psychically binding the anxiety" and barring "access to every possible occasion that might lead to the development of anxiety, by erecting mental barriers in the nature of precautions, inhibitions or prohibitions" (275). Libido or sexual excitement is converted into anxiety by repression, into an affect that doesn't know its own cause or means of satisfaction. In phobias this anxiety can be fixed in a phobic object whose presence then evokes the anxiety thereby contained. But this method of getting rid of anxiety comes "at the price of subjecting [oneself] to all kinds of inhibitions and restrictions" (275). One only defends against the anxiety by avoiding the phobic object. However, in Jeffreys's text, the defense is not to accept restrictions on the subject but to project them onto the transgressor of boundaries and to focus rejection and hatred on the figure of the interloping masculine presence. Here the choice of phobic object is overdetermined by the psychosocial rejection of the transwoman who is described as invading or usurping women's space from outside the boundary of inclusion. While transphobia affords some understanding at this level, a symptomatic analysis will prove even more effective.

According to Freud, the analysis of the sense of a phobia cannot be done directly, as a phobia is not a symptom but descriptive. For Freud, phobias "should only be regarded as syndromes which may form part of various neuroses" (1977a: 273) or, for our purposes, syndromes that form part of a distorted political position. That is to say that the mere description of a phobia, while an obvious place to begin, is not psychoanalytically effective because "the relation between anxiety and its objects" is of a "secondary nature" (282). Following Freud, we understand that the path to the formation of a phobia involves the conversion of a specific partial drive into anxiety by the repression of its content and the binding of anxiety in the phobic object. The analysis required here is the analysis of unconscious mental processes that connect the repressed drive to the anxiety and the anxiety to its phobic object (292). In analyzing the phobia of Little Hans, Freud claims that "the essence of Hans's illness was entirely dependent upon the nature of the [drive] components that had to be repulsed" (296).

The choice of phobic object is also at issue in analyzing the phobia, and, as our previous discussion shows, the transgressive trans-intruder is part of the meaning of this object choice. But the more effective analysis is to trace the psychic connections of the chain of unconscious signifiers from the desire at work in the drives to anxiety and to phobia. This is accomplished in psychoanalysis through an analysis of the associations of the patient and for our purposes through analyzing the significant aspects of the text in question that present themselves as laden with libidinal force. First we discuss the concept of "unwoman" as a symptom that underlies the phobia that takes transwomen as its object, and then we discuss its connection to the drives.

Unwoman as Symptom

We have seen that transphobia as a psychosocial phenomenon and as a political category pervades Jeffreys's discourse. Now we are concerned with the textual positioning of the transwoman as abject other, as the deceptive and treacherous nonwoman, indeed, as the disturbing figure of the unwoman. Transgendered women are not accepted as women by RLFs and so are considered to be failed boundary crossers. A man may be unmanned but never transformed into a "real" woman. The transwoman appears in the imaginary sphere as the unwoman, a figure as anxiety provoking as the undead for popular culture, the un-American for the politically paranoid, or the uncanny for the psychoanalytic tradition.

According to Žižek, "the 'undead' are neither alive nor dead, they are precisely the monstrous 'living dead'" (2006: 21–22), and this negative life is destructive of natural life like a kind of antimatter destroying matter. The un-American is the specter that haunts the fantasy of the ideal of American community; they appear to be like the real American but have a hidden evil purpose to destroy the American way of life. Likewise, in Jeffreys's text, transwomen are perceived not only as the "evil deceivers and make-believers" of Talia Bettcher's (2007) critique but also as possessing control over others. Signifiers of this power are reflected in the language of the text in which transpersons are variously seen to "occupy" (45), "extirpate" (46), "erase" (47), "usurp" (51), "highjack" (88), and "expunge" (100) women's bodies, experience, and/or space. Just as the un-American disrupts the impossible symbolic fiction of the all-American citizen, the unwoman disrupts the RLF dream of the exclusive women's community outside the control of men. The failure of the dream community gives way, not to a realization of the flawed nature of the idealized state, or to some failure in one's own belief, but to the feared and hated image of the other. As such, the phobic subject is caught up in what Žižek calls a "paranoiac obsession" with this other as the enemy (1996: 116).

Žižek (1996) employs the example of anti-Semitism in describing the logic of hatred in which the Jew is the object of fantasy. Like the unwoman, the phantasmatic Jew doesn't exist in reality but is feared even more because of "the gap" between the fantasized Jew and the living person: "The anti-Semitic discourse constructs the figure of the Jew as a phantomlike entity that is to be found nowhere in reality, and then uses this very gap between the 'conceptual Jew' and the reality of actually existing Jews as the ultimate argument against Jews" (108). The phantasmatic Jew is "a kind of uncanny double of the public authority that perverts its proper logic: he has to act in the shadow, invisible to the public eye, irradiating a phantomlike, spectral omnipotence" (110). And for Žižek, the specter as phobic object is not only to be feared and avoided but also seen to be persecutory. The phobic subject is also decidedly paranoid: "haunted" by images of what the other "is doing when out of my sight, of how he or she deceives me and plots against me, of how he or she ignores me and indulges in an enjoyment that is intensive" (116).

Applying this analysis to the RLF discourse, we can see that it is not the actual characteristics of the transperson—what they say or do—that incites the fear/hatred of the RLF. Rather, it is the latter's fantasy about the other's political and/or sexual omnipresence, "about 'their' strange sexual practices, about their secret hypnotic powers" (Žižek 1996: 105). Unlike nontransgender men, those more predictable opponents of women whose exercise of power and privilege on the basis of their difference is so easily discredited, transwomen are represented as sneaky, deceptive, and invasive, "usurping biological and existential womanhood" (Jeffries 2014: 51) in their false claim to be women. Deceitful and plotting, the unwoman is imagined to change her sex in order to betray and harm women, and to disrupt the possibility of a community of equals. What could be more uncanny?

For Freud, the uncanny is ambiguously familiar and strange. It is "produced when the distinction between imagination and reality is effaced, as when something that we have hitherto regarded as imaginary appears before us in reality" (1985b: 367). Is this not precisely what we mean when we declare something to be "unreal"? "The uncanny" is English for Freud's term, *das Unheimliche*, which is literally "unhomey": a strange but familiar element that revives anxiety because it is "something repressed which *recurs*" (363). The uncanny is the encounter with the embodiment of this strange but familiar other that represents the return of the repressed; it is "something which ought to have remained hidden but has come to light" (364). In this regard, Freud wrote of the return of the dead, of spirits and ghosts. In any case, these ambiguous others—the undead, the un-American, and the unwoman—all represent the evil other side of a shared fantasy of an ideal state or of an untroubled community for a political discourse. Where there is an encounter with the uncanny, with the falsely familiar, anxiety is provoked by the object whose "features function as indicators of a more radical strange-ness," as something "not quite human" (Žižek 1996: 105). This radical other is what must be excluded if the fantasy of political unity is to be maintained.

In Jeffreys's text, the uncanny as unwoman is attached to the disruption of the other as the model for identification and thus for one's own identity. A woman whose identity does not oppose but rather embodies the masculine disrupts the exclusion of masculinity as a category upon which RLF sexual identity is founded. Thus, the unwoman calls into question the homey group identification of radical lesbian feminism and the identities of its members upon which the fantasy of a women's community of equals is based. This concern appears, for example, in Jeffreys's complaint that transwomen are "hypermasculine" men who engage in a "ruthless appropriation of women's experience and existence" (2014: 7). More-over, legal and medical support for transgender rights is understood not only to "clash" with women's rights but also to threaten "communities of women" where "privacy and security from men's violence" is at stake (11). This power to exert control over women is attributed to the fantasy figure of unwoman, whose actions are characterized variously as homophobic, fetishistic, masochistic, voyeuristic, and criminal.

Psychoanalytic theory contends that one way to control or at least to channel the anxiety provoked by the anomalous is by taking an object as its target, and here the object of the phobia is the transwoman. This transphobia enables a defense against a generalized anxiety—the idea that sexual difference is not stable and fixed, or that the boundaries between man and woman are permeable—by localizing it in an object that can be avoided, denounced, or persecuted. While transwomen are the object of the phobia, the fantasized figure of unwoman is the symptom, and like other symptoms it haunts the imaginary of the phobic subject.

From Symptom to Drive

The unwoman as symptom is an uncanny figure that is both too much and too little. What is missing in the unwoman is a "true" female identity, which for Jeffreys means an experience and knowledge tied to a history of growing up in a female body. Although unwoman occupies the place of the object of desire for the RLF, she is not an acceptable object of desire for her because she is perceived to be an impostor who exercises male power through the gaze and the voice. What is too much is indicated by the drives represented in the symptom. For Lacan (as for Freud) drives are partial drives that have an "irrepressible character even through repressions" (Lacan 1981: 162). As representatives of libido (198), the partial drives obtain pleasure in an indirect way, not through possessing an object but by circulating around some object that is imagined to be missing or lost. This lost object (Lacan's "object a") is instrumental in the unconscious construction of subjective identity. Not an object of desire, the object of the drive can be "the foundation of an identification of the subject, or the foundation of an identification disavowed by the subject" (186). As object that causes desire, "object a" represents what is lacking in the object of desire that makes it desirable. As the object of the drive, it represents the surplus of enjoyment that is "anaclitically" attached to the functioning of needs, but it can also be the cause of anxiety when it is too closely encountered, as in the case of the phobic object. The encounter of the phobic object through the gaze and voice transforms sexual excitement into anxiety, and when desire is encountered in the other, it becomes a source of anxiety and aggression. It is how others enjoy their object that is at the heart of powerful emotions like hate, particularly where "others" are seen to enjoy excessively or somewhat differently. For Lacan, desires are dangerous, and this is particularly the case when they are alien.

The drives to be analyzed here can be seen to appear in the text's presentation of two vivid scenarios: the gaze that is the object of exhibitionism or voyeurism but uncanny when it is encountered out of its proper place, and the voice with its power of seduction as the ego's ideal but guilt inducing and persecutory when it speaks from the position of the superego. As unwoman, the transwoman is endowed with the power to control how women see themselves through the effects of what for Lacan are two fundamental objects of the drive: the gaze and the voice. As the phantasmatic scenarios concerning the invasion of intimate women's spaces reveal, the gaze and the voice together threaten to undermine the identity of the subject so addressed. The gaze is the reactive object of the scopic drive that petrifies: it is the gaze of the other that functions in the dialectic of imaginary identity originating in the mirror stage. The voice is the object of the invocatory drive that is erotic and seductive; but it also constitutes the voice of conscience and wields the power to persecute and to create guilt. Following a description of the two scenarios, we will analyze the nature of these drives and show how they function within those scenarios with respect to the unwoman, that intimate alien who subverts a type of subjective formation that is to be nurtured by the RLF discourse.

In the first scenario, the gaze of the transwoman is imagined to invade the public yet intimate space of the sex-segregated washroom, an exclusive cisgender women's space that transwomen also access. In this context, Jeffreys perceives a violation of women's right to privacy, security, and dignity, which includes "the forcing of women into the intimate proximity of men, some of whom have a clear interest in the sexual excitements that they can access by violating women's right to human dignity" (2014: 154). This passage exemplifies two aspects of the subject's encounter with the object of the drive. First, if the object is brought too close, it generates anxiety, which in this case takes the form of shame. Second, it is the other's excessive enjoyment that is disconcerting. Jeffreys's view is that like men, and especially those men who don women's clothing to engage in voyeurism (155), transwomen should be excluded from women's public toilets. Her knowledge of these voyeurs is gleaned from criminal reports of cross-dressed men who have been caught in the act, including "the direct targeting of women's excretory functions for observation, filming and sound recording" (155). Moreover, the pornographic industry includes photographs men "have taken by stealth, through hidden cameras, of women in toilets and locker rooms, defecating and urinating, or naked in showers" (154). Because *some* male voyeurs cross-dress to gain access to women's intimate spaces, transwomen, who are regarded as men who believe they are women, are also lumped in this category. Not only does Jeffreys count "men who seek to transgender . . . in the ranks of rapists and murderers of women" (176), she also misconstrues their greater likelihood to be criminalized as an indication that they "are more prone to criminal behaviour than other men are" (157).[10]

Jeffreys asserts that transwomen should also be excluded from other exclusively female public spaces such as prisons, women's shelters, and music festivals where their access is depicted as "forced" or as "an onslaught" (165). These metaphors are explicitly linked to rape by other RLF authors Jeffreys cites (163, 167). And the male gaze is clearly invoked in these intimate and exclusive female spaces where RLF identity and culture is meant to be "consolidated" (166). The transwoman's presence at the Michigan women's music festival is deemed a challenge to "the site's special and ideological remoteness from the everyday surveillance of the heteronormative gaze" (Maria Fowler, quoted in Jeffreys 2014: 166). The feared gaze of transwomen in the communal showers is also a male gaze that makes women "ashamed of their bodies" (Jeffreys 2014: 166), a shame that the women-only site was meant to preclude. The encounter with the gaze objectifies the subject and creates a sense of shame, just as the reaction against the seductive power of the voice generates guilt.

Equally controlling is the presence of the transwoman in the private life of her intimate partner. In the second vivid scenario, the transwoman's voice is imagined to have the ability to transform women's identities. For example, in the (formerly) heterosexual couple, transwomen are said to "highjack" women's lives (88), to exhibit "masculine privilege" (91), and to force their wives to take part in sexual activities "in support of their husbands' impersonation of womanhood" (94). Another example of what Jeffreys refers to as "parasitism" is the partners' "feeling that their husbands want to be them in a parasitic way, to take over their persona" (87). Even worse than these narcissistic and fetishistic demands that disrupt the heterosexual woman's identity is the "invasion" of "the most intimate of women's spaces"—the lesbian body (180). In this instance, the transwoman (as "male-bodied") is said to demand sexual access to her lesbian partner's body and to "guilt-trip lesbians into allowing penises into their bodies" (180). Jeffreys's complaint is that complying with these sexual demands undermines the lesbian partner's sexual identity, while failure to comply transforms her into a guilt-ridden subject who is accused of "transphobia or transmisogyny" (181). It is a double bind situation in which she is a victim.

Turning to an analysis of the drives, we will suggest that Jeffreys's concerns with the gaze in the women's washroom and with the voice in the intimate relationship are fantasy projections onto the transperson. What is there for the unwoman to see in the woman's washroom? Is it a real nakedness or bodily function or something even more intimate—the fragility of the subject's gendered identity in the form of a fantasy scenario of intrusion of something that must be kept at a distance? What is heard in the voice of the unwoman in the intimate relationship? Is it really the sexual requests of the other that constitute the violation of the lesbian partner, or is it something more unsettling—the erosion of her lesbian identity through a fantasy of being held captive to the demands of the (male) other? What is it about the drives of gaze and voice that enable us to understand the formation of the transphobia and its symptom?

For Freud (1984b), one of the partial drives is scopophilic, and like the other partial drives, one of its features is the ability of the drive to turn around on itself. In this case, the mechanism of turning around is through an identification with the other in which the aim of seeing/voyeurism can be transformed into that of being seen/exhibitionism. Freud's analysis of the scopophilic drive locates a preliminary narcissistic object in the subject's own body with a turning around from voyeurism into exhibitionism based on identification on the side of the subject of the drive: "The narcissistic *subject* is, through identification, replaced by another, extraneous ego" (1984b: 129). And for Freud, the object of the scopophilic drive "is not the eye itself" but "an object other than itself" (130), which means that the eye would be the source, not the object of the drive. In terms of Jeffreys's text, what is being seen in the women's washroom are not simply women's exposed bodies or bodily functions but the (male) gaze of the voyeuristic unwoman who is imagined to be deriving "sexual excitements" from observing women "defecating and urinating." This gaze undermines something crucial to the RLF subject: the refusal to be the object of the male gaze coming from the other.

For Lacan, it is the gaze that originates as the object of the scopic drive which concerns both the pleasure of sexual seeing and of "*making oneself seen*" (1981: 195). In discussing a work of Maurice Merleau-Ponty, Lacan accepts the idea of "the dependence of the visible on that which places us under the eye of the seer" (72). But for Lacan, the eye functions as a metaphor for something prior, for the gaze that is not the source of the drive but its object, or an instance of "object a."

The idea is that the gaze is a virtual object, an object that has been turned around on the subject such that the gaze is not a looking but a being looked at or a giving of the subject to be seen. For Lacan, "I see only from one point, but in my existence I am looked at from all sides" (72). This transformed object is not something conscious but a part of the unconscious structure of the subject in relation to its constitutive other: "The psychic object, once a real other, can no longer be seen or heard. Invisible and inaudible, it nonetheless gazes at us or speaks inside us from the outside, arousing anxiety" (Jaanus 1995: 125). For Freud as well, this incorporated psychical other can be either annihilating or enticing, and it might be for this reason that the drive for Lacan is the scopic drive, not the scopophilic drive in Freud's terms. *Scopic* is a more neutral term that allows for a transformation of content, while an erotic scopophilic drive can be changed into what might be called a desexualized "scopophobic" drive in which the fear of being looked at replaces the love of being seen. If the scopophobic drive is repressed, anxiety can be transformed into shame. In Jeffreys's account, this fear of being seen is indicated by the claim that the gaze of the other operates by "stealth" through hidden cameras that violate women's privacy. There is no pleasure here in seeing, except on the side of the other. The feared gaze of unwoman creates anxiety for women who can no longer be assured that cross-dressing men will be excluded from their previously sex-segregated space.

According to Lacan, the gaze takes the place of the imaginary other from which the subject draws an image of unity. The gaze is the part of the self in the other that gives the world a center and coherence, turning sensation into the experience of reality. But the gaze from the position of the other also turns the subject into an object, which is mortifying. The Sartrean figure cited by Lacan to describe the gaze is that of someone looking through a keyhole at a forbidden scene who hears a noise that signals he or she is being observed: "The gaze that surprises me and reduces me to shame. . . . the gaze I encounter . . . is, not a seen gaze, but a gaze imagined by me in the field of the Other" (1981: 84).[11] Through the gaze of the other, one is objectified, with the effect of producing shame—an affect that replaces scopophilic pleasure (84). According to Jacques-Alain Miller's interpretation, Sartre is "trying to grasp the subject's fall in the status of this shameful reject" (2006: 14). And Lacan makes use of this example because "it is an account of the emergence of the affect of shame as a collapse of the subject" (14). Unlike guilt, which is the effect of a judging other, shame is the result of a perceived loss of modesty by the subject who imagines herself being seen by the other or being caught in the act by the gaze of the other: "Shame is related to the jouissance that touches on what Lacan . . . calls 'that which is most intimate in the subject'" (13). The subject as objectified is petrified by the gaze as if being caught in the view of Medusa-like power of the drive. In Jeffreys's scenario, the intent of the unwoman's gaze is to make women objects for her perverse pleasure. This gaze robs women of their modesty, as their naked bodies are exposed in the washroom and communal shower, making women "ashamed of their bodies" (Jeffreys 2014: 166).

We can see why the gaze is also represented by the well-known idea of the evil eye, something against which one must be protected. It is something that structures reality but cannot be seen and is not visual but psychical. The eye has the power to analyze and separate things (Lacan 1981: 115), a power opposite to uniting things (the two powers that correspond, respectively, to Freud's distinction between the death drives and erotic drives). The eye as source and the gaze as object are structured as a death drive in their power to objectify the subject, to threaten annihilation and induce shame. In his account of Lacan's reading of shame, Miller notes that in other historical times a person might well die of shame in order to preserve their honor—the value and meaning of their life (2006: 18). According to Miller, Lacan points out that no one any longer dies of shame but that shame continues to carry the power of death—the "second death" (19), which is that of the "emblem" or "the master signifier that marks the subject with an ineffaceable singularity" (20). Psychoanalysts must keep in mind that the subject has a relationship "to what he is insofar as he is represented by a signifier" (19). This signifier will not be sacrificed, as it represents "that which is the most intimate, the most precious in his existence" (19). Thus we can see how the gaze of the other as object of the scopic drive induces a shame that reduces one to an object. An unconscious instance of the death drive, the scopic drive must be repressed in the name of preserving the honor and value of the subject. In Jeffreys's scenario, the fantasized fear is of rape and murder, but what is at stake here are the dignity and honor of women, emblems of their distinction that are threatened by the "intimate proximity of men" (2014: 154) in the gaze of unwoman.

The voice is the object of the invocatory drive, an object that also plays its part in the foundation of subjective identity. The voice is the other that speaks within me, and outside of my control. For Freud (1984a), it is the voice of conscience or the superego that speaks to me through establishing an ego ideal, a set of prescribed and/or prohibited ways of being. Modeled on the father as the "perceived obstacle" to the child's oedipal desire for the mother, the voice of the superego is a masculine voice that makes moral demands on the ego that it strives to fulfill (374). If the drive that corresponds to the demands of this internal voice is repressed, one experiences an unconscious sense of guilt, and the aim of the drive turns from love to hate, which for Freud produces an unconscious need for punishment and suffering (391). Alternatively, this drive can be externalized as aggression against the other and its representatives in the external world. However, this aggression increases anxiety in which the ego fears being "overwhelmed or annihilated" (399). In the fantasized scenario, we hear unwoman's demand for sexual access to women's bodies, one that lesbians may be "guilt-tripped" into accepting. Aggression toward transwomen is evident in the critique of their sexual demands as unwelcome assertions of male privilege, demands that threaten to undermine RLF identity. The voice of the unwoman must therefore be rejected because it appears as the voice of paternal authority coming from the other that is invasive.

Now we can understand what is so terrifying about unwoman. The unconscious desire from the side of the other takes the form of anxiety when the object of desire disappears and all that remains is a "pointing towards the object's place," which is now that of an "indefinite object" that appears as an internal danger to the integrity of the ego (Lacan 2015: 365). When the drives are located in unwoman as a masculine other, and when the object of desire (woman) has become undesirable, the only relationship to desire that remains is that of an unbearable anxiety. For Lacan, this is the purpose of phobia itself: "To sustain a relationship to desire in the form of anxiety" (366). What is terrifying about unwoman is that she represents a paternal authority that is otherwise refused by the RLF subject as an invasive limit on her enjoyment. Yet it is the limiting function of the symbolic father that enables the subject to have an identity in the first place, and a position from which to desire. The paternal function that limits one's enjoyment also protects the subject from being overwhelmed by the more intense love bond with the m(other), in which nothing is lacking and one cannot become a desiring subject. According to Lacan, "Anxiety is the final or radical mode in which the subject continues to sustain his relationship to desire, even if it is an unbearable mode" (365). One response to the unbearable anxiety threatening one's identity is aggression.

In his chapter "Aggressiveness in Psychoanalysis," Lacan indicates the importance of drawing out the patient's aggression toward the analyst, as it will represent "the patient's imaginary transference onto us of one of the more or less archaic imagos . . . and which has given its form to this or that agency of the personality through an act of identification (2006: 87–88). The form that aggression takes reveals a particular form of unconscious subjective identity that must be anticipated and responded to accordingly. His fourth thesis is that "aggressiveness is the tendency correlated with a mode of identification I call narcissistic, which determines the formal structure of man's ego and of the register of entities characteristic of his world" (89). Especially interesting for our analysis is his discussion of aggressive reactions in paranoia, which take the form of two "parallel series": belligerent actions on the one hand, and "imputations of harm" on the other (90).[12] According to Lacan, explanations people give for imputing harm to the other "run the gamut from poison (borrowed from the register of a highly primitive organicism), to evil spells (magic), influence (telepathy), physical intrusion (lesions), diversion of intent (abuse), theft of secrets (dispossession), violation of privacy (profanation), injury (legal action), spying and intimidation (persecution), defamation and character assassination (prestige), and damages and exploitation (claims)" (2006: 90). While we have focused on some of the ways in which harmful actions are attributed to the transwoman, readers of Jeffreys will notice that all of these harmful capacities are attributed either literally or metaphorically to her, or to the transgender ideology she represents. While the transwoman is perceived to influence her partner, to violate women's privacy, to spy and intimidate, transgender ideology is a kind of poison that corrodes lesbian communities, magically turning lesbians into "genderqueer" male-identified persons (Jeffreys 2014: 45), defaming the character of "real" women, and damaging RLF feminist politics. As Lacan predicts, the imputation of harm openly reveals "the role of aggressive intention in phobia" (2006: 88). Moreover, he makes the connection between aggression in phobia and the threat to the subjective structure of the subject, a connection that we also discovered in our analysis of the scopic and the invocatory drives at work in the fantasy scenarios of the text.

Anxiety and the Disappearing Lesbian Subject

As we understand them, the two fantasized scenarios in Jeffreys's text that represent both the signal anxiety and the symptom of the text are clearly based on the repression of two separate partial drives: the scopic and the invocatory.[13] These drives are portrayed as bringing their partial objects of gaze and voice into too close proximity to the subject, a proximity that creates anxiety leading to the disintegration of the subject's ego identity. The ego is caught between the gaze of the imaginary other and the demands voiced by the superego. For Freud, "the ego is the actual seat of anxiety"; it emits its libidinal energy as anxiety and represents "the fear of being overwhelmed and annihilated" (1984a: 399). The imagined encounters with the phobic object take the form of the intrusive male gaze of the unwoman in the washroom where anxiety is experienced as shame or loss of "dignity" (Jeffreys 2014: 154). They also take the form of the demanding male voice of the unwoman, which shifts the woman-identified woman partner into the position of male-identified woman partner, disintegrating lesbian identity from inside. Because of the eerie power of these encounters and their representations, they represent figures of the uncanny. The unwoman is the enemy within because despite her conscious intentions and feminine identity she represents the embodiment of the drives in the form of the male gaze and the masculine voice, two drives that threaten the ego with destruction and fill it with anxiety.

In this section, we present some textual evidence of the destructive effects of anxiety and the phobic response on the RLF subject. Experiencing herself as under attack, the RLF nevertheless remains unaware of how that experience is generated by her own fantasy of the unwoman who enjoys tormenting her with her voyeuristic gaze and her power to control. Knowledge of the phobia is produced even though this knowledge remains ineffective because it is unconscious. As we will suggest, this knowledge could become the basis for another political response if the untheorized anxiety located in the unwoman could be made accessible.

For psychoanalysis, when the basis of identity is undermined, the subject is alienated, and its meaning fades away: if I can no longer be certain of who I am, then my existence as a subject disappears. If our analysis is correct, then we should expect to find reference to this perceived threat to the subject in the text. Sure enough, in Jeffreys's text, repetition of the word *disappears* is rife. Used as a verb, it captures the idea of a process that is the effect of the other on oneself. According to Jeffreys, the transgender project "disappears the fixedness of sex" (2014: 5), "disappears biological reality" (184), disappears "masculine privilege" (9), disappears "the category woman" (161), and "disappears . . . all the experiences of" women (6). Most strikingly, it is a project that "disappears" lesbians themselves (3, 45, and 108), since "the very existence of 'women' and 'lesbians' has become doubtful" (48). What is not in doubt is that the transgender project for which unwoman is a metonymic emblem represents the fantasized annihilation of everything that holds meaning for the RLF. We contend, however, that while the disappearance of lesbian individuals is clearly a fantasy, the fading away of the RLF subject is *not* a fantasy. That is, the lesbian subject whose distinctive identity is based on a contradictory refusal of women's relationship to men in the assertion of female identity has become difficult to maintain. Given this existential threat to RLF identity and politics, a threat that is heightened with the increasing visibility and legitimation of transpersons, the repetition of the transphobic discourse with its drives and its symptom can be understood.

For the RLF whose identity is derived from a master signifier that is gendered female, honor and distinction as well as identity depend on its gendered specificity. It is the distinctive RLF identity that is undermined by the (imagined male) gaze and voice of the unwoman in the two fantasy scenarios we analyzed. We have suggested that what is at play in the tableau of the couple of unwoman and lesbian is the voice that is heard as male, at least in insistence and effects. The inner voice is that of the superego, which proclaims values and judges from the standpoint of the ego-ideal. Demanding what it wants from the subject, the voice comes from the Other and possesses the power to create guilt. As we have shown, the voice of the unwoman that demands sexual acquiescence of the lesbian partner creates guilt in the latter, whether she complies or not, and puts her sexuality into question.

These drive scenarios emphasize Lacan's point (2007: 182–83) that to lose one's distinction is to lose one's honor and so to be ashamed. For Lacan, shame is prominent in a society in which honor is the primary ethical force, but in contemporary Western society, this shame passes away along with the sense of honor only to become unconscious and a reaction to an encounter with the gaze. For the RLF, the loss of honor and distinction is experienced as real and as such supports the complaint about the harmful effects of the intrusive gaze of unwoman that underlies the transphobia. Moreover, as the RLF prides herself on being the subject who embodies and protects the honor of feminism itself, the perceived threat to her woman-identified identity also threatens to undermine feminism itself (Jeffreys 2014: 119). We can understand the threat to RLF subjectivity through the undermining of her sense of honor and value as signaled by the unwoman. This threat to the ego operates through two of the masters it must serve: the alter ego (how one sees oneself) and the superego (how one is judged or valued by the other). These masters are gendered male by the biography and structure imputed to the unwoman. One might say, following from this discourse and after Lacan, that anxiety is the affect of the real, shame is the affect of the imaginary, and guilt is the affect of the symbolic. Anxiety is annihilating, shame is mortifying, and guilt is condemnatory. What can be done with this sort of knowledge?

For both Freud and Lacan, the knowledge produced by the hysteric plays a formative role in the founding of psychoanalysis and the discovery of the unconscious. The hysteric produces knowledge about her symptoms, even though this knowledge is inaccessible to her. The importance of sustaining a sense of honor and the replacement of shame and guilt by aggression is a knowledge expressed in Jeffreys's text. This knowledge is also implicit in the RLF discourse in general, of which the text itself functions as a symptom. As with the knowledge produced by the hysteric, this knowledge has no power to affect the phobic stance of the RLF subject because it remains in the unconscious. As Lacan (1998: 16) indicates in his model of the discourse of the hysteric, the knowledge produced is "impotent" because it is unknown to the subject and therefore unable to dissolve the symptom.

We have shown that the subjective structure of the woman-identified woman can be undermined from two directions by two drives that constrain the ego and assail the particular identity of the RLF. The response of the RLF to transwomen as described in this text remains on the imaginary level in which drives are repressed and located on the side of the other and no identification with them or the unwoman is possible. The evil eye of the unwoman's gaze must be ejected from the protected and segregated site designated exclusively for ciswomen and her voice prevented from the domestic scene of seductive intimacy with the woman-identified lesbian life partner. The result of this dual-pronged threat provides the motive for a witch hunt of transwomen. Their persecution is analogous to that of the committee on un-American activities that persecuted those in the media who structured the gaze and the voice of Hollywood beyond the control of the American state. In both cases, then, a better politics would involve relating to the reality of the persons who are vilified than to the phobic imaginary of those who persecute them.

It is only by uncovering the true but inaccessible and impotent knowledge that the discourse of the RLF might be able to overcome the symptom of transphobia that on the surface holds no reasonable force. For a psychoanalytic patient, this process would require working with the unconscious knowledge produced to "traverse" the fantasy and identify with the symptom (Žižek 1991: 137). In our reading of the text, we assume that the symptom expressed is relevant to understanding a broader perspective because the text itself, with its contradictions and imaginary projections, is an expression of a discourse. Although unwoman appears as a representative of the unconscious drives involved in subjectivity, she indicates not an individual pathology but a contradiction inherent in the text that is positioned by a broader RLF discourse. As a figure of untheorized anxiety and aggressiveness, unwoman would be better understood as imaginary on the social and political level in which transphobia also appears. Žižek (1991: 140) suggests that there can be an experience of traversing the fantasy and identifying with the symptom in the political field as well, in which the fantasy concerns a shared symbolic fiction and the symptom that disrupts the fiction can be differently understood.

In Žižek's example of anti-Semitism, the symbolic fiction is that "civilized" persons are not racist and do not persecute Jews but are victims of a fantasized Jewish control. In our example of transphobia, the symbolic fiction is that RLFs are not transphobic and are victims, not perpetrators of persecution. In both accounts, denial and projection function to preserve the respective fantasies of civilized persons and honorable RLFs. For Žižek, the solution to these untenable political positions is to identify with the symptom in the form of the fantasized, excluded other. This identification would involve a recognition that one is responsible for producing the fantasized other as what must be excluded from one's own self-image. Such recognition would mean that the persecution of Jews is at the heart of "civilization" and that the persecution of transwomen is at the heart of an imagined harmonious community of women. For Žižek it is important to understand "how 'identification with the symptom' is correlated with 'going through the fantasy': by means of such an identification with the (social) symptom, we traverse and subvert the fantasy frame that determines the field of social meaning, the ideological self-understanding of a given society, i.e., the frame within which, precisely, the 'symptom' appears as some alien, disturbing intrusion, and not as the point of eruption of the otherwise hidden truth of the existing social order" (1991: 140). The hidden truth of the social fantasy of "civilized" persons is that it can be maintained only through the exclusion of its imagined uncivilized "others." And the hidden truth of the social fantasy of a RLF community based on a clear and biologically based female identity is that it can be maintained only at the expense of its border crossers, especially of those transwomen who represent the intrusion of phallic power.

While RLF discourse defines knowledge about the female subjective structure and the plight of the ego in opposition to its external male counterpart, the unwoman as the intimate alien subverts the subjective formation from the inside. The unconscious knowledge involved in the transphobic symptom is about "object a," the object that causes desire and around which the drives circulate in the forms of the gaze and the voice. These drives have been located on the side of the transgender other who is imagined to enjoy in ways that are not available to the RLF. Instead, identification with the unwoman would involve reclaiming those drives and recognizing that they are a product of one's own desire and fantasy.

To use the imaginary figure of unwoman as an implicit model in this text is a strategic impasse that creates more heat than light—anxiety, shame, and exclusionary hostility toward a class of persons who should be taken to be sisters and allies. Clearly there is no "Woman" or unwoman. Echoing Lacan's (1998: 7) famous statement that "the Woman does not exist"—that is, the fantasy image of "Woman" is the symptom of the man—we contend that the unwoman does not exist and is a symptom of RLF subject position and discourse. As symptom, specter, and ghost, unwoman might be resolved if the phobic mechanisms that call her into being could be understood, and then transwomen could be seen as just women. This corresponds to Lacan's version of the end of analysis: to identify with the symptom rather than allow it to have enough independence to haunt the subject. The symptom must be accepted as one's own creation and as imaginary. If we are all potentially unwomen, then we have to own the drives, and our capacity for enjoyment in all its multiple forms, forms that do not respect the equation of women and men with exclusively female and male bodies. Reflection and analysis then could shift the discourse to gain a purchase on the reality of transwomen. A different discourse might then include a validating ego ideal, an acceptance of identification with the symbolic father as a necessary moment in a process that would enable the establishment of a relationship to a lesbian (or other) partner who is neither the phallic father nor the engulfing phallic mother.

Projections, the choice of phobic object, the imputations of harm, and the imaginary scenarios staging the scene of the voice and the gaze as drive objects are imaginary formations that generate aggressiveness and function as obstacles to understanding. Taking this knowledge explicitly into account would enable a transformation of registers from the imaginary, in which things tend to repeat, to that of the symbolic, in which communication and articulation are possible and imaginary deadlocks can be resolved. With the imaginary register, a relationship is not with a real other but with an alter ego that is an imaginary other, in this case an uncanny other that generates anxiety. Our reflections do not provide a definitive solution but attempt to remove the roadblock of a specular relation with that part of the subject that is a symptom, a symptom that does not in reality exist. At the level of the symbolic, reality can be addressed and politics made possible. This might enable a transformed gender politics that addresses sexual others at a symbolic level, a politics that forges a relation to lesbian, feminist, and transgender subjects without harming one another.

Patricia Elliot, PhD, teaches courses on gender and psychoanalysis at Wilfrid Laurier University where she is professor in the Department of Sociology. She is author of *Debates in Transgender, Queer, and Feminist Theory: Contested Sites* (2010).

Lawrence Lyons, PhD, taught psychoanalysis and political theory at York University in Canada. Recently retired from the Department of Communication Studies, he continues to be an avid reader of Lacanian theory.

Notes

1. As Susan Stryker and Paisley Currah note, the terms *trans* and *transgender* are contested concepts that refer to "forms of gender crossing" as well as to "ways of occupying genders that confound the gender binary" (2014: 1). By "transwomen" we refer to those who may embrace either of these positions, although Jeffreys's concern is with those women who were ascribed a male sex at birth. We refer to those who share Jeffreys's beliefs about gender and transgender as RLFs, even though some radical lesbian feminists may not share these views. Some readers will be familiar with the less friendly acronym *TERF*, which stands for "trans-exclusionary radical feminist" (Goldberg 2014: 25). We also refer to the text as Jeffreys's text, even though half of the chapters were written with Lorene Gottschalk.
2. The experimental hormone-blocking drugs prescribed to children and teens are targeted here as particularly heinous. They are read as a form of "social engineering" (Jeffreys 2014: 123) intended to punish nonconformist and homosexual subjects.
3. See, for example, Amanda Stewart (2016).
4. Previous critiques of RLF assumptions may be found in Riddell 2006, Elliot 2010, Heyes 2003, and Shelley 2008, among others.

5. Jeffreys addresses transmen as well, but they are not the feared object because they are seen as women who seek to escape subordination, contrary to the transwomen who are believed to masochistically participate in that subordination.

6. Although Jeffreys cites Raewyn Connell's excellent analysis of gender (2014: 4), she misses its multilevel complexity and reduces gender to what Connell (2005) would call "hegemonic" forms of gender.

7. Intersexed persons are not threatening (or vilified) because they do not seek to transgress boundaries and they often contest the use of medical intervention on their bodies: "Intersexuality has a biological basis, whereas this book will argue that 'gender identity' is a mental condition" (Jeffreys, 9).

8. For a critique of this theory, see Elliot 2010: chap. 5.

9. It is interesting to note in this context that Jeffreys actually poses the question, "Are women a figment of men's imagination?" (2014: 6). Of course her response is no, except in the eyes of transwomen who "have an *idée fixe* that they are, themselves, women" (177).

10. For a critique of the criminalization of transgender persons, see Garcia 2014 and Spade 2011.

11. For Lacan, the field of the Other is that of social reality onto which the subject projects the gaze as imaginary. We use the small *o* ("other") to refer to the various instances of this imaginary other.

12. Although Lacan's example is in reference to paranoia, in Jeffreys's text we are dealing with a phobia in which the imagined harm attributed to the other is part of a neurotic defense, not a psychotic one. Indeed, for Lacan, phobia is considered "the most radical form of neurosis" (2015: 366).

13. These are only two of four such drives, but they are the ones that are expressed in the text's symptom, and the other two are pregenital.

References

Bailey, J. Michael. 2003. *The Man Who Would Be Queen: The Science of Gender-Bending and Transsexualism*. Washington, DC: Joseph Henry.

Bettcher, Talia Mae. 2007. "Evil Deceivers and Make-Believers: On Transphobic Violence and the Politics of Illusion." *Hypatia* 22, no. 3: 43–65.

Blanchard, Ray. 2005. "Early History of the Concept of Autogynephilia. *Archives of Sexual Behavior* 34, no. 4: 439–46.

Connell, R. W. 2005. *Masculinities*. Cambridge: Polity.

Elliot, Patricia. 2010. *Debates in Transgender, Queer, and Feminist Theory: Contested Sites*. Surrey, UK: Ashgate.

Freud, Sigmund. 1977a. "Analysis of a Phobia in a Five-Year-Old Boy." In *Case Histories 1: "Dora" and "Little Hans,"* translated by Alix Strachey and James Strachey, edited by Angela Richards, vol. 8 of *The Pelican Freud Library*, 169–305. Harmondsworth, UK: Penguin Books.

———. 1977b. "Fragment of an Analysis of a Case of Hysteria." In *Case Histories 1: "Dora" and "Little Hans,"* translated by Alix Strachey and James Strachey, edited by Angela Richards, vol. 8 of *The Pelican Freud Library*, 35–164. Harmondsworth, UK: Penguin Books.

———. 1984a. "The Ego and the Id." In *On Metapsychology: The Theory of Psychoanalysis*, edited by Angela Richards, translated by James Strachey, vol. 11 of *The Pelican Freud Library*, 339–407. Harmondsworth, UK: Penguin Books.

———. 1984b. "Instincts and Their Vicissitudes." In *On Metapsychology: The Theory of Psycho-analysis*, edited by Angela Richards, translated by James Strachey, vol. 11 of *The Pelican Freud Library*, 113–38. Harmondsworth, UK: Penguin Books.

———. 1985a. *Civilization and Its Discontents*. In *Civilization, Society, and Religion*, edited by Albert Dickson, translated by James Strachey, vol. 12 of *The Pelican Freud Library*, 251–340. Harmondsworth, UK: Penguin Books.

———. 1985b. "The Uncanny." In *Art and Literature*, edited by Albert Dickson, translated by James Strachey, vol. 14 of *The Pelican Freud Library*, 339–76. Harmondsworth, UK: Penguin Books.

Garcia, Nina. 2014. "Starting with the Man in the Mirror: Transsexual Prisoners and Transitional Surgeries Following *Kosilek v. Spencer*." *American Journal of Law and Medicine* 40, no. 4: 442–63.

Goldberg, Michelle. 2014. "What Is a Woman?" *New Yorker*, August 4.

Greer, Germaine. 1999. *The Whole Woman*. London: Transworld.

Heyes, Cressida. 2003. "Feminist Solidarity after Queer Theory: The Case of Transgender." *Signs* 28, no. 4: 1093–120.

Jaanus, Maire. 1995. "The *Démontage* of the Drive." In *Reading Seminar XI: Lacan's Four Fundamental Concepts of Psychoanalysis*, edited by Richard Feldstein, Bruce Fink, and Maire Jaanus, 119–38. Albany: State University of New York Press.

Jeffreys, Sheila. 2003. *Unpacking Queer Politics*. Cambridge: Polity.

———. 2014. *Gender Hurts: A Feminist Analysis of the Politics of Transgenderism*. London: Routledge.

Lacan, Jacques. 1981. *The Four Fundamental Concepts of Psycho-Analysis*. Edited by Jacques-Alain Miller, translated by A. Sheridan. Book 11 of *The Seminar of Jacques Lacan*. New York: W. W. Norton.

———. 1998. *On Feminine Sexuality, the Limits of Love, and Knowledge, 1972–73*. Translated by Bruce Fink. Book 20 of *The Seminar of Jacques Lacan*. New York: W. W. Norton.

———. 2006. *Ecrits: The First Complete Edition in English*. Translated by Bruce Fink. New York: W. W. Norton.

———. 2007. *The Other Side of Psychoanalysis, 1960–70*. Translated by Russell Grigg. Book 17 of *The Seminar of Jacques Lacan*. New York: W. W. Norton.

———. 2015. *Transference*. Edited by Jacques-Alain Miller, translated by Bruce Fink. Book 8 of *The Seminar of Jacques Lacan*. Cambridge: Polity.

Lawrence, Anne. 2008. "Shame and Narcissistic Rage in Autogynephilic Transsexualism." *Archives of Sexual Behavior* 37, no. 4: 457–61.

Miller, Jacques-Alain. 2006. "On Shame." In *Jacques Lacan and the Other Side of Psychoanalysis: Reflections on Seminar XVII*, edited by Justin Clemens and Russell Grigg, 11–28. Durham, NC: Duke University Press.

Morgan, Robin. 1978. "Lesbianism and Feminism: Synonyms or Contradictions?" In *Going Too Far*, 170–88. New York: Vintage.

Raymond, Janice. 1979. *The Transsexual Empire: The Making of the She-Male*. Boston: Beacon.

Rich, Adrienne. 1980. "Compulsory Heterosexuality and Lesbian Existence." *Signs* 5, no. 4: 631–60.

Riddell, Carol. 2006. "Divided Sisterhood: A Critical Review of Janice Raymond's *The Transsexual Empire*." In *The Transgender Studies Reader*, edited by Susan Stryker and Stephen Whittle, 144–58. London: Routledge.

Shelley, Christopher. 2008. *Transpeople: Repudiation, Trauma, Healing*. Toronto: University of Toronto Press.

Spade, Dean. 2011. *Normal Life: Administrative Violence, Critical Trans Politics, and the Limits of the Law*. Brooklyn, NY: South End.

Stewart, Amanda. 2016. "Survival. Activism. Feminism? Exploring the Lives of Trans* Individuals in Chicago." *Journal of Critical Thought and Praxis* 5, no. 1. lib.dr.iastate.edu/jctp/vol5/iss1/3.

Stryker, Susan, and Paisley Currah. 2014. Introduction to *TSQ* 1, nos. 1–2: 1–18.

Žižek, Slavoj. 1991. *Looking Awry: An Introduction to Jacques Lacan*. Cambridge, MA: MIT Press.

———. 1996. "'I Hear You with My Eyes'; or, The Invisible Master." In *Gaze and Voice as Love Objects*, edited by Renata Salecl and Slavoj Žižek, 90–126. Durham, NC: Duke University Press.

———. 2006. *The Parallax View*. Cambridge, MA: MIT Press.

Unthinkable Anxieties

Reading Transphobic Countertransferences in a Century of Psychoanalytic Writing

GRIFFIN HANSBURY

Abstract This article is adapted from a presentation the author gave at the Forty-Ninth Congress of the International Psychoanalytical Association in Boston, Massachusetts, in 2015. The author offers a reading of transphobic countertransference through a century of psychoanalytic literature on transgender patients, from Freud's applied analysis on the case of Schreber to today's relational trans-affirmative psychoanalysts. Through this reading, the author describes four basic "unthinkable anxieties" that appear to underlie transphobic countertransference reactions in cisgender analysts working with transgender patients. The author concludes that a relational psychoanalytic approach, with a focus on mentalization, can be a compassionate and transformative one for working with many trans patients. **Keywords** transgender, transphobia, psychoanalysis, countertransference

For over a century of history written by cisgender[1] psychoanalysts about transgender patients, beginning as early as Sigmund Freud's 1911 applied analysis of the gender-crossing German judge Daniel Paul Schreber, clinicians have revealed their attitudes and biases as they shaped psychoanalytic narratives about trans people. They have also, directly or indirectly, illustrated the types of psychic disruptions that may be experienced in the presence of trans patients. In this article, I turn the lens away from the transgender patient, the usual object of the professional's regulatory gaze, and onto the cisgender analyst through a review of the literature. This perspective offers a new view that is only just becoming possible. The field of psychoanalysis is in an exciting, and sometimes unsettling, moment of transition in which progressive cisgender analysts are discussing trans outside the often pathologizing question of etiology, while trans clinicians like myself are entering the profession, publishing and presenting on the topic. We can now just begin to ask: what happens when cis meets trans in the consulting room? Over the past century, the answer has often been some measure of transphobic countertransference.

TSQ: Transgender Studies Quarterly ★ Volume 4, Numbers 3–4 ★ November 2017 **384**
DOI 10.1215/23289252-4189883 © 2017 Duke University Press

Countertransference, positive, negative, and otherwise, is present in any therapeutic work. In transference, the patient transfers feelings and relationship patterns from the past onto the analyst. The analysis of the transference is essential and, many would say, it is *the* work of psychoanalysis. Countertransference refers to the analyst's emotions, impulses, and associations toward the patient, which also may be transferred from the analyst's past relationships. Freud first defined *countertransference* in 1910 as that "which arises in [the analyst] as a result of the patient's influence on his unconscious feelings" (144). The analyst's task, wrote Freud, was to "recognize this countertransference in himself and overcome it" (145). In this classical view, countertransference is a hindrance to the treatment, a pathological reaction produced by the analyst's own unresolved conflicts. Later theorists disagreed, arguing that countertransference is normal, expectable, and a useful tool for diagnosis and for understanding the patient's internal experience, "an instrument of research into the patient's unconscious" (Heimann 1950: 81). Countertransference, in this view, emanates from the patient and is received by the analyst as a kind of communication. Today, as psychoanalysis has evolved into relational and intersubjective models, it is generally agreed that countertransference is a cocreation of both analyst and patient. It is both personal to the analyst and diagnostic of the patient, and it is the analyst's task to parse which is which.

While countertransference has stopped being a problem in itself, it can still trouble the work. The analyst Heinrich Racker called its pathological expression "countertransference neurosis," deriving from persistent "oedipal and preoedipal conflicts as well as paranoid, depressive, manic, and other processes" in the analyst that "interfere with the analyst's understanding, interpretation, and behavior" (1957: 305) in the treatment. While the countertransference may help with the analyst's perception of the patient's unconscious processes, Racker explains, it may also "provoke neurotic reactions which impair his interpretative capacity" (1953: 313). I wonder if this phenomenon—or something similar to it—might arise in many analysts working with transgender patients. It could be thought of as a transphobic countertransference neurosis, even when the analyst is unaware of having any biases against transgender people.

Transphobia is a relatively new word. Most simply, it is to transsexuality (or transgender) what homophobia is to homosexuality, both a fear and a prejudice.[2] In the field of trans studies, Talia Mae Bettcher (2014) argues against the idea that transphobia is irrational. She writes, "Transphobia occurs in a broader social context that systematically disadvantages trans people and promotes and rewards antitrans sentiment. It therefore has a kind of rationality to it, grounded in a larger cisgenderist social context" (249). She then asks how this definition can explain "the nature of transphobia." In this article, I am working on the assumption that transphobia has at least a dual nature, both irrational (fear) and somewhat rational (organized into a prejudice that values cisgender over transgender). While it is the irrational I am most interested in here, a brief discussion of the prejudice (rooted in the irrational) may be useful, as both can come into play in the cis-trans analytic dyad.

Feminist psychoanalyst Elisabeth Young-Bruehl paired three basic forms of prejudice with three characterological types, focusing on the irrational underpinnings of prejudice. Obsessional prejudices like anti-Semitism, she wrote, serve to ghettoize and eradicate a feared group. Hysterical prejudices like racism sexually exploit and attack targets that "have become the eroticized objects of incestuous or otherwise transgressive desire." And narcissistic prejudices like sexism "justify attack on people who are perceived as threats to the identity and specialness or prerogatives of a group self-appointed as superior." For Young-Bruehl, homophobia takes all three forms, "depending on whether the primary motivation or purpose served is to eliminate, to sexually exploit, or to bolster narcissism by saying, 'We are not homosexual'" (2009: 252–53). Young-Bruehl did not discuss transphobia, and it would be a worthwhile endeavor to add it to her list. While a full exploration is beyond the scope of this article, I offer some brief thoughts on the subject, with an eye toward understanding the types of fear responses that might underlie the prejudice.

Transphobia as prejudice, like homophobia, comes in different forms. In one, the trans person is not viewed as legitimately transgender but as homosexual—a man disguised in women's clothing who aims to seduce a heterosexual man, or vice versa, as in the famous case of Brandon Teena, whose rapist-murderers annihilated him for the crime, in their minds, of being a lesbian dressed as a man to seduce a woman. In another form of transphobia, which I'll call institutionalized transphobia, governments, lawmakers, and other authorities attempt to control trans people, for example, barring them from using the appropriate public restrooms. In this case, the authorities and their supporters also deny the reality of trans, viewing trans women, for example, as perverse men who dress in female attire so they can enter women's restrooms and commit sexual assault. In both examples, which might be categorized as hysterical, following Young-Bruehl's model, the trans person is eroticized, depicted as a terrifying sexual aggressor and transgressor. In another, more controversial example, some cisgender female radical feminists attempt to exclude trans women from the category of "woman." This form of transphobia may best fit with Young-Bruehl's narcissistic type, a prejudice of what she calls "boundary establishment" (1996: 35).

This is hardly a complete list of the many possible forms of transphobia, but what each has in common is a denial of trans reality. Often in transphobia, the category "transgender" itself is denied as a reality, and the trans person is cast as really homosexual, really the gender they were assigned at birth. In this view, which has appeared in the psychoanalytic writing about transgender patients from the beginning, the trans person is seen as psychotic, in denial of corporeal reality, that is, the sexed body as immutable binary. I want to explore the possibility that the character of transphobia, as a denial of reality (transgender exists, sex is not binary), might be categorized as psychotic prejudice—as it often looks like one when it appears in countertransference descriptions in the analytic literature.[3]

In reviewing the literature, I identified four basic transphobic countertransference reactions. The analyst may fear that

1. I will be tricked, through a denial of reality, into homosexuality.
2. I will become ungendered or slip outside of gender.
3. My body will break apart and important pieces will be lost.
4. I will go crazy.

While the anxiety in such reactions is certainly not realistic, could it be categorized as neurotic?[4] As Freud first defined the two types (1926), realistic anxiety is the fear of a real and known external danger, while neurotic anxiety is "about an unknown danger . . . a danger that has still to be discovered" (165). That danger is an unconscious instinctual demand, often a sexual one. While it's possible that some transphobic countertransference reactions may arise from the analyst's instinctual demands and their attendant dangers (a heterosexual cisgender male, for example, may find his unconscious wish to be sexually penetrated aroused in the presence of a transgender woman), I suspect that much of transphobic countertransference emanates from an earlier point in psychic development—from the analyst's primitive infantile anxieties.

Though not a perfect one-to-one correspondence, in the list above I hear echoes to the English psychoanalyst Donald W. Winnicott's description of what he called "unthinkable anxiety," the psychotic anxieties of infancy. He listed the varieties (1965: 58): (1) "Going to pieces," (2) "Falling for ever," (3) "Having no relationship to the body," and (4) "Having no orientation." Such unthinkable anxieties are related to the infantile fear of annihilation. The infant, Winnicott explains, is constantly on the verge of these anxieties and is usually kept safe by a consistent maternal presence. But if the mother fails, the infant may go mad. "Madness here," wrote Winnicott, "simply means a *breakup* of whatever may exist at the time of *a personal continuity of existence*" (1971: 97). The infant's anxieties are unthinkable because they are preverbal, unattached to language. They are psychotic because they belong to such an early moment of psychic development. They can persist through life or reappear, triggered by stressors. Given the right circumstances, we all can lose ourselves, however momentarily, in the swirl of infantile psychotic anxieties.[5]

I conjecture that such unthinkable anxieties may arise in cisgender analysts when they experience a transgender patient as a breakup of personal continuity, a disruption to their own experience of reality and embodiment. Some fear losing a grip on their (sexual) orientation, leaving them disoriented. Others feel like their relationship to their gendered/sexed body is under threat. Or they may have the sensation of falling out of gender and thus out of the body. These primitive anxieties seem related to Wilfred Bion's "nameless dread" (1959, 1962) and later Thomas Ogden's "formless dread" (1988), the infantile terror of being uncontained, without boundaries, without form, without a legible and definable skin. These anxieties may be managed by the analyst with one or more defensive maneuvers, which can potentially damage the work and retraumatize the patient.

As I write this article, I am concerned that cisgender analyst readers who work with transgender patients might feel reprimanded or policed by my analysis and thus wary of exploring and exposing their countertransference reactions, afraid of a newly arisen transgender regulatory gaze that wags its finger and says, "Shame on you," in all its politically correct fervor. Doing my best not to wag that finger, while still highlighting potentially harmful outcomes of analytic work with trans patients, I want to make space to be curious about these countertransference reactions while challenging the defensive maneuvers used to manage them. We all have infantile and psychotic aspects. Negative countertransference happens to all analysts, and it seems to happen in ways specific to working as a cisgender analyst with transgender patients. It may come from transphobic prejudices in the analyst, conscious or unconscious.[6] It may come from early internal conflicts and other unprocessed material in the analyst. The analyst's goal is not to be without countertransference but to think it through and not act it out. To do that, when working with transgender patients, it is essential to have some awareness of what a transphobic countertransference might look and feel like.

To that end, and keeping in mind the two lists above, I will review the assorted fears and defenses as they appear throughout the analytic literature, beginning with what may be considered the first transgender case.

Freud on Schreber

In 1911, Freud published an analysis of Daniel Paul Schreber, the esteemed German judge who wrote the best-selling *Memoirs of My Nervous Illness* while hospitalized for psychosis. Freud never met Schreber but was enthralled by the judge's description of their[7] belief that God was turning them into a woman. Schreber's delusional paranoia, Freud concluded, was due to an "outburst of homosexual libido" (1911: 43). At the time, the idea of transsexuality was still, largely, unthought and unthinkable. Equating the wish to be the opposite sex with homosexuality was the prevailing viewpoint of the day, one that would guide psychoanalysts for generations.

What emotions stirred in Freud as he read Schreber's vivid writing? When Schreber stood at the mirror, torso bared and dressed in the "sundry feminine adornments" (21) of ribbons and necklaces, when they imagined their breasts and vagina, writing, "I am a woman luxuriating in voluptuous sensations" (quoted in Freud, 34), did it make Freud nervous? Excited? I was drawn to a curious note in the article. Freud states that his "unavoidable" task is to elucidate the etiology of Schreber's cross-gender wish, and if he fails to do so, he will be left in the "absurd position" of "a man holding a sieve under a he-goat while some one else milks it" (34). This simile is borrowed from Immanuel Kant's *Critique of Pure Reason*, from a passage about absurd questions met by absurd answers. In choosing the simile with its dreamlike, cross-gender image, Freud may have provided the first expression of the analyst's anxiety with the transgender patient, and the attendant defense deployed:

1. The analyst is afraid of confusing the sexes, as he believes his transgender patient does.
2. If he capitulates to this confusion of sexes, the analyst will join the trans patient in a shared psychosis.
3. So disoriented, the analyst (in this case, a male) will unwittingly place himself in close proximity to a penis.
4. To avoid this confusional, homoerotic outcome, he must develop a theory of the etiology of the patient's cross-gender wish. Containing the patient in theory is the only way to orient himself.

Since 1911, analysts have heeded Freud's imperative. With transgender patients, they did not want to end up confused, psychotic, and grasping the wrong goat.

After Schreber

Throughout the next decades, psychoanalysis had little to say about the phenomenon that had become known in the medical field as "transsexualism." In 1930, the influential Viennese analyst Otto Fenichel named the disconnect when he stated that cases of cross-dressers who felt "disgust . . . for the male genital" or "longing for that of the female would have to be examined analytically before we could make any pronouncement about them" (1930: 225). But such cases were not presenting themselves for psychoanalytic examination. That began to change after the emergence of Christine Jorgensen, the World War II soldier who famously transitioned on the cover of the *Daily News* under the headline "Ex-GI Becomes

Blonde Beauty." As Joanne Meyerowitz explains in *How Sex Changed: A History of Transsexuality in the United States*, "in 1952, the press discovered Christine Jorgensen and inaugurated a new era of comprehensive, even obsessive, coverage" (2002: 49). This marked a turning point in trans visibility. *Sex change* became a household term across the United States, more trans people—no doubt recognizing themselves for the first time in the image of Jorgensen—sought medical transition, and psychoanalysts got into the debate. Meyerowitz describes the moment as a "medical turf war" between physicians and psychoanalysts, between biological and psychological approaches to the problem of trans.

In the early 1960s, at the University of California, Los Angeles (UCLA), School of Medicine, psychiatrist and psychoanalyst Robert Stoller, along with colleagues like Ralph Greenson, established the Gender Identity Research Clinic (GIRC) for the study of gender-nonconforming children and adults. So began the modern relationship between psychoanalysts and transgender patients, a story that can be divined from the writings of Stoller and Greenson.

In his 1964 article "On Homosexuality and Gender Identity," Greenson presented what was likely the first case of a posttransition trans person in the analytic literature. The woman that Greenson calls "the trans-sexual paratrooper" (218) was not an analysand, however, but an interview subject at UCLA. Still, in this early account, we can see some of the countertransferential issues that continue to trouble psychoanalysis today. They frequently manifest as a problem with pronouns.

Greenson uses masculine pronouns when narrating the subject's past and continues through her transition, recalling how "he" had "his" penis and testicles removed, took estrogen injections, changed "his" name to a woman's, married a man, and adopted a child. It is only immediately after recounting the patient's surgery to construct a vagina does Greenson change her pronouns to feminine ones. It's a compelling moment for the pronoun switch. The mental image of a vagina seems to bring forth *she*. But then Greenson changes back, as if he himself had crossed a boundary from which he then recoiled. He reinstates the masculine pronoun, writing, "The trans-sexual paratrooper seemed to accomplish what Schreber hoped for and failed. He did transform himself into a woman and he did seem to obtain some form of 'cure'" (219). Reading the changing and reversing pronouns has a disorienting effect. Was Greenson also disoriented, on the brink of the unthinkable? Maybe he was attempting to contain himself with the masculine pronoun, asserting, in essence: I know this is really a man. I am not confusing the sexes. I might have gone crazy for a moment, but I am not crazy.

Robert Stoller took many trans patients into analysis and wrote extensively on them. Generally sympathetic, especially for the time, his writing is also laced with frustration for a population he described as "demanding" and "harassing" (1968). Stoller developed what would become an enduring grand narrative of transsexual etiology. Male-to-female transsexuals, he explained, were created by depressed, bisexual mothers who held them in an "endless embrace" (1973: 215), while the fathers failed to intervene. Female-to-male transsexuals suffered from the opposite problem—"too much father and too little mother" (1968: 205). Breaking away from mainstream ideas, however, Stoller also asserted that transsexuals were neither psychotic nor homosexual. He advocated surgery as the best treatment for adults, whose "malignant condition" (140), he decided, was incurable by analysis.

Through the 1970s and 1980s, as more gender clinics served more trans patients seeking hormones and surgery, dozens of articles on transsexuality appeared in the psychoanalytic literature. In reports of patients often described as difficult, insistent, and demanding (Limentani 1979; Socarides 1970), various writers concluded that transsexuality is "a personality and characterological disaster" (Limentani 1979: 149), a perversion (Limentani 1979; Socarides 1970), something "between perversion and psychosis . . . sharing many common borderline features" (Meyer 1982: 406), and a reaction to "extreme separation anxiety" and overidentification with the mother (Ovesey and Person 1973: 64). Charles Socarides railed against surgery, writing, "The creation of Mary Wollstonecraft Shelley's Frankenstein monster pales in comparison to this spareparts, 'tinker toy' type of surgery practiced on living, suffering, and needy human beings as therapy for what is a purely psychological disorder" (1973: 282).

Until the twenty-first century, psychoanalysis remained fixed on determining what went wrong in the development of gender identities unanimously diagnosed as disordered. In the face of unthinkable anxiety, thinking about etiology can be a powerful defense.[8]

Countertransference Revelations

If in the 1960s transgender patients and psychoanalytic thought on transsexuality coevolved as trans people began emerging into the daylight, in the 1990s another leap in that coevolution occurred. Trans activists and academics took up their own subjectivity, publishing their ideas while inventing new language. *Transgender* became a preferred, and more inclusive, term. At the same time, gay and lesbian analysts began coming out of their closets and changing the way the field thought about and talked about homosexuality, exemplified in Ken Corbett's interrogative shift, when he asked, "'How homosexuality?' (With what meaning and to what effect?) as opposed to what I consider to be the ill-conceived etiologic project of 'Why homosexuality?' (For what reason, cause, motive, or purpose?)"

(2001: 325). Relational psychoanalysis also became prominent, its proponents moving away from the classical drive theory that humans are motivated primarily by sexual and aggressive aims, and toward the idea that humans are primarily motivated by a need for relationship. Essentially launched by Stephen Mitchell in the 1980s, by the mid-1990s, relational psychoanalysis had emerged as an amalgam that included object relations theory, self-psychology, and psychoanalytic feminism, which helped to bring attention to ideas about social construction, especially as it pertains to sex and gender. In addition, relational analysis asks the analyst to be self-conscious in the work. After all, as the feminist relational analyst Adrienne Harris has written, "we cure with contaminated tools" (2011: 709). For relational analysts, the analyst-patient dyad is an intersubjective one, a mutual two-person psychology—distinct from the one-person psychology of classical analysis—and countertransference is cocreated. With this new focus, analysts began looking at themselves as well as their patients, and they started revealing their countertransference in print. Some bravely ventured to do so in writing about their work with trans patients.

In a 1993 article titled "Gender-Role Stereotypes and Clinical Process," Sue Shapiro makes brief mention of her countertransference with a female-to-male trans patient. Recalling the feminist relational analyst Muriel Dimen's assertion that "we do not always feel in gender, and when we do not, we feel anxiety" (Dimen 1991: 338), Shapiro describes her experience succinctly: "Our countertransference becomes most apparent in extreme cases, for example, in my work with a transsexual who suffers from extremely rigid expectations of male and female behavior—an apparent woman living in the 1990s who thinks of herself as a man who loves women in a 1950s sort of way. Sitting with her fills me with a nameless terror. I feel the ground under me giving way" (1993: 375). We do not know the patient's pronouns, only that Shapiro uses *her*, a possible act of "mispronouning," still a common and unchallenged practice in the 1990s. While she calls the patient a transsexual, Shapiro also seems to be positioning the patient as a lesbian, consistent with the view that transgender people are really homosexuals. From the one descriptive sentence provided, we don't know how the patient self-identifies, and we can't say for sure if the word choices come from the patient or the analyst. We could, however, say that the description is confusing and/or confused. And while one might agitate about the gender politics of a quarter century ago, it's more useful to look deeper. Something powerful is happening here, as evidenced by the two uses of the word *extreme*. In the next pair of sentences, Shapiro describes the unthinkable anxiety aroused in her in the presence of the patient. She is filled with "a nameless terror" and feels the ground give way. She seems to feel as if she is falling outside of gender, dangerously disconnected from her sense of self. This may be the first time in the literature that an analyst has named the particular dread that can be triggered in the presence of trans patients.

In his 1996 article, "Transsexualism: Some Considerations on Aggression, Transference, and Countertransference," Miguel Torres describes the fear he felt while working with a male-to-female patient, including "a vague but constant sensation of uncomfortableness, incomprehension and distress" when discussing surgery (19). Over time, as the patient became more feminine appearing, the analyst became more anxious, afraid that he might feel an attraction to the patient. He both "misgenders" and feels out of gender, writing, "I did not know how to treat him" (19), meaning he did not know how to behave in a gendered way toward his patient. But the word *treat* also points to another underlying anxiety when working with trans patients—the analyst may not know how to administer treatment. His thinking function becomes impaired by an unthinkable anxiety, a nameless terror, a dread that has not been put into words.

In her 1998 article, "A FE/Male Transsexual Patient in Psychoanalysis," Danielle Quinodoz describes the anxiety she felt with a posttransition trans woman. When opening the door to her office and seeing the patient's face for the first time, Quinodoz experienced an "intense hallucination," superimposing the face of a former male patient on this new patient's face (97). Quinodoz worried that "I was likely to get close to my own 'madness'" while working with a trans patient. The inability to "tell inside myself whether my patient was a man or a woman" became a persistent countertransference. Unable to get her bearings during the first session, having lost her "spontaneous reference points" (97), Quinodoz wonders, "Which one of us was 'mad'—the analyst or the patient?" (108). Once again, an analyst grapples with unthinkable anxieties in the presence of a trans patient. Will I lose a connection with my own body, gender, and sexual orientation? Will I go crazy (lose touch with reality)? Will I fall forever in confusion?

While these three analysts express awareness of their gender-anxious countertransference reactions to trans patients, not all analysts do. Perhaps none has been as unapologetic as the French psychiatrist and analyst Collette Chiland. In her 2000 article "The Psychoanalyst and the Transsexual Patient," she provides a veritable taxonomy of transphobic countertransference from her years as psychiatrist-in-chief at the Alfred Binet Center in Paris.

Initially, Chiland describes feeling confused when listening to trans patients, unsure of how to classify them diagnostically. Like many analysts, she finds refuge in a diagnosis. "At a pinch," she writes, "they could be classified as borderlines" (2000: 24). But Chiland denies feeling any confusion about the sexes. "I remain unruffled when confronted with transsexualism," she writes, because "I do not run the risk of being deceived by a possible male partner." She remains unconvinced that her female-to-male patients are men because "a man to me is ultimately someone capable of penetrating me virtually" (31). Again there appears the denial of trans reality and, possibly, the homosexual panic that often underlies transphobia.

Chiland names another common countertransferential reaction when she writes, "The analyst cannot remain emotionally aloof to the mutilation demanded by the patient" (30). (The word *mutilation* often appears in the literature on trans, as does the word *demand*—trans people are routinely characterized as self-mutilating and demanding.) Chiland makes note of a male analyst in her clinic's working group who "struggled with . . . castration anxiety" aroused by the "intensity and repetition" of a transfeminine patient's "demand" for gender-confirming genital surgery. Chiland wonders "whether women might tolerate transsexual patients better than men." The answer seems to be yes, at least for the unruffled Chiland. She will not fall out of gender. She will not feel the ground give way beneath her. No unthinkable anxiety, no nameless dread, will engulf her. "The grim determination of female patients to have their breasts removed has never inspired anxiety in me," Chiland says, "but only consternation" (29). In the dictionary, *consternation* is partly defined as "a sudden, alarming amazement or dread that results in utter confusion."[9] (The word is the same in French.)

Chiland makes decisions about her patients' pronouns that run counter to their requests. The discomfort that comes when treating transsexuals, she says, "begins with the problem of language" (31). Language is indeed a constant problem for trans people, whether it's finding words for sexed body parts or talking about oneself in the pretransition past. Pronouns are the most frequent source of language pain. While many people "slip" when trying to shift pronouns (I do that myself), others staunchly refuse to address trans people with the appropriate pronouns.[10] I am curious about what is behind a moment of mispronouning. When and why does a person "slip" and use the wrong pronoun? Why does a more adamant person refuse to pronoun correctly? Again, questions like these turn the lens away from the trans object and onto the regulatory other—who has become dysregulated when coming into contact with trans.

A language becomes even more of a problem for trans people when it applies grammatical gender not only to pronouns but to nouns and other parts of speech like adjectives and articles. French is one of those languages. On this point, Chiland is unyielding. For her frustration, she blames the patients: "One's ability to communicate with another person is often utterly thwarted by transsexuals," she says. Her response is rigidity. "My own approach is to explain to patients that I respect and have no desire to attack them, but that I shall not speak to them in their new gender" (31).

As we've seen so far from the literature, the cisgender analyst disturbed by a transgender patient may deploy a number of defenses to ward off unthinkable anxieties:

1. The analyst who fears her own ungendering may insist on the binary nature of gender. There are men and there are women, says this analyst, grounding herself in the split. If she is progressive, maybe even identifying as feminist, she might do what appears to be the opposite, casting the trans person as too rigidly gendered, holding too tight to a traditional gender binary.
2. The analyst who experiences castration anxiety (of breasts or penis) with a trans patient may cast the act of surgery as a "mutilation" and the patient as a Frankenstein monster. Disavowed are the male analyst's wish for a vagina of his own, and the female's wish for the breast-free embodiment of childhood.
3. The analyst who fears madness might project psychosis onto the trans patient while grasping for a diagnosis and a theory of etiology that can reassure the analyst that he still has the capacity to think.
4. The heterosexual analyst who is afraid of being deceived into homosexuality, having his or her own homosexual longings aroused, might refuse to acknowledge the patient in their appropriate gender, insistently mispronouning or intentionally using the patient's former name (an act of aggression known in the trans communities as "deadnaming"). If the analyst is homosexual, he or she might do the same in an attempt to ward off heterosexual longings stirred by a patient in the midst of transition. For example, a formerly lesbian patient transitions into an attractive man, stirring unresolved Oedipal conflicts and gender anxieties in his lesbian analyst.

Such anxieties arise. Their presence is not necessarily the problem. What the analyst does with them, too often, becomes the problem. Unthinkable anxieties must be thought. They must be put into words, spoken aloud or held in the mind. In this way, the analyst can help transgender patients move beyond their own nameless dread and unthinkable anxiety.

Language can be used as a defense against the unthinkable. It can also facilitate the transition of the unthinkable to the thinkable, a primary task of psychoanalytic work. In the 2000s, as psychoanalysis has opened, little by little, to trans experience, it has also accepted language from the trans communities. The word *transgender* began trickling into the analytic literature in the late 1990s. In 2000, *Studies in Gender and Sexuality* launched with the investigation of trans phenomena as part of its mission. Adrienne Harris noted that "a full conversation between transgender witnesses and psychoanalysts is still to be held" (2000: 228). That conversation would not take long. In the twenty-first century, the relationship between psychoanalysis and transgender has evolved into something utterly new.

Feminist relational analysts, like Virginia Goldner, have looked at trans subjectivity to understand cis subjectivity (2011). Patricia Gherovici (2010), Oren Gozlan (2011), and Patricia Elliot (2001) have used Lacanian theory to challenge the notion that psychoanalysis and gender-confirmation surgery must be mutually exclusive. Asking "How transgender" instead of focusing on "Why transgender," Avgi Saketopoulou has put forth a theory of "massive gender trauma, a clinical syndrome arising at the onerous intersection of the misgendering of transgender patients and the subjective, anguished experience of the natal body" (2014: 773). As an openly transgender analyst, I began publishing on the topic in 2005 (Hansbury 2005). Today, more trans clinicians are entering analytic training and publishing their ideas and experiences (Pula 2015). The conversation "between transgender witnesses and psychoanalysts" is happening, but the transgender witnesses are no longer only the objects of the analytic gaze; we are becoming analytic investigators ourselves. The language continues to evolve.

In the early 2000s, academics took up the word *cisgender*, which first appeared in the mid-1990s in transgender newsgroups on the nascent Internet. Carl Buijs, a trans man from the Netherlands, is often credited with its coinage. The earliest mention of *cisgender* I can find in the psychoanalytic literature dates to 2011 (Hansbury 2011; Ehrensaft 2011). Since then, *cisgender* has been anointed, included in the Oxford English Dictionary in 2015. It is also controversial, as some nontrans people do not identify with it and have concerns about reifying a cis-trans binary. I believe it is important to have this word, and the others branching from it. As the queer feminist blogger Emi Koyama wrote in 2002, the terms *cisgender*, *cissexual*, and *cissexist* "de-centralize the dominant group, exposing it as merely one possible alternative rather than the 'norm' against which trans people are defined." When turning our lens on the dominant group, these words enable us all to think and talk about a position that often goes unseen and thus unexamined. By naming the unthinkable anxieties in transphobic countertransferences, it becomes more possible to think and work them through.

Working Through

How does one get out of the knot of a transphobic countertransference and remain a thinking analyst without resorting to defenses that damage the work and harm the patient? A few analysts—mostly in the relational and feminist tradition—have demonstrated this in their clinical writing.

In her 2011 article "Crossing Over," Melanie Suchet describes a ten-year analysis with a patient who transitioned from female to male during the treatment. Suchet describes feeling confused, anxious, and uncertain. She owns the feelings as belonging to herself. When she struggles with the patient's new male name, she questions her own resistance. Taking an intersubjective approach (and correctly using gender pronouns), Suchet wonders, "How will his changing body affect my own? Perhaps I am afraid that his transitioning will rock my own gender stability" (183). Here she thinks and names one of the unthinkable anxieties surely felt throughout history by analysts with trans patients. Furthermore, she notes, "There is also a faint glimmer of envy; does he get to be both sexes?" (183).[11]

Hilary Offman, in her 2014 article "The Princess and the Penis: A Post Postmodern Queer-y Tale," describes a similar experience in her relational work with a female-to-male trans patient. Watching her patient stroke the new beard growing on his "formally delicate and pretty chin," writes Offman, "I could no longer ignore my own feelings of dismay. How could he be so happy about such a horrifying turn of events, I thought to myself, as I imagined with dread a similar growth of dark hair on my own face." Offman describes feeling confused, disoriented, disturbed, and perturbed by the patient's choice to "waste" his "natural loveliness" (76–77). On another occasion, as the patient contemplates surgery to remove his breasts, the analyst faces the frightening possibility of her own mastectomy. She wonders, "Why was I so freaked out" (77) by the patient's physical transition? She later answers her own question, in part, saying she felt "betrayed" by the patient's "decision to switch gender 'teams'" (81).

Suchet works through her countertransferential anxiety by imagining her patient's changing body in reveries and dreams, including one in which the patient removes his shirt and the analyst sees the absence of breasts, noting, "It feels okay." Offman chooses to disclose her countertransferential discomfort directly to the patient, using her own words to create a space in which their bodies and genders don't have to be the same.[12] In Danielle Quinodoz's earlier work with a posttransition trans woman, she imagined herself in "the role of parents at the beginning of a pregnancy, expecting a baby whose sex they could not yet know" (1998: 105). Like Suchet, she mentalized the patient's transgender body—that locus of so much unthinkable anxiety—creating a thinking space in her mind for the patient to exist in whatever form she took.

Mentalizing, the analyst Peter Fonagy has written, is "the capacity to conceive of conscious and unconscious mental states in oneself and others" (1991: 641). It is the capacity to self-reflect, developed in relationship to the primary caregiver's own reflective capacity. If the caregiver can accurately picture the child, then the child will have the chance to "find himself in the other" (Fonagy 2000: 1132). He is thought of—he is mentalized, his mind held in the mind of the other—and so he thinks and exists. But the psychic and embodied experiences of many gender-nonconforming children are not accurately reflected in the minds of their cisgender caregivers. Consistently misgendered, they are misrepresented, unable to find themselves in the other and thus unable to find themselves in themselves, a deeply distressing and disorienting state of being—one that can throw a child into unthinkable anxiety and nameless dread.

In her 2014 article "Mourning the Body as Bedrock: Developmental Considerations in Treating Transsexual Patients Analytically," Avgi Saketopoulou makes the case that trans patients' psychological problems "often result from the traumatic and unmentalized impact of being trans rather than being its originary cause" (780). She discusses how it is possible for a transgender patient to resort to psychotic solutions, such as the denial of existing genitals, to cope with the horror of having a body that does not fit one's self, and the "inability to process and digest the complicated discrepancies between her body and her gender experience" (785). As she imagines her way into the disorienting dissonance of living in a transgender body, Saketopoulou helps to mentalize her patients' bodies and genders, visualizing them vibrantly surviving (2011).

In her 2015 article "The Colonized Mind: Gender, Trauma, and Mentalization," Sandra Silverman writes of her work with a female-to-male trans patient in transition, exploring "what happens when a mind is not mentalized but colonized" (53), that is, invaded and controlled by another person's mind, in this case, by the patient's mother. While mentalization is about "making space," Silverman notes, colonization "is about destroying space" (53) controlling the colonized and preventing them from becoming their own separate selves. Silverman describes feeling, at times, "disoriented and unable to think" (56) while sitting with her patient. As she grapples with anxiety and analyzes her own possible biases, Silverman makes the space to hold in her mind the patient's potential selves. As she does so, the patient also begins to think himself into being, to play, and to mourn.

Throughout history, trained in the collective anxieties of the psychoanalytic field, too many practitioners have colonized[13] the psyches of transgender patients, inserting interpretations laced with unprocessed anxieties that destroy space instead of making space. What the most recent trans-affirmative psychoanalytic literature seems to be demonstrating is that transgender experiences—of both psyche and soma—require mentalization, a shared process between analyst and patient. As Adrienne Harris described it, mentalizing is "a capacity to hold another's experience, metabolize it, and reflect it in a way that can be reabsorbed. There is a flow of experience transforming gradually between and within each person. These experiences have a sensory, a linguistic, a motoric, an affective as well as a cognitive aspect. Mentalizing and being mentalized are full body/mind experiences" (2009: 11–12). In this way, the unthinkable gender/body anxieties of both analyst and patient may be transformed.

Conclusion

The countertransferential crisis between cisgender analysts and transgender patients is, in many ways, a crisis of thought. Trans people have often gone unmentalized from early life—unheld as themselves in the minds of caregivers, surrounding communities, and society at large. To be unthinkable, to oneself and to others, can leave a person in a state of confusion, a kind of fragmented blurriness that can look like all the diagnoses that have been put on trans people: psychotic, borderline, narcissistic, and so on. I have known this blurriness, this fragmentation, in my own practice with trans patients. While I don't consciously experience the feeling of "falling out of gender," the patient's unmentalized parts will inhabit my mind like a fog. Fragments arise, appearing and disappearing half-symbols and images thrown together without links to bind them into meaning. My countertransference at these times is to feel frustrated by the unknowing. I strain to cut through the fog and put the pieces together. I ask myself: what are my foggy fragments, and what are the patient's?[14]

If we agree that countertransference is a cocreation of both analyst and patient, then it is essential to ask: What aspects of the transphobic countertransference emanates from the patient? What part is a communication from the patient—about her own internal world and/or about how she was perceived and treated by early caregivers? What is the patient's own transphobia? Carrying the experience of being inexplicable or unimaginable, many trans patients enter treatment with the expectation that they will be misperceived by the cisgender clinician, even if he or she is a queer clinician. Conversely, they may expect that a trans clinician will understand them implicitly, but we are still two separate minds in a room together.

One of my trans patients speaks of regularly "falling out of focus" and into a state of feeling inexplicable. Others experience states of disembodiment or dissociation, sometimes with the horrifying sensation of body parts coming apart. Some describe a mysterious internal object that moves through the body, something primitive or unformed, like an insect or an alien. Some dream of strange, half-formed genitals that "make no sense." Still others describe feeling colonized or haunted by the minds of, usually, their mothers. My own thoughts on these phenomena are not fully thought—I continue to think them with my patients—but I will say that the transgender psyche sometimes seems especially porous, vulnerable to the evacuated anxieties of others. Gender nonconformity has the potential to terrify in its power to unmoor us from known locations of body and psyche. Do trans children become both triggers of and receptacles for their caregivers' gender anxieties? If so, trans patients are coming into treatment carrying not only their own gender trauma but their caregivers' as well. It is critical that analysts don't add to that burden with their own unthinkable anxieties about bodies and genders.

The analyst drowning in the confusional whirlpool of transphobic countertransference is unable and/or unwilling to mentalize the patient's psyche and soma. Resorting to her own defensive maneuvers, this analyst might try to force-feed thoughts, pushing indigestible and even toxic interpretations to answer the question "Why trans?" She might colonize the patient's mind with her own gender anxieties, potentially traumatizing the patient, reenacting earlier experiences of colonization from anxious caregivers who misgendered and misrepresented the gender-nonconforming child. The trans patient cannot find himself in the mind of this analyst, just as he could not find himself in the mind of his caregiver. He searches but finds only more unbearable, unthinkable anxiety and dread. But the analyst who mentalizes the unmentalized can get out of the whirlpool and get on with the healing work.

By loosening its grip on the analytic overpreoccupation with etiology—by moving away from the question "Why trans?" and toward "How trans?"—the field of psychoanalysis is beginning to open a space in which clinicians can analyze their own transphobic reactions and not drown in countertransferences that impede the work and harm the patient. This sea change, still very much under way, is made possible by a coevolution between cisgender and transgender analysts, activists, and academics who are writing and speaking, sharing their thoughts and words to collectively imagine a way of working and working through.

Griffin Hansbury, MA, LCSW-R, is a frequent presenter on transgender issues. His writing on the subject has appeared in several journals, including *Psychoanalytic Dialogues* and *Studies in Gender and Sexuality*. He received the 2015 Ralph Roughton Paper Award from the American Psychoanalytic Association. He is a psychoanalyst in private practice in New York City.

Notes

1. *Cisgender* refers to people who are not trans, that is, who experience their sex and gender as mostly congruent. The prefix comes from the Latin, meaning "on the same side," versus *trans*, meaning "on the other side." The cis/trans nomenclature is used in organic chemistry to describe the orientations of molecules. While trans and cis is a binary, I believe cisgender presents as a spectrum, like transgender, on which one can feel more or less congruence between one's sex and gender. Are trans and cis separate spectra or the two end points of the same line? Surely, there is a place along the way where trans and cis begin to blur.

2.   While societal hatred and intolerance of trans people can certainly influence an analyst's work with trans patients, I am more interested in looking at how transphobia's more subtle expressions—anxiety, discomfort, dislocation—affect the work.

3.   In this article, I am only looking at transphobic countertransference as it is revealed in published written accounts of cis analysts working with trans patients. An in-depth qualitative study of cisgender analysts' reactions to their transgender patients would be a worthy project for a researcher.

4.   Freud differentiated neurosis from psychosis: "Neurosis is the result of a conflict between the ego and its id, whereas psychosis is the analogous outcome of a similar disturbance in the relations between the ego and the external world" (1924: 149).

5.   For the analyst Melanie Klein (1946), we can always slip back into what she termed the paranoid-schizoid position of early infancy.

6.   The transgender analyst is not without internalized transphobia. I venture to say, from personal experience, that transphobic countertransferences take different forms in the trans analyst; however, a discussion of countertransference in the trans-trans analytic dyad is beyond the scope of this article.

7.   I cannot know what gender pronoun Schreber would have used, so I am opting for the gender-neutral *they/them*. And so I join a long tradition of analysts making a pronoun decision without the patient's input.

8.   This is not to disparage the search for genetic factors (though it should be admitted that analysts do not ask cisgender and heterosexual patients to mine the cause of their being cisgender and heterosexual, though the field more routinely expects that of queer patients). I am suggesting that an exclusive—or even primary—reliance on etiological queries can sometimes be used defensively by the analyst, and it often comes at the expense of healing possibilities.

9.   *Dictionary.com*, s.v. "consternation," accessed July 16, 2017, www.dictionary.com/browse /consternation.

10.   Recently, in some more progressive societies, this refusal has been deemed harassment. For example, in 2015, the New York City Commission on Human Rights began requiring employers to "use an individual's preferred name, pronoun and title (e.g., Ms./Mrs.) regardless of the individual's sex assigned at birth, anatomy, gender, medical history, appearance, or the sex indicated on the individual's identification" (NYCCHR 2017).

11.   I suspect that this envy underlies much of the transphobic countertransference we see in cisgender analysts. What happens to dissociated grief for gendered parts of the analyst's self that did not live out? Does the trans patient disturb this tender place, stimulating old longings to be both sexes?

12.   Many analysts seem to identify with the "same-sex" body of the patient; that is, female analysts may identify with the femaleness of the female-to-male patient in transition, so that medical transition is felt viscerally in the body of the analyst. One supervisee of mine experienced intense breast pain during the week when her transmale patient was undergoing and recovering from chest surgery (mastectomy) some three thousand miles away.

13.   In this context, the term *colonize* is used to describe a psychic process of invasion and control, and not a geopolitical one, though the metaphor works to describe a power struggle in which the powerful (cis/analysts) take over the (psychic) space of the oppressed (trans/patients).

14.   From a Kleinian/Bionian perspective, Judith Mitrani offers a useful description of such unmentalized experience: "Elemental sense data, internal or external, which have failed to be transformed into symbols (mental representations, organized and integrated) or into signal affects (anxiety which serves as a signal of impending danger, requiring thoughtful action), but which are instead perceived as concrete objects in the psyche or as bodily states which are reacted to in corporeal fashion (e.g., somatic symptoms or actions). Such experiences are merely 'accretions of stimuli' which can neither be used as food for thought nor stored in the form of memories" (1995: 70).

References

Bettcher, Talia Mae. 2014. "Transphobia." *TSQ* 1, nos. 1–2: 249–51.

Bion, Wilfred. 1959. "Attacks on Linking." *International Journal of Psycho-Analysis* 40: 308–15.

———. 1962. "The Psycho-Analytic Study of Thinking." *International Journal of Psycho-Analysis* 43: 306–10.

Chiland, Colette. 2000. "The Psychoanalyst and the Transsexual Patient." *International Journal of Psycho-Analysis* 81, no. 1: 21–35.

Corbett, Ken. 2001. "More Life: Centrality and Marginality in Human Development." *Psychoanalytic Dialogues* 11, no. 3: 313–35.

Dimen, Muriel. 1991. "Deconstructing Difference: Gender, Splitting, and Transitional Space." *Psychoanalytic Dialogues* 1, no. 3: 335–52.

Ehrensaft, Diane. 2011. "Boys Will Be Girls, Girls Will Be Boys." *Psychoanalytic Psychology* 28, no. 4: 528–48.

Elliot, Patricia. 2001. "A Psychoanalytic Reading of Transsexual Embodiment." *Studies in Gender and Sexuality* 2, no. 4: 295–325.

Fenichel, Otto. 1930. "The Psychology of Transvestism." *International Journal of Psycho-Analysis* 11: 211–26.

Fonagy, Peter. 1991. "Thinking about Thinking: Some Clinical and Theoretical Considerations in the Treatment of a Borderline Patient." *International Journal of Psycho-Analysis* 72, no. 4: 639–56.

———. 2000. "Attachment and Borderline Personality Disorder." *Journal of the American Psychoanalytic Association* 48, no. 4: 1129–46.

Freud, Sigmund. 1910. "The Future Prospects of Psycho-Analytic Therapy." In *Five Lectures on Psycho-Analysis, Leonardo da Vinci, and Other Works*, vol. 11 of *The Standard Edition of the Complete Psychological Works of Sigmund Freud*, translated by James Strachey, 139–52. London: Hogarth.

———. 1911. "Psycho-Analytic Notes on an Autobiographical Account of a Case of Paranoia (Dementia Paranoides)." In *The Case of Schreber, Papers on Technique, and Other Works*, vol. 12 of *The Standard Edition of the Complete Psychological Works of Sigmund Freud*, translated by James Strachey, 1–82. London: Hogarth.

———. 1924. "Neurosis and Psychosis." In *The Ego and the Id and Other Works*, vol. 19 of *The Standard Edition of the Complete Psychological Works of Sigmund Freud*, translated by James Strachey, 147–54. London: Hogarth.

———. 1926. "Inhibitions, Symptoms, and Anxiety." In *An Autobiographical Study, Inhibitions, Symptoms, and Anxiety, the Question of Lay Analysis, and Other Works*, vol. 20 of *The Standard Edition of the Complete Psychological Works of Sigmund Freud*, translated by James Strachey, 75–176. London: Hogarth.

Gherovici, Patricia. 2010. *Please Select Your Gender*. New York: Routledge.

Goldner, Virginia. 2011. "Trans: Gender in Free Fall." *Psychoanalytic Dialogues* 21, no. 2: 159–71.

Gozlan, Oren. 2011. "Transsexual Surgery: A Novel Reminder and a Navel Remainder." *International Forum of Psychoanalysis* 20, no. 1: 45–52.

Greenson, Ralph. 1964. "On Homosexuality and Gender Identity." *International Journal of Psycho-Analysis* 45: 217–19.

Hansbury, Griffin. 2005. "Mourning the Loss of the Idealized Self: A Transsexual Passage." *Psychoanalytic Social Work* 12, no. 1: 19–35.

———. 2011. "King Kong and Goldilocks: Imagining Transmasculinities through the Trans–Trans Dyad." *Psychoanalytic Dialogues* 21, no. 2: 210–20.

Harris, Adrienne. 2000. "Gender as a Soft Assembly." *Studies in Gender and Sexuality* 1, no. 3: 223–50.

———. 2009. "You Must Remember This." *Psychoanalytic Dialogues* 19, no. 1: 2–21.

———. 2011. "The Relational Tradition: Landscape and Canon." *Journal of the American Psychoanalytic Association* 59, no. 4: 701–35.

Heimann, Paula. 1950. "On Counter-Transference." *International Journal of Psycho-Analysis* 31: 81–84.

Klein, Melanie. 1946. "Notes on Some Schizoid Mechanisms." *International Journal of Psycho-Analysis* 27: 99–110.

Koyama, Emi. 2002. "Cissexual/Cisgender." Eminism.org, June 7. www.eminism.org/interchange /2002/20020607-wmstl.html.

Offman, Hilary. 2014. "The Princess and the Penis: A Post Postmodern Queer-y Tale." *Psychoanalytic Dialogues* 24, no. 1: 72–87.

Limentani, Adam. 1979. "The Significance of Transsexualism in Relation to Some Basic Psychoanalytic Concepts." *International Review of Psychoanalysis* 6: 139–53.

Meyer, Jon. 1982. "The Theory of Gender Identity Disorders." *Journal of the American Psychoanalytic Association* 30, no. 2: 381–418.

Meyerowitz, Joanne. 2002. *How Sex Changed: A History of Transsexuality in the United States*. Cambridge, MA: Harvard University Press.

Mitrani, Judith. 1995. "Toward an Understanding of Unmentalized Experience." *Psychoanalytic Quarterly* 64, no. 1: 68–112.

NYCCHR (New York City Commission on Human Rights). 2017. "Gender Identity/Gender Expression: Legal Enforcement Guidance." www1.nyc.gov/site/cchr/law/legal-guidances -gender-identity-expression.page#1 (accessed June 21, 2017).

Ogden, Thomas. 1988. "On the Dialectical Structure of Experience—Some Clinical and Theoretical Implications." *Contemporary Psychoanalysis* 24: 17–45.

Ovesey, Lionel, and Ethel Person. 1973. "Gender Identity and Sexual Psychopathology in Men: A Psychodynamic Analysis of Homosexuality, Transsexualism, and Transvestism." *Journal of American Academy of Psychoanalysis* 1, no. 1: 53–72.

Pula, Jack. 2015. "Understanding Gender through the Lens of Transgender Experience." *Psychoanalytic Inquiry* 35, no. 8: 809–22.

Quinodoz, Danielle. 1998. "A Fe/Male Transsexual Patient in Psychoanalysis." *International Journal of Psycho-Analysis* 79: 95–111.

Racker, Heinrich. 1953. "A Contribution to the Problem of Counter-Transference." *International Journal of Psycho-Analysis* 34: 313–24.

———. 1957. "The Meanings and Uses of Countertransference." *Psychoanalytic Quarterly* 26: 303–57.

Saketopoulou, Avgi. 2011. "Minding the Gap: Intersections between Gender, Race, and Class in Work with Gender Variant Children." *Psychoanalytic Dialogues* 21, no. 2: 192–209.

———. 2014. "Mourning the Body as Bedrock: Developmental Considerations in Treating Transsexual Patients Analytically." *Journal of the American Psychoanalytic Association* 62, no. 5: 773–806.

Shapiro, Sue. 1993. "Gender-Role Stereotypes and Clinical Process: Commentary on Papers by Gruenthal and Hirsch." *Psychoanalytic Dialogues* 3, no. 3: 371–87.

Silverman, Sandra. 2015. "The Colonized Mind: Gender, Trauma, and Mentalization." *Psychoanalytic Dialogues* 25, no. 1: 51–66.

Socarides, Charles W. 1970. "A Psychoanalytic Study of the Desire for Sexual Transformation ('Transsexualism'): The Plaster-of-Paris Man." *International Journal of Psycho-Analysis* 51: 341–49.

———. 1973. Review of *Sexuality and Homosexuality: A New View*, by Arno Karlen. *Psychoanalytic Quarterly* 42: 280–83.

Stoller, Robert J. 1968. *Sex and Gender: On the Development of Masculinity and Femininity.* London: Hogarth and the Institute of Psychoanalysis.

———. 1973. "The Male Transsexual as 'Experiment.'" *International Journal of Psycho-Analysis* 54: 215–25.

Suchet, Melanie. 2011. "Crossing Over." *Psychoanalytic Dialogues* 21, no. 2: 172–91.

Torres, Miguel. 1996. "Transsexualism: Some Considerations on Aggression, Transference, and Countertransference." *International Forum of Psychoanalysis* 5, no. 1: 11–21.

Winnicott, Donald. 1965. *The Maturational Processes and the Facilitating Environment.* International Psycho-Analytical Library 64. London: Hogarth and the Institute of Psycho-Analysis.

———. 1971. *Playing and Reality.* London: Tavistock.

Young-Bruehl, Elisabeth. 1996. *The Anatomy of Prejudices.* Cambridge, MA: Harvard University Press.

———. 2009. "Childism—Prejudice against Children." *Contemporary Psychoanalysis* 45, no. 2: 251–65.

The Queering of a Cisgender Psychoanalyst

HILARY OFFMAN

Abstract When the author's patient Sam first came out as trans, both analyst and patient assumed he would benefit from switching from an ostensibly cisgender psychoanalyst like the author to someone transgender, like him. In the end, Sam decided to stay with the analyst, all while transitioning from female to trans male and then giving birth to his biological offspring. The analysis profoundly affected the analyst to such an extent that she can no longer even casually refer to herself as merely "cisgender" without adding quotations around the term and the qualifier "ostensibly." As someone assigned female at birth, the analyst might not have expected to need to make such stipulations. Whereas initially, the analyst could only see Sam's possible gains from a potential switch to a trans analyst, she later realized that something might also have been lost. When Sam decided to stay with the analyst, she worried about being a supportive and good enough "trans-parental" object for him but later realized how the psychoanalytic process could be endangered by the wrong kind of "transpositive" attitude. In this article, the author explores the concept of cisgender, asking about the ways in which queer theory and dialectical psychoanalysis can constructively inform each other, and the ways in which the author's own "queering" experience contributed significantly to the clinical process.

Keywords cisgender, transgender, psychoanalysis, psychotherapy, clinical

When faced with difference beyond our comfort level, it is a human tendency to want to pair like with like. There was a time when a cisgender female therapist like me, unaware of her own naïveté, could easily be convinced that her transgender male patient might be better treated by someone like him, someone with the expertise to "treat" something that she knew nothing about. When Sam first presented in my office, I was in no way considered an expert in anything gender related but merely a newly graduated psychiatrist with room to provide follow-up care for a very despondent young woman. Sam had recently been discharged from a local psychiatric hospital, after having been treated for what seemed like a first episode of psychosis. Back then, Sam identified as "she," even though at the time she ironically looked more masculine to me than he does now.

TSQ: Transgender Studies Quarterly * Volume 4, Numbers 3–4 * November 2017 **405**
DOI 10.1215/23289252-4189892 © 2017 Duke University Press

We ended up working together for a long time in psychoanalysis around issues of developmental trauma and insecure attachment, frequent dissociation into traumatic self-states, and a dearth of reflective capacity. For many years, the issue of gender didn't even come up.

It wasn't until well into the therapy that Sam decided to come out as trans. Because of it, his friends thought it was important that he switch his therapist from a "normal" one like me to one who understood both what it meant to be trans and what it meant to pursue the process of transitioning, and at first Sam agreed with them.

It turned out that the trans expert therapist wasn't available, so Sam decided to wait, and he eventually opted to not even try to change therapists. Instead he chose to stay in therapy with me, an ostensibly "cisgender" psychiatrist who, at the time, also happened to be a psychoanalytic candidate ready for her first official training case. I can't help but notice as I write these words how I can no longer even casually refer to myself as merely cisgender, needing to add not only quotations around the term but also the qualifier, "ostensibly." Given that the term *cisgender* was coined "to describe the condition of staying with birth-assigned sex or the congruence between birth-assigned sex and gender identity" (Enke 2013: 235), one might think that, as someone born a biological female who always has identified her gender as female, I wouldn't need to make such stipulations. And yet, I cannot bring myself to accept that term as I would have when first introduced to it.

From the perspective of contemporary psychoanalytic theory, if both the analysand and the analyst feel that they have changed as a result of the process, this marks a successful therapeutic encounter (Slavin and Kriegman 1998). With respect to my own experience, I can safely say that I found the analysis with Sam to be both challenging and transformative to such a degree that I now realize I wouldn't be the analyst I am today without having been affected by this process. At the outset of Sam's transitioning, I could focus only on what Sam might have gained by a potential decision to switch from me to a trans analyst. When Sam ultimately decided to stay with me, I worried a lot—and still do—about being a supportive and "good enough trans-parental object," much in the spirit of Donald Winnicott's "good enough mother," one who "starts off with an almost complete adaptation to her infant's needs, and as time proceeds she adapts less and less completely, gradually, according to the infant's growing ability to deal with her failure" (1953: 94). So when I learned about the term *transpositivity*, defined by Rupert Raj as "respect for and acceptance of people who identify as 'trans'" (2002: 30), at first it resonated for me as a depiction of the way I thought I was with Sam that was both possible and accurate.

That is, it resonated until I learned what it meant in terms of clinical orientation and practice; Raj adds that a transpositive therapist expresses "an attitude that is respectful, sensitive, accepting, validating, affirming, empathic, caring, compassionate, encouraging, supportive, and mutually trusting and trust-worthy" (9). I realized that no matter how "transpositive" I had tried to be, I had not in any way managed to pull off this degree of unrelenting supportiveness with Sam, or for that matter with any other patient of mine. Moreover, I believe that complying with Raj's recommendations would subject any psychodynamic therapy to such constraints as to undermine its very premise, ignoring the part of Winnicott's definition of "good enough mother" that stresses the importance of allowing the infant the gradual opportunity to learn to cope with the mother's imperfect attunement. In that sense, I began to wonder whether, if Sam had left to seek the expertise of someone trans, something might have also been lost, that there might have been something important about my being cis and his being trans that contributed to the work so much that it motivated me to explore the ways in which too much transpositivity could actually become a barrier to a productive psychoanalytic relationship.

Despite having never heard of the terms *cisgender* or *transpositivity* when I first met Sam, he chose to transition from identifying as female to identifying as a trans male, and then to get pregnant and give birth, all with me as the psycho-analytic anchor (Offman 2014). But even after writing an entire article devoted to our clinical process and formulation, I still want to examine why I automatically assumed a transgendered "expert" would be the best choice of psychoanalyst for someone like Sam, as he entered into this life-changing process, and why I no longer believe that to be the case. I wondered whether I was reacting to some-thing specific about the process of transitioning gender, a transformation of mind and body that could at times be considered hazardous—whether I was correct in assuming that he would be in better hands with someone who "knew the ropes," someone who could guide and protect him more than I could. After all, even in progressive communities such as the one Sam and I fortunately inhabit, claiming trans identity is no laughing matter, and violence against those identifying as gender variant remains disturbingly high (Bauer et al. 2015; Stotzer 2009). In fact, Sam recently reminded me just how scared I was all those years ago when he insisted on being a pioneer user of male-designated change rooms without explicit permission, after having told me violent stories about what happened to those "caught" pushing the boundaries of conventionality. Given that these risks and challenges were associated with just existing as trans, something I had never personally experienced, I questioned whether as a privileged cisgendered person I even had the right to comment. It is precisely as someone who begins from the assumption that she has no right to comment that I write this article, concerned about whether an opportunity is wasted by dismissing the opinion of someone worried about that very possibility.

Over the course of its history, psychoanalysis has had a lot to say about the kinds of patients considered ideal for the process (Kantrowitz, Singer, and Knapp 1975) and even now, those in the process of transitioning gender have not typically been included among them. When I first met him, Sam could barely tolerate his own affect, but slowly, over time, our work deepened significantly and with it, our mutual commitment toward each other and our process. I could feel something shift in me as I let myself be guided by him into what was then, for me, a foreign and uncertain realm. By the time I made my own unconventional decision to choose Sam as my first psychoanalytic control case, I began to realize that something within me also wanted to transition in its own right, but it was not until more recently that I began to think more about what that was.

Right from the beginning, I was drawn to the field of relational psychoanalysis, impacted by postmodern theory through its "antifoundationalism, the undercutting of any claims to certain knowledge or values" (Mitchell 1996: 49). According to Stephen Mitchell, one of the founders of the relational movement, "the best position for the clinician in the land of postmodernism includes, in claiming considerable knowledge about many things, not claiming to know things we don't know, and probably never will know. And I think this also serves as a model for the most helpful approach for the analysand in sorting out their own choices and shaping their own experience" (57). For someone personally uncomfortable with orthodoxy in general, who purposefully sought a psychoanalytic home away from what felt like arbitrary and constraining convictions, such words spoke to my very soul. I had come to dread the seemingly stock criticisms of psychoanalytic purists, dismissing anything outside the territory already established as acceptable and correct using phrases such as, "well that's all well and good, but that's *not* psychoanalysis." Not only could I never understand how some psychoanalysts could be so sure of what was and wasn't psychoanalysis, but I also could not convince myself such certainty was remotely possible, or even desirable. I was ready for a psychoanalytic world where knowing wasn't always the point, ready for an opportunity to lean "antinormative," and fortunately I was not alone.

Years earlier, it was Irwin Z. Hoffman, one of the relational psychoanalytic movement's most influential writers, who first guided me away from a "blank-screen concept" of psychoanalysis, "the idea that the analyst is not accurately perceived by the patient as a real person, but that he or she serves rather as a screen or mirror to whom various attitudes, feelings, and motives can be attributed, depending upon the patient's particular neurosis and its transference expression" (1998: 97). Instead, Hoffman directs us toward an appreciation of a different kind of therapeutic relationship in which there is a "full appreciation of the inevitability and usefulness of the analyst's personal involvement in the analytic process" and the idea that psychoanalysts are "able to use their emotional experience or countertransference, broadly defined, to enhance their understanding of their patients and to open up new therapeutic potentials in the process" (193). In my early training in psychiatry, like most therapists of my cohort, I had been indoctrinated by my supervisors with therapeutic neutrality and nondisclosure as overriding principles, prevailing tenets of a traditional, classical psychoanalytic model. After years of clinical experience, however, and what I considered an enlightened exposure to postmodern thinking, I had dismissed these ideas as impossibilities.

So for me, this relational understanding of the potential role of the analyst was pivotal and represented a new beginning. I learned from Stephen Mitchell, the "father" of the relational movement, that drive theory's perspective on mind could be understood as "fundamentally monadic; something inherent, wired in, prestructured, . . . pushing from within . . . in the form of endogenous pressures" (1988: 3). By contrast, Mitchell describes a relational-model version of mind as "fundamentally dyadic and *interactive*"; in this contemporary understanding "above all else, mind seeks contact, engagement with other minds" (3). Exposure to other pioneering relational writers such as Lewis Aron helped me further reframe my understanding of the analytic dyad as a mutually asymmetrical process, in which transference and countertransference are viewed as coconstructed: "The relational approach that I am advocating views the patient-analyst relationship as continually established and reestablished through ongoing mutual influence in which both patient and analyst systematically affect, and are affected by, each other. A communication process is established between patient and analyst in which influence flows in both directions. This approach implies a "two-person psychology" or a regulatory-systems conceptualization of the analytic process" (1991: 33). As a "two-person psychology," contemporary relational theory stands in contrast to drive theory's "one-person" model, in which the subjectivity of the patient is considered to be the sole focus.

Likewise, Jessica Benjamin exposed me to the developmental nature of "mutual recognition," which represents a "separate trajectory from the internationalization of object relations [in which the] subject gradually becomes able to recognize the other person's subjectivity, developing the capacity for attunement and tolerance of difference" (1990: 33). As Sam and I negotiated the ways in which we felt similar to and different from each other, I was guided by Benjamin's idea that "the other must be recognized as another subject in order for the self to fully experience his or her subjectivity in the other's presence. This means, first, that we have a need for recognition and second, that we have a capacity to recognize others in return—mutual recognition. But recognition is a capacity of individual development that is only unevenly realized" (35) Clinical work demands a great deal from all of us who dare to practice it; I relied on these contemporary psychoanalytic ideas to guide me in my work with Sam, through several unanticipated curves. For example, it could not have been predicted that just when Sam was eagerly contemplating the possibility of a flat chest as a desired outcome of his "top surgery," I was contemplating the same possibility for myself, but with intense dread. A cousin of mine had tested positive for the BRCA2, the gene that causes a predisposition to breast and ovarian cancer; she had undergone a prophylactic double mastectomy for the purpose of disease prevention. Given the extensive history of breast cancer in my family, and my own mother's (early and therefore treatable) diagnosis of ovarian cancer, I decided I had no choice but to pursue genetic testing. Awaiting the results of my blood test with trepidation, my irritation with Sam's desire for surgery intensified. How could I listen empathically to someone talking with such great enthusiasm about the prospect of cutting his breasts off, while I was desperately trying to keep my own? In the end, I decided to come clean and tell Sam about my dilemma, deciding that it was better for him to know where I was coming from, so that we could openly discuss what the possibility of surgery meant for both of us. Sam went ahead and had the top surgery, pumped breast milk for his newborn daughter from those very breasts that, as a result, are no longer completely flat, and remains ecstatic with the end result. I tested negative for the breast and ovarian cancer gene and remain equally ecstatic in my surgical avoidance.

Without first gaining an appreciation of the role and importance of the analyst's subjectivity and its exploration in the countertransference, I would not have been able to explore the meaning and impact of the mutually complex process surrounding this enactment. Building on Heinrich Racker's (1957) idea of countertransference identification, Hoffman explains further that "our countertransferential attitudes are more pervasive, consequential, and potentially useful than what has traditionally been considered to be the case" (1998: 74), which encouraged me to more bravely and openly explore my own feelings, so different from those of Sam as he innovated gender. I had come to agree that when one chooses to practice psychoanalysis relationally, by definition this comes with the awareness that we not only (inevitably) impact our patients but also may find it morally irresponsible not to do so (Hoffman 2016). In such cases, we are not choosing whether but how we do so and which impacts we aim to have.

When Sam began testosterone treatment as part of his transition, before he made the decision to discontinue it to become pregnant, his voice began to lower, and the structure of his face began to change. As he lovingly stroked the emerging dark beard on his formerly delicate and pretty chin, at first I could only imagine with great dread the appearance of a similar growth of dark hair on my own face. In time, those uncomfortable feelings began to abate, and I felt proud of my unfazed reactions. But as I learned to deal with our somewhat obvious differences, Sam began to find himself "preoccupied with all things pregnant." Since I had become pregnant during the time of Sam's therapy sessions, he had already witnessed me experience the very thing in which he was now so desperate to participate, and I noted with irony the shift into more familiar territory. Sam and I began to talk more about the experience of carrying a child, and he openly expressed how much he enjoyed our "sharing like a sisterhood of girlfriends." But now I was finding myself a bit confused again, wondering what so much alikeness meant in the context of our different gender identities.

When I first published an article about my clinical work with Sam (Offman 2014), people asked me how I could "stand it," how I could deal with the confusion of working psychoanalytically with someone in the process of becoming a trans male, getting pregnant, giving birth, and then continuing to reinvent himself as the baby's father. Early on, I did get mixed up, like when he called the oral sex he and his partner performed on their biologically female parts "blow jobs," or when he used the pronoun *they* to speak in a politically correct, gender-neutral fashion about a single individual. Even to this day I struggle to understand how Sam could so easily relinquish the title of "Mommy" in favor of "Daddy," when he was the one who endured such a difficult pregnancy and childbirth. I wrote about how it felt to get used to the ways in which I had to turn my head upside down to accommodate Sam's innovations, and how in time I came to experience this seemingly simple process as quite profound, thrilled by my growing ease pairing previously incompatible words like "when *he* had a C-section."

I could feel a sense of my own transitioning and development as I surrendered to the dialectical pull of sameness, letting it expand me in the way in which I was always hoping to expand Sam. All my life I had struggled with a feeling that I never fit in, and I commonly admonished myself for this failure of conformity, believing that if I had the ostensible trappings necessary, there was something wrong with me if I was still unable to pull it off. I began to find the idea of applying the term *queer* to this feeling personally compelling, while at the same time trying to acknowledge the ways in which I was appropriating it. As I felt myself lured by the notion of participating in the construction of my own identity, I wondered that though cisgender might indeed be who I am, maybe it isn't necessarily how I always feel, that maybe I can call myself queer in that I often identify as someone other than the person I appear to be. Though I am not trans, I might occasionally still be able to *feel* trans, partly because I had somewhere to change from, having started as cis in the first place. Initially faced with the necessity of altering the way I experienced gender variance, I have come to cherish the ways in which I was encouraged to reinvent and develop myself and to think about the ways in which doing so impacted Sam's therapy. To me, this kind of thinking can represent a form of personal psychoanalytic activism, a way of being transpositive without necessarily predetermining what that means.

I am fortunate to have been clinically affected by the psychoanalytic paradigm shift described by Mitchell (1988) as it moved away from its more traditional focus on cognition and insight, toward a focus on process and affect; the ways this philosophical shift informed me mark the impact of the psychoanalytic process on both me and Sam. My earliest psychoanalytic education insisted that gender identity was fixed and binary and that my homosexual classmate was "abnormal." However archaic-seeming and upsetting, it gave me the incentive to find a new psychoanalytic home, to take my own leap of faith away from the psychoanalytic training institute preferred by most MD-psychiatrists like me, to another with a broader commitment to both past and future, a move that I like to think represented my early "queering." It was not until much later in my relationship with Sam that I was exposed to contemporary queer theory, courtesy of such well-known and expert writers in this area as Benjamin (1995, 1996), Corbett (1997, 2008), Dimen (1991, 1995), Goldner (1991, 2003), and Harris (1996, 2005). Goldner confirmed for me that while "the modernist viewpoint within psychoanalysis conceives of sex and gender as universal psychic phenomena . . . postmodern traditions in both feminist theory and psychoanalysis conceive of gender and sexuality as emerging in and through history and culture and thus consider them to be fluid and variable social categories" (2003: 113). In his article describing the ways in which "all human development is infused with an interplay between centrality and marginality," Ken Corbett (2001: 313) explains how the term "'queer' obtains its very meaning and energy through its oppositional relation to normal social realities" (319). Similarly, queer theorists such as Annamarie Jagose write that "these days it almost goes without saying that queer is conventionally understood to mean 'antinormative'" (2015: 26) and that "queer theory's signature critique of the normative has often gone hand in hand with its celebration of the antinormative" (27). Robyn Wiegman and Elizabeth A. Wilson also note "how profoundly the history of queer theorizing has been shaped by an antinormative sensibility, one that unites the multiple and at times discordant analyses that comprise the queer theoretical archive into a field-forming synthesis" (2015: 2). In this way, antinormative thinking can be thought of as part and parcel of what defines thinking queer in the first place, a position from which to explore the world that is both valid and important.

Hoffman, who writes that the psychoanalytic process often "takes a leap forward when [analysts] have deviated from their more customary ways of working, when they have thrown away the Book," asks us to consider "to what extent [is] a deviation from tradition or from a stance that seem[s] more 'psychoanalytically correct' an important or even essential part of the therapeutic action of the experience?" (1998: 194). Although it didn't occur to me when I first encountered this idea, now I can't help but find it quite queer in its sensibility, in the way it evokes a feeling of defiance and a refusal to passively accept the status quo or prevailing agenda. But it is important to note that at the same time Hoffman endorses the potential value of spontaneously and idiosyncratically deviating from the "normative," he does not in any way advocate privileging the "antinormative" either. He recognizes that throwing away the book can become as fixed a position as refusing to ever give it up: shutting down the very potentials we were hoping to expand in the first place, leaving us with fewer options from which to choose any potential course of action.

In that sense, equating queer with antinormative represents thinking that isn't very psychoanalytic: it doesn't reflect the dialectical thinking that is the crucial theoretical premise of a contemporary relational psychoanalytic viewpoint. According to Hoffman's theory of dialectical constructivism, to think psychoanalytically we must ensure that while any given dialectical component may appear in the foreground at any given time, the other is always held in the background—that though we look for "obviously contrasting features" (1998: 200) inherent in any given polarity, it is also crucial to "find the effects of each pole on the other, and even aspects of each pole represented within the other" (200). In this way, the analyst establishes a "dialectical interplay between ritual and spontaneity, between what is given and what is created, between what is role-determined and what is personal, between constraint and freedom" (223). It also means that from a psychoanalytic perspective, neither transgender nor cisgender identities can fully exist without a consideration of the other.

Corbett further suggests that not only have traditional psychoanalytic models tended to privilege the "normative logic of centrality" (2001: 313) over marginality but also that "postmodern theories have enabled the queer as the ideal nonnormative, noncentral citizen . . . who articulates his own set of cultural imperatives and injunctions, including his own brand of mental freedom" (315). On the one hand, I love the idea that by labeling myself "queer" I get to locate myself in this place of "mental freedom," but at the same time I agree with Corbett that privileging the margin over centrality is just as problematic as privileging centrality over the margin.

I'm pleased that queer theory is also now starting to question its exclusive allegiance to antinormativity as an underlying premise, asking what will happen to the field as, over time, queer itself becomes less queer, less marginal (Wiegman and Wilson 2015). This summer, at the Canadian National Exhibition in Toronto (founded in 1879 and currently one of the largest fairs in North America), new custom-designed single-person washrooms were provided in place of the traditional gender-based group ones. On the doors, replacing typical gendered instructions were the proud words, "We don't care" (Keenan 2016). To many, cisgender and transgender represent logical opposites of a gender polarity, but to consider only this possibility severely limits their potential interpretations. To think critically and psychoanalytically about what appears to be a binary opposition, we must consider the ways in which cisgender and transgender are and are not opposites, along with the ways in which they dialectically affect and inform each other. And to do that, we need to explore how the term *cisgender* was created in the first place.

According to A. Finn Enke, to fully understand the evolution of the term *cisgender*, one needs to first understand that its usage came about in the context of the "transgender liberation movement" and its burgeoning efforts to "recognize and to address the connections among many different forms of gender-based oppressions and the economic, nationalist, and racist structures that buttress those oppressions in a world that was (and still is) an explicitly and often silently trans-exclusive and disenfranchising space" (2013: 236). The motivations of this liberation are not hard to understand. After all, as Enke describes, "it is hard to overstate how dramatically sex/gender congruence, legibility and consistency within a binary gender system buy a privileged pass to social existence, particularly when accompanied by the appearance of normative race, class ability and nationality. The term 'cisgender' was to name that privileged pass" (237). To me, not only does this definition seem perfectly acceptable, but I also find the idea of creating a new word to direct a different kind of attention to it to be an appealing and logical part of our evolution.

Susan Stryker further explains how the term *cisgender* is meant to be an improvement on the term *nontransgender*: "The idea behind the term is to resist the way that 'woman' or 'man' can mean 'nontransgendered woman' or 'nontransgendered man' by default, unless the person's transgendered status is explicitly named; it's the same logic that would lead someone to prefer saying 'white woman' and 'black woman' rather than simply using 'woman' to describe a white woman (thus presenting white as the norm) and 'black woman' to indicate a deviation from that norm" (2008: 22). Part of me completely resonates with what Stryker is trying to get us to see, particularly since Sam has shared with me how powerful it felt from an activist's perspective to define *cis* in terms of trans, instead of it always being the other way around by default. And yet at the same time, I can't get rid of the feeling that careful defining of terms doesn't determine the way in which these ideas play out in any given clinical situation, when the use and appropriation of terms cannot be preestablished but require examination by that particular dyad for their idiosyncratic meaning in that time and space. From a psychoanalytic point of view, there remains a certain quality of aptness that we cannot legislate no matter how hard we try, and not only that, there remains the question of whether we should even be trying to do so in the first place.

Enke further explains that despite the ways in which cisgender has been defined, "cisgender does not stay put. It is even now traversing contexts, and—like genders and many other substituents—it is changing in the crossing. . . . Nowadays, cisgender commonly implies staying *within* certain parameters (however they may be defined) rather than *crossing* (or trans-ing) those parameters" (2013: 235). Maybe this explains why it is that people seem to be reacting to the use of the term *cisgender* in unanticipated ways. In a Huffington post blog called "I Am NOT Cisgendered," J. Nelson Aviance (2016) explains why he rejects the label "cisgender," even though he is not transgendered nor does he dispute the match between his gender assignment/biology and gender identity. To him, being called "cisgendered" is more akin to being labeled "normatively gendered," an idea that he finds "prescriptive and limiting." He argues, "If 'cisgendered' means your gender identity matches the social construct attached to the sex you were assigned at birth, then there cannot be a male gender identity that acts outside those normative social boundaries. And if you say there is a variation on gender identity and live as a man, then you negate the many variations on what it means to 'be a man' or even to 'live as a man'" (Aviance 2016). Whether or not one agrees with Aviance's position, it's hard to argue with the idea that he personally finds being labeled "cisgender" by default as "aggressive and hurtful," claiming that "you don't get to make a reductive statement about my gender identity or how I embody my gender while trying to argue for recognition of the diversity of other people's embodied genders." I see his point. While he recognizes his own potential privilege, he does not derive privilege from identifying as cisgender or from embodying a normative gender identity. Rather, he feels prevented from expressing a stance on his own gender identity–essentially, feeling silenced. Once cisgender becomes conflated with the idea of normativity, then we have to accept that even if the label is accurate, any given individual might feel unacceptably constrained by its application.

Stryker, Paisley Currah, and Lisa Jean Moore wrote that "the time [is] right for bursting transgender wide open" (2008: 12), and I couldn't agree more. Enke agrees, also explaining that if "trans invokes a person's (or body's) orientation in space and time . . . cis theoretically must also be *effected through* time and space, despite the presumption of stasis" (2013: 239). But this means that from a psychoanalytic perspective, if we are committed to bursting transgender open, then we must also consider the value of bursting cisgender open too, despite, or perhaps especially, while we acknowledge its normative privilege. Though like Corbett

I find "much to be admired in the postmodern explanation of the ways in which power and norms shape our subjectivities," I also remain "troubled by the prospect that, through our incessant deconstruction of patterns of enculturation, we run the risk of undervaluing our needs to be recognized by others" (2001: 329). We need to consider a "post-postmodern" position that includes more than one way of thinking (Hansbury 2011; Offman 2014). Wiegman and Wilson agree that we need a "more studied consideration of the character of norms to rethink the conceptual framework that sustains antinormativity . . . to show that norms are more dynamic than queer critique has usually allowed" (2015: 2). So now it seems that queer theorists are also imploring us to consider the power and potential of the normative in the antinormative, incorporating the dialectical thinking so cherished in a contemporary psychoanalytic perspective.

Thinking dialectically has helped me in my work with another psycho-analytic patient, this one a thirty-nine-year-old cisgender homosexual male who, though emphatically uninterested in transitioning his gender identity, still complains that he passes as conventionally male far too readily. Patrick is big and tall and appears very masculine but is also conspicuously self-conscious, all while working in a very "manly" profession. In all the years I have known him, Patrick has had precisely one intimate encounter, even though he has always longed for intimacy, more than anything else. Now that he has his own apartment and the potential for privacy, we have both struggled to find ways to make this happen for him, but to no avail. Although Patrick has some close friends, he is unable to open himself up to them, where they would encounter his longing—amidst his wildly colorful and outrageous scarves and necklaces, items that might seem to belong to a very different man than the one he outwardly appears to be.

Patrick and I have been working determinedly for him to safely tolerate wearing these items in ways and places that are not secret. Each foray has felt both exhilarating and dangerous for him, but in venturing out, he has had to face the unanticipated and harsh reality that, no matter how many enchanting items he layers on his body, no matter how fetching they are, it doesn't change the way people interpret his gendered self—he just can't make other people see him as anything other than essentially male. And yet, Patrick doesn't feel that he can exist for one minute longer as the kind of male for which he is so ostensibly privileged to pass, one he doesn't feel is good enough for him to physically or emotionally connect with anyone.

Patrick's best friend happens to be a trans woman, who openly underwent complete surgical reconstruction with the full knowledge of their entire social group. But despite Claire's "audacity," Patrick has been surprised to find that she is the one most uneasy with his new look, noticing with dismay how it was "dif-ficult for her" to accept his shiny, newly painted nails. To Patrick, though Claire reads as trans, she seems to "think cis." When Patrick pulls out pretty, delicate items to put on while they roam her edgy but "accepting" neighborhood, Claire politely and gently suggests that he put them away, for fear there will be "second glances" that she would rather avoid. Patrick feels that since Claire now "passes" as female, that it's not up to her to comment on the ways in which he, and not she, stands out by wearing items considered traditionally feminine. It has been hard for Patrick to accept Claire's perspective, feeling constrained and judged by it as if the ways in which Claire interprets transgender define the ways in which he must interpret cisgender.

I considered myself sufficiently queered by Sam to enter somewhat "expertly" into this exploration of gender identity with Patrick. When he couldn't convince others in his life to see him the way he wanted, Patrick turned to me, formally presenting each new shirt, necklace, or purse for my approval with such serious ceremony that it felt impossible to react otherwise. I convinced myself that unwavering encouragement made me a good self-object, that by consistently praising each risk-taking, antinormative move, I was helping propel Patrick toward doing so with an actual potential partner. Over time, Patrick expanded his choices to ones so "impossibly cute and adorable" that they literally included neon rainbow unicorns, items not particularly attractive to an urban professional hipster like me with a penchant for black and gray. What had started out as seemingly innocent approval seeking had somehow morphed into needing confirmation that covering himself with neon rainbow unicorns would prevent people from noticing the large bear behind the curtain of extreme and delicate femme. As I looked into his imploring eyes, I realized it wasn't fair to lead Patrick on, avoiding the terrible feeling of disappointing him. While in this case the trans piece wasn't as much about transitioning gender as it was about transitioning reality, I had to finally admit that being too transpositive had shut down our process instead of maximizing its potential. In the end, we had to abandon our default privileging of the antinormative, to think dialectically about the ways in which the normative also played an important role in Patrick's experience, beyond the obvious polar differences. Now when Patrick shows off his latest purchases, somehow even more "fey" than before, he does so with the awareness that I would not be caught dead in any of them. And now when he displays his elaborately intricate, brightly colored nail designs for me to appreciate, I thrust my own professionally manicured, dependably light pink, and short-nailed medical hand at him so we can laugh at our disparate tastes. Though we both might identify as queer, we are playing with ideas of normativity and antinormativity, centrality and marginality, without ever having to decide which version is better.

Through exploring mutually how the meaning of queer has changed for both of us, Patrick and I have come to understand that his friend Claire's identity requires her to flip the gender binary in a way that his does not—that the ways in which she wants to be female and the ways in which he wants to be not-that-kind-of-male are neither the same nor different, though still somehow related. Without having discovered the queerness latent in my own cisgender identity, I don't think we could have come to understand that what Patrick really wants is to be the kind of cisgender male he feels he is and to have it be considered normative—or at least accepted—by the rest of the world. He is tired of passing for the man he is not and wants instead for his antinormativity to pass, as he becomes more authentically himself: "I think cisgender has been taken to mean something that maybe it doesn't—just like trans—what does it really mean?—I have a dick and I don't want it to fall off—I don't want to renovate—I'm happy with the house—but that doesn't mean I'm happy with masculinity and maleness and male culture—maybe I'm NOT comfortable with being cisgender after all—why can't we just have perfectly normal antinormativity?" As a result, Patrick and I are now focusing less on what he is not and more on what he might be. While he may still have no desire to transition his physicality in any way, we have come to agree that he needs to transition something, and how that something is defined will need to be of his own construction, something not necessarily preapproved or even sanctioned by the society in which we currently live. If we can find a way for him to do so, and have him live to tell the tale, we both believe it just might facilitate the discovery of, and participation in, the kind of shared life he wants and deserves so much. And in the same vein, if we allow queer theory and psychoanalytic theory to inform us and each other, then we can facilitate the creation of space not only for queer normativity and mainstream antinormativity but also for other dialectical potentials we have yet to encounter. I, for one, look forward to that exciting challenge.

These days, I like thinking about how far I have come—that my automatic assumption that a transgender analysand would do better with a transgender psychoanalyst seems like one that would no longer enter my mind in the same way it did. Instead I think about the ways in which this process queered me, and how my background in contemporary psychoanalysis helped me to remain open to unforeseen potentials when thinking about whom and how we treat. I have a much greater respect for what it means to be a nonexpert in this field, and little desire to propose any certainty about what it means to be transgender or cisgender from a psychoanalytic point of view. Hansbury (2011) asks us to consider whether cisgender psychoanalysts work differently than transgender psychoanalysts, but since we can't really know what we mean when we label someone "transgender" or "cisgender," we can't really answer that question. Yet I greatly respect Hansbury for asking it in the first place because it is precisely this kind of queer challenge from which all psychoanalytic thinking can benefit. All we can ask is that we do our best to think dialectically, to consider both the normative and the antinormative, the center and the margin, the queer and the not queer, and all the ways in which they inform and impact each other, allowing ourselves to be guided in each psychoanalytic moment by that which does not foreclose possibility but instead, as Enke puts it, encourages us to become "accessible in more ways than we can imagine" (2013: 244).

Hilary Offman, MD, FRCPC, is a psychiatrist and psychoanalyst in private practice in Toronto, Canada. She is a graduate and faculty member of the Toronto Institute for Contemporary Psychoanalysis and a lecturer and supervisor in the Department of Psychiatry, University of Toronto. She is also the author of "The Princess and the Penis: A Post Postmodern Queer-y Tale" (2014).

Acknowledgment

I would like to thank Brian Chisamore, MD, FRCPC; Adriano Bugliani, PhD; Brenda Rowlandson Grad Dip Psychotherapy; and Irwin Z. Hoffman, PhD, for the time, comments, and encouragement that greatly helped me in the writing of this article. Clinical material was published with permission. Names and personal details have been changed to protect privacy.

References

Aron, Lewis. 1991. "The Patient's Experience of the Analyst's Subjectivity." *Psychoanalytic Dialogues* 1, no. 1: 29–51.

Aviance, J. Nelson. 2016. "I Am NOT Cisgendered." *Huffington Post*, July 18, 2014, updated February 2, 2016. www.huffingtonpost.com/j-nelson-aviance/i-am-not-cisgendered_b_5598113.html.

Bauer, Greta. R., Ayden I. Scheim, Jake Pyne, RobbTravers, and Rebecca Hammond. 2015. "Intervenable Factors Associated with Suicide Risk in Transgender Persons: A Respondent Driven Sampling Study in Ontario, Canada." *BMC Public Health* 15, no. 1: art. 525.

Benjamin, Jessica. 1990. "An Outline of Intersubjectivity: The Development of Recognition." *Psychoanalytic Psychology* 7, supplement: 33–46.

———. 1995. "Sameness and Difference: Toward an Overinclusive Model of Gender Development." *Psychoanalytic Inquiry* 15, no. 1: 125–42.

———. 1996. "In Defense of Gender Ambiguity." *Gender and Psychoanalysis* 1, no. 1: 27–43.

Corbett, Ken. 1997. "Speaking Queer: A Reply to Richard C. Friedman." *Gender and Psychoanalysis* 2, no. 4: 495–514.

———. 2001. "More Life: Centrality and Marginality in Human Development." *Psychoanalytic Dialogues* 11, no. 3: 313–35.

———. 2008. "Gender Now." *Psychoanalytic Dialogues* 18, no. 6: 838–56.

Dimen, Muriel. 1991. "Deconstructing Difference: Gender, Splitting, and Transitional Space." *Psychoanalytic Dialogues* 1, no. 3: 335–52.

———. 1995. Introduction to *Psychoanalytic Dialogues* 5, no. 2, 157–63.

Enke, A. Finn. 2013. "The Education of Little Cis: Cisgender and the Discipline of Opposing Bodies." In *The Transgender Studies Reader 2*, edited by Susan Stryker and Aren Z. Aizura, 234–47. New York: Routledge.

Goldner, Virginia. 1991. "Toward a Critical Relational Theory of Gender." *Psychoanalytic Dialogues* 1, no. 3: 249–72.

———. 2003. "Ironic Gender/Authentic Sex." *Studies in Gender and Sexuality* 4, no. 2: 113–39.

Hansbury, Griffin. 2011. "King Kong and Goldilocks: Imagining Transmasculinities through the Trans-Trans Dyad." *Psychoanalytic Dialogues* 21, no. 2: 210–20.

Harris, Adrienne 1996. "Animated Conversation: Embodying and Gendering." *Gender and Psychoanalysis* 1, no. 3: 361–83.

———. 2005. *Gender as Soft Assembly*. Hillsdale, NJ: Analytic.

Hoffman, Irwin Z. 1998. *Ritual and Spontaneity in the Psychoanalytic Process: A Dialectical-Constructivist View*. Hillsdale, NJ: Analytic.

———. 2016. "The Risks of Therapist Passivity and the Potentials of Constructivist Influence." *Psychoanalytic Dialogues* 26, no. 1: 91–97.

Jagose, Annamarie. 2015. "The Trouble with Antinormativity." *differences* 26, no. 1: 26–47.

Kantrowitz, Judith L., Judith G. Singer, and Peter H. Knapp. 1975. "Methodology for a Prospective Study of Suitability for Psychoanalysis: The Role of Psychological Tests." *Psychoanalytic Quarterly* 44: 371–91.

Keenan, Edward. 2016. "New Ex Washrooms Are a We-Don't-Care Dream." *Star* (Toronto), August 27. www.thestar.com/news/gta/2016/08/27/new-ex-washrooms-are-a-we-dont-care-dream-keenan.html.

Mitchell, Stephen. A. 1988. *Relational Concepts in Psychoanalysis*. Cambridge, MA: Harvard University Press.

———. 1996. "Gender and Sexual Orientation in the Age of Postmodernism: The Plight of the Perplexed Clinician." *Gender and Psychoanalysis* 1, no. 1: 45–73.

Offman, Hilary. 2014. "The Princess and the Penis: A Post Postmodern Queer-y Tale." *Psychoanalytic Dialogues* 24, no. 1: 72–87.

Racker, Heinrich. 1957. "The Meanings and Uses of Countertransference." *Psychoanalytic Quarterly* 26: 303–57.

Raj, Rupert. 2002. "Towards a Transpositive Therapeutic Model: Developing Clinical Sensitivity and Cultural Competence in the Effective Support of Transsexual and Transgendered Clients." *International Journal of Transgenderism* 6, no. 2: 1–43.

Slavin, Malcolm Owen, and Daniel Kriegman. 1998. "Why the Analyst Needs to Change: Toward a Theory of Conflict, Negotiation, and Mutual Influence in the Therapeutic Process." *Psychoanalytic Dialogues* 8, no. 2: 247–84.

Stotzer, Rebecca L. 2009. "Violence against Transgender People: A Review of United States Data." *Aggression and Violent Behavior* 14, no. 3: 170–79.

Stryker, Susan. 2008. *Transgender History*. Berkeley, CA: Seal.

Stryker, Susan, Paisley Currah, and Lisa Jean Moore. 2008. "Introduction: Trans-, Trans, or Transgender? The Stakes for Women's Studies." *WSQ* 36, nos. 3–4: 11–22.

Wiegman, Robyn, and Elizabeth A. Wilson. 2015. "Introduction: Antinormativity's Queer Conventions." *differences* 26, no. 1: 1–25.

Winnicott, Donald W. 1953. "Transitional Objects and Transitional Phenomena—A Study of the First Not-Me Possession." *International Journal of Psychoanalysis* 34: 89–97.

Putting the "Trans" Back in "Truth"

A Psychoanalytic Take on Gender's Authenticity

HANNAH WALLERSTEIN

Abstract This article concerns the concept of "truth" in relation to transgender studies. Historically, transgender claims to gendered truth have been pathologized as either refusing reality or assuming it locatable. In order to listen to such claims with greater rigor, the author proposes a rethinking of the concept of truth in relation to subjective life. This article attempts as much, by charting out a psychoanalytic definition of truth not as correspondence but as translation. To do so, it follows this thread, beginning in Freud's work and then as it is elaborated in the work of Wilfred Bion. It then turns to implications for thinking gender, and transgender phenomenon more specifically, concluding with an interview with Joy Ladin, in which gender transition is proposed to facilitate a more "truthful" relation to reality.
Keywords gender, truth, psychoanalysis

This article concerns the concept of "truth" in relation to transgender studies. Historically, transgender people have been criticized for both rejecting and (incorrectly) believing in truth. The former criticism assumes what Susan Stryker, following Frederic Jameson, terms a modernist "mirror-style representational" theory in which the relationship between representation (gender) and referent (sex) is understood as "strictly . . . mimetic" (2006: 9). In short, man mirrors maleness, and woman mirrors femaleness. What follows is a correspondence theory of truth, in which anyone who claims a gender outside the assumed gender/sex correlation is seen to be falsely representing his or her biological sex. The latter criticism, coming from a postmodern sensibility, ironically accuses the transgender subject of supposing precisely the correspondence theory of truth that grounds the first critique. The argument goes as follows: in attempting to reconcile sexed materiality with gender identity, the transgender subject asserts the necessity of a correlation between sex and gender.[1] In psychoanalytic versions of this critique, transgender people are articulated as eclipsing the space between representation and reality (Millot 1989; Shepherdson 2006). Often within

TSQ: Transgender Studies Quarterly ★ Volume 4, Numbers 3–4 ★ November 2017 **421**
DOI 10.1215/23289252-4189901 © 2017 Duke University Press

a Lacanian framework, here changing the body becomes synonymous with a fantasy that the real of sexual difference can be fully aligned with the representational system of gender.

Put bluntly, whether one sits on the modern or postmodern end of the spectrum, transgenderism has made many theorists nervous when it comes to thinking truth. Rather than assume the transgender person's claim to an often "inescapable and inalienable" (Stryker 2006: 10) gendered truth is either delusional or ignorant of the postmodern turn, I follow others (Stryker 2006; Farley and Kennedy, 2016) in proposing that such claims demand a rethinking of the concept of truth in relation to subjective life. This article hopes to contribute to such a task, by charting out a psychoanalytic definition of truth not as correspondence but as translation.[2] To do so, it will outline this thread, beginning in Sigmund Freud's work and then as it is elaborated in the work of Wilfred Bion. It will then turn to implications for thinking gender, and transgender phenomena more specifically. Lastly, in conversation with an interview with Joy Ladin, it will propose that the act of gender transition may rework the relation between representation and reality, facilitating a more "truthful" relation to otherness within and without.

Before continuing, a few clarifying remarks are in order. First, in line with other contemporary psychoanalytic engagements with gender and sex (Gherovici 2010; Gozlan 2015; Farley and Kennedy 2016), this article will define gender as a representational system through which the subject relates to sexual difference and define sexual difference as an unknowable unconscious reality that inaugurates human subjectivity. Second, a word on scope: while transgender studies has highlighted the need for new frameworks for thinking truth, the theoretical concerns of this essay are not restricted to those who are transgender or gender nonconforming. As will become clear, this article contends that we all must enter a translational process in order to experience gender as subjectively true, a process that entails estrangement and creative engagement for all.

Truth, the Sham, and the Transfer

In "Analysis Terminable and Interminable" (1937a) Freud writes, "The analytic relationship is based on a love of truth—that is, on a recognition of reality . . . it precludes any kind of sham or deceit" (248). Two relations are proposed: truth as the recognition of reality, and as opposed to the sham. We will come back to both. But first, what truth is Freud speaking about? And what does it mean to "love" it?

Freud's essay "Screen Memories" (1899) is his first to explicitly take up the question of truth. The paper introduces the concept of screen memories to explain seemingly "emotionally insignificant" memories from childhood. Freud proposes that these early memories hide while bearing evidence of other conflictual (i.e., repressed) memories: "What is recorded as a mnemic image is not the relevant experience itself . . . [but] another psychical element closely associated with the objectionable one" (307). This is due to conflict: a compromise has been formed between the "principle which endeavors to fix important impressions" and that which "resists" objectionable ones. To begin, then, Freud posits a double relation to truth—on the one hand, a desire to recognize reality ("to fix important impressions"), on the other, a resistance to any such effort.

To elaborate his theory, Freud sets up a dialogue between himself and a fabricated analysand, a "man of university education, aged thirty-eight" (309), in which the unconscious meaning of a screen memory is revealed. We now know that the content Freud offers is entirely autobiographical. This screening of his screen memory is striking, since, as Evelyne Ender (2005) points out, Freud's generous use of personal examples in the *Interpretation of Dreams* makes it unlikely Freud would resort to such a rhetorical strategy out of bashfulness. How, then, do we account for Freud's use of a fictional dialogue in order to reveal the truth behind memory?

Ender answers that such a dialogic structure both articulates the undecidability of memory's relation to truth and allows Freud to express his ambivalence toward such undecidability. She compares Freud's dialogue to the act of remembering itself: "Like any other rememberer, Freud must have felt the split between the 'I now' and the 'I then' . . . offer[ing] a vivid reminder that we all ultimately view the 'film' of our memories through the eyes of a self very different from the subject in the picture" (95). This split contaminates any sense of memory as an accurate (read, honest) harbinger of objective reality. Ender goes on to chart how Freud uses the two characters to voice his own ambivalence about such implications: his analysand gets carried away, asserting that the screen memory is pure fiction, while Freud plays the scientist who cautions against such radically constructivist claims.

But in addition to the problem of accuracy Ender elucidates, there is a different type of truth at stake in the dialogue. Regardless of whether the screen memory has some connection to past material reality or is entirely fabricated, it serves a purpose both Freud and his fabricated analysand come to be certain of. Freud summarizes: the memory "is calculated to illustrate the most momentous turning points in your life, the influence of the two most powerful motive forces—hunger and love" (1899: 316). What is most "true" then about the memory is not its rendition of objective reality but the unconscious drives it screens. Freud compares it to the sham: "There is a common saying among us about shams, that they are not made of gold themselves but have lain behind something that is made of gold" (307). Thus we arrive at an unconscious truth that is not opposed to deceit but expressed through it and only revealed, I contend, in dialogue with an other.

When Freud returns to a conceptualization of psychoanalytic truth in his late paper "Constructions in Analysis" (1937b), he places it specifically in this act of transfer, elaborating the dialogic structure he intuited in "Screen Memories." The paper is responding to the critique that psychoanalysis follows a "Heads I win, tails you lose" logic: if the patient agrees with an interpretation, the analyst assumes himself correct; if the patient disagrees, the analyst still assumes his accuracy, chalking the patient's refusal up to resistance. Freud argues that while psychoanalysis does not take a patient's conscious rejection of an interpretation at face value, neither does it hold her or his conscious acceptance in high regard. Nor is the analyst's determination of what is true trusted in and of itself. Instead, Freud points to the importance of the intersubjective exchange. He defines the two roles: The patient has knowledge (it is the truth of his experience that is at stake) and also the need not to know it (the experience of interest is that which is repressed). The analyst has neither the experience nor the inhibition and thus acts as the decoder: "His task is to make out what has been forgotten from the traces which it has left behind or, more correctly, to construct it" (258–59). Like the screen memory, his task is ambiguously both passive (hearing "traces") and active (constructing their meaning). How then does he know when his "decoding" is correct "enough"? Only through its effect on the patient: "If the construction is wrong, there is no change in the patient; but if it is right or gives an approximation to the truth, he reacts to it with an unmistakable aggravation of his symptoms and of his general condition" (265). Put differently, we know we are wrong when no contact is made, when there is a lack of transfer. Indeed, Freud points to confirmation being clearest when the patient continues with a translation of his own, "when a patient answers with an association which contains something similar or analogous to the content of the construction" (263). It is the indirect response, the translation into the patient's own language that marks the arrival at subjective truth.

Bion's Contribution

Where Freud raises the importance of exchange to subjective truth, Wilfred Bion expands on the necessary context for such an exchange to lead to growth. Truth is arguably one of Bion's most central concepts, leading neo-Bionian thinkers to theorize a truth-drive at the heart of his contribution (Grotstein 2004). He famously compares truth to food: "Healthy mental growth seems to depend on truth as the living organism depends on food" (1965: 38). Yet regardless or perhaps because of its central import, truth is difficult to define in Bion's work. He relates it and even exchanges it for "O," a concept comparable to Lacan's real, which refers to the senseless, formless, "ultimate reality" that underlies all knowledge but can never itself be known (1970: 27). But there are subtle differences. For one, truth and falsehood relate to the realm of thoughts, where reality is thought about (recall Freud's positing of truth as the re-cognition of reality). In addition, while reality encompasses all that is, truth seems to be particular to and possessed by individual entities. So Bion speaks of the "absolute truth in and of an . . . object" (30). To be clear, Bion is not referring here to an object in its conventional sense, a thing that can be known in some direct way, but to the psychoanalytic object, which operates at the border between psychic and material reality. Grotstein follows out both these distinctions by defining truth as a personal relation to reality: "Truth . . . constitutes our emotional comprehension and acceptance of reality, both inner and outer. . . . Put another way, reality always is. Truth constitutes our personal, emotional, subjective acceptance of it as our truth and the truth" (2004: 1094).

The capacity to accept reality is for Bion no easy task. It is never entirely possible and is approached only through the alpha function, or the transformation of unbearable experience into thoughts. This is in its origin an entirely interpersonal affair. Bion narrates its development through the act of breastfeeding. First, the infant is hungry and experiences this sensation as a bad object: "It is associated with a visual image of a breast that does not satisfy but is of a kind that is needed. This needed object is a bad object. All objects that are needed are bad objects because they can tantalize" (1962: 84). The infant thus attempts to evacuate the bad breast. If he is fed with "milk, warmth and love," then he experiences taking in the good breast and—at the same time and "indistinguishable" from the taking in—"evacuating the bad breast" (34). Over time the bad object is felt to be "removed [from the good breast] and re-introjected" (90). If the mother is able to receive the infant's projected objects and provide meaning to them, then "they [the objects] are felt to have been modified in such a way that the object that is re-introjected has become tolerable in the infant's psyche" (90). Bion terms this maternal receptiveness "reverie": a "state of mind which is open to the reception of any 'objects' from the loved object . . . whether they are felt by the infant to be good or bad" (36). In her reverie, the mother acts as a "container" to the unbearable experience that, now "contained," is transformed into something thinkable. Put back into the breast-feeding exchange, the "'wanted' breast is [now] felt as an 'idea of the breast missing' and not as a bad breast present" (34). The infant has thus accepted a piece of reality, encountered true thought, and can now do something to alter his situation.

Alternately, when maternal reverie is absent and relations between the infant and breast are dominated by envy, projected elements are not contained but instead "stripped" of the "good and valuable elements," leaving the infant forced to re-introject only "worthless residue" (96–97). In contrast to the experience of containment, Bion describes this as a state of "withoutness": "It is an internal object without an exterior. It is an alimentary canal without a body" (97). Such a structure cannot think about reality but can only evacuate it—thus truth is inapproachable, and growth does not occur. So Bion defines the lie as an evacuation of meaning: the liar "denudes the environment of significants . . . [only] harbor[ing] thoughts if he does not need thoughts to contribute to his significance and [only tolerating] . . . thoughts that do not do so" (1970: 104). This is both a rejection of the environment and of its impact on the self (a fantasy of omnipotence).

In resonance with Freud's thinking in "Constructions in Analysis," Bion applies this same interpersonal exchange to the analytic dyad's elaboration of truth. He writes of the analyst's reverie as a receptiveness to the patient's projected elements, or a "becoming O": "In order to know the truth one must become it." This "at one-ment" can be "felt" but not directly known. It is importantly not identification: "There can be no geometry of 'similar,' 'identical,' 'equal'; only of analogy" (1970: 89). The contact of becoming is not merging, then, but translation. Grotstein clarifies:

> To become not as fusion but in the "become" process the analyst is evoked, provoked or "primed" . . . to respond to the analysand's emotions and associations with his/her private, native emotions that are independently summoned within him/her . . . to enter within his/her own unconscious to locate and to summon (unconsciously) those emotions and experiences that are apposite to the hidden emotional truths of the analysand with which they symmetrically resonate, thereby achieving a "common sense." (2004: 1085)

It is specifically the resonance between two—a resonance dependent on both the willingness to be impacted by the other qua other (i.e., not via merging) and the capacity to translate such impact into a personal language—that leads to the progressive uncovering of truth.

To summarize, subjective truth is here defined as a personal relation to/ acceptance of reality, based on the tolerance of separation (the breast is absent) and the (therefore necessary) act of translation. To be clear, the translation at stake is not between languages, in which an already inscribed meaning is rearticulated and correspondence becomes possible. Instead, it is the forming of meaning out of an encounter with something fundamentally unknowable and without sense. This is translation as creative act, the development of a form out of that which has none.

Returning to gender, I contend that truth defined as such allows us to attend to gendered experience with greater nuance. If, following Bion's paradigm, gender is of the order of thought (i.e., representation), and sexual difference is of the order of unknowable reality, then we can take seriously gender's relation to sex and questions of truth, without collapsing into a positivist conception of gender as corresponding to sex in some predetermined way. Instead, it would be gender's difference from sex that renders gender a potential vehicle for meaningful engagement with sexed existence. Revisiting Bion's developmental formulation, three subjective possibilities ensue: gender could be experienced as a direct harbinger of sex, in which case it would feel too real and foreclose questions of subjective truth; gender could be used to evacuate the reality of sex, in which case it would feel subjectively false; or gender could be used to establish a personal relation to sexed existence via translation, in which case it would feel subjectively true.

Truth and Gender Transition

While a full look at the implications of such a model for transgender studies is beyond the scope of this essay, here I will address two consequences that directly concern the critiques with which I opened. First, thinking truth as translation demands a repositioning of the transgender subject in relation to normative gender development. Far from being anomalous, the transgender subject's assertion of truth here renders explicit the discord at the heart of all sexed embodiment and the creativity necessary for any gender identity to become subjectively true. Second, such a framework opens up ways of reading the reconciliation between body and gender identity often at play in gender transition. While it is indeed possible that changing one's body may reflect a collapsing of space between representation and reality (the first of the subjective possibilities outlined), it is also possible that changing the body may articulate a different, translational process. Here, acting on the body would not be a flight from truth or the limits of symbolization but, rather, the establishment of a personal relation to one's own materiality that renders the space between representation and reality both bearable and generative. To claim a gender and body[3] as one's own would then not foreclose the radical otherness of sexual difference, but it would put it to creative use.

"Gender and the Syntax of Being"

To illustrate how transitioning genders may facilitate a more "truthful" relation to reality, I will conclude with an interview from Krista Tippett's podcast *On Being* with Joy Ladin (2014), the first openly transgender professor at an Orthodox Jewish institution. During the interview, Ladin discusses her subjective experience prior to, during, and after gender transition. Here all three phases will be outlined.

Prior to her transition, Ladin describes herself as without subjecthood, as "a persona not a person." She articulates a state of absence: without a relation to space (a "cardboard cutout") and embodiment more generally ("without a body," "with a body that felt like a cross between a mask and a tomb"). At best, she remained hidden; at worst she had already passed. At another point, Ladin describes her prior experience of gender as "eating her alive." Gender here does not provide access to reality but takes it over—sucking out space for a subject to exist.

Without space to be, as Ladin describes, others are both out of reach and far too close. She narrates an inability to make contact with her children: "When my children hugged me, it felt like they were hugging nothing, like their love was pouring into an empty space where I should have been." Simultaneously, Ladin describes a need to fend off and control the other's gaze, lest it be too humiliating or rejecting. She developed a system of rules meant to keep herself in hiding (don't play with dolls, don't look at women, don't use flowery language). Paradoxically, because Ladin's gender felt so wrong, it took over everything: "I was thinking about gender all the time. It was boring. It was exhausting." In her experience of gender as annihilating presence, staving off contact became a full-time job.

So Ladin describes her decision to transition genders as a moment of differentiation. She narrates contemplating suicide as a way out of the impact her gender transition would have on loved ones, and a particularly useful moment when her therapist commented, "You have to stick around for your children to reject you." I find this statement quite lovely because it gets at two different types of aggression: one in which the self is sacrificed in order to bypass (and thus protect from) the suffering and aggression of others, and the other in which the self asserts its presence, something akin to Donald Winnicott's "ruthlessness" (1945), in which space is claimed from the other in order to exist. In the suicidal act, the other looms unbearably large and is in need of protection (it cannot tolerate my being), while in the ruthless act there is faith in an object relation that withstands aggression and difference; rejection becomes not destructive but foundational to growth.

Second to the establishment of a subjective space is a process of getting to know via translation. Ladin discusses her transition as a discovery from the "outside in": "I had no idea what I looked like. I couldn't even make choices about what colors look good on me or not, what do I like what don't I like, because I had never seen myself. So the external was my gateway into a whole bunch of self-defining preferences, choices, decisions, experiments." She offers the example of choosing an outfit: "'I'm going to wear that because I love that.' The love is what's the real self and the expression is more superficial but for me I needed to create a . . . visible female self first, and then that self had to go out in the world and start developing a history and establishing a history with people." Unlike her prior state in which exposure was avoided at all costs, Ladin now has a gendered place from which to receive thoughts about herself. Experiences in external reality become a means of learning about internal reality, creating a history of desire from which to orient forward.

Such subjective contact with reality leads to the development of personal responsibility. Ladin articulates this in reference to God:

> The two most important things about being a Jew are living in gratitude and living in joy. And [for most of my life] I wasn't able to do either. . . . I was a walking complaint about existence because it all felt wrong to me and I would say to God, you know, that's your fault. And now that I live as myself and I've been given this incredible miracle, now, unfortunately, I don't have that out. So when I'm talking to God I am obligated to be grateful and joyful. . . . I'm often not, but now I see that that does reflect ways that I need to grow as a person, and not some existential raw deal that I was given. And that's pretty extraordinary. I feel that only recently have I been able to serve God.

Through the act of gender transition, Ladin moves from a place of contingency (the "raw deal I was given") to responsibility for a life decidedly hers. God's dictum "be grateful, be joyful" becomes not a taunting fantasy impossibly out of reach but an ideal just far enough as to inspire work ("I need to grow as a person"). In short, God (and I would add gender) become not the stealers of Ladin's being but markers of the space necessary for becoming. It is in this space that true thought grows—both radically other and uniquely one's own.

Hannah Wallerstein is a postdoctoral fellow in psychodynamic psychotherapy and psychoanalytic studies at the Austen Riggs Center.

Acknowledgments

Thank you to Elissa Marder for seeing my interest in translation, to Mark Stoholski for your generous engagement with this text, and to my anonymous readers for your thoughtful suggestions.

Notes

1. For more on this tension within gender studies, see Prosser 2006.
2. For another lucid and complementary psychoanalytic elaboration of truth in relation to transgender children, see Farley and Kennedy 2016.
3. While the concept of the body has not been considered in any detail in this article, I do think it relates to the process of translation described. Put briefly, my guess is that only when gender functions as an effective translator to sexed existence, a process that may be facilitated by bodily modification, does the body come to exist as psychic home.

References

Bion, Wilfred R. 1962. *Learning from Experience*. London: Rowman and Littlefield.

———. 1963. *Elements of Psycho-Analysis*. London: William Heinemann Medical Books.

———. 1965. *Transformations*. London: William Heinemann Medical Books.

———. 1970. *Attention and Interpretation*. London: Tavistock.

Ender, Evelyne. 2005. *Architexts of Memory: Literature, Science, and Autobiography*. Ann Arbor: University of Michigan Press.

Farley, Lisa, and R. M. Kennedy. 2016. "A Sex of One's Own: Childhood and the Embodiment of (Trans)gender." *Psychoanalysis, Culture, and Society* 21, no. 2: 167–83.

Freud, Sigmund. 1899. "Screen Memories." In *Early Psycho-Analytic Publications*, vol. 3 of *The Standard Edition of the Complete Psychological Works of Sigmund Freud*, translated by James Strachey, 299–322. London: Hogarth.

———. 1937a. "Analysis Terminable and Interminable." In *Moses and Monotheism, An Outline of Psycho-Analysis and Other Works*, vol. 23 of *The Standard Edition of the Complete Psychological Works of Sigmund Freud*, translated by James Strachey, 209–54. London: Hogarth.

———. 1937b. "Constructions in Analysis." In *Moses and Monotheism, An Outline of Psycho-Analysis and Other Works*, vol. 23 of *The Standard Edition of the Complete Psychological Works of Sigmund Freud*, translated by James Strachey, 255–70. London: Hogarth.

Gherovici, Patricia. 2010. *Please Select Your Gender: From the Invention of Hysteria to the Democratizing of Transgenderism*. New York: Routledge.

Gozlan, Oren. 2015. *Transsexuality and the Art of Transitioning: A Lacanian Approach*. London: Routledge.

Grotstein, James S. 2004. "The Seventh Servant: The Implications of a Truth Drive in Bion's Theory of 'O.'" *International Journal of Psychoanalysis* 85, no. 5: 1081–1101.

Ladin, Joy. 2014. "Gender and the Syntax of Being: Identity and Transition." Interview with Krista Tippett, *On Being* (audio podcast), December 11. www.onbeing.org/programs/joy-ladin-gender-and-the-syntax-of-being-identity-and-transition/.

Millot, Catherine. 1989. *Horsexe: Essay on Transsexuality*. New York: Autonomedia.

Prosser, Jay. 2006. "Judith Butler: Queer Feminism, Transgender, and the Transubstantiation of Sex." In *The Transgender Studies Reader*, edited by Susan Stryker and Stephen Whittle, 257–280. New York: Routledge.

Shepherdson, Charles. 2006. "Selection from *The* Role *of Gender and the* Imperative *of Sex*." In *The Transgender Studies Reader*, edited by Susan Stryker and Stephen Whittle, 94–102. New York: Routledge.

Stryker, Susan. 2006. "(De)Subjugated Knowledges: An Introduction to Transgender Studies." In *The Transgender Studies Reader*, edited by Susan Stryker and Stephen Whittle, 1–18. New York: Routledge.

Winnicott, D. W. 1945. "Primitive Emotional Development." *International Journal of Psycho-Analysis* 26: 137–43.

"There Is Nothing Missing in the Real"

Trans Childhood and the Phantasmatic Body

JACOB BRESLOW

Abstract In 2012, a Colorado elementary school district barred Coy Mathis, a six-year-old trans girl, from using the girls' restrooms under the justification that her foreshadowed future adult male sex organ would make the other girls currently using the restroom uncomfortable. Responding to this moment as indicative of antitrans discrimination more broadly, this article undertakes a psychoanalytic interrogation of how this exclusion was structured by the coming together of the trans child and the phantasmatic body. Centering the ambivalent political and psychic work of the body as phantom, and the trans child's phantasmatic body in particular, the analysis puts Freudian and Lacanian understandings of the penis/phallus into conversation with biographical narratives of trans childhood. Thus, it argues that both trans-affirmative and transphobic narratives that temporally position the phantasmatic body of the trans child do so in nuanced and complex ways that structurally complement, rather than challenge, each other's terms.

Keywords trans children, psychoanalysis, narrative, transgender theory, embodiment

S peaking to the media in February 2013, Kathryn Mathis, a middle-aged white woman living in Colorado with her husband and their five children, defended her and her husband's decision to file a discrimination complaint on behalf of Coy, their six-year-old daughter:

> We got a call one evening, it was the principal and he said he wanted to set up a meeting with us to discuss options for Coy's future use of the restroom.... It came out that Coy was no longer going to be able to use the girl's restroom and they were going to require her to be using the boy's restroom or the staff bathroom or the bathroom for the sick children. (Mathis, quoted in Whitelocks and Greig 2013)

This decision was made, the principal explained, because the Fountain–Fort Carson School District believed that it was no longer appropriate for Coy, a trans girl, to share the space of the restroom with the other girls. Fearing for their child's safety, and upset that the school district was abruptly curtailing their previous

TSQ: Transgender Studies Quarterly ★ Volume 4, Numbers 3–4 ★ November 2017 **431**
DOI 10.1215/23289252-4189910 © 2017 Duke University Press

support of Coy's gender identity, the Mathis family took her out of school and filed a discrimination complaint.

In a letter by W. Kelly Dude, the school's attorney, he justified the district's stance by putting into question Coy's sexed embodiment, her gender identity, and, crucially for this article's argument, her location in childhood. Dude, who excuses his use of male pronouns for Coy as "not [an] attempt to be disrespectful, but because I am referring to male genitals" (2012), made the following statement:

> The District's decision took into account not only Coy but other students in the building, their parents, and the future impact a boy with male genitals using a girls' bathroom would have as Coy grew older. . . . I'm certain you can appreciate that as Coy grows older and his male genitals develop along with the rest of his body, at least some parents and students are likely to become uncomfortable with his continued use of the girls' restroom. (2012)

On the premise of Coy's potential and future male genitalia, and the discomfort they would allegedly create, the school district argued that it would be inappropriate for her to continue to use the girls' restrooms.[1] What does it mean, I ask, to regulate access to a space based on the future possibility of adult male genitals? What does it mean, particularly in this case, when the possibility itself of adult male genitalia is both uncertain—hormone and surgical interventions for trans girls shift the temporality and necessity of obtaining future male genitals—as well as foreshadowed? Thinking through these questions, this article's analysis is not specifically directed toward the gendered regulation of public space.[2] Rather, it is an interrogation of how this exclusion works through the coming together of the trans child and the phantasmatic body.

In order to articulate the ambivalent political work of this particular pairing, I draw on Gayle Salamon's framing of the body as phantasmatic (2004, 2006, 2010). Salamon, who works with Sigmund Freud's concept of the bodily ego ([1923] 1955), Kaja Silverman's (1996) reading of the Jacques Lacan's mirror stage ([1949] 1977), and Maurice Merleau-Ponty's phenomenological framing of the body (1962), argues that these concepts are useful for understanding and advocating for trans subjectivity and embodiment. The phantasmatic body, Salamon writes, "shows that the body of which one has a 'felt sense' is not necessarily contiguous with the physical body as it is perceived from the outside" (2004: 96), and, Salamon argues, "a phantasmatic body part cannot be considered *not-body* simply because of its nonmateriality" (2006: 100). In other words, understanding the body (in whole or in part) as phantasmatic—rather than as a pregiven biological entity that is straightforwardly material—means recognizing that *all* bodies are continuously and laboriously produced through feelings, desires, phantasies, and the processes of identification (and therefore recognition and misrecognition). For Salamon, understanding the body as phantasmatic thus complicates what she calls "the nature of bodily being" (2010: 2) because it means acknowledging that one's sense of one's body as a "unified whole" is itself phantasmatic. "Within psychoanalysis," Salamon writes, "one is not born a body, but becomes one" (2004: 105).

For Salamon, the phantasmatic body is a productive site of theorization for trans subjects and trans theory precisely because it allows for a "resignification of materiality itself" (2004: 117). This resignification is important, Salamon argues, because it could open up avenues for bodies to "manifest sex in ways that exceed or confound evident binaries" without pathologizing them (2004: 95). Understanding the body as phantasmatic, as something that one becomes through alteration and prosthesis, as well as through fantasy, desire, and identification, could thus allow for affirmations of materiality, for the potential to "create and transform the lived meanings of [the body's] materialities" (2004: 120). Adding to Salamon's analysis, I argue that interrogating the temporality of the phantasmatic trans body—and specifically the phantasmatic construction of a trans body as ambivalently located in childhood—complicates the potentials for affirmation and depathologization. Here, the ambivalent temporal evocation of the trans child's body can both affirm and insist on the livability of a trans child's embodiment (as we shall see below). But, central to this article's argument about the political ambivalence of the trans child's body, this is not the only work that the phantasmatic body allows for. Building on my wider research on the ambivalent political and psychic life of childhood (Breslow 2017a, 2017b), this article centrally asks how phantasies of childhood, children's bodies, and trans bodies work both for and against a trans politics. Analyzing the phantasmatic trans body and childhood through the psychoanalytic frames of Freud and Lacan, as well as the uptake of their work within trans, feminist, and queer scholarship, I situate this article within a body of work that argues for the importance of psychoanalysis within trans critique (Cavanagh 2016; Elliot 2001; Farley and Kennedy 2015; Gherovici 2010; Goldner 2011; Gozlan 2011; Salamon 2004, 2010). At issue, then, are not just the ways in which psychoanalytic approaches provide the particular languages of fantasy, recognition, projection, and disavowal to help understand the violent gendered logics behind antitrans discrimination policies like the one that barred Coy. Also at stake are the ways in which a particular psychoanalytic reading of childhood—that long-standing object of psychoanalytic inquiry and conjecture—illuminates investments in sex, gender, and embodiment that a trans project can interrupt.

In this article, I begin with Coy's precarious location in childhood as a springboard to interrogate the investments at work in two competing fantasies operating here: first, that sexual difference and bodily inhabitation are simultaneously inconsequential and hypervulnerable during childhood; and, second, that children occupy a space prior to bodily (and specifically genital) awareness. What do these fantasies mean, I ask, particularly when the gendering of boyhood and girlhood is so intense? What role does the fantasy of children's ignorance of sexual difference and sexual anatomy—a fantasy certainly not held within Freudian psychoanalysis (cf. Freud [1907] 1963)—play in the psychic life of the gender binary, and what demands does it make, of femininity, of (cis)girls, and of trans children in particular? Reiterating this article's focus on the ambivalence of the child, I alternatively ask: what are the promises and limitations for a critical trans project when trans people evoke this particular duality of the child's positioning within and before sexual difference? In answering these questions, this article turns, initially, to Freud's and Lacan's analyses of the role of the penis/phallus as they structure psychosexual development, and as they shed light on the school district's decision to exclude Coy. In the following section, I turn to a selection of narratives of trans childhood (including, but not exclusively about Coy) found in autobiographies, biographies, published interviews, and testimonials, wherein the trans child's phantasmatic body operates as a justificatory device through which trans narratives of self-discovery and transition are legitimated. By doing so, this article advocates for a critical psychoanalytic interrogation of the phantasmatic body of the trans child—one that opens up trans critique to the ambivalences of the child's body and its temporal positionings.

Disavowing the Psychic Brutality of Gender

Against the school district's claim that Coy would introduce an otherwise absent discomfort into the same-sex space of the girls' restroom, psychoanalysis, despite being a variegated field that includes many (sometimes contradictory) approaches, such as relational, Freudian, Lacanian, object-relations, and feminist psychoanalytic theories, might nonetheless suggest that gendered recognition and psychosexual development—particularly in relation to girls and femininity—is anything but comfortable. While *comfort* is not, of course, a psychoanalytic term, we can see in Freud's discussion in "Femininity," for example, that the process of psychosexual development through which "a woman develops out of a child with a bisexual disposition" ([1933] 1955: 416) is one that is born out of relationships between women (between mother and child) involving hostility, hate, reproach, and ambivalence (420). Freudian psychoanalysis, then—despite having been rightly castigated by many trans and feminist scholars for its pathologization of trans people and women, and for its overwhelming phallocentrism—is helpful here in relationship to Coy not only because it questions the presence and source of discomfort within allegedly same-sex spaces but also because it does not assume as natural or necessary the link between femininity and female embodiment.[3]

Indeed, for Freud, as well as for the early feminist psychoanalysts like Karen Horney ([1926] 1967) and Helene Deutsch (1946), the assumption that embodiment explains psychosexual development not only needs to be questioned; it is also most difficult to explain in regards to female embodiment and femininity (Freud [1933] 1955: 416). For instance, Horney, who challenged Freud's phallocentrism and the wider discipline's androcentrism ([1926] 1967: 54), argued that one of the key stages in the Oedipus complex for women—the girl's turning away from her mother, what she called the girl's "flight from womanhood" (64)—is not a natural or given process but is, rather, "reinforced and supported by the actual disadvantage under which women labor in social life" (69). Along these lines, Gayle Rubin, a feminist theorist and social scientist, argues that what is commonly understood as a "normal" disposition (a "normal" that Freud puts in quotes intentionally) might best be understood as a form of gendered violence: "The creation of 'femininity' in women in the course of socialization is *an act of psychic brutality* . . . Freud's essays on femininity [are] descriptions of how a group is prepared psychologically, at a tender age, to live with its oppression" (1975: 196, emphasis added). In arguing, from a sociopolitical perspective, that normative gendering is not a fact of biology but instead a process of integrating misogyny into the psyche (cf. Beauvoir 1949; Grosz 1994; Martin 1996), Rubin asserts that it is not a girl's potential failure to achieve normative femininity that should be of concern (as it is within at least a normative reading of Freud). Rather, Rubin contends, concern should be directed at the conditions under which the desired outcome is produced, precisely because it is produced as desired (and as natural) despite only being achieved through an act of psychic brutality. In this sense, the idea that the girls' restroom is a space of comfort might be understood as a disavowal of the violence of normative gendering, as it seeks to name the communality of that gendered experience as having nothing to do with anxiety or resentment. This analysis in and of itself might be productively understood as a trans-affirmative position, for in its universal questioning of the attainment of masculinity or femininity, psychoanalysis dislodges the uneven burden placed on trans subjects to defend, justify, and assume a particular body and identity.[4] Within this framing of psychoanalysis, that is, all gendered positions—cis, trans, and otherwise—must be explained in a framework that includes, but is not reducible to, the body.

But more needs to be said about the relationship between this disavowal and questions of the body from within psychoanalytic, rather than sociopolitical, explanations. The role that the body plays in producing gendered subjects is, however, a complicated one—one that differs across various psychoanalytic accounts, and even across various readings of Freud. In a particular biologically determinist reading of Freud's outlining of the Oedipus complex (such as within Horney, Beauvoir, Jones [1912] 1923, and Deutsch)—a reading that many challenge and that I shall also challenge—the girl begins her move from polymorphous sexuality to "normal femininity" (Freud [1933] 1955: 424) only after acknowledging real physical anatomy: the presence or absence of the penis comes to signify for the child either their own masculinity and authority (in boys) or their own inferiority and femininity (in girls). This understanding of the Oedipus complex fits within, indeed structures, a straightforward reading of the transphobic exclusion of Coy. It is precisely, in other words, the district's biologically determinist reading of sex, as well as its disavowal of the psychic brutality of psychosexual development that, on the surface, justifies its exclusion.

We can see this taking place in Dude's justifying of Coy's exclusion, wherein it was the assumption of the visual recognition of Coy's "male genitals" (Dude 2012) by the other girls in the same-sex space of the restroom that was produced as the precise act by which the girls would recognize their own inferiority, and their discomfort would arise. This is explicit in the fourteen-page decision by the court. Steven Chavez, the director of the Colorado Civil Rights Division and author of the decision (which sided with Coy), had to argue against the district's contention that if Coy were allowed to use the girls' restroom on the basis of gender identity it would set a harmful precedent: "The Respondent [the school district] also proffers 'what-if' scenarios, such as a request coming from 'a male high school student with a lower voice, chest hair and with more physically mature sex organs who claims to be transgender and demands to use the girls' restroom after having used the boy's restrooms for several years'" (Chavez 2013: 8–9). The link between the projection of Coy into an older male body—"as Coy grows older and his male genitals develop along with the rest of his body" (Dude 2012)—and this phantasmatic figure of the older, hairy, and sexually mature man is more than simply evidence of the district's creative gendered imaginary. In this narrative, the school district locates the site of gendered violence and vulnerability as taking place in the meeting of opposite sexed (and aged) bodies; reproducing the biologically determinist Freudian narrative almost directly, the school district lifted Coy out of childhood and into a postpubescent male body, eliciting the Oedipal moment of genital recognition between the girl and her father. In locating Coy's body as being the phantasmatic penis that produces this discomfort, the district overemphasizes the act of perception, assuming that it—rather than the meanings already assigned to the perceived organ (to which I next turn)—is the source of discomfort. The violence of sociocultural norms about femininity and the insidious hierarchy that marks the female body as inadequate is thus disavowed precisely by being projected onto Coy's body in the district's fantasy of Coy's penis.

However, as Jacqueline Rose argues, this biological reading of Freud and, I am arguing, its use within the exclusionary logic of the Fountain–Fort Carson School District "systematically [fall] into a trap" (1982: 28). This reading is problematic, Rose writes, because it fails to recognize that "the concept of the phallus in Freud's account of human sexuality was part of his awareness of the problematic, if not impossible, nature of sexual identity itself" (28). Central to this misreading, Rose argues, is the failure to grasp that the process that Freud describes for achieving femininity is a process formed through a patriarchal society that itself delineates and produces the "fact" of sexual difference. Here, sexual difference, in Rose's account, is not exactly the sexual difference of Luce Irigaray (1993), Rosi Braidotti (1993, 2003), or Drucilla Cornell (1994)—for whom sexual difference is "both an epistemological approach and a creative process" (Foster 1999: 435). While Rose shares with them an analysis of symbolic relations, she understands sexual difference to be a structure of constriction (rather than creative liberation) by which the incredible range of gendered possibilities, performativities, and subjectivities that could come into being—and indeed can even be imagined—are limited into fewer and fewer options (Rose and Malabou 2016).

As such, sexual difference, for Rose, is different from anatomical difference, even, and precisely, as the latter comes to figure the former. Anatomical difference (mistakenly understood as naturally binary), Rose writes, "becomes the sole representative of what [sexual] difference is allowed to be" (1982: 42). If we take Rose's point about the figuring of sexual difference by anatomical difference, then the assumed effects of seeing, and being affected by, the anatomical body can be understood as the consequences of a misrecognition. The body one sees, in other words, is the body produced through language, desire, fantasy, and identification. The girl in the Oedipal triangle thus begins the process of becoming feminine not in the very moment she sees the genitalia of her mother and father but, rather, in the moment she comes to identify with her body's signification. As Rose writes:

> Freud gave the moment when boy and girl child saw that they were different the status of a trauma in which the girl is seen to be lacking (the objections often start here). But something can only be *seen* to be missing according to a pre-existing hierarchy of values ("there is nothing missing in the real"). What counts is not the perception [of the penis] but its already assigned meaning [the phallus]—the moment therefore belongs in the symbolic. (1982: 42)[5]

Restating this in relationship to Lacan's concept of privation, the girl child does, in a material sense, not have a penis; and yet, while this not-having is a real absence, the real, for Lacan, cannot be lacking—the vagina does not lack a penis—and as such it is only when the girl perceives the penis as being absent (as not being where it should be) that she reads her body as lacking in relationship to the phallus and thus the symbolic.[6] The fantasy of being deprived of an object that she never had and is not missing is thus not just the initiating division for the girl, it is also the catalyst by which she comes to notice anatomical difference itself.[7] It is therefore the slip between the anatomical body and the phantasmatic body that begins this process.

For Lacan, that is, anatomy is not at all central to the process of psychosexual development (what he calls "sexuation"); rather, the symbolic meanings that are ascribed to anatomy are. He writes: "[The] facts reveal a relation of the subject to the phallus that is established without regard to the anatomical difference of the sexes" ([1958] 1977: 576). Lacan thus shifts Freud's language from the penis to the phallus and argues for a reading of Freud's Oedipus complex along the lines of the symbolic rather than the anatomic (indeed he argues that such an anatomic reading of Freud is an inaccurate one). For Lacan, it is not whether or not one has a penis but whether one represents, within the structure of desire, what it means to "have" or "be" the phallus (582).[8] The phallus, for Lacan, is thus a signifier—indeed *the* privileged signifier—by which sexual difference is introduced. It is not, Lacan writes, "an object (part-, internal, good, bad, etc.). . . . Still less is it the organ—penis or clitoris—that it symbolizes" (579). Rather, the phallus is a signifier whose function is to designate meaning and to position one within sexual difference through one's relationship to it. "Clinical experience has shown," Lacan writes, not that "the subject learns [of its location within the structure of desire by] whether or not he has a real phallus, but in the sense that he learns that the mother does not have it" (579).

This shift from penis to phallus is important here for a few reasons. First, it reiterates my analysis of Coy's exclusion because it insists that it is not the presence or absence of a penis that is at issue but, rather, the meaning assigned to the phallus. Being thus related to the symbolic, rather than the anatomical, the question of where gendered violence comes from absolves Coy from the equation and instead points to the hierarchal values ascribed to bodies within the symbolic. But secondly, the question of the phallus is important because taking it seriously means interrogating the question of temporality in the move between anatomical and sexual difference. Time is important for my analysis here because, as I have already demonstrated, the demand for Coy's exclusion was justified both through a narrative of her phallic body, as well as through a removal of her from the space of childhood. Interrogating the phantasmatic body's temporality, I follow the insightful work of Patricia Gherovici, a Lacanian psychoanalyst whose book *Please Select Your Gender* (2010) proposes a rethinking of sexual difference and advocates for a depathologization of transgenderism within psychoanalysis. For

Gherovici, who draws upon Morel (2000b), sexual difference must be understood in relationship to time. "We need to stress both the temporal and spatial aspects of the word *difference*" (2010: 195), Gherovici writes. Drawing upon the French verb *différer*, which suggests both to differ and to defer, Gherovici advocates for the concept of difference to be understood within its double meaning—"[the] temporal (to postpone, to delay) and the nonidentical" (195). In this light, the first temporal register of sexuation, Gherovici writes, takes place "in the reality of anatomy, that is, in a mythically 'natural' difference" (193). The second, she argues, is the subsequent temporal register of sexual difference, "and it is here that 'anatomy' is interpreted according to values of difference brought about by the signifier" (193). Put simply, Gherovici argues, "children notice anatomical differences *only after the symbolic event* brought about by the threat of castration. Anatomy, with its chromosomes, gametes, and genitalia, becomes *then* part of a mythical Real that acquires signification on this second stage, when the values of the sex assigned at birth are structured and a sexual positioning is assumed" (106, emphasis added). For Gherovici, this temporal dimension is important because it helps her to understand the unconscious reasons some of her trans clients understood, as children, that the error of their anatomy was somehow going to be corrected over time (194). For my argument, the temporality of sexuation is additionally important for the critique it engenders in relationship to Coy's exclusion.

In a way, the Fountain–Fort Carson School District proposed its own mapping of sexuation as a temporal concept, even as it did so to justify its rescinding of support for Coy. Explaining their previous leniency in relation to Coy's gender, the district argued that they had been caught unaware: "The reason [Coy's presence in the girl's restrooms] has not been 'an issue' to date is that fellow students and even the other teachers in the building are not aware that Coy is a male and at his young age, he may appear to be a female" (Dude 2012). This reasoning—based on the premise of an understandable yet inaccurate collective (mis)reading of the child's body—used the signification of gender to stand in for Coy's anatomical sex. In other words, the temporary (mis)reading of Coy as female, premised on her "young age," negated the very need to know whether she had a penis. For the district, the slippage between sexual and anatomical difference was so entrenched within the gendered embodiment of childhood that the chain of signification operated in reverse; appearing as a female, Coy was understood to occupy the position of lack. Read primarily through her signification, Coy was known to not have a penis.

In this sense, the district's argument that Coy had "not yet" or "only just" become problematically located in the girls' restroom suggests that their reading of her signification had a temporal dimension. The district's slippage between sexual and anatomical difference thus extended only to the limits of childhood. When read as a child, she, like the rest of the girls, inhabited a space within the district's framing of psychosexual development prior to sexual difference (prior to the threat of castration)—in which anatomical difference was present but not yet perceived or perceivable. For a moment, that is, all the girls, including Coy, were understood within the realm of the real where nothing is missing. For the district, to be a child is to be unaware of anatomical difference, to be prior to the threat of castration and the real's acquisition of signification. In this sense, the district's previous support for Coy was thus premised not on whether she had a penis but on whether she was a child. In their reversal of the decision to support Coy, the district corrected their supposedly mistaken (mis)reading of her gender by correcting their reading of her age. Coy became "a male high school student" (Chavez 2013: 8), and she had "grow[n] older [and] develop[ed]" (Dude 2012). Coy was thus not only projected into a phantasmatic phallic body, as I discussed above in relationship to Freud; she was also projected into adulthood. By forcing this doubled projection simultaneously, Coy's exclusion was justified through the transphobic evocation of her phantasmatic body.[9]

Narratives of Trans Childhood

In this section, I turn to narratives of trans childhood because I want to explore the ways they both complicate and align with the temporal positioning of the trans child and the phantasmatic body that I have just critiqued. My turn from psychoanalytic texts to a collection of trans narratives is not, however, a distancing from psychoanalysis. Rather, following the work of Jay Prosser (1998), who deftly threaded together trans narratives of the mirror scene with the Lacanian mirror stage ([1949] 1977), I turn to trans narratives of childhood to connect them to the psychic and political life of childhood embodiment discussed above.[10] Indeed, one of the questions that Salamon raises about the phantasmatic body's relevance for trans theory is precisely about the relationship between materiality and narrative, and I want to offer the pairing of temporality and childhood here as an initial response to her provocation. Responding to Prosser's *Second Skins* (1998), in which Prosser explored the materiality of transsexual narratives, Salamon asks, "Though it is certainly possible to make claims about the relation between materiality and the figural, or materiality and narrative, it seems doubtful that that relation, in either case, is one of simple correspondence. . . . What kind of materiality is it whose purchase on 'reality' is so tenuous as to be constantly threatened by the power of discourse to undermine or unseat it?" (2004: 119). Salamon's concern is the way in which Prosser articulates bodily materiality as if transsexuals can have, through narrative, an unproblematic and uncomplicated production of the flesh. Indeed, Salamon argues that psychoanalytic theory would challenge any straightforward claim to a body. Agreeing with Salamon's caution about the relationship between narrative and materiality, I want, still, to think further about the work that trans narratives do—particularly when these narratives justify the fulfilling of the demand for a child's transition through the temporal interplay between anatomic and sexual difference as discussed above.

When narrated through what Elspeth Probyn (1995) calls the "event"—or what Carolyn Steedman (1992) calls the "form"—of childhood, the claims to one's rightful or honest inhabitation of gender are understood to gain further legitimacy. Writing about the use of childhood in narrative more generally, Steedman argues, "Childhood [is] a *form*: an imaginative structure that allows the individual to make an exploration of the self. . . . [It] is a taken-for-granted means of understanding the human subject, of locating it in time and chronology, and 'explaining' it" (1992: 11). In this light, we might understand childhood's narrative form as functioning similarly to the Lacanian mirror. Put simply, the mirror stage—at first described by Lacan as taking place in infancy when a child is actually confronted with their mirror image, and then broadened more generally out to a structure of subjectivity—describes the formation of the ego through a process of identification whereby one identifies with one's own specular (and alienating) image ([1949] 1977, [1951] 1953). It is with this image, which presents the body as whole (a gestalt) rather than fragmented, that one identifies one's self. In this sense, the very formation of the ego, Lacan argues, relies on a phantasmatic body: it relies on an act of identification with a perception of a body. And yet anything can be a mirror, and childhood, as a phantasmatic "point of pure identity" (Rose 1984: 5), as a product of adult desire, functions as a mirror whose specular image grants adults, as Lee Edelman writes, the fantasy of "unmediated access to Imaginary wholeness" (2004: 10).

In trans memoirs, Prosser argues, mirror scenes (often taking place within childhood) prefigure the future acquisition of the transsexual's "fleshy materiality." "The childhood mirror scene," Prosser writes, "functions simultaneously as autobiographical and as transsexual prolepsis, foretelling and naturalizing this plot of sex change, suggesting that, in the imaginary (the mirror) the [future organ] has been there all along" (1998: 102). In this light, Prosser argues, "it is not simply in the clinician's office but in the very conception of transsexual subjectivity that autobiography subtends (supports and makes possible) transsexuality" (115). In this section, then, I extend Prosser's analysis by interrogating the use of childhood in trans narratives to legitimate claims to a gendered selfhood.[11] Take, as an initial example, the following narrative from Jaime Cortez's *Sexile* (2004), an explicit and beautifully illustrated graphic biography of Adela, a trans woman who fled Cuba for the United States, where one version of this phantasmatic development is articulated. In three panels at the beginning of the text, Adela recalls being a child and thinking, "I couldn't wait to grow up because I knew that when I turned 10 my dick would fall off my pussy would grow and finally I'd become a complete girl" (2004: 6). These words, written in white against the black silhouette of a nude child figure, narrate the fantasy scene, as the young figure's penis falls off and is replaced by a vulva. Adela's remembering of her childhood understanding of genital development demonstrates a creative reimagining of the body (akin to that of Gherovici's clients) that allows her to use her partial awareness of puberty and genital becoming to find hope in her body's wished-for ability to intervene.

Unfortunately, as Adela and other trans children learn, the body does not intervene in its trans becoming on its own. Sometimes, faced with this dire reality, the child takes their body into their own hands. In an interview for the *Huffington Post*, Sarah, the mother of a young trans girl named Danann, relates a story in which her daughter's precocious self-awareness led to Danann doing just that:

> [At the age of four] Danann began insisting she was a girl. . . . One morning we were getting ready to go to church, and Danann said she didn't want to go. I asked why, and he said, "I don't think God is that great. He made a mistake when he made me," and pointed to his penis. . . . Just a few weeks later I walked into the kitchen, and Danann had taken scissors and was getting ready to cut off his penis. (Edwards-Stout 2012)

A similar distressing scenario is relayed in a newspaper article for the *Metro* by Kerry, the mother of a girl named Danni:

> Kerry McFadyen, from Scotland, has let her child, Daniel, live as Danni, after she realised she was more interested in dolls than footballs. The 32-year-old knew that Danni, who is now six-years-old, should have been her daughter when she caught her with a pair of scissors. Kerry explained how she found Danni in the bathroom with a pair of scissors "above his bits." She said: "I tried to be calm and asked him what he was doing, and he told me he was about to cut off his willy so he could be a girl." (Mann 2015)

In these narratives, trans children's refusing of their sexed bodies—an attempt at chopping off a penis, or creating a narrative of development that understands genitalia as swapping at puberty—troubles the cultural understanding that children lack an awareness of genitalia and their significance. These narratives raise interesting and critical questions about the assumptions of children's embodied knowledge of sex and gender that could complicate the logics behind many antitrans discrimination policies. And yet, these questions—about the universality of children's genital awareness, or the cultural refusal to acknowledge children's sexual knowledge, or even the presumption that cis girls, more so than trans girls, are traumatized by the presence of a penis—are often swept aside, as the work they are required to do is that of affirming the naturalness or truthfulness of trans identification.[12]

The naturalization of trans identity operates in these narratives through the stronghold of the assumption of children's genital ignorance—or, rather, the disavowal of their knowledge—which means that when trans children articulate an awareness of mistaken genital presence, their recognition of anatomical difference is understood as preemptive and exceptional. And it is precisely this exceptionality that allows for these narratives to justify trans children's trans identities.[13] Indeed, I am arguing that it is precisely when the trans child is believed to transgress the normative child's inability to recognize that anatomical difference figures sexual difference that their claim to a rightful inhabitation of another gender is naturalized. The trans child, in other words, precociously moves into what Gherovici called the second temporal stage of sexuation. It is this exceptional knowledge, as evidenced by the childhood narratives presented here, that positions trans children in a peculiar (and I would argue ambivalent) relationship to both gender and childhood that is naturalized precisely through its nonnormative temporality (cf. Castañeda 2014). In this sense, the ambivalent positioning of childhood as prior to and formed by various types of knowledge of sexual difference allows the idea of childhood to both naturalize gender identity and to delegitimize trans desire as childish. In a framework in which trans children are not deemed mature enough to know their gender and are too young to be appropriately aware of their sex, the trans child only needs to state an awareness of the genitalia they have to be understood as having a precocious or asynchronous gendered development.

A similar temporality was central to a feature article about Coy published in *Rolling Stone*. The article, "About a Girl: Coy Mathis' Fight to Change Gender" (Erdely 2013), which uses male pronouns for Coy up until she is described as having been properly diagnosed with gender identity disorder at age four, gives credence to Coy's desire to transition and to use the girls' restrooms through a narration of her early childhood:

> [Kathryn Mathis] told no one of her suspicion about Coy [being gay]—it felt creepily premature to speculate about the sexuality of a kid still in diapers. Then one night in January 2010, Kathryn was tucking him in for bed under his pink quilt, and Coy, then three, seemed upset. "What's wrong?" she asked. Coy, his head resting against his kitty-cat-print pillow, hugged his pink stuffed pony with the

glittery mane that he'd gotten for Christmas and said nothing, his mouth bent in a tight frown. "Tell me," Kathryn urged. Coy's chin began to quiver.

"When am I going to get my girl parts?" he asked softly.

"What do you mean?"

"When are we going to go to the doctor to have me fixed?" Coy asked, tears now spilling down his cheeks. "To get my girl parts?" (Erdely 2013)

Like the other narratives I have relayed above, in this account, Coy's gender identity becomes all the more justified, naturalized, and necessary to establish in her daily life, precisely through her awareness of her genitalia (and their mismatch with her gender) at a moment in time when to even speculate about her sexuality is deemed "creepily premature." This narrative of Coy's knowingness as the impetus for her transition uses the device of childhood to cohere a gendered selfhood to her, but it does so by reifying this understanding of childhood (childhood as genital ignorance) through Coy's shocking break of the cultural fantasy—what Rose (1984) calls the "impossibility"—of childhood itself.

As such, while the narrative of Coy's fantasy of an impending medical fix to her distressing anatomy justifies her rightful occupation of the girls' restrooms, and of femininity and femaleness (for her parents, if not for her school), its effectiveness in doing so maintains the space of childhood as that which is defined by its ignorance. Coy is thus produced as a girl both through her location within childhood and through her narrativized break from it, and it is this break that was also used against her by her school district. Indeed, in the school district's logic, it was Coy's assertion that she was a girl—and thus her acknowledgment that her body included incorrect and unwanted genitalia at a time in which children (and particularly girls) are not supposed to have an understanding of their anatomy—that produced the concern around her presence and propelled her into the realm of male adolescence. Coy was thus explicitly excluded from the girls' restrooms because she disrupted the normative timing of the recognition of (and identification with) sexual difference: at six years old, her bodily awareness cast aside her actual body, being understood as so asynchronous to childhood itself that the district, in its limited bodily imagination, understood her as already having mature, adult, male genitalia.

Conclusion: Already Truly Being

I want to conclude by suggesting that narrative itself played a central role in this temporal and subjective positioning, and by arguing for a further consideration of some of the teachings of Freudian psychoanalysis. As I argued above, trans lives and trans narratives are intimately intertwined. As Prosser writes, "Transsexuality is always narrative work, a transformation of the body that requires the remolding of the life into a particular narrative shape" (1998: 4). Therefore, what trans narratives expose, Prosser argues, is a collective desire for coherence and bodily integrity such that "transition does not shift the subject away from the embodiment of sexual difference but more fully into it" (1998: 6). Prosser thus contends that before critiquing trans autobiographies "for conforming to a specific gendered plot," one that establishes one's self and one's gender as coherent and linear, "we need to grasp the ways in which the genre of autobiography *is* conformist and unilinear" (115).[14] Autobiographical narratives, Prosser writes, function precisely by taking the randomness of life events and endowing them with "chronology, succession, progression—even causation" (116). The work that trans narratives do thus specifically asserts a trans person's "claim to already (truly) be" the gender they identify with (119).

Because the narratives that Prosser is reading are ones written by adults about their current gender identity—and thus their returns to childhood are a reading back onto childhood of their coherent gendered selves—the linearity of them is retrospective: it builds a coherence that begins in adulthood and reads that self back into the past. However, in most of the narratives that I have been working with here—and certainly for Coy—the subject at stake is a child, and thus their constructions of coherence, linearity, chronology, and causation jut them into an adulthood that has not yet come to be. Relying on narrative structures that evoke and pivot around the phantasmatic body of the trans child, this question of already truly being becomes more complex. Body narratives that implant the child subject "more fully into" sexual difference and define them as "already (truly) being" an adult future self thus create the conditions under which a transphobic rereading is also made possible. Put simply, for those advocating on Coy's behalf, this narrative entrenchment in a future sexual difference, and this linear production of a future self that has always been, relied on childhood as narrative to stake the rightful claim that Coy must be recognized as a girl. For those working against her, however, those same structures of entrenchment and "already currently being" a particular gendered and sexed self functioned as the device through which her phantasmatic adult male body could already be read onto her. If, as Salamon argues, "to affirm a materiality [that is culturally abjected] is to undertake a constant and always incomplete labor to reconfigure . . . the materiality of our bodies [and] the lived meanings of those materialities" (2004: 120), then perhaps part of the project of affirming trans embodiment is also reconsidering the demands this affirmation makes in relationship to normative conceptions of time.[15] For indeed, Freud's work suggests two final things that might be of use here. First, Freud ([1905] 2016, [1907] 1963, [1908] 1955) insists, as we must, that we need to be more open to thinking about the child's relationship to gender and sexuality. Moreover, Freud's model of the unconscious—one that emerges within a childhood that we keep returning to and never have a mastery over—suggests that we inhabit time in multiple and nonlinear ways. Psychoanalysis, as a language through which we can understand our bodies and psyches as having a relationship to time that is contested and multifarious, is thus necessary for our continued advocacy for girls like Coy, even as it challenges us to articulate such affirmations in ways that complicate what it means to live in a body.

Jacob Breslow is a teaching fellow in transnational sexuality and gender studies at the Department of Gender Studies, London School of Economics. He has a book chapter titled "The Queer Story of Your Conception: Translating Sexuality and Racism in *Beasts of the Southern Wild*" in the anthology *Queer in Translation* (2017).

Notes

1.   The school claimed that it was not discriminating against Coy based on sex, seeing as she was "a male" and was not being denied access to the boy's restroom (Chavez 2013: 5–6). It also argued that even if it *was* discriminating against Coy for not letting her use the girls' restroom, this practice was sanctioned by the Colorado Civil Rights Commission (Dude 2012).

2.   For more on the regulation of restrooms, see Cavanagh 2010.

3.   Psychoanalysis, Salamon argues, "has historically been used to relegate [trans people] to the realm of pathology and abjection" (2010: 13). For a critique of this long-standing pathologization and its relationship to the pathologization of women and femininity, specifically within psychology, see Tosh 2016. According to Jay Prosser (1998: 9), transsexuality was first "invented" in 1949 when a trans man was diagnosed as a "psychopathic transsexual" (Cauldwell 1949), and as such it has always had an ambivalent relationship to diagnosis. For a few challenges to Freud's phallocentrism, see Beauvoir 1949, Britzman 2006, Chodorow 1978, Horney 1967, Irigaray 1985a and 1985b, and Klein (1928) 1986.

4.   Making this argument, of course, requires a depathologized use of psychoanalysis—or what Patricia Gherovici describes as a "depathologization of transgenderism" (2010: xiii)—as Freud himself would distinguish between "normal" and "pathological" gendered attainment.

5.   Rose's citation is from "The Phallic Phase and the Subjective Import of the Castration Complex" (Lacan [1968–76] 1982). This article was not written by Lacan but by a member of the school he founded in 1964.

6.   The real, for Lacan, is one of the three orders of psychoanalytic phenomena (the other two being the imaginary and the symbolic), and it is defined as that which is outside language and which absolutely resists symbolization.

7.   Because the fantasy of being deprived an object that is not missing is located in fantasy, we could additionally say that this temporality is true, in a sense, for the trans girl. As I demonstrate in the following section, the fantasy of being eventually deprived of an object that she has and does not want is also the catalyst by which she notices anatomical difference. For Geneviève Morel (2000a), this is described in relationship to the phallus

and the real, wherein the male-to-female transsexual reasons as such: "You see that I have a penis, and you say I have a phallus. But I do not experience that phallic jouissance. Then, cut off my penis and *you will not make the same mistake*" (186, emphasis added, as cited in Gherovici 2010: 164–65).

8. Unpacking the notion of having and being in relationship to the threat of castration, Judith Butler (1993: 84) writes that "being" the phallus can be understood as being able to wield the threat of castration, while "having" the phallus suggests that one suffers from castration anxiety, that one fears the loss of the phallus.

9. Here, it is clear that the phantasmatic body is not just a question of gendered embodiment— it is additionally laden with questions of age and temporality.

10. The focus on childhood as a narrative form has been addressed by other scholars (Ames 2005; Gherovici 2010; Prosser 1998), but I argue that it requires further critical attention within this scholarship, particularly in relation to the psychic work that childhood itself as an ambivalent structure of power and subjectivity allows for in these narratives.

11. Trans people's claims to their gender are constantly repudiated, questioned, criminalized, and ignored (Feinberg 1996; Halberstam 2005; Spade 2011; Stanley and Smith 2011). Using narratives of gendered discovery in childhood is one of the ways these violences are countered, and while my intention is not to criticize trans people for responding to the uneven demand to justify their identities, I do want to think through, along with trans people, the consequences that these narratives have for our understandings of how childhood, sex, and gender coconstitute meaning for one another.

12. On this point, Rose argues that this recognition should be a point of coalition for trans and feminist theory: "A further reason why trans and feminism should be natural bed-fellows is that male-to-female transsexuals expose, and then reject, masculinity in its darkest guise. . . . If you want more than anything in the world to become a woman, then chances are there is somewhere a man who, just as passionately, you do not want to be" (2016).

13. In making this argument, I am not suggesting that there is no difference between cis and trans children; rather, my concern is for the ways in which this cultural fantasy of children's anatomical ignorance requires trans children to be projected out of childhood in order for their claims to their rightful inhabitation of their gender to be accepted.

14. It is thus important to disentangle the linearity within particular trans narratives from the understanding that a child, or childhood, is linear, or that narrative itself is linear. For more on narrative's "performative dynamic" and intersubjective structure, see Huffer 2013. For the complexity of children's narratives, see Treacher 2006.

15. See, in this regard, the autobiography of Janet Mock (2014), as well as the documentary *I'm Yours* (dir. Chase Joynt, 2012).

References

Ames, Jonathan, ed. 2005. *Sexual Metamorphosis: An Anthology of Transsexual Memoirs*. New York: Vintage Books.

Beauvoir, Simone de. 1949. *The Second Sex*. London: Vintage Classics.

Braidotti, Rosi. 1993. "Embodiment, Sexual Difference, and the Nomadic Subject." *Hypatia* 8, no. 1: 1–13.

———. 2003. "Becoming Woman: Or Sexual Difference Revisited." *Theory, Culture, and Society* 20, no. 3: 43–64.

Breslow, Jacob. 2017a. "The Theory and Practice of Childhood: Interrogating Childhood as a Technology of Power." PhD thesis, The London School of Economics and Political Science.

———. 2017b. "The Queer Story of Your Conception: Translating Sexuality and Racism in *Beasts of the Southern Wild*." In *Queer in Translation*, edited by B. J. Epstein and Robert Gillett, 129–43. London: Routledge.

Britzman, Deborah. 2006. "Little Hans, Fritz, and Ludo: On the Curious History of Gender in the Psychoanalytic Archive." *Studies in Gender and Sexuality* 7, no. 2: 113–40.

Butler, Judith. 1993. "The Lesbian Phallus and the Morphological Imaginary." In *Bodies That Matter*, 57–91. New York: Routledge.

Castañeda, Claudia. 2014. "Childhood." *TSQ* 1, nos. 1–2: 59–61.

Cauldwell, D. O. 1949. "Psychopathia Transexualis." *Sexology* 16: 274–80.

Cavanagh, Sheila. 2010. *Queering Bathrooms: Gender, Sexuality, and the Hygienic Imagination*. Toronto: University of Toronto Press.

———. 2016. "Transsexuality as Sinthome: Bracha L. Ettinger and the Other (Feminine) Sexual Difference." *Studies in Gender and Sexuality* 17, no. 1: 27–44.

Chavez, Steven. 2013. "Determination." June 17. State of Colorado Department of Regulatory Agencies.

Chodorow, Nancy. 1978. *The Reproduction of Mothering: Psychoanalysis and the Sociology of Gender*. Berkeley: University of California Press.

Cornell, Drucilla. 1994. *Transformations: Recollective Imagination and Sexual Difference*. New York: Routledge.

Cortez, Jamie. 2004. *Sexile*. Los Angeles: The Institute for Gay Men's Health.

Deutsch, Helene. 1946. *The Psychology of Women: A Psychoanalytic Interpretation*. London: Research Books.

Dude, W. Kelly. 2012. "Re: Coy Mathis/Fountain–Fort Carson School District" (Letter to Michael D. Silverman). Transgender Legal Defense and Education Fund, December 28. www .transgenderlegal.org/media/uploads/doc_491.pdf.

Edelman, Lee. 2004. *No Future: Queer Theory and the Death Drive*. Durham, NC: Duke University Press.

Edwards-Stout, Kergan. 2012. "Mother of Transgender Child Speaks Out." September 11. kerganedwards-stout.com/transgender-child/.

Elliot, Patricia. 2001. "A Psychoanalytic Reading of Transsexual Embodiment." *Studies in Gender and Sexuality* 2, no. 4: 295–325.

Erdely, Sabrina. 2013. "About a Girl: Coy Mathis' Fight to Change Gender." *Rolling Stone*, October 28. www.rollingstone.com/culture/news/about-a-girl-coy-mathis-fight-to-change-change -gender-20131028.

Farley, Lisa, and R. M. Kennedy. 2015. "A Sex of One's Own: Childhood and the Embodiment of (Trans)gender." *Psychoanalysis, Culture, and Society* 21, no. 2: 167–83.

Feinberg, Leslie. 1996. *Transgender Warriors: Making History from Joan of Arc to Dennis Rodman*. Boston: Beacon.

Foster, Johanna. 1999. "An Invitation to Dialogue: Clarifying the Position of Feminist Gender Theory in Relation to Sexual Difference Theory." *Gender and Society* 13, no. 4: 431–56.

Freud, Sigmund. (1905) 2016. *Three Essays on the Theory of Sexuality*. Edited by Philippe Van Haute and Herman Westerink, translated by Ulrike Kistner. London: Verso.

———. (1907) 1963. "The Sexual Enlightenment of Children (An Open Letter to Dr. M. Fürst)." In *The Sexual Enlightenment of Children*, edited by Phillip Rieff, 17–24. New York: Collier Books.

————. (1908) 1955. "On the Sexual Theories of Children." In *The Essentials of Psycho-Analysis*, translated by James Strachey, 376–89. London: Penguin Books.

————. (1923) 1955. "The Ego and the Id." In *The Essentials of Psycho-Analysis*, translated by James Strachey, 439–83. London: Penguin Books.

————. (1933) 1955. "Femininity." In *The Essentials of Psycho-Analysis*, translated by James Strachey, 412–32. London: Penguin Books.

Gherovici, Patricia. 2010. *Please Select Your Gender: From the Invention of Hysteria to the Democratizing of Transgenderism*. New York: Routledge.

Goldner, Virginia, ed. 2011. "Transgender Subjectivities: Theories and Practices." Special issue, *Psychoanalytic Dialogues* 21, no. 2.

Gozlan, Oren. 2011. "Transsexual Surgery: A Novel Reminder and a Navel Remainder." *International Forum of Psychoanalysis* 20, no. 1: 45–52.

Grosz, Elizabeth. 1994. *Volatile Bodies: Toward a Corporeal Feminism*. Bloomington: Indiana University Press.

Halberstam, Judith. 2005. *In a Queer Time and Place: Transgender Bodies, Subcultural Lives*. New York: New York University Press.

Horney, Karen. (1926) 1967. "The Flight from Womanhood: The Masculinity-Complex in Women as Viewed by Men and by Women." In Horney 1967: 54–70.

————. 1967. *Feminine Psychology*. London: Norton.

Huffer, Lynne. 2013. *Are the Lips a Grave? A Queer Feminist on the Ethics of Sex*. New York: Columbia University Press.

Irigaray, Luce. 1985a. *This Sex Which Is Not One*. Translated by Catherine Porter and Carolyn Burke. Ithaca, NY: Cornell University Press.

————. 1985b. *Speculum of the Other Woman*. Translated by Gillian Gill. Ithaca, NY: Cornell University Press.

————. 1993. *An Ethics of Sexual Difference*. Translated by Carolyn Burke and Gillian C. Gill. London: Athlone.

Jones, Ernest. (1912) 1923. *Papers on Psycho-Analysis*. London: Baillière, Rindall and Cox.

Joynt, Chase, dir. 2012. *I'm Yours*. www.youtube.com/watch?v=5NZjUH5XZys.

Klein, Melanie. (1928) 1986. "Early Stages of the Oedipus Complex." In *The Selected Melanie Klein*, edited by Juliet Mitchell, 69–83. Harmondsworth, UK: Penguin Books.

Lacan, Jacques. (1949) 1977. "The Mirror Stage as Formative of the Function of the I as Revealed in Psychoanalytic Experience." In *Écrits*, translated by Alan Sheridan, 1–7. London: Tavistock.

————. (1951) 1953. "Some Reflections on the Ego." *International Journal of Psycho-Analysis* 34: 11–17.

————. (1958) 1977. "The Signification of the Phallus." In *Écrits*, translated by Alan Sheridan, 281–91. London: Tavistock.

————. (1968–76) 1982. "The Phallic Phase and the Subjective Import of the Castration Complex." In *Feminine Sexuality: Jacques Lacan and the École Freudienne*, edited by Juliet Mitchell and Jacqueline Rose, translated by Jacqueline Rose, 99–122. Houndmills, UK: Macmillan.

Mann, Tanveer. 2015. "Toddler Becomes Britain's Youngest Transgender Child after Mum Found Her Trying to Cut Off Her 'Bits.'" *Metro*, December 7. metro.co.uk/2015/12/07/boy-6 -becomes-britains-youngest-transgender-child-after-mum-found-him-trying-to-cut-off -his-willy-5549667.

Martin, Karin. 1996. *Puberty, Sexuality, and the Self: Boys and Girls at Adolescence*. London: Routledge.

Merleau-Ponty, Maurice. 1962. *Phenomenology of Perception*. London: Routledge.

Mock, Janet. 2014. *Redefining Realness: My Path to Womanhood, Identity, Love, and So Much More*. New York: Atria Books.

Morel, Geneviève. 2000a. *Ambigüedades sexuales: Sexuación y psicosis (Sexual Ambiguities: Sexuation and Psychosis)*. Buenos Aires: Manantial.

———. 2000b. "Psychoanalytical Anatomy." In *Sexuation*, edited by Renata Salecl, 28–38. Durham, NC: Duke University Press.

Probyn, Elspeth. 1995. "Suspended Beginnings: Of Childhood and Nostalgia." *GLQ* 2, no. 4: 439–65.

Prosser, Jay. 1998. *Second Skins: The Body Narratives of Transsexuality*. New York: Columbia University Press.

Rose, Jacqueline. 1982. "Introduction—II." In *Feminine Sexuality: Jacques Lacan and the École Freudienne*, edited by Juliet Mitchell and Jacqueline Rose, translated by Jacqueline Rose, 27–58. Houndmills, UK: Macmillan.

———. 1984. *The Case of Peter Pan, or the Impossibility of Children's Fiction*. London: Macmillan.

———. 2016. "Who Do You Think You Are?" *London Review of Books* 38, no. 9: 3–13.

Rose, Jacqueline, and Catherine Malabou. 2016. "Sexual Difference and the Symbolic: What Future?" Audio podcast, Birkbeck Institute for the Humanities, London, June 14. Backdoor Broadcasting Company. backdoorbroadcasting.net/2016/06/sexual-difference -and-the-symbolic-what-future/.

Rubin, Gayle. 1975. "The Traffic in Women: Notes on the 'Political Economy' of Sex." In *Toward an Anthropology of Women*, edited by Rayna Reiter, 157–210. New York: Monthly Review.

Salamon, Gayle. 2004. "The Bodily Ego and the Contested Domain of the Material." *differences* 15, no. 3: 95–122.

———. 2006. "'The Place Where Life Hides Away': Merleau-Ponty, Fanon, and the Location of Bodily Being." *differences* 17, no. 2: 96–112.

———. 2010. *Assuming a Body: Transgender and Rhetorics of Materiality*. New York: Columbia University Press.

Silverman, Kaja. 1996. *The Threshold of the Visible World*. New York: Routledge.

Spade, Dean. 2011. *Normal Life: Administrative Violence, Critical Trans Politics, and the Limits of Law*. Durham, NC: Duke University Press.

Stanley, Eric, and Nat Smith, eds. 2011. *Captive Genders: Trans Embodiment and the Prison Industrial Complex*. Oakland, CA: AK.

Steedman, Carolyn. 1992. *Past Tenses: Essays on Writing, Autobiography, and History, 1980–90*. London: Rivers Oram.

Tosh, Jemma. 2016. *Psychology and Gender Dysphoria: Feminist and Transgender Perspectives*. New York: Routledge.

Treacher, Amal. 2006. "Children's Imaginings and Narratives: Inhabiting Complexity." *Feminist Review*, no. 82: 96–113.

Whitelocks, Sadie, and Alex Greig. 2013. "Transgender Child, Six, Wins Civil Rights Case to Use the Girls Restroom at School in Colorado." *Daily Mail*, June 24. www.dailymail.co.uk /news/article-2347149/Coy-Mathis-Transgender-child-6-Colorado-wins-civil-rights-case -use-girls-bathroom-school.html.

Stalled on the Stall

Reflections on a Strained Discourse

OREN GOZLAN

Abstract The title of the article, "Stalled in the Stall," is a commentary on the present state of discourse surrounding transsexuality, particularly concerning access to the gendered bathroom. It points to an irony: media representations of transsexual and transgender identities include myriad of expressions, bringing to view the notion of identity as partial, contradictory, and not easily read. And yet, the popular media talk and discussions on the transsexual subject are mostly by way of the bathroom: worries about accommodations, rights, and problems concerning violence and access. In this article, the author plays with the stall as a signifier that allows us to hypothesize about unconscious phantasies and desires that structure the encounter for and with transsexuality and stall our capacity to think analytically. The nature of the debate, the author suggests, repeats the history of homophobia and transphobia. Associating to the stall as an emotionally charged space linked to innermost primal phantasies and anxieties may shed light on the ways in which some dilemmas seem to be stalled on a particular object and may allow the exploration of the phantasies that underscore the capacity to imagine gender with psychoanalytic sensitivity. The clinic too is affected by a magnetizing pull toward sameness; certitude replaces difference in which the body is often mystified as known. Beyond the fixations that are well documented, the article raises two new questions: Can a turn to the clinic help us understand our mindless state in the bathroom? And, in turn, can the bathroom, as a primal scene of natality, be fantasized as a thought experiment with which to think about the clinic?

Keywords transsexualty, primal scene, sexual difference, anality, parental couple, indifference

In the Jim Crow era, bathrooms—along with water fountains and lunch counters—were places that might be marked with "white only" signs. The bathroom has also been a battleground for women and handicapped workers fighting for equal treatment in the workplace. Because of the nature of things people do in the bathroom, it can be a space where they feel exposed or vulnerable and therefore resist change. It is also, as transgender icon Janet Mock says, "the great equalizer for all of us."
—Katy Steinmetz, *Time*

The title of the article is a commentary on the present state of discourse surrounding transsexuality but also an inquiry into the phantasies[1] that underscore the capacity to imagine gender with a psychoanalytic sensitivity. It points to an irony: media representations of transsexual and transgender identities include myriad of expressions, bringing to view the notion of identity as partial, contradictory, and not easily read. And yet, the popular media talk on the topic of transsexuality unfolds mostly by way of the bathroom: worries about accommodations, rights, violence, and access. One side of the debate approaches bathroom access as a matter of rights and equity, whereas those who argue that bathroom access should be granted according to birth sex seem to be mobilized by a mass hysteria over the image of "the monstrous transsexual," ushering in old stereotypes of transsexuals as predators or pedophiles threatening children with sexual violence. Prevalent in this mythology is the idea that transgendered individuals deceive and stall in their attempt to "fool everyone" about their "true" gender identity. The terms of the debate, I suggest, repeat some of the main tropes in the history of homophobia and transphobia that defend against the loss of a fantasized "naturalness of gender" (Halberstam 2005; Katz 1995). The discourse, I argue, is stalled in the stall.

Significantly, the argument against access manipulates the concern over the so-called safety of children as means of suppression of nonconforming sexual identities and as excuse for reactionary politics. Once the figure of the child is strategically introduced in the debate as an object in need of protection from imaginary threats, we need to wonder why other real threats—poverty, malnutrition, or gun violence, to name a few—do not elicit the same degree of hysteria. This selective preoccupation with the safety of children reveals that what is at stake is rather different: a failed attempt at projecting one's anxiety onto the other and a refusal to contain and process the question of gender identity and sexual difference as a universal quandary. The bathroom itself has become a contested space laced with phantasies of control and expulsion, abjection, anxiety, relief, anticipation, and hate and a signifier for the universal dilemmas around sexual difference enacted in the question of who is allowed in and who is expelled out. What is at stake in allowing the trans subject into the bathroom of their choice? What rudimentary anxieties find voice in the demand for entry and the attempt at exclusion in the bathroom space? I will focus on the space of the bathroom as signifier, as a kind of trope, and as an entry path into the question of inclusion and exclusion, recognition, and otherness as it is enacted through the gendered bathroom debate.

There are four kinds of stalling that we can observe in discourses around transsexuality: the view of gender as known and determined by an assigned gender at birth, the conception of the transsexual subject as a threatening figure that is both ruined and ruining nature, the narrow view of transsexuality as a question concerning the gender nonconforming alone rather than a universal feature of gender identity, and lastly, the view that transsexuality can be understood as an individual issue without considering the apparatus—cultural, institutional, medical—on which transsexuality's shifting definitions and understandings lean. These stalled discursive positions reflect the fact that, despite changes brought about by public discourse, social movements, and technological advancements, transsexuality continues to haunt us as a dilemma concerning the universal conundrum of sexual difference and gender identity as constituted through complex negotiations of psychic and sociosymbolic demands essential to our constitution as desiring, embodied subjects. To the extent that the presence of the transsexual in the bathroom reminds us that our bodies are not given, transparent, or legible, it operates as an enigmatic message that is met simultaneously with openness and resistance, receptiveness and fear, curiosity and hate. The bathroom, then, may be a productive space to elaborate on the phantasies, desires, and anxieties that structure the encounter for and with transsexuality as well as the ways in which these unconscious resonances stall our capacity to think.

My focus is an analytic one, and therefore I am less concerned with presenting arguments in favor of the right to access and more with exploring the instability of the phantasy of gender: how this instability manifests itself in the contentious space of the bathroom, and how the responses to the question of access may be entangled with unconscious significations and burdened with infantile remnants. Psychoanalysis has a long history of conceptualizing the toilet, anal eroticism, and the psychology of excretion, and it might be useful to return to these theories in order to grasp the oral and anal aggression manifesting in the current public discourse. The dilemma for the clinic concerns the question of how the signifier of the bathroom can be used to dislodge our saturated minds from the rather rigid terms of the debate and to prevent it from being flushed down the toilet. Beyond these fixations, which are well documented, the article raises two questions: As we shift our view of the bathroom from a situation of access or exclusion to an emotional situation, can our relation to "the stranger in the bathroom" change? And conversely, would thinking about the bathroom encounter as a "strange situation," as a confrontation with difference, change our relation to the stranger within?

Social theorists such as Sheila Cavanagh (2010), Mary Anne Case (2010), and Terry S. Kogan (2010) link the debate over the exclusion of transgendered people to the history of the bathroom as a space of segregation of racialized peoples and to the "cissexist body politics" (Cavanagh 2010: 111) and heteronormative sexism that regulates gender and shapes the very architecture of the toilet. While these interventions help us understand the historical connections between various forms of oppression and exclusion of difference—racial, classed, and gendered—the question remains as to why the bathroom has become so central in discussions about transsexuality. There are two bathrooms to discuss: the public bathroom and the psychic bathroom, by which I mean the phantasies, anxieties, and defenses that animate libidinality. There is something about the space of the bathroom, I suggest, that makes it a fertile ground for conflict and struggle over the body and what it means to be embodied. Indeed, the bathroom is a threshold space between public and private realms, a place of rushed encounters, of secrecy and hiding, but also of revealing and exposing. The body loses its composure in the bathroom and becomes abject through leakages of waste, fluid, and smells—excretions reminding us of the constitutive vulnerability and helplessness of the condition of being embodied. This confrontation with the abject body, makes "the boundaries and limitations of our selfhood ambiguous and indicates our physical wasting and ultimate death" (Covino 2004: 17). There is something about the confrontation with the enigmatic, abject body at the stall, ours and others, that stalls our capacity to think and that frames the presence of "the transsexual in the bathroom" as an emotional situation charged with the affective vicissitudes of our own bathroom history. Just as the bathroom reminds us of the boundaries and limitations of our finite bodies, it reminds us as well of the fragility of the ideality of gender that is at a constant risk of collapse.

Embedded in the bathroom are uncanny returns of familiar yet estranged scenes. We are surrounded by mirrors, projecting and returning the image of our and others' bodies. The fragmented images in the mirror create a jolting "story of the eye" being told from the blind spot of phantasy, reminding us what is in store for the self in bathroom encounters: confusion of tongues, murky borders, and unanticipated conflict. The scenes in the bathroom are always compounded by cross-projections. The projections associated with the mirror stage—longing for recognition, belief in the image, and wish for approval—turns the other into a mirror, investing chance encounters with idealization and aggression. The self we wish to project cannot be captured in the mirror's image, which proves elusive, and our sexuality, like the bodily odors of the bathroom, diffuses the distance between the other and the self. The bathroom is a place where we face our abject body, the body that leaks, expels, and smells, a body that "draws me toward the place where meaning collapses" (Kristeva 1984: 2), where the boundaries between self and other become diffuse, and where the other's gaze is simultaneously craved and feared, idealized and suspected.

Bathrooms have always been spaces of scrutiny and secrecy, where we are most vulnerable to the other's gaze. It is a space where we confront our body as abject and vulnerable while in close and undesired proximity to strangers, and although this tension makes any bathroom interaction potentially fraught, for the transsexual subject it is infinitely more complicated and dangerous than the mere possibility of being yelled at or expelled. As Cavanagh (2010) observes, the gendered codes of the bathroom support the illusion of the binary of gender, and the mere misrecognition of one's identity can potentially lead to abuse or violence. Yet descriptions are not explanations, and while sociology seems to offer us a solid ground to map the power dynamics in the bathroom with a clear delineation of oppressor and victim, it also risks staying within a phantasy of the transparency of human interactions, in which the imaginary and symbolic qualities of this power, its repetitions and investment, are often denied or disavowed.

What is foreclosed, we may ask, when the discourse is stalled? I suggest that stalled discourses foreclose a move to understand gender in an expansive way that may reveal all that is uncertain and unknown about the complex constitution of our gender identities and about the pressing phantasies and anxieties circulating in cultural representations and taking shape around the presence of the transsexual individual in the bathroom. This includes the view of the transsexual subject as a Frankenstein-type monster who believes he can give birth to himself or herself, as a pathetic character who deceives themselves and others, or as a damaged body ruined by and ruining nature. Following Jacques Lacan's notion of the imaginary, we may argue that the image of the transsexual is stalled between imaginary and symbolic significations. On the one hand, the transsexual individual is completely othered and burdened with fictional attributes that fix them as monstrous, abject, or pathetic; on the other hand, we fail to recognize the arbitrary nature of the symbolic coordinates that shape the ideality of gender as dichotomous, natural, permanent, and cohesive and therefore the extent to which the very notion of transsexuality as a gender identity is constituted as such through such coordinates. What, then, can an exploration of the bathroom scene, understood as an emotional situation, reveal about the imaginary and symbolic connotations of the presence of the transsexual individual in the bathroom?

Irritable Bowel

The bathroom calls upon a history of one's libidinal relation to expelling and satisfying bodily needs. And yet, our history of toilet training also tells us that the bathroom is not just a place of satisfaction but also a place of frustration and hate where excrements represent both abjection and aggression. I have suggested that the public bathroom is an affectively charged space and that entering a public bathroom elicits a series of anxieties: a sense of urgency, a dire need for relief, a difficulty to do so, the anxiety of not finding a bathroom, of wanting to go in and rushing to get out. It is a dangerous place for many but also a place for pleasure—a place where strangers meet and, not unfrequently, a place for casual sex. Invested with childhood phantasies and significations, the bathroom brings us back to the history of our first encounter with a set of rules and prohibitions. Indeed, the bathroom is the setting where those struggles emblematic of the anal phase meet the imaginary equations of gender, and we may wonder about the unconscious carryover of our history of toilet training to the scene of the gendered bathroom.

Sigmund Freud posited the body as our first object-relation: a reservoir of pleasure and pain, a site of persecution, love, and creativity to suggest a corollary between bodily organs and psychosocial processes. From the body emerge archaic modes of symbolic equations that are later replaced by representations. Through his analysis of the Wolf Man, the Rat Man, and Little Hans's "lumpf," Freud ([1909] 2001: 64) suggests an unconscious link between feces and money, and feces and babies, as well as a confusion between anus and the vagina and between love making and sadistic attacks, which add to the complexity of the child's identifications and disidentifications. Organs and thoughts, Freud's mapping of the psychosexual stages suggests, go hand in hand (Britzman 2015). While the weaning associated with the oral phase primes the infant for loss, the anal stage has its corollary in the social preoccupation with the tension between public and private, passivity and activity, and controlling and expelling the other. On the way to object love, Freud reminds us, we also encounter our wish to be penetrated, a fear of being castrated, a desire to attack the other, a wish to have a baby, to give a gift, and so on.

In his 1908 paper "Character and Anal Eroticism," Freud establishes a connection between obsessions and anal eroticism and identifies its three salient characteristics: order, parsimony, and abstinence ([1908] 2001: 169). Tidiness, cleanliness, greediness, stinginess, stubbornness, and persistence are tied, Freud hypothesized, to the pains and pleasures of toilet training. The child for Freud is an erotic being whose sexual attention progresses along psychosexual stages that correspond to the erotogenic zone dominant in each stage. The child's enjoyment in withholding and expelling feces is also emblematic of her conflicts over separation/individuation and hence related to identification and object choice, love, and hate.

The emotional world, Karl Abraham reminds us, is a toilet. And the toilet of the emotional world is a place where things are wasted and saved, attacked and treasured. In his paper "The First Pre-genital Stage of the Libido" (1916), he writes that sexual arousal, love, and aggression are organized, in the anal stage, around retention and expulsion and correspondingly, that passivity and activity constitute the representational precursors of what, in the genital face, will be understood as sexual difference around the presence and absence of the phallus.

In 1962, Paula Heimann renewed psychoanalysis's interest in the psychosexuality of anality with an essay titled "Notes on the Anal Stage." While

Heimann appreciates the ways in which oral phantasies, anxieties, and equations will be carried to the anal stage, in which the "anus can be equated with the mouth and faeces with food" (406), anal eroticism, she observes, is a subject matter in and of itself that organizes specific concerns around mastery and sadism and "is distinguished by ambivalence in regards to active and passive, male and female aims" (407).

Heimann's theorization compels us to consider the bathroom scene as a place of blockage, where things get lodged and refused to be let go, a place of omnipotence and transferential torrents marked by a desire to please and possess, but also as a place where we confront desire's inevitable failure, and hence loss. However, what sets my discussion apart from one concerned with toilet training is that I am here speaking about adults meeting in their bathroom of choice. But I am also suggesting that the desire to cling to the demarcations of the gendered bathroom and the aggression enacted in the compulsion to exclude may carry traces of anal psychosexuality. To what extent do the organizing desires and affects of anality manifest in the dynamics of exclusion in the gendered bathroom? In other words, how are mastery, aggression, ambivalence, and infantile understandings of sexual difference enacted in the anxieties around bathroom access?

Sphincter Morality

On the surface, the debate in the United Stated about safety versus rights revolves around whether to pass a bill banning transsexuals from accessing bathrooms consistent with their gender identity. Public discourse, for and against, tends to revolve around three fantasized positions: victim, bully, and ally. The structure of "doer and done to," oppressor and victim, which assumes a clear demarcation between victim and aggressor, plays out in the bathroom, making it an emotionally charged space linked to our innermost primal phantasies and anxieties. These positions were known to us before in our childhood toilet training. It is the case that the rules that regulate bathroom behavior and that concern privacy, control, cleanliness, and the like belong to our childhood. If we start there, we can conceptualize toilet training as a benign trauma, a place where both parents and children experience a great deal of anxiety and often mistake training with punishment. The child is told to defecate in the "right place" at the "right time," she is told not to mess around with the warm inviting stool, and she is punished for attempting to eat it. Shame and disgust are soon associated with excretion and, because of its anatomical proximity, with the child's sexual organs. The child is beholden to the parents' authority but also defies what is experienced as parental intrusion and coercion.

To understand the bathroom dilemma as an enigmatic situation that animates infantile psychic conflicts and resolutions, we need to bring into focus superegoical anxieties, defenses, and pleasures whose formation is closely tied with the "dos and don'ts" of toilet training: a situation in which, for the first time, compliance with parental demands is strongly enforced. Donald Meltzer (1992) claims that the qualities of the anal phase turn the mind into a claustrum, where defenses such as projective identification, symbolic equations, and withdrawal accompanied by sadistic attacks become paramount. There is also a danger in the bathroom that is reminiscent of a primal scene, with its merging of sexuality and violence and the amalgamation of the child's parental figures into the "combined parent-figure." According to Melanie Klein, the combined parent-figure is a child's primitive phantasy of "the mother containing the father's penis or the whole father; the father containing the mother's breast or the whole mother; the parents fused inseparably in sexual intercourse" (1975: 79). In Klein's and Wilfred Bion's (1977) theorization, the combined parental couple, imbued with colossal annihilating and castrating power, forms the basis of the child's tyrannical, sadistic, and primitive superego. The combined parental couple, in short, is a persecutory bad object internalized as a tyrannical superego, a superego that, when the ego is threatened, responds in typical paranoid-schizoid fashion: with splitting into good/bad objects, aggression, and retaliation.

I'm putting forward the idea that the entrance of a gender-ambiguous person into the bathroom may activate primitive superego defenses in response to perceived threats to the self's imagined gender coherence. A door opens, suddenly somebody appears. Is it a man or a woman? What is her/his purpose in the bathroom? How does that perceived gender ambiguity play in this particular space? There is ambivalence over seeing and not seeing, in which the fiction of gender confronts its unintelligibility, and what cannot be deciphered is turned into shit. The entrance of an ambiguously gendered person into a gendered bathroom brings into question the subject's comfortable phantasy of intelligibility while revealing that the coherence between gender presentation and genitalia is, invariably, a mere assumption. Indeed, and this is a key aspect of the conflicts over bathroom access, the notion that all individuals are "essentially, originally, in the first place, always have been, always will be, once and for all, in the final analysis, either 'male' or 'female'" (Garfinkel 1967: 122) is radically called into question in the bathroom encounter, and this moment of unavoidable interpellation of one's gender certainty will bring forth projective identifications in those who feel threatened by this interpellation: the psychic response of turning the ambiguous other into shit that needs to be expelled is, I would argue, the defining mode of "bathroom policing."

There is an unconscious compliance, I suggest, in policing the bathroom that turns the passive position in relation to internalized parental authority into a ferocious projection. Persecutory anxieties related to confusion and loss of certainty mobilize sadistic attacks that are simultaneously compliant, defiant, and retaliatory. Just as in the anal claustrum, thought in the bathroom encounter may be foreclosed and our minds lost. The wish to expel the transsexual subject from the gendered bathroom enacts an identification with the parental command that protects the subject from the menacing possibility of not knowing (his or her own) gender. There is a refusal to acknowledge that the bathroom is a public space and, as such, a place of difference, where we meet as strangers. The usual questions that we encounter as we enter—"Am I in the right bathroom?" and "Can I control myself?"—are agonized through our encounter with the other, and although there is a bare equality that belongs to the bathroom (we all need to go), the encounter with the enigmatic other elicits a confusion of gender categories that threatens our omnipotence: "I can tell who is male and who is female."

On the surface, placing the two scenes side by side—toilet training and the anxiety over the presence of the transsexual in the bathroom—seems nothing but farfetched. Indeed, we are trying to grasp something that seems removed from our understanding, and we are trying to fetch it through associations. The bathroom scene of our childhood reveals how our identity is constituted through identifications with multiple positions in relation with the other. Regardless of our confidence in our ability to position ourselves in relation to others, our symbolic location depends on the other's agreement. The agreement, however, is a place of conflict.

For the transsexual person, the bathroom situation typically repeats a long history of expulsions and exclusions that may recapitulate an old struggle with an internalized other who urges us to do the "right thing" and whose recognition we crave. It is also in the toilet that we get our first whiff of gender as division. For the transsexual subject, the entrance to the bathroom confers or denies a right of passage that asserts or threatens their relation to the internalized other through the implicit question: how successful are you at passing? I have been arguing that the presence of the transsexual in the bathroom is a reminder that the bathroom is a public place where the other has to be contended with, and therefore, it is perceived as a threat to one's omnipotent desire for control. The presence of the transsexual disrupts the fantasized coordinates of gender that hold in place our essentialized understanding of sexual difference. Within the anal claustrum ruled by projective identification, the question "if you are this, then what am I?" is lived as persecutory. The gender-ambiguous other has not only "intruded" into the bathroom, but they have cracked the walls of the claustrum itself, and now there is a confrontation with an intruder who is also the intruder within and who is also perceived as being in disguise. Confronting the other in oneself through the encounter with the unintelligible other subverts the demand from the internalized other—you must be x or y—and threatens cisgender cohesion. The transsexual is a reminder that the so-called cisgender—a term revealing an essentialist trope of origin—is not alone in the bathroom, that he or she is not a sole creator of him- or herself and that his gender identity is also beholden to the other. What is attacked is what cannot be known; it is a powerful blow to narcissistic unity and a reminder of the fluidity and changeability of gender, hence, of temporality.

We may imagine the "bathroom police" standing for the parental function in toilet training: a primitive, punitive, and prohibitive moral stance sadistically enacting an exclusion of the gender-ambiguous other. For the bathroom police, this enforcement of the "law of gender" allows them an identification with the parental couple and a fulfilment of their imagined desire: a gesture that affords them both recognition and pleasure. But we may also imagine that, for the bathroom police, the "monstrous transsexual" could be easily identified with the combined parental couple, an imagined fused figure of the parents—and the genders—that confuses, excludes, and distresses. The combined parental couple, joined in coital *jouissance*, reminds the child of the pain of exclusion: "you cannot come in here," "we are complete without you." From this perspective, we could imagine the expelling of the gender-ambiguous other as a reversed enactment of the pain and anger of infantile exclusion, as a repetition of the primal scene from an active and empowering position that turns "I can't come in" into "you must stay out." If, at the level of the imaginary, the transsexual subject is perceived as dangerously fusing two genders and as a reminder of parental *jouissance* stealing the child's gratification, aggression against this combined figure would help to keep objects apart and differentiated—so that genders remain whole and known—and allow an identification with parental authority while accessing the couple's forbidden *jouissance*.

A Transsexual Is Being Yelled At

Reading Freud's essay "A Child Is Being Beaten" ([1919] 2001), the reader is at once drawn into a passive stance. It is a child-observer's mesmerizing orchestration of a scene in his own mind. The scene involves the child's masturbatory gratification that shifts his position from one of helplessness—of being dethroned by a rival—into a sadistic one—observing a rival being beaten—, but there is also the child's unconscious identification with and envy of a rival receiving the paternal beating: "My father beats me because he loves me." Here, love is confused with punishment, a phantasy that propels the wish to be handled passively by the father in a gesture equated with care and possession. Through the beating phantasy, Freud explains the contradictory wishes that structures one's relation to others. Freud's elaborations on the structure of phantasy through the beating scene illustrate intricate relations between sexuality, gender, and punishment—simultaneously feared and desired—for what we are and what we are not. There is an equation between being beaten and being loved because in this phantasy the child being beaten constitutes the ultimate passive recipient. In Freud's formulation, the beating phantasy articulates a passion for being handled, a longing for merging with the other through one's surrender, but simultaneously and paradoxically, it also signifies an escape hatch through its very orchestration: in shifting his identification with the child who is being beaten to one with the sadistic beater, the child omnipotently eschews the craved but dangerous merger.

I suggest that "A Child Is Being Beaten" allows us to consider the bathroom scene as a conflation of contradictory positions: between victim and perpetrator, passive and active, bully and ally. "A Child Is Being Beaten" illustrates how the passivity inherent to the act of observation may function as a defense against ownership of desire. There is something being cancelled out, I suggest, in current discourses that focus either on the "danger" of the gender-neutral bathroom or on the transsexual as victim of discrimination and intolerance. And what gets cancelled is the subjectivity of the transsexual person themselves. In limiting our analysis to the brute "reality" of the bathroom encounter, we run the risk of repeating the conflation of the real of the body—forever and universally inaccessible—with its signifiers—whose multiple psychic meanings exceed sociocultural significations. What is left behind is the question of desire and the dread of internal difference that is unsymbolizable. Will treating the bathroom analytically, as a phantasy scene, give us a way into the social dread that is enacted in the bathroom? The dread of the other, of the leaking body? The question becomes then, does the bathroom encounter give us insight into the difficulties we face in thinking about transgender work in the clinic, where the singularity of the unconscious comes to bear?

Indeed, according to Freud, there are many competing and shifting positions in the beating phantasy that play on the dial of love and hate. But the defining feature of the beating phantasy is that none of the positions actualized in this scene can be understood separately but only in terms of their complementary function in the phantasy's configuration; therefore, the logic that structures these positions is relational. Similarly, the bathroom scene exemplifies the ways in which the body is tied from the outset to the other and cannot be relied upon as an unambiguous marker of identity or selfhood. In the bathroom encounter, sexual difference is constructed through a play of projections and distortions in which observing and being observed become one and the same thing, things that cannot be seen are invented, and what can't be seen turns scary. What thoughts are beaten in or out of one's mind in the bathroom? Does the claustrum from which "the anal eye" emerges equate the transsexual with a fused parental couple when the difference between them becomes too hard to bear? Is there envy of the entity that, in one's mind, is in possession of all the goods that gender can offer? Is the beating an attempt to expel what one cannot digest? Or does the uncertainty of gender threaten a tenuous coherence borne of fetishistic certitude? If the distinction between victim and victimizer, beating and being beaten is inherently unclear in the unconscious, will the structure of the beating phantasy helps us paint a picture of the bathroom scene as a fraught experience?

The anxieties associated with the bathroom, the tension between privacy and being exposed, and the possibility of being expelled, misrecognized, or misread, remind us that the bathroom is not just a place where we take care of our business but also a place where we perform our gender from the moment we enter the door. If we open the bathroom scene to its primal beginnings, we see traces of hatred, defense, phantasies, and murderous wishes. There is an omnipotent phantasy of gender certainty that one confronts right at the door and, when called into question, it transforms into superego anxiety—guilt or shame—that gets lodged in the toilet. What starts with a question, "Are you in the 'right' place?" soon becomes persecutory: "Are you a man or a woman?" We feel watched and are watchful of the other whose projections will encounter ours. We all possess an anus—as noted by Pier Paolo Pasolini's observation that "we are all equal from behind" (2008) and rehearsed in Janet Mock's claim that the bathroom is "the great equalizer for all of us" (quoted in Steinmetz 2015). Yet, this apparent truth is routinely negated in the public bathroom that is anything but neutral. In the bathroom, our phantasies meet the other and hence the limits of our fantasized omnipotence. The encounter with the other returns us to our constitutive susceptibility and dependency, which manifest in feelings of insufficiency in which comparisons are being made. There is a regression in the bathroom that recalls our infantile gazing at our father's penis or our mother's breasts, a regression that activates our infantile sexual theories, which now return as persecutory. Preoccupation with size and looks, how big, how quick, and how far are often played out in the bathroom scenes of our adolescence and childhood. Hence, anyone entering the bathroom is already under the influence of primal phantasies, partial objects, and contradictory identifications.

The bathroom police is an aggressor who may be actively "beating" the gender-ambiguous intruder but who is also and simultaneously observing a trans being beaten—both in the actual bathroom but also in the bathroom of public discourse where unfounded suspicions, attacks, and accusations are thrown around like feces. In Freud's reading, the beating phantasy is closely tied to superego anxiety, in which beating the other articulates an alliance with parental authority while simultaneously enacting the child's wish to separate. Beating off the strange other is also a beating of the stranger in the self; the act of expulsion enacts an eschewal of the enigmatic tension between the self and its otherness. In other words, in the exclusion of the transsexual, there is a denial of the enigmatic nature of sexuality that always introduces difference (separation). As such, what is also expelled is the paradox of one's origin: for it is the other to whom I am beholden, and our constitutive susceptibility and dependence on the other's desire gives birth to our subjectivity.

The often painful bathroom encounters with gender difference reveal the ways in which the body is not a good enough boundary and what is seen cannot be distinguished from our projections/evacuations. This suggests that there is tyranny at play that bears its weight on all the characters in the bathroom scene: an internal tension between ideal ego—the tyranny of culture and parental ideality of gender—and ego ideal—the phantasy of what the other has—that makes desire persecutory.

To understand the complexity of the bathroom scene, I therefore suggest, we must step back into the fun house of mirrors, partial identifications and projections, where the dynamics of beating, looking, and being beaten that Freud identified in the childhood scene may reawaken in these circumstances. In the bathroom, where the body becomes public, it is at risk of being handled in a way that can no longer recognize its singularity. For the victimizer, the desire for a fixed sense of self and other makes the appearance of conflict or incongruity unbearable. But the wish for a conflict-free and congruous gender image may also be present for the transsexual subject who wishes to be recognized as coherent and read "correctly." In the absence of such clear legibility, identifications in the bathroom prove unstable, and the positions taken by both parties become murky. Who is the protector, victim, or aggressor? Both sides feel under attack and feel a need to protect something that is imagined to be destroyed by the other, and hence both become susceptible to persecutory anxieties.

Beating phantasies are scenes of shifting identifications: they protect us against perceived loss of love and from feelings of rivalry and envy, and they also allow us to escape dangerous mergers with the other. The bathroom, I argue, is a nonneutral and psychically complex space, ripe for the return of the repressed. There, the wish for recognition from the other meets its opposite: the fear of being (mis)recognized as something unwanted or undesired, in excess or in deficit of the image we wish to project. In the bathroom space, "identity" becomes a fraught and persecutory demand to conform that is tied to the desire to be recognized and included. Understood as an emotional situation, the transphobic bathroom attack is an uncanny primal return: an imagined encounter with the monstrous combined parent, a refusal of a fantasized primal sadistic intercourse (condensed in the image of the transsexual), a fear of the other invading me, a reversed enactment of this invasion through transphobic intrusive violence, an acting-out of my sadistic desire to know. The violent encounter in the bathroom enacts an attempt at separating myself from an other with whom one is psychically fused in projective identification.

The insistence on identity as coherent, legible, and sovereign, on both sides of the debate, structures the bathroom scene as a closed and rigid dynamic in which the fixed positions of aggressor, victim, and ally cannot be escaped or overcome. If kicking out and being kicked out are complementary actions, acts mirroring each other in the claustrum that is the gendered bathroom, what kind of kick would release us from this asphyxiating space? What psychic shift would allow us to imagine the bathroom encounter otherwise?

An Analyst Is Being Beaten

The conflation of victim/victimizer positions makes the bathroom a site of repetition where mastery and passivity, love and hate, return and turn into their opposite. On both sides, there is an appeal for recognition that turns into persecutory anxiety. The transsexual individual demands recognition and equal access, but when the encountered response is "you do not belong here," the wish for love turns into hatred, and the other, into a persecutor. For the bathroom police, what must be obeyed is an anachronic, internalized symbolic order that must be defended against what is experienced as an attack: a wrecking of one's gender, a threat to cohesiveness, an incomprehensible otherness, and an anticipation of aggression or retaliation. But for the bathroom police, it is not only one's imagined self-coherence that is threatened: it's the very integrity of the symbolic order, with its clear gender demarcations, that needs to be safeguarded and upheld. The bathroom police gives itself the right to represent and defend a frail symbolic order. Indeed, when the deviant transsexual happens to be beaten, misgendered, outed, yelled out, or barred, the bathroom actualizes an old scene of allegedly justified punishment.

Might a turn to the clinic open the mind locked in the bathroom stall? Can analysis help us understand our mindless state in the bathroom? And conversely, can the bathroom, as a primal scenario of childhood, serve as a thought experiment through which to reflect on the clinic? The psychoanalyst, however, is not in the bathroom and is often not seen as someone who has genital or excretory organs. But the analytic clinic, I suggest, runs the risk of turning into a toilet when thinking becomes stalled, when anxiety and aggression are projected and evacuated, and when the difference between self and other blurs. And so both analyst and patient are confronted with a series of questions: Who is the patient identifying herself with? From which position is the patient speaking? Whose desire is he enacting? Who and what is the analyst for the patient? We can imagine the analyst as a transsexual subject encountering the projections and disavowals of the patient's policing superego. Here too, the analyst's thinking is at risk of becoming stalled by ideality, and she or he may problematically identify with the position of the subject supposed to know. From this position, the analyst may attempt to educate the patient on the logic of making the bathroom an inclusive space or to become an ally to the patient through identifying with her helplessness. Yet, I would argue that the analyst may learn to occupy a transsexual stance through an increased capacity to accept reality as an always shifting compromise formation, never absolute and always in question. The primal shift from the "pleasure of shitting" to the prohibition that commands us to "get rid of it" reminds us that we need to loosen up our ties to an idealized story, even at the risk of becoming undone by uncertainty and incompleteness. Such risk is constitutive of the clinic. And while conflicts over access to the bathroom involve very real concerns over transphobia and its dangers, for the analyst, this "reality" must also represent the limits of our imagination, and, as such, we need to overcome the claustrum mindset that reduces the bathroom scene to an encounter between victim and victimizer.

There is a necessary mismatch between the clinic and everyday life that I am trying to grapple with here. Of course, the psychoanalyst also "goes to the bathroom" and works with retentive and excretory metaphors and associations, but she is, most definitely, not the police of the bathroom. In fact, analysis is the only space in which one can think about the patient's history of digestion, indigestion, and evacuation, that is, of what is internalized and expelled. When there is a wish to flush away pain, conflict, or anger, the analyst functions as a psychic toilet for our projections that we fear may return in retaliation. In the consulting room, we deposit our "dirty secrets" (Lemma 2014: 1) and act out perverse phantasies such as attack or release in the form of evacuation of affect or an emotional "dumping" on the analyst or the analytic space. The anxieties, anticipations, and phantasies accompanying us to the bathroom—around dirt and cleanliness, expelling and withholding, hiding and revealing—also shape the nature of the clinic: we see the analyst as friend or foe, we feel triumphant or humiliated, rejected or understood, misread, recognized, or "found out." Analysis, I suggest, dislodges the apparently transparent logic of the bathroom scene and opens it up to "the risks of freedom and imagination" (Britzman 2016: 4). Once we are willing to consider phantasy as constitutive of the bathroom scene, we may attempt to understand how this scene articulates the ways in which sexuality, with its enigmatic qualities, exerts pressure on the *I* that is always reliant on the "eye" of the other.

I argue that while prejudice must be met with a revolt that transforms public policy, something must be transformed too for those who advocate rights of equality and access. Listening to the other's words as an enigmatic message, whose author or addressee is unknown, does not automatically or necessarily transform reactionary discourses or win our rights. And yet, this form of listening is, in my view, necessary to liberate our narrative from its asphyxiating friend/foe logic and to open it up to the unrepresentable, the unknown, and the unintelligible, allowing the subject to locate herself in a narrative that both precedes and exceeds her. There is an emotional transformation that is required in moving away from brute facts and toward symbolization, and this is where analysis resides. The analytic stance offers a way to pose "in-difference" as a way out of the ideality that structures the bathroom encounter, where the enigmatic message of the other places us within the realm of difference in relation to the self.

In "Instincts and Their Vicissitudes" ([1915] 2001), Freud positions indifference in opposition to love and hate, and while love and hate can easily turn into its opposites, in indifference the ego is not invested "with interest" toward the external world and is unconcerned with satisfaction. Freud claims that the capacity to observe one's observation, to suspend attention and hover over language, comes at the cost of an inevitable alienation. In, or within, the realm of difference is the only position that does not revert into love or hate and that requires the capacity to tolerate one's ambivalence and to listen to the other's desire as enigmatic. In-difference requires distance and estrangement, and these qualities are both needed and promoted in analysis in order to counteract our tendency to fall into idealization and the "delusion of clarity of insight" (Meltzer 1976: 141) with its promises of immediate understanding and irrefutable certainty. Meaning, Freud suggests, is made out of gaps, absences, associations, and slips, and what allows analysis its play is the pleasure we take in not understanding. If relating within difference or in-difference grants associations their freedom, could it loosen our hold on meaning and allow us to imagine what it would mean to experience the bathroom scene otherwise? What would it mean to respond within difference or in-difference?

Contemporary struggles over rights of access to the gendered bathroom reveal that the mind is lost between two opposite poles. On the one hand, there is an anxious bathroom police, whose urge to eschew the unintelligible other matches the urgency of defecation: words are evacuated and meaning is lost as soon as they are uttered. On the other hand, there is a transsexual subject hanging onto the literalness of the other's words ("get out," "you are not allowed here," "you have made a mistake"), which, much like fecal matter, once taken in, can no longer stand for something other than an attack. It is difficult to take distance from the words that are uttered, but in identifying with the projected transphobic content, the subject risks reenacting the very ideality that sustains the gendered bathroom, an ideality within which we are framed as soon as we cross the door. Both stances, I suggest, are emblematic of a constipated mind refusing to let go. The clinging to certitude of meaning hides an infantile confusion of tongues, but if we withhold the temptation to immediately understand, the bathroom scene may be read as enigmatic: Who is speaking? From which position? What answer is expected through this interpellation? To whom are these words addressed?

Indeed, we may wonder, is there a sexual investment involved in driving the transphobic phantasy? One dimension is the constellation of primal anxieties and aggression that the social incurred that is played out and hyped up in the gendered bathroom. There is an aggressiveness in constructing gender in the first place that is being displaced on the other. There is a splitting that is part of sexuality and that forms basis for a social contract. The idea of transphobia, I propose, has to be understood as an unconscious dilemma. If we understand the bathroom as a place of anxiety because it relates to questions of the body (e.g., an erotic place and a place of shame), we may also consider transphobia as involving eroticism and libidinal investments. The transphobic person, in this view, "gets off" on their anxiety, on confirming their identity as an autoerotic phantasy of self-sufficiency (there is no other) imbued with the urgency of knowledge. The phantasies culminating in the refusal to let go or the urgency of evacuating is animated and gets caught up in the bathroom, which the social has turned into a harsh, cruel place.

I would suggest that, at the level of the imaginary, the anxieties of the transsexual entering the bathroom and of the transphobic wishing to expel her are structurally linked. Both positions can be described as an attempt to avoid transitioning, understood as a psychic position that can tolerate the threshold between the self and what is other to it: both its internal self-difference and its difference from the external other. The transsexual defends their right to choose the bathroom that matches their gender identity, while the transphobic demands that people must use the bathroom that matches their biological sex. There is, however, a gap between the bathroom sign (male/female) and one's biological sex as much as there is a gap between the bathroom sign (male/female) and one's gender identity. From this perspective, one could argue that what the transphobic experiences as threatening is not the discontinuity between sex and gender—a continuity that, in the bathroom space, is never "known," only assumed—but the gender-ambiguous person's failure at passing. As the Center for American Progress's Sarah McBride notes, "Transgender men, who are likely to have a birth certificate with an 'F' on it, are often indistinguishable from cisgender men" (quoted in Steinmetz 2016). Insofar as these political positions deny the gap between the signifiers men/women and biological sex *and* gender identity, they are identically different: two sides of the same coin. Both positions, I suggest, constitute defensive positions against transitioning, that is, against acknowledging one's self-difference and one's difference from the external other.

As an enigmatic scene of anxiety, the bathroom encounter reveals a phantasy about the libidinal world that is not only operative behind the closed doors of the bathroom but also outside it: identity is both an imposition and a plea for acceptance. We are all interlopers, trespassers who get to enjoy the fragile illusion of legitimacy only when the other bestows recognition upon us. In the bathroom encounter, it is the transsexual who is refused this recognition and therefore left in the precarious position of having to contain the universal panic of not-being, of failing to pass.

For the transsexual subject entering the bathroom, there may be an anxious anticipation of a confrontation that recapitulates, repeats, and confirms a long history of refusals and rejections. The confirmation of one's fear of bullying or violence certainly leads to confusion, anger, and helplessness. But if there is a deferred quality to our anxious anticipation, could a repeated attack be experienced not as repetition of compulsion but as repetition with difference? As difficult as it is to avoid the anticipation of danger, one may wonder if refusing to orient one's entrance into the bathroom by the desire for the other's recognition may allow oneself to occupy a position of in-difference. Between fear and the desire for recognition, I suggest, there is also a capacity for anticipation that belongs to the analytic space.

I have argued that the anxious anticipation of an attack and the disavowal of the existence of transsexuality are ways to avoid psychic conflict. Existential fights over authenticity and truth as well as the fear of the transitioning body believed to be fake, inauthentic, or monstrous reveal the ways in which all transformations—conceptual, psychical, or physical—are subject to paranoid-schizoid ideation that defends us against loss, fragmentation, or aggression. Identity, understood as the capacity to walk in many worlds (internal world, outside world, and next to others) without disintegrating, is a precarious position. Identity does not stand still, and once recognition is actualized, there is a desire for more.

The clinic, Deborah Britzman reminds us, must encounter "more that we know" (2016: 4), and so, to open up a path to the destiny of desire, one must confront the difference within one's own narrative, to allow the story its variation. Transsexuality confronts us with an alterity that introduces a difference to our narrative of gender. Yet for the transsexual subject, the desire for a comfortable release in the bathroom also involves understanding how the anticipation of the other's attacks orients the patient's desire. Could the fear of being "found out," for example, repeat an unconscious demand "not to believe"—a repeated encounter with a primal incorporation of parental rejection? It is hard to think of our own ideality in moments when we encounter the murderous rage of those we fear or want to retaliate against. Can we break free of the mesmerizing phantasies that stall us in the stall? The work of analysis involves moving from the passive position of "this is happening to me" to a responsibility to symbolize, and, as I have been arguing, this transformation, this transitioning, requires us to learn in-difference.

Indeed, if our ties to the sociosymbolic order are contingent and arbitrary and therefore difficult to loosen up or predict, then transitioning out of what has become stalled in the claustrum of the bathroom necessitates a turn from the imaginary to imagination. Yet the work of analysis is not one of explanation but reconstruction of our constitutive failure in incorporating ourselves fully into this sociosymbolic order. The fact that the subject always already exceeds the symbolic coordinates that shape her into being is precisely what grants her the degrees of freedom out of which the work of analysis emerges.

In the clinic, analyst and patients struggle through the lure of the imaginary that promises full recognition and mimetic symmetry, an ever-present danger that accompanies the always-in-transition story of origin. This danger exists for both transsexual and cisgender subjects as they enter the bathroom. The clinic too is affected by a magnetizing pull toward sameness, in which certitude replaces difference and the body is often mystified as known. The patient wants to flush her pain in the analysis and then gets pissed off when the toilet won't flush away. They have a theory of how to get rid of the emotional mess, but the shit keeps coming back. And yet, analysis is also the only place in which one can think about one's history of digestion and indigestion, in which what is expelled from the narrative also allows for its transformation. Patient and analyst think together about the patient's constitutive dilemmas and deadlocks, about what it means to feel shamed, punished, or misrecognized. The analyst's capacity to maintain and tolerate in-difference to meaning—sometimes against the patient's desire for blind loyalty—means that the analyst must listen with equal attention to the most "painful and outrageous aspects of the human heart" (Jaqueline Rose, cited in Britzman 2016: 4), to the ways in which we are complicit in our own suffering, to our propensity to avoid responsibility for ourselves. And so the question of whether the analyst can listen otherwise to the pain of exclusion, the injury of being hated, and the agony of being barred without repeating the victimization must also orient the transsexual subject as they enter the bathroom.

Oren Gozlan, PsyD, C Psych, ABPP, is a clinical psychologist and a psychoanalyst in private practice. He is the chair of the Gender and Sexuality Committee of the International Forum for Psychoanalytic Education. Gozlan has published numerous articles in psychoanalytic journals. His *Transsexuality and the Art of Transitioning: A Lacanian Approach* won the American Academy and Board of Psychoanalysis's annual book prize for books published in 2015. He is also the winner of the 2016 Symonds Prize from the journal *Studies of Gender and Sexuality* for his article "The Transsexual Turn: Uncanniness at Wellesley College." His edited collection *In Transition: Current Critical Debates in the Field of Transsexual Studies* is forthcoming.

Note

1.   *Phantasy* refers to unconscious fantasy.

References

Abraham, Karl. 1916. "The First Pre-genital Stage of the Libido." In *Selected Papers on Psychoanalysis*, 248–79. London: Hogarth.

Bion, Wilfred R. 1977. *Second Thoughts: Selected Papers on Psychoanalysis*. London: Karnac Books.

Britzman, Deborah. 2015. *Melanie Klein: Analysis, Play, and the Question of Freedom*. New York: Springer.

———. 2016. "Thoughts on Misogyny: A Response to Dr. Leticia Glocer Fiorini's Paper." Paper presented at the Forty-Fourth ATTPPP Scientific Session, Toronto Institute of Psychoanalysis, Toronto, April 2.

Case, Mary Anne. 2010. "Why Not Abolish the Laws of Urinary Segregation?" In *Toilet: Public Restrooms and the Politics of Sharing*, edited by Harvey Molotch and Laura Norén, 211–25. New York: New York University Press.

Cavanagh, Sheila. 2010. *Queering Bathrooms: Gender, Sexuality, and the Hygienic Imagination*. Toronto: University of Toronto Press.

Covino, Deborah Caslav. 2004. *Amending the Abject Body: Aesthetic Makeovers in Medicine and Culture*. Albany: State University of New York Press.

Freud, Sigmund. (1908) 2001. "Character and Anal Erotism." In vol. 9 of *The Standard Edition of the Complete Psychological Works of Sigmund Freud*, edited and translated by James Strachey, 169–75. London: Vintage Books.

———. (1909) 2001. "Analysis of a Phobia in a Five-Year-old Boy." In vol. 10 of *The Standard Edition of the Complete Psychological Works of Sigmund Freud*, edited and translated by James Strachey, 1–149. London: Vintage Books.

———. (1915) 2001. "Instincts and Their Vicissitudes." In vol. 14 of *The Standard Edition of the Complete Psychological Works of Sigmund Freud*, edited and translated by James Strachey, 111–40. London: Vintage Books.

———. (1919) 2001. "A Child Is Being Beaten: A Contribution to the Study of the Origin of Sexual Perversions." In vol. 17 of *The Standard Edition of the Complete Psychological Works of Sigmund Freud*, edited and translated by James Strachey, 175–77. London: Vintage Books.

Garfinkel, Harold. 1967. *Studies in Ethnomethodology*. Malden, MA: Blackwell.

Halberstam, Judith. 2005. *In a Queer Time and Place: Transgender Bodies, Subcultural Lives*. New York: New York University Press.

Heimann, Paula. 1962. "Notes on the Anal Stage." *International Journal of Psycho-Analysis* 43: 406–14.

Katz, Johnathan Ned. 1995. *The Invention of Heterosexuality*. Chicago: University of Chicago Press.

Klein, Melanie. 1975. "Some Theoretical Conclusions Regarding the Emotional Life of the Infant." In *Envy and Gratitude and Other Works, 1946–1963*, 61–93. London: Delacorte.

Kogan, Terry S. 2010. "Sex Separation: The Cure-All for Victorian Social Anxiety." In *Toilet: Public Restrooms and the Politics of Sharing*, edited by Harvey Molotch and Laura Norén, 145–64. New York: New York University Press.

Kristeva, Julia. 1984. *Powers of Horror: An Essay on Abjection*. New York: Columbia University Press.

Lemma, Alessandra. 2014. *Minding the Body: The Body in Psychoanalysis and Beyond*. New York: Routledge.

Meltzer, Donald. 1976. "The Delusion of Clarity of Insight." *International Journal of Psycho-Analysis* 57, nos. 1–2: 141–50.

———. 1992. *Claustrum: An Investigation of Claustrophobic Phenomena*. London: Karnac Books.

Steinmetz, Kathy. 2015. "Everything You Need to Know about the Debate over Transgender People and Bathrooms." *Time*, July 28. time.com/3974186/transgender-bathroom-debate/.

———. 2016. "Why LGBT Advocates Say Bathroom 'Predators' Argument Is a Red Herring." *Time*, May 2. time.com/4314896/transgender-bathroom-bill-male-predators-argument/.

Žižek's Antagonism and the Futures of Trans-Affirmative Lacanian Psychoanalysis

CHRIS COFFMAN

Abstract This essay uses Slavoj Žižek's recent writings about transpeople—and their reactions to him—as a way to reconsider the contributions that Lacanian psychoanalysis could make to trans theory. Affirming that there is already considerable value to trans-affirmative theorizing in the work of Shanna Carlson, Patricia Gherovici, and Gayle Salamon, this essay nonetheless argues that Žižek's work offers—despite itself—a way of traversing the fantasy of sexual difference that structures Lacanian accounts of gender. By going beyond the assumption that the antinomy that structures subjectivity must always and only be named "sexual difference," this essay creates an opening for thinking sex, gender, and sexual difference otherwise.
Keywords transgender, transsexuality, psychoanalysis, Jacques Lacan, Slavoj Žižek

Slavoj Žižek has never been a friend of North American multiculturalism, and his recent pronouncements about transpeople are no exception. His 2016 piece entitled "The Sexual Is Political" has justifiably elicited unfavorable responses from the press. The *Los Angeles Review of Books*, for example, recently published a retort by Che Gossett that asks how Žižek dares "to write about trans subjectivity with such assumed authority while ignoring the voices of trans theorists (academics and activists) entirely" (Gossett 2016). It is worth noting that the refusal to engage transpeoples' perspectives to which Gossett points is part of a larger pattern in Žižek's work. Rather than carefully investigate and respond in an informed fashion to the North American debates to which he so often refers, Žižek often reacts superficially and sensationalistically. In "The Sexual Is Political," he avoids the difficult task of engaging recent Lacanian scholarship on transgender by intellectual peers such as Shanna Carlson, Patricia Gherovici, and Gayle Salamon, drawing instead on a *Wikipedia* article to construct an inaccurate and superficial genealogy of trans* discourse that conflates transgender with

TSQ: Transgender Studies Quarterly ★ Volume 4, Numbers 3–4 ★ November 2017
DOI 10.1215/23289252-4189929 © 2017 Duke University Press

so-called postgenderism. Using this strategy, he treats transpeoples' lives as mere manifestations of North American "political correctness" run amok and misses the opportunity to explore the ways his Marxist rearticulation of Lacanian psychoanalysis could work in the service of the goals of trans* theory rather than negate its claims.

A perfectly reasonable response to Žižek's spectacle would be to ignore him and thereby reduce his power: to throw his writings in the "GENERAL WASTE" bin to which, in one of the most objectionable analogies in "The Sexual Is Political," he compares those people hailed by the "+" in the formulation "LGBT+" (Žižek 2016c). An alternative approach—one that acknowledges and pushes back against his capacity to get under our skin—might instead interrogate the reasons for which his thinking is tripped up by transgender phenomena, and the reasons for which trans-affirmative psychoanalytic thinkers are so tripped up by him. Examining these matters reveals that what is at stake in the way Žižek spins diversity issues is not only the desire to provoke the kinds of controversies that fuel academic celebrity but also the very terms of the philosophical system through which he apprehends gender. Manifestations of transphobia in Žižek's writing reveal aporias within his philosophical system and therefore ways in which some of his ideas can be rearticulated in the service of a trans-affirmative mode of Lacanian psychoanalysis.

In "The Sexual Is Political," Žižek reiterates and rearticulates claims that will sound familiar to frequent readers of his work. For instance, he explains—and hardly for the first time in his oeuvre—that "the reason for this failure of every classification that tries to be exhaustive is not the empirical wealth of identities that defy classification but, on the contrary, the persistence of sexual difference as real, as 'impossible' (defying every categorization) and simultaneously unavoidable. The multiplicity of gender positions (male, female, gay, lesbian, bigender, transgender . . .) circulates around an antagonism that forever eludes it" (2016c). The first sentence in this passage does not advance a claim that will be new to those familiar with Lacanian theory. It is the explanation of sexual difference that animates every one of Žižek's books. And it is also the account that is behind Carlson's query, in the 2014 initiatory issue of *TSQ*: "What happens when we take a trans look at the formulas" of sexuation through which Jacques Lacan reformulates sexual difference in his twentieth seminar, *Encore*, without assuming "the formulas' positions to be occupied by (only) the 'men' and 'woman' of normative imaginings?" (2014: 169). This is a good question, one about which Žižek, in 2016, appears to be in agreement with the trans* theorists he claims to oppose.

Žižek's oppositional style has contributed significantly to the rift between theories of "gender" and Lacanian explanations of "sexual difference" and "sexuation," however. These distinctions, although meaningful, are not as divisive as they seem. Part of the problem lies in the incommensurability fostered by translation: *sexual difference* and *sexuation* enter English as translations of the French terms *la différence sexuelle* and *l'identité sexuée*, whereas *gender*—a concept introduced by English-language feminisms grounded in sociological accounts of "gender roles"—does not have a French equivalent. The French word *genre* instead invokes the concept of literary genre and also, grammatically, marks what English speakers would call "anatomical sex."[1] Unlike these social, linguistic, and biological distinctions, Lacanian terms such as "sexual difference" and "sexuation" refer to psychical structures that emerge from within the dialectic of desire.

As Ellie Ragland explains, "Lacan coined the term *sexuation* to describe a subject's choice of sex as masculine or feminine in assuming an active or passive position vis-à-vis his or her object of desire"—that is, to describe "the way a subject is split by language (or not)" through Oedipalization (2004: 65–67). Moreover, "the formulas of sexuation" articulated in Lacan's *Seminar Twenty* "provide the logical matrix" for the "deadlock" in the real that forces the subject to choose between masculine and feminine positions within the dialectic of desire (Salecl 2000). Carlson asserts that these two stances cannot be reduced to "'gender' as we might more conventionally conceive of it," insofar as they "signal two different logics, two different modes of ex-sistence in the symbolic, two different approaches to the Other, two different stances with respect to desire, and (at least) two different types of jouissance" (64). Within these two "psychic identifications," the "masculine identifies primarily with the symbolic order of language and social conventions, while the feminine identifies with the real of affect, loss, and trauma" (Ragland 2004: 179). However, this results not in the binary opposition between the "masculine" and the "feminine" that Lacan and Žižek are often accused of perpetuating but, rather, in an antagonistic clash between two fundamentally incommensurate positions.

Despite Lacan's stress on psychical positioning, his thesis that "sexuality is structured—that is, imposed from the outside"—is "compatible with sociological feminisms" in some ways, as Ragland notes (74). Even though his thinking diverges from sociologists' arguments about gender "role behavior," he demonstrates that "one 'learns' one's sexual identifications—one's sexuation—from the symbolic order" as a correlative of "imaginary identifications, not biological anatomy" (74). Ragland explains that "Lacan recast the Freudian cause of human *behavior and motivation* away from anatomy and biology to the subjective sexual identifications he called differential structures of desire. Each structure of desire establishes a pattern connecting it to jouissance depending on the way lack . . . is filled in reference to the Father's Name . . . and the object (*a*) that marks the primordial subject as real" (98). As Ragland observes, the antiessentialist character of Lacan's work creates overlaps between his thinking and sociologists' accounts of gender. These two lines of thinking are not equivalent to one another, however, for Lacanians and gender theorists diverge in their understandings of the mechanisms that lead to gender diversity. But if we stress their theories' intersections rather than their divergences, then we can see the complex interplay between the psychical and the social that is at work in the contemporary proliferation of genders.

Because—as Ragland puts it—"sexual difference is not innate" but rather symbolic—that is, because sexuation "does not" determine "one's biological sex, but the position one occupies in reference to the masculine *all* of knowledge, or the feminine *not all* of knowledge"—this theory may be adapted for queer and trans* theory because the subject is free to choose between the "masculine" and "feminine" positions without regard to anatomical differences (125, 179). Moreover, these psychical differences set into motion numerous possibilities for social gender. In her cross-reading of Lacan with systems theory, Judith Roof points out that one of the functions of the "castration complex"—even when strictly defined—is to propel "a perpetual process of sorting differences into difference as the symbolic condition for desire" (2016: 60). Roof's interpretation of Lacan's account of "subjective sexuation" acknowledges that subjects may adopt "multiple postures and attitudes in relation to difference"—possibilities that may include a variety of transsubjectivities (60).

In the past, Žižek and trans-affirmative psychoanalytic thinkers have parted ways not over the second-order manifestations of gender that are at stake in the above remarks but about what—until recently—he has presumed to be sexual difference's fundamental intractability as the constitutive antagonism that sets that multiplicity of genders into motion. In 2012, I published an article entitled "Queering Žižek" that sought to expose the internal contradictions within Žižek's thought and develop their potential for furthering the work of queer and trans* theory. I demonstrate that, contrary to Žižek's claims in various writings from 1989 to 2012 about the intransigence of sexual difference, his positing of class struggle as an antinomy that functions analogously to that of Lacanian sexual difference reveals that both are contingent and available for "ideological struggle and transformation" (Coffman 2012). Žižek repeats this move in "The Sexual Is Political" in his claim that "the other great antagonism is that of classes" (2016c).[2] Reiterating this assertion with a difference in the second of two replies to "The Sexual Is Political," he acknowledges the multiplicity of antagonisms by defining "class struggle" as comprising not only "the workers' struggle" but also "Third World crises" and "the plight of immigrants and refugees" (2016b).[3] In so doing, Žižek confirms my argument despite himself.

Despite his prior insistence that sexual difference is transhistorical and unchangeable, in 2016 Žižek finally concedes that "the LGBT trend is right in 'deconstructing' the standard normative sexual opposition, in de-ontologizing it, in recognizing in it a contingent historical construct full of tensions and inconsistencies" (2016c). Thus, without admitting it, in "The Sexual Is Political" he ultimately accepts a point Judith Butler repeatedly made in *Bodies That Matter* and *Contingency, Hegemony, Universality* despite his vehement resistance throughout the 1990s. Yet even in Žižek's 2016 reformulation, he finds himself acknowledging the contingency of "the standard normative sexual opposition"—which I see as indicating that it is a fundamental fantasy available for traversal—without admitting that it is available for this kind of rearticulation (2016c).

Herein lies the problem with Žižek's subsequent claim that "transgenderism is ultimately an attempt to avoid (the anxiety of) castration," an anxiety that he presumes to exclusively concern sexual differentiation (2016c). He formulates its cause as a worry: "Whatever choice I make, I will lose something, and this something is NOT what the other sex has" (2016c). This formulation implies that there are only two possibilities for sexual differentiation. Yet as Roof explains, "if we dismiss Freud's Oedipal chamber drama and understand castration more figuratively as the moment individuals begin to recognize difference—that they are separable and perpetually separated from their environment and from others around them—castration . . . signals the point when a polymorphous lack of differentiation gives way to differences and taxonomies"—ones that are "multiple," provisional, and subject to change (2016: 59–60). Roof's argument demonstrates that the proliferation of labels for genders and sexualities in the United States—which Žižek accounts for in Lacanian terms with a "+" that symbolizes the "one exceptional element which clearly does not belong to it and thereby gives body to +" (2016c)—is compatible with Lacan's thinking. Žižek, though, unjustifiably asks transpeople to bear the burden of this positioning in a way that heterosexual and cisgender people do not.

Lacan need not be interpreted this way. As Kaja Silverman has demonstrated, castration is fundamentally linguistic rather than sexual in nature (1992: 112). And as Mari Ruti (2008: 488) explains, "language generates lack," which "in turn generates desire." Because desire circulates around the *objet a*, an endlessly deferred phantasmatic object, the "subject . . . lacks not simply some locatable object [e.g., a penis] but . . . lacks being as such," as Carlson elaborates (2010: 51). Castration thus does not necessarily lead to the dramas of Oedipalization or the theaters of the phallus so commonly revived in mainstream psychoanalytic writing but, rather, to our most fundamental existential condition: what Ruti (2008: 485) calls "ontological lack." Thus if, as Silverman (1992: 112) argues, the name of the father is only one among a wide variety of possible "signifiers that impart a retroactive significance to the lack introduced by language," it is possible for that signifier to be replaced by another. An authentic act in the real—rather than the symbolic and imaginary resignifications that Butler calls for in *Bodies That Matter*—could replace the name of the father with another signifier and thereby render sexual difference either incidental or irrelevant to desiring subjectivity (Coffman 2012). In other words, the "antagonism" in the "real" to which Žižek refers may be "unavoidable," but its consequences are not inalterable, nor need the difference it concerns necessarily be sexual. Nor need "transgenderism" be understood as "ultimately an attempt to avoid (the anxiety of) castration," as Žižek claims (2016c).

Trans-affirmative Lacanian psychoanalysis has not yet explored the implications of the possibility that an act in the real might rearticulate the terms of the constitutive antagonism that mobilizes a variety of genders. Carlson, for example, explores one possibility for trans* theorizing available within a conventionally Lacanian account of sexual difference as the antagonism underlying diverse genders. In her own inflection of the arguments through which strict Lacanian theorists such as Žižek and Joan Copjec conceive of sexual difference as real and therefore unchangeable, she argues that "with respect to sexual difference, we must insist on the ways in which, for Lacan, the terms *masculine* and *feminine* signal two different logics, two different modes of ex-sistence in the symbolic, two different stances with respect to desire, and (at least) two different types of *jouissance*. Nothing here indicates 'gender' as we might more conventionally conceive of it" (Carlson 2010: 64). This distinction implies that, although every speaking subject must come to occupy either the masculine or feminine position, a person's positionality does not constrain their options for gender expression. It also allows Carlson to make the case that the subjectivity of the "transsexual subject" who "strives to pass *and/or* . . . identifies with one gender or another with an apparent degree of certainty" is "psychically no different than any other subject who lines up under one banner or the other" (64). This argument enables her important observation that "'transsexuality' is not in and of itself any more extreme a type of symptom than is 'man' or 'woman'" (64–65). Moreover, Carlson's reasoning allows her to assert that "the transgender subject—as someone who is not necessarily or only very strategically invested in 'passing' as one gender or another . . . , as someone who may be invested in embodying a gender that would attest to what he or she may define as the constructedness of gender . . . —would be the human subject as such" (65). Clearly, there are powerful possibilities for trans-affirmative theorizing available even within strict interpretations of Lacan.

Salamon also works within a conventional reading of Lacan, and when she writes about the real, she does so to argue that Jay Prosser's *Second Skins* (1998) underestimates the implications for trans* embodiment of Lacan's account of the split subject. Salamon stresses the way in which transsubjectivity entails the production of a sense of "bodily coherence" through symbolic and imaginary "recognition" and "misrecognition" (2010: 24). Underscoring the dangers of Prosser's insistence "that the transsexual body is 'unimpeachably real,'" Salamon charges that this claim "ends up landing him squarely in the Real," in all its "plenitude and fullness"—a positioning that is problematic because it leaves the transsexual "outside of language, outside of meaning, outside of the symbolic, outside of relation, outside of desire"—in a space of "radical abjection and death" (41). Although I concur with her critique of Prosser, find her Lacanian account of trans* embodiment incredibly useful, and share her desire for a reading of Lacan that situates transgender subjectivity within rather than outside "language" and "relation," I also see possibilities for altering the terms of the real (41).

Carlson hints at such a possibility when she argues that Stephen Whittle, in the foreword to the first edition of *The Transgender Studies Reader*, implicitly positions transpeople as engaging in what Žižek, interpreting Lacan, calls the "ethical act" (Carlson 2010: 68; Žižek 1998). To make this claim, she equates what Ragland describes as "the suffering of hysteria," with its refusal to accept the premise that "either one is masculine or one is feminine" (Carlson 2010: 67–68; Ragland 2006: 85), with Whittle's statement about the sacrifices made by trans* studies' pioneers: "It has been through this articulation of the imposition of gendering on us by others that the position of suffering of those with trans identities has been heard" (Carlson 2010: 67–68; Whittle 2006: xv). However, by valorizing the potentially revolutionary potential of the feminine position—and therefore Lacan's association of femininity with hysteria—to theorize the transperson's questioning of gender ("Am I a man, or am I a woman, and what does that mean?"), she implicates her analysis in some of his more questionable assertions about femininity (Carlson 2010: 65). These claims become especially problematic when she quotes Ragland's statement that the hysteric's self-questioning puts her "at risk of being overtaken by the real in both the symbolic and the imaginary" (Carlson 2010: 67; Ragland 2006: 69). Although Carlson finds in the hysteric's and the transperson's "suffering" the beginnings of the "ethical act"—and therefore the seeds of "social transformation"—her argument also reproduces the pathologizing elements of Lacan's account of femininity and thereby points to the need for trans* theorists to continue to challenge the underlying assumptions of his discourse (Carlson 2010: 65–68).

I see less pathologizing and more expansive ways for trans* theory to conceive of the "ethical act" and its capacity to initiate "social transformation" (65–68). As Žižek and others argue, Lacan's later writings suggest that by engaging in an authentic act, it is possible to traverse the fundamental fantasy that shapes subjectivity. Distinct from daydreams and everyday fantasies, what Lacanians call the "fundamental fantasy" is an unconscious formation that orients the subject by providing a sense of life's potentialities and constraints.[4] The process of traversing—that is, going beyond—the fundamental fantasy creates the possibility for the emergence of "a new *point de capiton*" (the "quilting point" that links the three orders) and therefore "a new structuration of the imaginary, symbolic, and Real," as I have put it elsewhere (Coffman 2013: 49). Žižek describes the "act" as *"symbolic suicide,"* a strategy for "withdrawing from symbolic reality that enables us to begin anew from the 'zero point,' from that point of absolute freedom called by Hegel 'abstract negativity'" (1992: 49). Traversing the fundamental fantasy asks the unhappy subject to engage the real and temporarily embrace a state of "subjective destitution" (Žižek 1996: 166). This sets a process of profound change into motion—one that entails the "radical transformation of the very universal structuring 'principle' of the existing symbolic order" as well as the coordinates of the imaginary and real that are quilted to it through the *point de capiton* (Žižek in Butler, Laclau, and Žižek 2000: 220).[5] This overhaul of the symbolic order creates, in turn, the conditions through which a new fundamental fantasy—and therefore a new form of subjectivity—can emerge.

As Ruti observes, the resulting "disbanding of fantasies . . . allows us to begin to imagine alternative ways of living and relating" (2010: 1). Yet Lacan's account of traversing the fundamental fantasy was inconsistent and not yet fully worked through by the time of his death (Coffman 2013: 46). Theorists writing in his wake have been left to develop its potential consequences for subjectivity and have laid out several prospects for what might lie beyond the fundamental fantasy's traversal. These developments all hinge on the *sinthome*, the individual mode of *jouissance* Lacan theorizes in *Seminar Twenty-Three*. Lorenzo Chiesa points to the way this "unconcluded" aspect of "Lacan's work" can be generative: "New inventions of his own reinvention of Freudian psychoanalysis" can emerge as scholars further define and clarify the concept of the *sinthome* and its possible functions (2007: 189). This inventiveness animates the most exciting developments in trans-affirmative Lacanian psychoanalysis.

In one reading—the one to which I have already referred—traversing the fundamental fantasy by embracing the *sinthome* can reconfigure the relationship between the symbolic, imaginary, and real orders. Although this interpretation is associated with Žižek—a writer to whom one would not intuitively look for a theory that enables transsubjectivity—in my view his account of the fundamental fantasy's traversal offers considerable promise. It is important to note that unlike Prosser's transsexual—whose subjectivity is permanently bereft of imaginary and symbolic support—the subject who traverses the fantasy only temporarily experiences subjective dispossession. The brief "passage through 'symbolic death'" that takes place by traversing the fundamental fantasy allows the subject to alter and thereby reanimate their position within "language," "meaning," "the symbolic," "relation," and "desire" by engaging the real in conjunction with the other two orders (Žižek 1999: 262; Salamon 2010: 41). Ruti notes that despite Lacan's otherwise powerful critique of ego psychology and the "narcissistic" aspects of fantasy, there are cases in which it is vital to "reconstitute the ego" when it has been "profoundly injured" by oppression (2008: 493). Yet she also observes that the "act" through which one traverses the fundamental fantasy "is essentially an encounter with the real which jolts the subject beyond the social coordinates of its existence, potentially allowing it to rupture the parameters of whatever is oppressing it" (Ruti 2010: 12). This account suggests that by engaging the real, traversing the fundamental fantasy can shift the symbolic's most oppressive terms while maintaining the underlying structure of the Lacanian triad that provides psychical support for vulnerable subjects.

The prospect that an act in the real might reconfigure the terms of the real, imaginary, and symbolic but not abolish the Lacanian triad is important to trans* studies because, as Salamon demonstrates, transpeople often rely upon recognition by the other as they live out their embodiments in contexts that risk their symbolic erasure. Although in keeping with Lacan's account of the imaginary, she acknowledges that every recognition is a form of *mis*recognition, Salamon—like Ruti—makes a compelling case for the capacity of the imaginary and symbolic orders to support transgender embodiment, despite the misprisions and inconsistencies they also engender. I thus see considerable potential for trans* psychoanalysis in a theory of traversing the fundamental fantasy. This process enacts what Ruti calls "a radical reconfiguration of the normative order" but does not abolish the underlying structure provided by the Lacanian triad and its supporting fantasies (2010: 11).

Another possible outcome of embracing the *sinthome* involves suturing a breach in the Lacanian triad and thereby creating a "partially individuated symbolic" instead of traversing the fundamental fantasy (Chiesa 2007: 189). Chiesa, following Lacan, sees this solution at work in James Joyce's writings, which employ the *sinthome* to repair a rupture of the three orders and thereby fend off psychosis (Lacan 2016). In *Seminar Twenty-Three*, Lacan explains that "the sinthome"—an antiquated word for "symptom"—is "the fourth ring" that ties together the Borromean knot he had previously described as a triad comprising the real, imaginary, and symbolic orders (2016: 3, 12). Although the three circles of the knot usually interlock in such a way that they cannot be severed because "a knot is something that can be botched," in some cases "a mistake" in the triad's construction leaves it potentially separable and the subject at risk for psychosis (80, 76). Evidence from the "unconscious" reveals "that there are piles of" such "botched cases" (80). To account for the fact that relatively few such cases culminate in psychotic breaks, in the seminar on the *sinthome* Lacan replaces the aforementioned triad with a tetrad—"the imaginary, the real, the symptom . . . and the symbolic"—whose new element, the "symptom" or "sinthome," creates "the possibility of binding" the three other terms together (12). Embracing the *sinthome* allows the subject to stave off psychosis even when the Borromean knot has been "botched" (80). Lacan says that "should the symbolic thereby come free, as I once noted it would, we have a way of mending it, which is to fashion what I defined for the first time as a sinthome. This is the item that enables the symbolic, the imaginary, and the real to go on holding together, even though here none of them are actually holding on to any of the others anymore due to the two mistakes" (77). He further specifies that the *sinthome* is "that which enables the trefoil knot, not to go on forming a trefoil knot, but rather to maintain itself in a position that *looks like* it is forming a trefoil knot" (77). This ability to create the appearance of a knot, even in the case of a "mistake" that has undermined the integrity of its construction, makes the *sinthome* potentially effective as a means for which "the Borromean link to be mended" and the real, imaginary, and symbolic orders to be brought back into alignment (76).

In *Seminar Twenty-Three*, James Joyce serves as Lacan's primary example of a subject who has knotted the three orders back together through the *sinthome*, which in his case was writing. However, early psychoanalytic work on transgender by Catherine Millot (1991) used these claims about Joyce to pathologize transsexuality. This is the theory of the *sinthome* to which Žižek responds when he claims, inadequately, that he doesn't "think that the idea to conceive transgender identity as a 'sinthom' in Lacan's sense is of great use" (2016b). While he is completely right to refuse to "see transgender individuals as potential psychotics who avoided psychosis by creating a sinthome," in his rejection of this theory's most transphobic formulation he overlooks other possibilities for its trans-affirmative uses (2016b).

For Lacan, staving off psychosis is not the only use to which the *sinthome* can be put; it is also available to those whose Borromean knot has not been "botched" (2016: 80). In these latter cases, the *sinthome* is merely "neurotic" (42). In *Seminar Twenty-Three*, Lacan identifies "the father" as one such "symptom, or . . . sinthome," that is "*im-ply-cated*" in the "enigmatic bond between the imaginary, the symbolic, and the real" (11). As Ragland explains, this development in Lacan's thinking implies that—unlike his thinking in his much earlier seminar on the psychoses—"the Father's Name signifier need not be the 'imaginary daddy' of contemporary conceptualization, then. It can also be a signifier such as 'the outsider,' or a river god, rather than the actual progenitor, or even the mother's brother," among many possibilities (2004: 120). "The point is that this signifier represents the symbolic order as the *effect* of difference. Both sexual difference . . . and distance from the drives . . . make the social order possible" (120). This argument, which suggests that "the father" is only one of multiple possibilities for the *sinthome*, furthers the movement away from Lacan's earlier presentations of the Name-of-the-Father and the phallus as determinative signifiers and points to the possibility that other signifiers could just as effectively carry out their structural functions (Lacan 2016: 11). As a result, "the Oedipus complex," too, is only "a symptom" and its structuration of desire contingent (13). This change in Lacan's thinking has several important consequences for queer and trans* theory. First, his identification of "the father" as an interchangeable *sinthome* revises the claim he made in *Seminar Three: The Psychoses* that the subject needs to accept the name of the father as master signifier to become a speaking subject rather than a psychotic (11). By superseding this argument in *Seminar Twenty-Three*, Lacan obviates Butler's and my divergent critiques of the homophobia and transphobia at work in *Seminar Three* and Žižek's interpretation of it (Butler 1993; Coffman 2006). Moreover, when Lacan identifies "the father" and "the Oedipus complex" as *sinthomes* in *Seminar Twenty-Three*, he suggests that they could be supplanted by other formations—an act that could mobilize novel possibilities for desire and gendered embodiment (Lacan 2016: 11–13).

It is in this latter vein that Gherovici employs Lacan's theory of the neurotic *sinthome* to critique Millot's approach and initiate a line of thinking in which transsexuality involves a form of "art that can allow someone to love, work, desire" (Gherovici 2014: 258–59). Gherovici defines the *sinthome* as "a creative knotting together of the registers of real, symbolic, and imaginary" and "as the trace of the unique way someone can come to be and enjoy their unconscious" (2012: 261; 2014: 253). Stressing that "Lacan defines the *sinthome* as an artifice . . . a creation, an invention," she observes that it offers a valuable contribution to theories of "transgenderism because it offers a novel way to think about sexual difference"—a way that is not dependent "on the phallus or the Name-of-the-Father" as symbolic anchors (2012: 261, 267). Gherovici also finds in the *sinthome* a means of understanding writings about transition as examples of the "*Künstlerroman*, 'a novel of the artist'" (266). As such, transsexuals use writing to "help embody sexual difference" (267). The act of "writing the memoir" engages the "unsymbolizable"—the real—and thereby "grants a different form of embodiment in which the body finds its anchor in the sea of language" (2014: 255, 255, 262). Writing also becomes the means through which transsexuals find their "creative *sinthome*" and offer themselves up "for deciphering" by others (2012: 279–84). Through this reading of the *sinthome*, Gherovici reworks Lacanian theory to affirm transsexuals' desire to transition. This enables her to "argue for a depathologization of transgenderism" that repudiates Millot's claims (2014: 258).

In explaining the way transsexuals can identify their "creative *sinthome*," Gherovici suggests that they achieve what I elsewhere call a reconfigured "structuration of the imaginary, symbolic, and Real" (Gherovici 2014: 262; Coffman 2013: 49). This is a valid account of a way transsubjectivity can be achieved by embracing the *sinthome*, but there is also another possibility. Gherovici's argument suggests that the transsexual alleviates suffering by finding a new way of inhabiting a symbolic order constituted through the terms of Lacanian "sexual difference." She asserts, for instance, that "the body is marked by the conundrum of sexual difference," rather than existential lack more generally (262). Her argument—and the form of transsubjectivity for which she advocates—thus remains governed by what I call "(hetero)sexual difference": "The way in which certain uses of Lacanian psychoanalysis . . . rest on a circular ideology in which sex, gender, and sexuality are mutually constituted in heterogendered terms through the inscription of a putatively foundational antagonism between masculine and feminine" (Coffman 2012).

In my view, trans* psychoanalysis stands to benefit not only from Gherovici's interpretation of the *sinthome* but also from a theory of traversing the fundamental fantasy through an authentic act. Existing scholarly explications of the *sinthome* suggest that in some instances, embracing the *sinthome* can suture breaches of the Lacanian triad that might otherwise lead to psychosis (as in Joyce's situation), and that in others embracing the *sinthome* can reconfigure the imaginary, symbolic, and real to alleviate nonpsychotic forms of suffering (as in Gherovici's example of the "creative *sinthome*" whose inventiveness enables transsexuals' transitions). These are both valid interpretations of Lacan's concept of the *sinthome*. There is also, however, a third possibility: embracing the *sinthome* can allow the subject to traverse—and thereby reconfigure—the fundamental fantasy, profoundly altering the unconscious underpinnings of subjectivity.[6] I have argued elsewhere that queer theory would benefit from traversing the fantasy of "(hetero)sexual difference" so as better to "register the many possible configurations of desiring subjectivities" (Coffman 2012). Trans-affirmative psychoanalysis, too, would benefit from a theory that stresses that "sexual difference" is a fantasy available for traversal. Given Lacan's understanding of embodiment as arising through signification in the Other, such a theory would expand our understanding of the varied options available for trans* embodiment (262).

The outcome of fantasy's traversal has been theorized in two different ways. The way to which I have already referred—which is developed in Žižek's work as well as that of Chiesa (2007) and Yannis Stavrakakis (1999)—entails the creation of a temporary void in subjectivity that is quickly covered over by a reformulated version of the Lacanian triad of the real, imaginary, and symbolic orders and their constitutive fantasy. Another way—articulated in the work of

Juliet Flower MacCannell (2008), Paul Verhaeghe and Frédéric Declercq (2002), and especially Ed Pluth (2007)—derives from what I describe elsewhere as a more "radical reading of Lacan's" seminars (Coffman 2013: 49). This interpretation holds that "everyone" may "create their own *sinthome* at the place of the lack of the Other" and thereby dispense with the need to anchor their subjectivity with the symbolic's outworn props such as "the Name-of-the-Father" (Verhaeghe and Declercq 2002: 52). Pluth further clarifies that this process of "direct investment in signifiers as such" ultimately replaces the subject's original "investment in fantasy" (2007: 163). As I have observed earlier, Pluth offers an open-ended interpretation of Lacan's theory of the "act" that stresses the subject's "ability to touch the Real and bring its impasses into signification," thereby creating "the possibility of shifting the terrain of signification" (Coffman 2013: 53).

Either of these approaches would allow us to go beyond Carlson's positioning of sexual difference as the constitutive antagonism and see it as potentially subject to transformation. The forms of transsubjectivity that are best sustained through the symbolic and imaginary recognitions Salamon describes can still be effectively theorized through a theory of traversing the fundamental fantasy that emphasizes the emergence of a reconfigured symbolic, imaginary, and real; those that require fewer supports could proliferate within the open-ended and postmodern approach to signification that no longer depends upon recognition in the Other.

The latter solution offers another route to Carlson's insight that "there is something transgendered about the human subject, and that this transgenderism transcends notions of gender" (2010: 66). Her argument demonstrates the transgender potential inherent in even the strictest readings of Lacan—those in which "sexual difference" remains the name for the "impasses" set into motion by existential castration (66). The grounds for such interpretations are legible in *Encore*, which relies upon formulations such as "[a] woman seeks out a man" and "[a] man seeks out a woman" to stake out sexual difference's terrain (Lacan 1998: 33). Lacan nonetheless also claims in *Encore* that "men, women, and children are but signifiers," thereby underscoring their status as discursive constructions (33). He also asserts elsewhere in *Seminar Twenty* that "the apparent necessity of the phallic function turns out to be mere contingency" (94). The more radical implications of these statements—which hint at the flexibility of gender constructs yet remain undeveloped in Lacan's own thinking—have been drawn out in more recent psychoanalytic thought. Roof, for example, argues that "Lacan's theory of subjective sexuation" offers "multiple possibilities for individual positioning in relation to" Lacanian sexual difference—possibilities "that interpret this difference through vectors that simultaneously define difference as binary and leave the binaries behind" (2016: 60). Moreover, I argue both here and elsewhere that

Lacanian "sexual difference" itself is a fundamental fantasy that is available for traversal: a movement that further mobilizes and thereby "transcends" gender (Carlson 2010: 66).

As a strategy for moving beyond the continued antagonisms of Žižek's ideologically contingent antagonism, Lacan's theory of traversing the fundamental fantasy has much to offer trans* psychoanalysis. Yet given Žižek's simultaneously defensive and provocative style and his apparent lack of willingness to engage serious psychoanalytic scholarship in trans* studies, it may well be that further elaboration of these claims would be best served by detaching itself from his discourse. After all, the rhetoric at work in "The Sexual Is Political" is not new to his writing. I end "Queering Žižek" by turning an early example of Žižek's transphobia against itself to demonstrate that his writings, despite his "vehement resistance" prior to 2016, reveal Lacanian "sexual difference" to be a fundamental fantasy that is available for traversal (Coffman 2012). In *The Indivisible Remainder*, he offers the example of a man who "dress[es] up as a woman and commit[s] suicide in public" as his "best candidate" for the authentic act that would prompt a traversal of the fantasy (1996: 170). In "Queering Žižek," I do not "endorse" this "inflammatory" statement but nonetheless observe that it marks "a startling concession" on Žižek's part "that the fundamental fantasy of (hetero)sexual difference is contingent, ideological, and subject to traversal" (Coffman 2012). Though in 2016 he finally acknowledges sexual difference's contingency, he continues to defend against that insight's implications for his theory. *The Indivisible Remainder* thus offers an illustration of the potential perils of traversing the fundamental fantasy, stressing that its outcome is not always positive and could even be destructive.

Similarly, "The Sexual Is Political" discusses a case from 1926 Turkey—the execution of the "very masculine-looking" Şalcı Bacı for wearing a fedora in defiance of the Hat Law (Žižek 2016c). Asserting that "rather than undermin[ing] sexual difference," Bacı "stood for this difference as such" by embodying "the impossible-Real of antagonism," Žižek uses her situation to argue—contra Butler—that "the formula of sexual antagonism is not M/F (the clear opposition between male and female) but MF+, where + stands for the excessive element which transforms the symbolic opposition into the Real of antagonism" (2016c). In "A Reply to My Critics"—which Žižek published in the *Philosophical Salon* in response to criticism of "The Sexual Is Political"—he repeats this argument while clarifying that it implies that "it is not transgender people who disrupt the heterosexual gender binaries; these binaries are always-already disrupted by the antagonistic nature of sexual difference itself" (2016a). However, unlike the reference to suicide in *The Indivisible Remainder*, Bacı does not function in "The Sexual Is Political" (or in Žižek's follow-up pieces) as an example of a subject who traversed the fundamental fantasy. Instead, Žižek uses her positioning as the "impossible-Real" to build up to the claim that it is not "sexual difference" but "the fantasy of a peaceful world where the agonistic tension of sexual difference disappears" that would be traversed (2016c). This argument rests on the overly strict Lacanian interpretation of gender variance that I addressed above.

That this line of thinking appears in "The Sexual Is Political" also makes clear that Žižek has not (or at least had not in the summer of 2016) read Carlson's 2010 article on "Transgender Subjectivity and the Logic of Sexual Difference," which quite rightly argues that "'transsexuality' is not in and of itself any more extreme a type of symptom than is 'man' or 'woman'" (2010: 65). In Carlson's analysis, "transgenderism," too, "figures not as a solutionless solution to the impasses of sexual difference but, rather, as an expression of the logic of sexual difference" (65). Although I advance here a Lacanian theory according to which "transgenderism" is not necessarily "a feminine solution," I concur with Carlson's assessment that neither "transsexuality" nor "transgenderism" need be positioned as any more exceptional than "'man' or 'woman'" (65). Rather, these are all options among the varied "differences" in gender that can emerge through the dialectic of desire (Roof 2016: 60).

More worrisome, even, than Žižek's positioning of transpeople as emblematic of sexual "difference as such" is the echo in "The Sexual Is Political" of the tacit approval he gives to violence against transpeople in *The Indivisible Remainder* (Žižek 2016c). In the context of an essay that exploits—by purporting to address—North American political movements seeking to secure transpeoples' safe access to public restrooms, Žižek's inability to see the injustice at work in Bacı's fate points to the limits of his argument. Although he is right that apparently "'normal' heterosexuals" also "often find it difficult to recognize themselves in prescribed sexual identities" because of the incommensurability that subtends all forms of subjectivity, he misses the ways that those who differ *openly* from heteronormative genders and sexualities are systematically at risk for violence in ways that heterosexuals and cisgender people are not (2016c). His ending assertion of the need to go beyond "the fantasy of a peaceful world where the agonistic tension of sexual difference disappears" thus avoids confronting the issues of social justice that trans* activists raise (2016c).

In the first of the two responses to his critics that Žižek subsequently published in the *Philosophical Salon*, he reiterates this concern that "the universal fluidification of sexual identities unavoidably reaches its apogee in the cancellation of sex as such" (2016a). Žižek's continued conflation of "transgender" and "postgender" makes this slippery-slope claim unconvincing (2016a). Yet he rightfully observes in his second response piece that some of his opponents, too, made themselves unpersuasive by operating within the narrow intellectual confines of "tweet culture," which relies upon superficial "snaps," "retorts," and "outraged remarks" rather than lengthier and more thoughtful forms of "argumentation" (2016b). Moreover, it is noteworthy that although he continues to decry his interlocutors' "self-righteous Political Correctness," his replies to them are both devoid of the callous dismissals that characterized his initial response in "The Sexual Is Political" to recent political contestation over transpeoples' need for safe access to public restrooms (2016b; 2016a). Both follow-up essays offer analysis that explicitly demonstrates Žižek's growing recognition that transpeople are regularly faced with injustices that emerge from "the violent imposition of gender norms" (2016a). He continues not to see, however, that transpeople are disproportionately burdened with these threats and acts of violence because they are structurally coerced into emblematizing the "antagonism" at work in even the most "normative" manifestations of sexual difference (2016a). Even though Žižek concedes in response to his critics that he "fully support[s] the struggle of transgender people against their legal segregation" and is "deeply affected by their reports of their suffering," he does not admit that his own philosophical system risks compounding their problems (2016a). Instead, he transforms their suffering into an ethics, asserting that "the ethical greatness of transgender subjects resides precisely in the fact that they" embody "the deadlock of subjectivity even more radically than other more 'normalized' subjects" (2016b). These claims reveal Žižek's own need to traverse the fantasy of (hetero)sexual difference that grounds his arguments—a movement that would relieve transpeople of the disproportionate burden they currently bear for what he rightly describes as an existential condition that is "universal" (2016a).

Žižek ultimately argues that transpeople achieve "ethical greatness" by refusing to embrace the *sinthome*, undergo temporary "depersonalization," and traverse the fantasy of (hetero)sexual difference (2016b). By contrast, Susan Stryker's introduction to the 1998 "Transgender Issue" of *GLQ* implicitly presents one way of achieving transsubjectivity by traversing the fundamental fantasy of (hetero)sexual difference. Viewed through the lens of my arguments in this essay, the passage that Stryker strikingly grafts from Lacan's "The Freudian Thing" into her text now shines in a different light. Stryker deliberately rips the passage from its original context, in which Lacan stages "the impulsive leap into the real through the paper hoop of fantasy" as an ineffective means of acting out in the imaginary order (Lacan 1977: 139). Placed in the context of the 1998 *GLQ* issue, however, this passage from Lacan offers up Stryker's own transition as an *avant la lettre* example of what I would call an act in the real (Stryker 1998: 151). She builds up to the citation from Lacan with the explanation that in the 1990s, informed by S/M and drag praxis as well as my graduate school exposure to speech-act theory, I began to see transsexuality not as an inauthentic state of being but rather as yet another communicational technology through which I could attend to the care of my self. It was a medico-scientific, juridico-legal, psycho-therapeutic apparatus for generating and sustaining the desired reality effects of my gender identifications through the manipulation of bodily surface, thereby extending those effects beyond dungeons or drag bars into more widely shared social spaces. Audience, I finally decided, was everything, and transsexual technology would be my vehicle for which Jacques Lacan called, in another context, "an impulsive leap into the real through the paper hoop of fantasy." Becoming "a transsexual" implied nothing more than the willingness to engage with the apparatus for one's own purposes. (151)

Here, Stryker reframes the passage from "The Freudian Thing" as a metaphor for the way her transition has enabled her to traverse the fantasy and reconfigure her relationship to the symbolic.

As Lynda Hart argues in a Lacanian analysis of lesbian S/M, the "'Real'. . . is precisely the possibilities of the imaginary that are located at the very limits of representation. Or, what representation fails to limit" (1998: 67). And as Stavrakakis argues, traversing the fundamental fantasy by engaging the *sinthome* requires that one take on "an impossible representation" so as "to 'represent' the impossible or rather to identify with the impossibility of its representation" (1999: 134). Hart argues that S/M is one way of accomplishing this task: it engages this border between the imaginary and the real, simultaneously mobilizing the "mirroring gaze of the lover"—who "promises to 'fix' us, to offer us constancy and coherency"—and pushing the limits of its representations to provoke the encounter with the real that could prompt the fundamental fantasy's traversal (1998: 160). Hart's theory acknowledges the oppressed subject's need for a fantasy to provide imaginary and symbolic support for their being but figures the theater of S/M as a venue in which to safely push its limits.

Similarly, Stryker's autobiographical anecdote in *GLQ* stresses the importance of "S/M and drag praxis" in the shaping of her transsubjectivity (1998: 151). These practices allow her to see "transsexuality" as part of an "apparatus for generating and sustaining the desired reality effects of my gender identifications through the manipulation of bodily surface" (151). This resonates with Hart's assertion that "Lacan's 'Real' is impossible, but through psychoanalytic time, it becomes the 'real-impossible.' For if the 'Real' is a psychic space that cannot be occupied, it is because it is not ocular. That is, it does not take place in the time or space of the ideological illusion called 'reality' because it exceeds a specular economy. Nonetheless, it does produce 'reality-effects,' not in spite of but due to its extra-metalinguistic status" (161). Thus, if the theaters of drag and S/M set an encounter with the real into motion, it is not to render it visible. The "reality-effects" of these practices are visible, but only as second-order phenomena. Stryker's personal narrative thus reveals the way in which transgender embodiment can be thought of as emerging in the gap between what Hart calls "the body" and "the flesh" (1998: 10). Both "illusions," the "'body' keeps us anchored in the worlds we have constructed in 'reality,'" and the "'flesh' is a place toward which we reach that always exceeds our grasp" (10). This formulation nuances the claim that Salamon makes via the phenomenology of Maurice Merleau-Ponty in her analysis of Lana Tisdell's remark in *Boys Don't Cry* that she has seen Brandon Teena "in the full flesh": trans* embodiment does not simply emerge as a phenomenon propped up through imaginary and symbolic (mis)recognition—as Salamon suggests—but rather subsists in the interstices of the imaginary, the symbolic, and the real (2010: 58).

This means that engagement with the real does not permanently consign Stryker to the dreaded realm of "abjection and death" that Salamon associates with Prosser's argument "that the transsexual body is 'unimpeachably real'" (Salamon 2010: 41). Instead, Stryker inscribes herself within a reconstituted network of "language," "meaning," "the symbolic," "relation," and "desire" (Salamon 2010: 41). In so doing, she exemplifies Lacan's account, in *Seminar Twenty*, of the emergence of embodiment through the process of coming to enjoyment through signification. As Ragland observes in explaining Lacan's concept of the fundamental fantasy, he connects "the body to language by way of unconscious fantasy": "He calls the fantasy a 'canker' that appears in the guise of enjoying the body—enjoying the Other as body, as well—in such a way as to disorganize one's experience of one's own body" (2004: 5). This subject "enjoys itself only by 'corporizing' (*corporiser*) the body in a signifying way"—a dynamic in which "enjoying (*jouir*) has the fundamental property that it is, ultimately, one person's body that enjoys a part of the Other's body" and in which "that part also enjoys" because "the Other likes it more or less" (Lacan 1998: 23). As Ragland explains, this theory suggests that "language creates one's imaginary body and defines one as a signifier that represents a subject for another signifier in a chain of articulations" (2004: 43). Lacan further notes that "a certain Sadian flavor" is at work in this dynamic—"an ecstatic, subjective flavor suggesting, in fact, that it is the Other who enjoys" (23–24).

When read in the context of recent queer expansions of Lacan's account of sexuation—rather than through the heterosexist vocabulary that animates Lacan's *Seminar Twenty*—this argument resonates productively with Hart's and Salamon's work. By suggesting that play with the signifier renders flesh incarnate— and that the fundamental fantasy is implicated in this practice—Lacan's thinking opens up a way of theorizing trans* embodiment as emerging through the encounter with the other via the Other. As Ragland explains, "insofar as certain *sinthomes*—identificatory *sinthomes* that are real knots—create the 'self' as a series of knots concerning the mother's unconscious desire and the place of the Father's Name signifier in the social realm, they can be undone. Lacan called this 'using the symbolic to work on the real'" (2004: 190–91). For Hart and Stryker, the practice of S/M provides a means of traversing the fundamental fantasy, undoing the knots between the three orders, and creating a new *sinthome*—one that, in the latter case, enables the achievement of transsexual embodiment.

Although Ragland asserts that "*sinthomes* always concern one's place in the masculine or feminine," whether that need continue to be the case in a trans-affirmative psychoanalysis is open to question (2004: 191). When Lacan argues that "man and a woman . . . are nothing but signifiers" who "derive their function from this, from saying [*dire*] as a distinct incarnation of sex" and in so doing demonstrate that "the Other . . . can thus only be the Other sex," the meaning of "the Other sex" in this formulation is subject to interpretation (2016: 39). Moreover, this process of signification in the other involves the exchange of the phantasmatic *objet a*—that which the desiring masculine subject mistakes as the cause of desire (127). It is important to note that Lacan describes the *objet a* as "*a*-sexual [*a-sexué*]" (127). Tim Dean emphasizes that this account of the *objet a* offers queers a theory of sexuality in which desire is "largely independent of gender"—a claim that opens up possibilities for theorizing diverse sexualities (2000: 216). I will add that, in an alternate translation, Lacan's description of this object as "*a-sexué*" also suggests that it is not subject to sexuation, even as the rest of *Seminar Twenty* insists that sexuation is driven by the incommensurate difference between masculinity and femininity (1998: 127). Lacan writes, for example, that "the Other presents itself to the subject only in an *a*-sexual form. Everything that has been the prop, substitute-prop, or substitute for the Other in the form of the object of desire is *a*-sexual" (127). Thus, despite the ease with which the meaning of "the Other sex" might be understood within the binary terms of *man* and *woman* that govern Lacan's own rhetoric, if we remain open to the varied "differences" he would reduce to "difference," then we can theorize the many different forms of embodiment that can emerge through signification—including trans* embodiment (Lacan 1998: 39; Roof 2016: 60).

Irreducible to the real, even as it is encountered via the Other, this process of embodiment partakes of both the "body" and the "flesh" as Hart defines them (1998: 10). If we understand the flesh as "a place toward which we reach that always exceeds our grasp"—and therefore as that which one can but need not necessarily choose to bring into closer alignment with one's body—then this theory can account for the varied decisions transpeople make with regard to contemporary options for physical and hormonal transition (10). Here I use the phrase "bring into closer alignment" rather than claim that the subject can fully align the flesh with the body, to underscore the importance of Lacan's argument that the subject is always split and subtended by internal divisions (10). Theorized in this fashion, transgender subjectivity need not be understood as a search for "ontological consistency," as Žižek claims (2016c). Nor need transgender embodiment be understood as "unimpeachably real," as Prosser would argue (Prosser, quoted in Salamon 2010: 41). Instead, it could be seen as yet another modality of split subjectivity.

Moreover, Lacan's assertion in *Seminar Twenty* that "there's no such thing as a sexual relation. It's only speaking bodies . . . that come up with the idea of the world as such," provides further support for Damon Young and Joshua J. Weiner's assertion that "the so-called anti-social thesis" in queer theory is a false binary, "as if queer social negativity engendered no bonds and queer collectivities did not take shape precisely in relation to some negation or incommensurability" (Lacan 1998: 126; Weiner and Young 2011: 224). Although Weiner and Young stress those forms of "incommensurability" that subsist "within the social," their point pertains to the world-making possibilities at work in individual and intersubjective modes of "incommensurability" as well (224). Lacan emphasizes that embodiment is achieved through a process that also invents the very "idea of the world as such," even as his exclusive references to "men" and "women" offer an impoverished sense of the gendered worlds it could entail (1998: 126).

Stryker's prolific work with word and image in the field of trans* studies uses signification to open up possibilities for new worlds of gendered embodiment. What she formulates as a "communicational technology" Gherovici understands as an "art"—one through which "writing" touches the "unsymbolizable" to remake "embodiment" (Stryker 1998: 151; Gherovici 2014: 255, 262). Whereas Gherovici's argument is grounded in transsexual memoir—a genre that also features prominently in Prosser's archive—my expanded account of the potential that the Lacanian *sinthome* holds for trans* studies also provides a means of reading the forms of embodiment at work in what Pamela Caughie calls the "transgenre" (2013: 503). Her concept of the "transgenre"—which builds upon Sandy Stone's 1991 suggestion that transpeople be considered "a *genre*—a set of embodied texts" who promise "*productive* disruption" of existing constructs (Stone 1992: 165)—allows her to offer a model of "transsexual life writing" whose "temporality of embodiment" differs from that offered in Lili Elbe's memoir (Caughie 2013: 519). Caughie's argument—that Virginia Woolf's fantastic novel *Orlando* offers a trans* inflection of Elizabeth Freeman's "queer vision of how time wrinkles and folds" (Freeman 2007: 163)—positions Orlando as a figure of "future embodiment," "as the deliberate shaping of a narrative of a life that might be lived, and liveable" (Caughie 2013: 519). I propose that narratives such as *Orlando* can be as effective for writing the *sinthome* as the transsexual memoirs Gherovici has considered. Defying the conventions of realist representation that typically ground autobiography, and shuttling back and forth in time to facilitate the imagination of hypothetical worlds, texts such as Woolf's allow for the perpetual reinvention of possibilities for gendered embodiment, possibilities that may or may not be grounded in bodily transitions or in the limited range of gendered pronouns that have heretofore governed Lacanian psychoanalysis.

However one might describe the "art" of trans* embodiment, written or otherwise, Lacanian approaches to transsubjectivity stress the importance of engaging the signifier in ways that touch the real (Gherovici 2014: 255). This engagement with the real can also involve traversals of the fundamental fantasy. As Stryker observed during her remarks at the opening session of the 2016 Trans* Studies Conference at the University of Arizona, "trans people know about deep change" (2016). This reformulation emphasizes profound subjective transformation, as do Lacanian accounts of traversing the fundamental fantasy. As Pluth explains about the "acts" that prompt traversals of the fundamental fantasy, "it is not the case that someone is simply changed by an act: he or she is reinaugurated as a subject" (2007: 102). Whether this movement reconstitutes the terms of the symbolic, imaginary, and real or whether it clears the way for what I elsewhere call "a more open-ended account of signification" than Lacan's early theory of the symbolic orders would allow, traversing the fundamental fantasy creates subjectivity anew (Coffman 2013: 47). This act enacts "deep change," yet it is important to note that Stryker's 2016 formulation does not hinge on transition as the only means of profound subjective transformation. Instead, she gestures out toward the broadest possible implications of "deep change" for gender and subjectivity.

In "A Reply to My Critics," Žižek insists that "transgender people . . . bring out the antagonistic tension which is constitutive of sexuality" in all its modalities, and that because they "bring out the anxiety that underlies every sexual identification," transpeoples' "message is universal" (2016a). When Carlson similarly observes that "there is something transgendered about the human subject, and that this transgenderism transcends notions of gender," she distinguishes transgender from transsexual using psychoanalytic arguments I would not (2010: 66). Yet importantly, her universalizing formulation both extends Žižek's thinking and sidesteps its greatest dangers. Her insistence on the "transgendered" aspects of all forms of subjectivity tacitly acknowledges his point that even apparently heteronormative subjects experience the incommensurability of the "masculine" and the "feminine" (Carlson 2010: 66). At the same time, her articulation of a Lacanian theory of transsubjectivity provides Lacanians with a way of seeing it as viable rather than as a misguided "attempt to avoid (the anxiety of) castration" (Žižek 2016c).

Both Žižek and Carlson remain faithful to Lacan's argument that sexuation mobilizes only "masculine" and "feminine" positions, however. Although Lacanians have a long history of opposing "historicist" and "rhetoricalist" readings of Lacan, I see no good reason to lock his theory of subjective sexuation into the language of "men" and "women" that was available to him in the 1970s (Copjec 1994; Dean 2000; Lacan 1998: 33). Lacan himself insists in *Seminar Twenty* that "men, women, and children are but signifiers" (1998: 33). Rather than reading Lacan more literally than he himself read the texts of the founder of psychoanalysis in his return to Freud, I propose that trans* theorists are especially well equipped to expand not only the vocabularies through which we talk about gender but also those with which we discuss sexual difference and sexuation. As Ragland demonstrates, Lacan's rereading of Freud may have been attentive to the letter of his text, but it was also transformative, tending to detach his predecessor's insights from anatomical difference and to consider instead their ramifications at the level of the signifier (Ragland 2004). If Freud is what Michel Foucault calls an "initiator" of a "discursive practice" that subsequent theorists revised and transformed, Lacan—who initiated first structuralist and then poststructuralist modes of psychoanalytic thinking—must be read similarly: not as a thinker whose own vocabulary need lock the formulae of sexuation into place for all time but as a theorist whose most radical insights reveal possibilities for their reformulation (Foucault 1977: 132). Žižek's own work, which usefully grafts Lacan's theory of the constitutive antagonism into other contexts such as class struggle, reveals—despite his denials—how generative further rearticulations of Lacan promise to be.

Trans* psychoanalysis is ideally positioned to engage in a transformative rethinking of Lacan's account of sexuation: one that goes beyond the limited vocabulary at work in the claim that "men and women are sexuated psychically, not biologically" (Ragland 2004: 179). Such a psychoanalysis should take the process of returning to Lacan's texts not as a mandate worshipfully to recite the master's mantras in antiquated vocabularies that are unresponsive to contemporary concerns but, rather, as an opportunity to mobilize repetitions of his ideas with twenty-first-century differences. If we graft Carlson's statement that "there is something transgendered about the human subject, and that this transgenderism transcends notions of gender" into the context I have offered in this essay—one in which Lacanian sexual difference is a fundamental fantasy available for traversal and need not permanently remain the only antinomy that structures the field of possibilities for gender and desire—then both her observation and Stryker's notion of "deep change" take on new resonances (Carlson 2010: 66). Rather than insisting upon "the antagonistic nature of *sexual* difference"—as do faithful Lacanians such as Žižek who consider "sexual difference" to be irreducible—we need to start talking about "the antagonistic nature of . . . difference" as the constitutive antagonism that drives desire, class division, and a variety of other social processes (Žižek 2016a, emphasis added). As Ruti observes, "the aim of Lacanian analysis" is to "loosen" constrictive "fantasies in order to create space for alternative life plots and directions, and in so doing expand the subject's repertoire of existential options" (2008: 498). Traversing the fundamental fantasy and engaging in "deep change" point to the contingency of both (hetero)sexual difference and the formulae of sexuation Lacan elaborates in *Seminar Twenty* (Stryker 2016). These kinds of transformations create myriad possibilities for "undoing" (Butler 2004) and redoing not only gender but also sexuation and sexual difference: ways in which we can understand not only "men" and "women" but also many other ways of being "sexuated psychically" as viable positionalities for desiring subjectivity (Ragland 2004: 179).

Chris Coffman is professor of English at the University of Alaska Fairbanks. She is the author of *Insane Passions* (2006) and *Gertrude Stein's Transmasculinity* (forthcoming in 2018) as well as numerous articles on modernist literature and queer theory.

Notes

1.   Pamela Caughie (2013) notes that in recent years "the French, for whom the word 'genre' (gender) refers not to sexuality but to linguistics, have begun to use 'transgenre' to translate the English 'transgender'" (502). At the time of this writing, this welcome development has not yet arrived in Lacanian approaches to transgender.
2.   This claim is followed by a series of preposterous analogies between sexual identities and class positions that only confirm Žižek's lack of familiarity with LGBT issues in North America.
3.   Žižek's claim that there is a "lack of contact" or "antagonism even" between "the struggle for sexual liberation" and these other struggles is baffling, however, given the currency of intersectional feminist and queer political analysis (2016b).
4.   For further explanation of the concept of the "fundamental fantasy," see Coffman 2012, Coffman 2013, Ruti 2008, and Ruti 2010.
5.   See Žižek's *The Sublime Object of Ideology* (1989) for a detailed discussion of the way in which the *point de capiton* quilts the three orders.
6.   See Chiesa 2007, Coffman 2013, Pluth 2007, Stavrakakis 1999, and Žižek 1989 for divergent accounts of the *sinthome* and Lacan's arguments about traversing the fundamental fantasy.

References

Butler, Judith. 1993. *Bodies That Matter: On the Discursive Limits of "Sex."* New York: Routledge.

———. 2004. *Undoing Gender.* New York: Routledge.

Butler, Judith, Ernesto Laclau, and Slavoj Žižek. 2000. *Contingency, Hegemony, Universality: Contemporary Dialogues on the Left.* London: Verso.

Carlson, Shanna. 2010. "Transgender Subjectivity and the Logic of Sexual Difference." *differences* 21, no. 2: 46–72.

———. 2014. "Psychoanalytic." *TSQ* 1, nos. 1–2: 169–71.

Caughie, Pamela. 2013. "The Temporality of Modernist Life Writing in the Era of Transsexualism: Virginia Woolf's *Orlando* and Einar Wegener's *Man into Woman.*" *Modern Fiction Studies* 59, no. 3: 501–25.

Chiesa, Lorenzo. 2007. *Subjectivity and Otherness: A Philosophical Reading of Lacan.* Cambridge, MA: MIT Press.

Coffman, Chris. 2006. *Insane Passions: Lesbianism and Psychosis in Literature and Film.* Middletown, CT: Wesleyan University Press.

———. 2012. "Queering Žižek." *Postmodern Culture* 23, no. 1.

———. 2013. "The Unpredictable Future of Fantasy's Traversal." *Angelaki* 18, no. 4: 43–61.

Copjec, Joan. 1994. *Read My Desire: Lacan against the Historicists.* Cambridge, MA: MIT Press.

Dean, Tim. 2000. *Beyond Sexuality.* Chicago: University of Chicago Press.

Foucault, Michel. 1977. "What Is an Author?" In *Language, Counter-Memory, Practice*, 113–38. Ithaca, NY: Cornell University Press.

Freeman, Elizabeth. 2007. Introduction to "Queer Temporalities," special issue, *GLQ* 13, nos. 2–3: 159–76.

Gherovici, Patricia. 2012. "The Transsexual Body Written: Writing as Sinthome." In *The Literary Lacan: From Literature to Lituraterre and Beyond*, 259–90. London: Seagull Books.

———. 2014. "The Art of the Symptom: Body, Writing, and Sex Change." In *A Concise Companion to Psychoanalysis*, edited by Laura Marcus and Ankhi Mukherjee, 250–70. Hoboken, NJ: John Wiley.

Gossett, Che. 2016. "Žižek's Transgender Trouble." *Los Angeles Review of Books*, September 13. lareviewofbooks.org/article/zizeks-transgender-trouble/.

Hart, Lynda. 1998. *Between the Body and the Flesh: Performing Sadomasochism.* New York: Columbia University Press.

Lacan, Jacques. 1977. "The Freudian Thing." In *Écrits: A Selection*, 114–45. New York: Norton.

———. 1993. *The Psychoses, 1955–56.* Book 3 of *The Seminar of Jacques Lacan*, edited by Jacques-Alain Miller, translated by Russell Grigg. New York: Norton.

———. 1998. *Encore, 1972–1973.* Book 20 of The *Seminar of Jacques Lacan*, translated by Bruce Fink. New York: Norton.

———. 2016. *The Sinthome, 1975–1976.* Book 23 of The *Seminar of Jacques Lacan*, edited by Jacques-Alain Miller, translated by A. R. Price. Cambridge: Polity.

MacCannell, Juliet Flower. 2008. "The Real Imaginary." *S: Journal of the Jan van Eyck Circle for Lacanian Ideology Critique* 1: 46–57.

Millot, Catherine. 1991. *Horsexe: Essay on Transsexuality.* New York: Autonomedia.

Pluth, Ed. 2007. *Signifiers and Acts: Freedom in Lacan's Theory of the Subject.* Albany: State University of New York Press.

Prosser, Jay. 1998. *Second Skins: The Body Narratives of Transsexuality.* New York: Columbia University Press.

Ragland, Ellie. 2004. *The Logic of Sexuation: From Aristotle to Lacan*. Albany: State University of New York Press.

———. 2006. "The Hysteric's Truth." In *Reflections on Seminar XVII: Jacques Lacan and the Other Side of Psychoanalysis*, edited by Justin Clemens and Russell Griggs, 69–87. Durham, NC: Duke.

Roof, Judith. 2016. *What Gender Is, What Gender Does*. Minneapolis: University of Minnesota Press.

Ruti, Mari. 2008. "The Fall of Fantasies: A Lacanian Reading of Lack." *Journal of the American Psychoanalytic Association* 56, no. 2: 483–508.

———. 2010. "Life beyond Fantasy: The Rewriting of Destiny in Lacanian Theory." *Culture, Theory, and Critique* 51, no. 1: 1–14.

Salamon, Gayle. 2010. *Assuming a Body: Transgender and Rhetorics of Materiality*. New York: Columbia University Press.

Salecl, Renata. 2000. Introduction to *Sexuation*, edited by Renata Salecl, 1–9. Durham, NC: Duke University Press.

Silverman, Kaja. 1992. "The Lacanian Phallus." *differences* 4, no. 1: 84–115.

Stavrakakis, Yannis. 1999. *Lacan and the Political*. London: Routledge.

Stone, Sandy. 1992. "The *Empire* Strikes Back: A Posttranssexual Manifesto." *Camera Obscura*, no. 29: 150–76.

Stryker, Susan. 1998. "The Transgender Issue: An Introduction." *GLQ* 4, no. 2: 145–58.

———. 2016. Untitled remarks at the opening session of the Trans∗ Studies Conference at the University of Arizona, Tucson, September 8.

Verhaeghe, Paul, and Frédéric Declercq. 2002. "Lacan's Analytic Goal: Le Sinthome or the Feminine Way." In *Re-inventing the Symptom: Essays on the Final Lacan*, edited by Luke Thurston, 59–82. New York: Other.

Weiner, Joshua J., and Damon Young. 2011. "Introduction: Queer Bonds." *GLQ* 17, nos. 2–3: 223–41.

Whittle, Stephen. 2006. Foreword to *The Transgender Studies Reader*, edited by Susan Stryker and Stephen Whittle, xi–xvi. New York: Routledge.

Žižek, Slavoj. 1989. *The Sublime Object of Ideology*. London: Verso.

———. 1992. *Enjoy Your Symptom! Jacques Lacan in Hollywood and Out*. London: Routledge.

———. 1996. *The Indivisible Remainder: An Essay on Schelling and Related Matters*. London: Verso.

———. 1998. "From 'Passionate Attachments' to Dis-identification." *umbr(a)*, no. 1: 3–17.

———. 1999. *The Ticklish Subject: The Absent Center of Political Ontology*. New York: Verso.

———. 2016a. "A Reply to My Critics." Philosophical Salon, *Los Angeles Review of Books*, August 5. thephilosophicalsalon.com/a-reply-to-my-critics/

———. 2016b. "Reply to My Critics, Part Two." Philosophical Salon, August 14. thephilosophicalsalon.com/reply-to-my-critics-part-two/.

———. 2016c. "The Sexual Is Political." Philosophical Salon, August 1. thephilosophicalsalon.com/the-sexual-is-political/.

Is the Phallus Uncut?

On the Role of Anatomy in Lacanian Subjectivization

JORDAN OSSERMAN

Abstract This article examines the role of anatomy in Lacan's theory of the phallus, focusing on a fundamental question insufficiently addressed in Lacanian thought: Does the penis really matter, and if so, why and how? The question is addressed by analyzing Lacan's work on the imaginary and symbolic dimensions of the phallus alongside a series of examples in which a subjective relation to the biological organ is particularly fraught, beginning with the case of David Reimer, a man who was raised a girl after losing his penis to a botched circumcision, and moving on to accounts from trans people and circumcised men who attempt foreskin restoration. The varying ways in which subjects strive to symbolize an imaginary encounter with lack are foregrounded, and anatomically determinist theories of sexual difference are challenged. Anatomy is shown to play a fundamental but nondeterministic role in the process of assuming a desiring position.
Keywords circumcision, David Reimer, Jacques Lacan, phallus, anatomy

The story of David Reimer, also known as the "John/Joan case," was first analyzed within the domain of queer theory in Judith Butler's essay "Doing Justice to Someone" (2004). Born in 1965 and assigned male along with his identical twin, David suffered from a botched circumcision that severely mutilated his penis. His parents sought the help of the psychologist John Money, who had become famous for his controversial views on gender (see Downing, Morland, and Sullivan 2014). Money advised them to raise David as a girl, whom they named Brenda, and keep secret the knowledge of his original embodiment and medical accident. This once celebrated experiment in gender (re)construction was widely decried a failure after David publicly revealed the tremendous gender dysphoria he experienced as a child and his decision, upon learning the facts of his birth, to declare himself a man and undergo medical masculinization treatments (see Colapinto 2000). Despite his apparent triumph over the trauma of his past, David eventually chose to end his own life.

TSQ: Transgender Studies Quarterly ★ Volume 4, Numbers 3–4 ★ November 2017 **497**
DOI 10.1215/23289252-4189938   © 2017 Duke University Press

Butler's essay unsettled the facile conclusions that many drew about David Reimer's story. His life was not a testament to gender essentialism against social construction, but, complex and singular, it was lived under the intense and relentless surveillance of people who treated David's every word "as evidence for or against a true gender" (2004: 70). However gender is ultimately inscribed, Butler argued, the question of how we choose to read it remains as fraught, and socially mediated, as ever.

Yet, David's story raises additional questions regarding the processes through which an individual comes to understand his or her physical body in relation to sexed subjectivity. Moving beyond Butler, I believe that a careful appraisal of certain aspects of Lacanian theory can make a useful contribution to our understanding of the often painfully felt discordances between subjective embodiment and anatomy.[1] To do this, I want to up take Shanna Carlson's call, in her short essay on psychoanalysis in the first issue of *TSQ* (2014: 171), for "work [that] needs to be done with the 'phallic function,' perhaps beginning with radical rereadings of the phallus as the signifier for the subject's lack-in-being." What is the relation between the anatomical organ and the "phallic signifier"? This brings us to the fraught topic of the alleged "phallogocentrism" of Lacanian theory (see, for example, Butler 1993). Indeed, if psychoanalysis is to withstand the criticism it has faced, then it must be made to answer the question: Does the penis really matter, and if so, why and how? Through an examination of clinical and biographical material—concerning transgender people and men who seek foreskin restoration—alongside Lacanian theory on the phallus and sexual difference, I hope to help elucidate the fundamental but nondeterministic role that anatomy plays in the process of assuming a desiring position as a subject. Examining the linkages between David Reimer's struggles and those of other groups of people provides a useful entry point into this problematic.

David's history has been noted for its many intersections with intersex and transgender concerns. Prior to David's "coming out" as a man, Money marshaled the case as justification for his medical standards for the treatment of intersex people: infants born with ambiguous genitalia should have them surgically "corrected" to resemble whichever sex the surgeon can more easily achieve (usually, the female sex) (Fausto-Sterling 2000: 66–71). The child, he argued, would adapt equally well to the norms of whichever sex had been surgically assigned. Money also pioneered relatively liberal sexual-reassignment protocols for adult transsexuals, overseeing one of the earliest male-to-female (MTF) surgical reassignments performed on US soil under the auspices of his Gender Identity Clinic in Johns Hopkins (Colapinto 2000: 37). When Brenda, at the age of eight, refused to undergo further vaginal construction surgery (presented to her as the necessary correction of a genital defect), Money had one of his transsexual patients attempt to convince Brenda of the benefits of the surgery (137). Brenda ran away in terror; the event precipitated the parents' confessing to Brenda the truth of her past and Brenda's subsequent transformation into David. Thus, neither intersex nor transgender in self-identification, David changed from boy to girl to man, a trajectory involving undergoing the same medical treatments that intersex and transgender people also often navigate, first, as Butler puts it, "in the name of [Brenda's] normalization," and finally, "in the name of [his return to] nature" (2004: 66): "He is, in his own view, a man born a man, castrated by the medical establishment, feminized by the psychiatric world, and then enabled to return to who he was to begin with" (65).

David's story resonates powerfully with yet another group of people, one that most commentators have overlooked: so-called intactivists, those who believe that infant male circumcision is medically and ethically unjustified and who campaign against the practice (see Osserman 2016). A subset of intactivists include men who attempt "foreskin restoration" to (re)grow the part of their genitals they feel to have traumatically lost. For them, circumcision is often thought of as a kind of medical castration, and the various skin-tugging techniques and implements they discuss on Internet forums represent the promise of a return to natural phallic wholeness (Kennedy 2015). David's story has been shared on intactivist websites as an extreme example of the dangers of circumcision (Chapin 2012).

Indeed, those who would allegorize David's life might consider the decision to circumcise him, the first of a long series of surgical interventions on his genitals, as the originary crime initiating his medico-psychological drama. David and his identical twin brother were delivered from the hospital foreskins intact (they were born in Canada where, unlike in the United States, circumcision is not practiced routinely), but both developed problems with urinating in the first few months of infancy and were diagnosed with phimosis, a condition in which the foreskin encases the head of the penis too tightly. Their doctor recommended that they both be circumcised. This was presented as an ordinary, low-risk procedure, and the parents readily consented. David was taken to the operating room first. The physician in charge used a new machine that, by an uncertain combination of technical malfunction and medical malpractice, burned off a significant portion of his penis. The doctors decided not to circumcise David's brother that day and, in a cruel twist of irony, his urinary problem eventually resolved itself without medical intervention (Colapinto 2000: 10–13). In fact, intactivists argue that doctors often misdiagnose as phimosis what is the natural state of the foreskin, which loosens as the boy's body matures, and that many physicians neglect nonsurgical alternatives to foreskin-related problems (CIRP 2008).

"Intersex," "trans," "intactivist": these three categories make an unlikely convergence in the case of David Reimer. What brings them together here is the question, made urgent in David's life, of what to do, or not to do, with a penis—and the consequences that follow.

Desire and Lack

Lacanians are fond of stressing the difference between the penis and the phallus (see, for example, Ragland-Sullivan 1982: 10; Lemoine-Luccioni 1982: 70). To "confuse" the two, it is held, is to make a fundamental error that erases the distinction between the biological organism and the psychoanalytic, desiring subject. Those who would accuse Lacan of covert biologism and gender essentialism rarely find their concerns allayed by the simple invocation of this distinction (Gallop 1987: 133–56; Butler 1993).

The phallus and the penis are not the same, and I will attempt to explain why. But, I find it both unhelpful and disingenuous that Lacanians so often shy away from explicitly examining the relation—even if it ends ultimately in a nonrelation—between the two. Some might be tempted to make Lacan "friendlier" to a critical audience by suggesting that the concept of the phallus, as the originary signifier of lack, can be maintained without the pesky penile referent: if the phallus is not really about the genitals, why not call it something more neutral, or neutered?[2]

Psychoanalysis, as a form of inquiry and knowledge, is concerned with the place where the desiring and *embodied* subject articulates herself in speech. To attempt to entirely divest the concept of the phallus from a relation to the sexual body is to turn psychoanalysis into a kind of pure semiotics, in which signifiers are considered wholly independent of the corporeal subjects who utilize them. While it is true that Lacan promoted a certain autonomy of the signifier—a call for analysts to listen to patients' speech *à la lettre*, rather than against the background of any presumed interior motive—concepts like the phallus exist in order to help understand, metapsychologically, what propels a living, bodily being into speech and into taking up a position in relation to lack. Though this need not necessarily prioritize the genitals, there are reasons worth exploring for why that bodily zone might become an important nodal point; this is made sharper when we consider the concerns of those who experience a need to alter their genitals in order to more satisfactorily inhabit a desiring position.

Lacan's central concern is the problem of lack and the ways that language both compensates for and reproduces, on a higher level, an originary experience of loss. There are various ways one could narrate this original loss. We can say that it concerns the moment when the infant first appreciates that it is not in a state of unity with the mother or its primary caregiver (hereafter, the "first Other"): that it is a separate body, receptive to pain and injury, that must find a way of articulating its needs to the Other in order to survive. In its first cry, and more dramatically in its first moments of speech, the infant sacrifices the illusion that it might exist as a homeostatic, self-sustaining unit. Moreover, by making use of a language that is not its own—the "mOther tongue," in Fink's formulation (1997: 7)—it gives up an imagined autonomy, alienating itself in the "discourse of the Other," which will give rise to the sensation that words are never quite adequate to describe one's inner experience, and the phenomenon of speech whose meaning exceeds or subverts what one intended to convey. This originary loss is not a chronological but a mythological moment, constructed retroactively, after the subject has entered into language and reckons with the sense of a lost *jouissance*, an unreachable primal pleasure or oneness (see Fink 1997).

This feeling is encapsulated by an anticircumcision activist, who writes in a blog post, "I don't know anything other than the sex life I've had, yet I can't help but wonder what my sex life could be like had I been allowed to keep the body nature designed" (Gualtieri 2012). For him, circumcision represents an irrecoverable loss in the form of a brutal separation from nature. It is not that he can remember the pleasures the foreskin once conferred—he would have been too young to appreciate them—but, rather, he experiences a painful, unbridgeable gap between what is and what, he imagines, could have been. For him, this is a loss that could, and ought to, be prevented, and one wonders whether the fantasy of undoing this loss, and the ability to blame concrete perpetrators, might serve a defensive function, providing an alibi for suffering and shielding him from an encounter with a more fundamental and unsettling loss.[3] This, indeed, is the Lacanian position: that behind every measurable, material loss lies the one for which we can never account, undo, or mitigate, in the face of which we must construct some kind of compromise to go on living. The problem of the phallus opens up at precisely this juncture, as a concept charged with both compensating for and holding open a lack that moves from the imaginary to the symbolic—from the body-image to language (and back again).

The Phallus: Imaginary and Symbolic

It is easiest to appreciate the relation between anatomy and Lacan's theory of the phallus if we begin our examination at the level of the imaginary. In his essay "Subversion of the Subject," Lacan (2006b) gives an account of the original registration, or "negativization," of the phallus in the imaginary mirror image.

In the mirror stage, the child is confronted with an image of itself from outside, a unity that appears superior to its internal experience of its body as inchoate and fragmented, promising wholeness and proprioceptive mastery. This is reinforced by an Other who encourages the child to recognize itself in its reflection ("Look, that's you!"). Psychoanalytically, this should be understood as an erotic phenomenon. The image of my body as a functional unit is enticing, and my libido becomes narcissistically invested in it. However, complete identification with the mirror image is impossible: there is always a gap between the external image of my body and my intuitive sense of embodiment. Moreover, such unity is undesirable, for if I were to completely coincide with my image, then my subjectivity would be soldered to the Other—there would be no distance between what I am and what the Other (here understood as the set of images/signifiers with which I am induced to identify) represents me as (Lacan 2006a: 75–81; Lacan 2006b; Van Haute 2001).

For this gap in the imaginary to be appreciated, it must somehow be registered. Something must stand for the failure of the body to be completely represented by the specular image. (This is, more generally, a central tenet of Lacanian theory: a lack only "counts" if it can register itself, however paradoxically, within the space in which it is lacking.) Lacan (2006b: 696) chooses to name this "something" the phallus: "This choice is allowed because the phallus—that is, the image of the penis—is negativized where it is situated in the specular image."

What does it mean for the phallus to be "negativized . . . in the specular image"? The child not only finds its body parts positively represented in the mirror image; it is also encouraged, by its caregivers, to recognize and enjoy them, as in games like "this little piggy went to the market," in which the toes are identified, delimited, and tickled. The genital zone is a unique exception to this process. No matter how liberal one's parents may be, there is almost always a certain reticence toward the child's genitals. The "negativization" of the phallus involves the way that the genitals are designated as an exceptional zone of the body image, invested if not with shame then at least with the sense that their relation to the Other is uniquely problematic (Fink 2004: 136). Thus Lacan suggests that the imaginary phallus is exempted from the libidinal investment in the specular image and thereby functions as the (necessary) gap between the image and the subject.

But why does Lacan designate the imaginary phallus as "the image of the penis" and not the genitals more generally? Prior to sexual difference, the negativization of the phallus might be thought to occur in the same way for boys and girls. However, it is when sexual difference opens up in the imaginary that Lacanian theory comes closest to anatomical determinism. This is an area in which scholars working within the intersections of psychoanalysis, transgender studies, feminist theory, and queer theory have offered important interventions into more orthodox Lacanian thought (see, for example Carlson 2010; Cavanagh 2015, 2016; Elliot 2010; Gherovici 2010; Gozlan 2014; Salamon 2010).

For Lacan, writes Van Haute (2001: 183), "the phallus marks for both sexes a crack in the specular image," but it does so in different ways: "An organ that might have been there for girls, and for boys, one that might have not." Both sexes experience a lack in relation to the image, but one is characterized more by the specter of loss (leading to the question, what must I do to preserve this?), the other by the sense of it already having gone (or not having emerged yet). Lacan (2006b: 696–97) offers an interesting explanation for why the penis—as that which is visually apparent yet excluded from the libidinal "immersion" in the specular image—comes to symbolize the phallus for both sexes: "Insofar as a part remains preserved from this immersion, concentrating in itself the most intimate aspect of autoeroticism, its position as a 'pointy extremity' in the form predisposes it to the fantasy of it falling off—in which its exclusion from the specular image is completed as is the prototype it constitutes for the world of objects."

In the visual order, the anatomical peculiarity of the penis—the fact that it appears as a "pointy extremity"—lends itself to the (prototypically Freudian) fantasy that this prized organ might fall off. The penis is thus held to be the first imaginary representative of the phallus not because of any apparent advantages over the vagina but because it presents itself as uniquely precarious, prone to detachment and the traumatic loss of autoerotic pleasure. The morphology of the penis—the simple fact that it protrudes from the body—coincides with its psychical inscription ("negativization") as something exceptional in relation to the other body parts, in order to produce the fantasy that this unique and excessive presence may all too easily become an absence. This, in turn, implies that those who have registered that they do not possess such an organ would develop a different relation to the imaginary phallus from those that do (though not nec- essarily an inferior one—it may, after all, be a relief to be freed of the necessity to erect phallic defenses).

This is perhaps Lacan's most "isolated" account of the imaginary phallus vis-à-vis the visual image of the penis, in the mythological time before the phallus has become an instrument of symbolization. In other instances, Lacan describes the relation between the biological penis and the signifying function of the phallus in different terms. For example, in seminar ten, Lacan enters into a dis- cussion on the importance of the loss of erection during sex: "Detumescence in copulation deserves to hold our attention as a way of highlighting one of the dimensions of castration" (2014: 168). If we take into account related remarks (45–46), he appears to suggest that what makes the penis uniquely "phallic" is that it visually indicates, in a seemingly concrete way, the presence or absence of sexual desire. The anatomical peculiarity of the penis visually lends itself to representing (one aspect of) symbolic castration: the split between the "natural" body and the subjective experience of enjoyment (linked to language). The flaccid penis sug- gests to the viewer that enjoyment escapes the subject's mastery. Moreover, the penile binary flaccid/erect allows for an initial bodily representation of the dia- lectics of presence/absence necessary to enter into signification. As Teresa Brennan writes, "The visual recognition of sexual difference is a channel connecting the heterogenous experience of the feeling, sensing body to something that is alien to it: the differential structure of language" (1989: 4).[4]

Additionally, in seminars three and four, Lacan (1997, 1998) discusses the child's registration of imaginary phallic lack in relation to his or her appreciation of the mother's desire for the father's penis, and of the apparent superiority of the paternal sexual organ. The child finds his or her genitals traumatically inadequate in comparison with the father's, ushering him or her into a sexually differentiated position of lack.[5] This brings us close to the problematics of the symbolic phallus, which we will discuss in a moment. For now, I wish to note that this account of the relation between the penis and the phallus relies on the child's interpretation of the Other's desire. The penis is significant here not because of any inherent anatomical function but because of the role it plays in the mother's desire. It is a process that would potentially be modified under alternative social structures (in which the penis is not valorized) and child-rearing scenarios.

How can we reconcile these accounts of the imaginary phallus with gender-nonconforming experience? Does the existence of those who possess a penis but occupy a feminine relation to the phallus, or vice versa, undermine Lacan's theory? Such gender-bending imaginary phallic dynamics are illustrated in an analyst's account of her assigned-female-at-birth analysand's process of transition. The patient wished to experience sexual and emotional vulnerability but felt that he could tolerate doing so only from the position of a man. He fantasized about wearing a strap-on and receiving oral sex, "letting someone take me over as I fall back on the bed and they are on top of me" (Suchet 2011: 178). He explained to the analyst that "masculinity is fragile, more fragile than femininity, so you need something biological, concrete to affirm it" (178). In this account, it appears that the analysand identified with a masculine relation to the imaginary phallus (one still threatened by the specter of loss). He eventually decided to alter his body in order to live this relation more fully. The phallic image as described by Lacan condensed something fundamental about the subject's relation to his body, but the possession of a biological penis was not the ultimate determinant.

To think about this problem within the terms of Lacanian theory, we might remember that to speak of any one of the registers of the imaginary, symbolic, or real in isolation from the others is always a reductive abstraction. One's assumption of the lack—that is, the trace of the real—within the imaginary always occurs in relation to the signifiers of the Other, and to desire—that is, the symbolic. This is not a chronological process, beginning with the childhood registration of anatomy and ending with symbolization, but a continuous and retroactive one, in which later significations, routed through the distorting effects of the unconscious, can dramatically impact imaginary identifications. For what is it at stake is not any kind of unmediated empirical reality but the psychical consequences of the relation between representation and the body, the fantasmatic interpretations of what the body means.[6] According to the later Lacan, in order to achieve some measure of stability, the subject must find its own singular (and necessarily nonconformist) way to "knot" together these relations between the different registers, with what he called the *sinthome*—hence the interest in the concept by those trying to bridge Lacanian psychoanalysis and trans concerns (see Cavanagh 2016; Gherovici 2010; Gozlan 2014). The question facing psychoanalytically informed transgender theory is thus: how can we appreciate the unique role of anatomy in subjectivization without slipping into anatomical determinism?

Let us move now into a discussion of the symbolic phallus in its role as a bridge between speech and the body, enabling the subject to ascend from the imaginary attempt to fill the lack in the Other to an acceptance of lack as the condition of desire (symbolic castration).

In its first manifestation, the lack in the Other "appears . . . as an enigma, an overwhelming emptiness that has no limit," writes Charles Shepherdson (2000: 70). The child perceives that there is something unfulfilled in the first Other. The Other's unpredictable comings and goings, and presences and absences, suggest to the child that something is wanting, or that the Other wants something for which the child cannot account.

The child will try any number of techniques to secure the first Other's love and attention, to fill in the Other's lack so that it will not look elsewhere for satisfaction. In Lacanian terms, this is the attempt to "be" the phallus for the Other. It is an imaginary pursuit, as, like the registration of the "crack" in the specular image, it is organized around the flawed hypothesis that there is a concrete "thing" that is lacking or threatened, which, if secured, will allow for unity and wholeness (Chiesa 2007: 60–96).

As language intervenes, this lack in the Other becomes differentiated and diffuse. It is no longer an imagined "thing" but rather a complex desire of the Other's. The child can now endeavor to decipher the Other's desire, whether through its attention to the Other's overt expressions of dissatisfaction or, more fundamentally, the unsaid or "beyond" consubstantial with signification: the gaps between signifiers, the fact that speech always evokes the possibility of more to be said. It is here that the symbolic phallus emerges, as the signifier that stands for the desire of the Other, "the privileged signifier . . . in which the role of Logos is wedded to the advent of desire" (Lacan 2006a: 581). This signifier functions as a veil, covering over the traumatic emptiness that the child has encountered with a positive signification (581).

Replacing the pursuit of imaginary completion with a relation to the symbolic phallus is a complex achievement. The child must find a way to accept that the first Other's desire is not for itself as an imaginary phallus but for something beyond, belonging to the order of language, culture, and society. In the more traditional Oedipal narrative, this is represented by the figure of the father, presumed bearer of the symbolic phallus, who puts a limit on the child's incestuous bond with the mother and compels the child to pursue socially acceptable alternatives. However, what matters for Lacan is not the physical father but the introduction of a third term, a structural place beyond the "(m)Other"-child dyad. The symbolic phallus thus becomes the means through which the child appreciates the larger network of socially viable positions it can inhabit. The child cannot "be" the phallus for the Other, but it can take on various phallic signifiers: interests, accomplishments, and ways of being in society that it deems desirable. These desires are never wholly independent of what one thinks the Other—which is no longer solely the first Other—wants/lacks. Rather, they are the subject's symbolic interpretations of the desire of the Other, once it has accepted the prohibition against/impossibility of the incestuous completion of the first Other (see Hook 2006; Chiesa 2007: 60–96).

This process of entering into signification begins from the subject's own body and moves outward. The child learns to differentiate the various parts and functions of its body in the imaginary and applies this rudimentary form of signification to its relations with the world. For example, a child sees a running tap and may think it is urinating (Leader 2011: 52). Gradually, the autonomy of the signifier will increase, such that "running tap" acquires a unique signification of its own; its connection to the body will be repressed and manifested only unconsciously, such as when the sound of a running tap incites the need to urinate. Thus, the dynamics involved in the passage from the imaginary to the symbolic are a kind of psychic acquisition and negotiation of signifying operations. The phallus is held to be the initial instance of this operation: through a process of metaphorical substitution, the imaginary organ (which, we recall, is already lacking) is transformed into a signifier, its connection to the body diminished but never totally extinguished. This signifier, the paradoxical signifier of lack, corresponds to the necessary gap in signification itself, the minimal difference required to set the chain of signifiers in motion (Van Haute 2001: 174). In other words, a subject finds a place for itself in language, without being *reduced* to language, by aligning its bodily encounter with imaginary lack to the lack in signification.

Mrs. G, a patient of the psychoanalyst Robert Stoller, starkly illustrates the potential difficulty involved in moving from the imaginary to the symbolic phallus. For most of her life, she was certain that there was a permanently erect penis inside her body. The penis appeared to serve a protective function, as she drew on the idea of it during moments of psychic distress, using it, in her words, "like a weapon" (Stoller 1974: 26). In the course of her therapy, she became less prone to psychotic breakdowns and more capable of handling difficult situations. In one such case, she suddenly remarked, "It would be nice if I had something like other people had instead of a penis to use in the same way that other people use whatever it is they have. I don't know what it is they have, but I know it's not a penis" (27). To relinquish the apparent security of a concrete object (or organ) in exchange for the symbolic phallus requires the subject to pose difficult questions and to find a way of symbolizing an unsolvable enigma.

Lacan (2006a: 581–82) underscores the dialectical process through which this interrogation of the symbolic phallus generates a subjective relation to desire: "The fact that the phallus is a signifier requires that it be in the place of the Other that the subject have access to it. But since this signifier is there only as veiled and as ratio of the Other's desire, it is the Other's desire as such that the subject is required to recognize—in other words, the other insofar as he himself is a subject divided by the signifying *Spaltung*." One confronts the fact that the Other is lacking and therefore desiring through the problematics of (the Other's desire for) the phallus. Because the phallus is a signifier, its significance can be grasped only through a relation to the Other. Yet in the struggle to discern the meaning of the phallus and consequently the Other's desire, one is ultimately forced to encounter the "otherness" of one's own desire.

To summarize: if, for Lacan, the child's earliest registrations of presence/ absence are thought to condense around the image of the penis, it is at the symbolic level that the child is held to make a dialectical advancement, replacing this imaginary struggle with the question of symbolizing the encounter with lack. The symbolic phallus "positivizes" the lack that the imaginary phallus represents, by expanding the range of "phallic possibilities" beyond the anatomical.

This does not mean that the penis is completely out of the picture. Consonant with our earlier provisos that the imaginary, symbolic, and real must always be thought of in tandem, the idea is that the desiring position one assumes as a response to the lack in the Other (symbolic phallus) is a more sophisticated analog of sorts to one's earlier relation to the negativized imaginary phallus. The assumption of subjective lack in the symbolic "maps onto" the sexually differentiated "crack" in the specular image, such that the effects of (and responses to) castration resonate from one register to the other.[7]

David Reimer's journey toward inhabiting a masculine position following the revelation of his past offers another helpful example of the dynamics involved in a subject's navigation from the imaginary to the symbolic phallus (see Gherovici 2010: 145–47). After his first of two phalloplasties, David took on a caricatured masculinity. He used the money awarded to him by the hospital that damaged his penis to purchase an expensive van with which he intended to "lasso some ladies," dubbing it "The Shaggin' Wagon" (Colapinto 2000: 187). However, his first sexual encounter ended disastrously, as he was forced to confront the inadequacies of his surgically (re)constructed penis. His second phalloplasty improved the organ's functionality, giving him the confidence to pursue a more successful relationship. With the trauma over his embodiment now somewhat lessened, his masculine identification also shifted. He gave up some of his earlier machismo and constructed a more nuanced identity, less attached to imaginary phallic insignia. His subsequent reflections on masculinity and withering critique of his medical treatment movingly demonstrate the difference between imaginary phallic ideals and the identificatory breathing space opened up by the symbolic:

> If I had grown up a boy without a penis? Oh, I would still have had my problems, but they wouldn't have been compounded the way they are now. . . . You know, if I had lost my arms and my legs and wound up in a wheelchair where you're moving everything with a little rod in your mouth—would that make me less of a person? It just seems that they implied that you're nothing if your penis is gone. The second you lose *that*, you're nothing, and they've got to do surgery and hormones to turn you into something.
>
> . . . From what I've been taught by my father, what makes you a man is you treat your wife well, you put a roof over your family's head, you're a good father. Things like that add up much more to being a man than just *bang-bang-bang*— sex. I guess John Money would consider my children's biological fathers to be real men. But they didn't stick around to take care of the children. I did. That, to me, is a man. (261–71)

Subjected to the violence of a culture that reduces sexual difference to the imaginary anatomical binary, David eventually articulates the view that, much as "bodies matter," the quest for psychical integrity and the inhabitation of sexed embodiment cannot take place solely on the imaginary plane. Neither his childhood anatomy, nor what he surgically acquired, finally determined his symbolic sexual positioning. Tragically, the circumstances surrounding David's suicide suggest that his realization may not have been secure enough to overcome the trauma of being forced to live as the passive object of Money's desire.[8]

Sexual Difference and the Phallus

In his earlier work, Lacan (2006a: 582–83) puts forth the theory that sexual difference involves assuming one of two possible relations to the symbolic phallus, that of "having" or "being." We are no longer speaking of the (imaginary) organ but, rather, the lack that the symbolic phallus represents. Is a subject preoccupied with possessing the signifier of desire (masculine), or with being that signifier, manifesting the lack that incites desire (feminine)?

Mark Rees's (1996) account of the unexpected satisfaction he experienced after being rejected by a woman offers an interesting illustration of Lacan's formulation. While seated in a concert, the recently transitioned Rees began to flirt with a woman nearby: "Her enthusiasm waned when she discovered that I was short (5′4.5″). It did, however, give me a few weeks' 'romance,' discovering where she lived and sending her flowers. . . . Although outwardly unsuccessful, the encounter did boost my confidence in myself as a passable male" (97). Although Rees did not possess the attribute that would secure this woman's affections— height, which he provides in a precise measurement, metonymically evoking penis size/a lacking imaginary phallus—he was reassured by the fact that his desirability was measured against masculine phallic criteria. If masculine and feminine subjects experience castration in different ways, Rees's desire, at one level, is to occupy a recognizably masculine relation to castration. "In my dreams I was forever pursuing a desirable woman but never quite reaching her," he writes (40), demonstrating a masculine form of desire, of longing for possession of the desired object.

Yet, the opposition of being/having the phallus, pertaining to the symbolic expression of sexual difference, can be misleading insofar as it may lend itself to the attempt to "diagnose" one's "true" sexual positioning as male or female. In the example above, could not Rees's desire be interpreted as a straightforward case of feminine penis envy? Did Rees want to have the phallus, or be seen to be lacking it? Would this type of reasoning not potentially invalidate trans self-identity by presuming to determine one's "real" gender identity?

It is important here to clarify the different meaning of sexual difference as it is theorized in psychoanalysis against the more commonplace notion of gender identity. For psychoanalysis, sexual difference concerns the desiring position one adopts in relation to castration, to the phallus; it is the way in which a subject copes with the impossibility of phallic wholeness. Masculinity involves the pretense that the phallus may ultimately be obtained, and femininity a more fundamental confrontation with its absence. In his later work, Lacan (1999) substantially develops this idea, formulating sexual difference in terms of a tension between modalities of *jouissance*, phallic *jouissance*, and a hypothesized *jouissance* "beyond the phallus" (or "non-all"). The concern is with how the subject derives enjoyment vis-à-vis the impossibility of phallic wholeness. Much has been said about Lacan's definitive move beyond anatomy in his "formulas of sexuation" (80; see, for example, Soler 1995; Morel 2000). Less remarked on is the fact that, with this latter theorization, one is no longer in a position to diagnose a subject as "truly" masculine or feminine, for "the 'formulas of sexuation' does [*sic*] not determine two kinds of subjects, but they express a field of tension in which each subject moves" (Van Haute and Geyskens 2012: 151). A subject experiences *jouissance* that can be characterized as "masculine" or "feminine," but this does not predetermine their symbolic identity as man, woman, or neither.

Gender, on the other hand, involves cultural representations (and hierarchies, power relations, etc.) *of* sexual difference; it is a mode in which the impasses of sexual difference are symbolized (see Elliot 1991). The way in which a culture, or an individual, produces and engages with gendered signifiers is necessarily contingent. The donning of feminine makeup may be a way of displaying one's castration to incite the other's desire—as the wearing of a tie may be a way of showing one has the phallus—but these acts may equally serve different purposes. As Carlson (2010: 63) writes, psychoanalysis has traditionally allowed a "too easy capitulation of the terms *feminine* and *masculine* to 'gendered' readings."

The examples we have examined so far show that imaginary phallic morphology plays a role—not predetermined by anatomy—in a subject's sexual positioning and in the way one chooses to represent one's positioning. Reimer's phalloplasties helped him symbolize a more complex masculinity; Rees's invocation of height helped him locate himself within a masculine economy. Both were driven not by phallic success but by the need to negotiate phallic inadequacy. However, the specific way in which one performs gender does not transparently denote one's desiring position. Though not unrelated, desire (what you want) is different from identification (who you want to be, and be seen as) (Rose 2016); trans identity, like queerness, involves a complex and messy mixture of both, and what compels a subject to take on such an identity will always be unique to that subject.

Psychoanalytically, what is crucial is not which kind of relation one occupies to castration but simply that one assume a symbolic relation to lack, moving from the fixation on imaginary phallic repair/completion into a desiring position engendered by the confrontation with and symbolization of loss. It is through assuming a symbolic position—rather than simply acquiring a set of gendered attributes—that a subject is able to participate in the social. As Rees (1996: 95) puts it, after assuming his masculinity, "Now my burden had been lifted I was enabled to look beyond myself to the world." Nevertheless, it may often enough be the case that for some subjects, the ability to assume a desiring position is predicated upon an intervention in the body, a subjective act in which one may free oneself from an "enslaving compulsion to become the desire of the Other" (Elliot 1998) by bringing the body into closer alignment with one's own desire.

Here we can locate Catherine Millot's mistake in *Horsexe* (1990), her notorious Lacanian analysis of transsexuality. Transsexuals, she argues, believe that, "by ridding themselves of the organ, they can also be rid of the signifier which, because it sexuates them, also divides them" (143). For her, to lose one's original genitals is a psychotic endeavor to overcome the loss inherent in signification, with potentially catastrophic consequences. This theory presumes that transsexuality exists in a cultural vacuum. It neglects the fact (perhaps more obvious today than when Millot wrote her book) that transition occurs within a heavily symbolically mediated context in which surgery often functions as a "rite of passage" (Bolin 1998) ushering a subject into a symbolic network. Anatomical change does not necessarily throw one into the abyss of the real. Rather, it can just as readily be a means of reknotting a particularly fractured relation between the real of the body, symbolic desire, and the imaginary phallus. Millot thus fails to consider that, for some, changing one's body may be a necessary step toward enabling the symbolization of imaginary lack.

The psychoanalyst Alessandra Lemma (2013) substantiates my claim in her account of her work with a male-to-female transsexual patient, Ms. A. In the early stages of the therapy, pretransition, Lemma was concerned that Ms. A, who suffered from severe panic attacks, seemed to be developing a rigid (imaginary) identification with her, going so far as to imitate Lemma's physical appearance and attire, which were linked to Ms. A's childhood attempts to secure her distant mother's love by dressing up in her clothes. After undergoing sex-reassignment surgery (SRS), she experienced disappointment that her new body was not as feminine as she had fantasized, painfully elaborating on this in the therapy. Over time it emerged that Ms. A did not envy her analyst's apparent femininity but, rather, "her perception that I inhabited a desired body and that could desire. Indeed she spoke about her perception of me as 'alive' and at ease with myself" (286). In a crucial therapeutic moment, Ms. A brought in old photos of herself as a boy and discussed with Lemma the traces of her pretransition self she cannot erase—symbolizing her sense of lack. Gradually, Ms. A adopted a more individualized femininity. Her panic attacks subsided, and "her experience of herself in the open spaces of life that she had once so feared, was one of greater potentiality" (286). In Lemma's account, it appears that Ms. A unsuccessfully attempted to repair the lack in the Other through imaginary compensation but was enabled by the combination of SRS and symbolization within the therapeutic space to secure her place as a desiring subject.[9]

Lacking Foreskin

While gender transition can involve any number of bodily alterations, foreskin restoration concerns a single organ: the circumcised penis. Nevertheless, some men experience complex psychic struggles surrounding the question of the foreskin.

In 1991, John Money—the psychologist responsible for David Reimer's gender reassignment—published an article in the *Journal of Sex Research* detailing the motivations of five circumcised men who attempted foreskin restoration through either surgery or stretching techniques. Four of the men had directly contacted Money's clinic in order to give an account of their experience and/or seek advice—one wrote to Money after seeing him in conversation with a transsexual woman on a late-night television show—and a fifth volunteered to share his experience on Money's request. Money focused on the erotic lives and fantasies of these men, responding in part to an earlier article in the *Archives of Sexual Behavior* (Mohl et al. 1981) that claimed that foreskin restorers were all homosexual and exhibited psychiatric disorders. Each man profiled was quite different in his motivations and life history, yet interestingly, all had very complex psychological and erotic relations to the absent foreskin.

One man dated the awakening of his desire to regain his foreskin to the time after he had an injured little finger surgically restored. "The constant reminder of seeing it has further intensified my feeling about replacing the missing foreskin," he said, drawing our attention to the phantasmatic bodily (in)congruities that feature in the imaginary register (Money 1991: 150). Although heterosexual, the man would regularly masturbate to pornography of men with intact foreskins. Another man, who also identified as heterosexual, discussed a period in his life when he cruised gay bars: "It seemed to me at that time that the guys to whom I expressed an interest, and liked because of their foreskins, rejected me for apparently reducing them to a little flap of skin" (151). After an unsuccessful attempt at foreskin restoration, it was within the visual-erotic field that he also managed to relinquish this desire, explaining that watching pornography of circumcised men "just sort of soothed my psyche, just to realize that it doesn't really make that much difference anymore" (152). Finally, a gay Jewish man with a penchant for collecting and repairing antique household appliances explained to Money that he became "fascinated with the challenge of restoring his foreskin" as an extension of his hobby: "It was as though, with a foreskin, he would become a one-of-a-kind model, namely a Jew who had a functionally restored foreskin" (153). Money writes that he was so successful that he was "accepted for membership in a brotherhood of The Uncut"—the nature of this fraternity is unspecified—and had "no additional body-image concerns" (154). Money concludes that in all cases, foreskin restorers "illustrate the marvelous complexity of the sexology of the body image in its relationships to erotic imagery and practices and to sexual orientation" (155).

Contemporary autobiographical accounts of foreskin restoration are usually less explicitly erotic, focusing much more on the subject's anger and alleged trauma over his circumcision, and the sense of wholeness and reclaiming of bodily autonomy he experiences through the restoration process. For example, one man complains, "People who have lost legs or [undergone] a mastectomy, everyone rallies behind them when they are pursuing self-image changes. But when it comes to men regaining what they lost, men who have been altered, where's their support to do this?" (Swanson 2015). However, Money's apparent prurience aside, the complicated intersection of desire with the attempted restitution of loss is unmistakable in all foreskin restoration narratives. Internet forums where men exchange techniques and advice are full of visual progress reports, in which men participate in (barely latent) homoerotic penis comparisons and marvel at the surplus of pleasure that restoration affords them.

Contrary to restorers' claims that they are simply retrieving an original nature that has been robbed from them, the ideals they attempt to achieve demonstrate the uniquely human unsatisfiability of desire, the fact that desire is grounded in lack. For example, the inventor of a foreskin restoration device did not stop after he achieved a "natural" foreskin length but documented his continued growth beyond the maximum "coverage index" (the name restorers have given for the degree to which the foreskin covers the head of the penis). His customers express identification with this limitless desire; one writes, "I can only imagine what it must be like to have full coverage 24/7!" (Kennedy 2015). These men have assumed a position of desire catalyzed by their attempt to fill in the lack in the imaginary (represented by the absent foreskin). Perhaps some find this a preferable alternative to confronting an endowment that they cannot control.

* * *

The wish to change one's gender is different from the wish to regrow one's foreskin. However, both situations involve the attempt to symbolically register loss and inhabit a relation to it, one that goes beyond the simple correction of a fault and connects in profound ways to the need to assume a sexed—that is, lacking/desiring—subjectivity.

Lacanian theory offers a way to account for what is at stake in a bodily intervention. Whereas, for example, the Jewish man (who interwove his desire for foreskin restoration with his repairman hobby) indicated a successful symbolization of imaginary lack, other foreskin restorers seem limited by fantasies of wholeness and imaginary restitution. One restorer's account appears to succumb to a superegoic imperative that does not suggest a high degree of subjective agency: "Learning of restoration changed me, slowly at first, but radically. I discovered a debt I inherited. Not my fault, but I owe wholeness to myself. The cost of restoration is mine. I must pay" (Carlisle 2016: 84). Similarly, trans narratives often describe the need to move beyond punishing gender ideals in order to successfully embrace transition. Rees (1996: 106) writes of counseling a trans male friend who "was obviously impatient to be 'fully male' and was working very hard to fulfill his perceived stereotype. We have to be realistic. His longings for what was impossible cost him a great deal."

Though it clearly plays a supporting role in symbolization, there is no simple answer to the function of the penis in the assumption of sexed subjectivity. Anatomy is involved in the registration of lack in the imaginary and, consequently, the never-ending journey toward subjectivization. Sometimes one must lose a penis to gain a relation to the phallus; other times, one must simply stretch some skin. Accounts of bodily intervention, whether trans, foreskin restorer, or otherwise, do not reveal to us the universal import of any single organ. What they do reveal is that physiology is only the starting point—necessary but insufficient—for desire to take shape.

Jordan Osserman is a PhD candidate in gender studies and psychoanalysis at University College London. His dissertation examines the significance of male circumcision from a psychoanalytic perspective. A summary of his research, titled "On the Foreskin Question," appeared in *Blunderbuss Magazine*.

Notes

1. For a sustained critique on the limits of Butler's theory of gender performativity in relation to trans embodiment, see Jay Prosser (1998: 21–60; see also Namaste 2000). Prosser convincingly argues that Butler's emphasis on sex as constructed fails to account for the psychic need, demonstrated in transsexual autobiographies, to inhabit a sexed body: "In transsexual accounts transition does not shift the subject away from the embodiment of sexual difference but more fully into it" (6). Prosser also criticizes Lacanian theory for an "ocular centric" account of the body that neglects its materiality, and for understanding transsexual surgery in terms of lack rather than the acquisition of wholeness (61–98). I believe that these latter criticisms wrongly portray the psychoanalytic theory of the split subject as inherently transphobic and naively idealize the desire for wholeness. This article is in part a defense of Lacanian theory in response to criticisms such as Prosser's. (See also Elliot 2001 for a sympathetic critique of Prosser.)

2. Tim Dean (2000: 32) attempts a more sophisticated version of the queer salvaging of Lacan in *Beyond Sexuality*, when he argues that Lacan's later concept of the object a "supersedes" the phallus.

3. The sense of an infinite, punishing gap between one's lived experience and a fantasied ideal of pleasure also corresponds to the Lacanian revision of the Freudian superego (Lacan 1999: 3; Žižek 2005: 54–68). Foreskin restoration advocates mobilize this superegoic dynamic as a means to bring additional circumcised men into the fold. For example, on the FAQ of a restoration website, the answer to the question in the heading "I'm Not Missing Anything by Being Circumcised; Why Should I Restore?" begins, "With no accurate means of comparison, the circumcised man does not know what he is missing. A man, colorblind from birth and thinking his sight is normal, might also never question his condition" (NORM 2016).

4. It is also worth considering the comic dimension of Lacan's morphological theory of the imaginary phallus. How can the entire psychic edifice of sexual difference rest on the

presence/absence of a pathetic, detachable little organ? Perhaps in pointing to the essential arbitrariness of the phallus, Lacan is also comically desanctifying it. For an extended treatment on this theme, see Alenka Zupančič (2008: 183–211).

5.   See Chiesa 2007 for an impressive exegesis of Lacan's work on this theme.

6.   Butler makes a similar interpretation of the relation between anatomical morphology and the phallus in "The Lesbian Phallus and Morphological Anatomy" (1993). However, she stages her argument in opposition to Lacanian theory. Neglecting to examine any of Lacan's work on the imaginary dimension of the phallus, she accuses him of performing a "repudiation of the anatomical and imaginary origins of the phallus" (47), which she interprets as a symptom of the heteronormativity allegedly underwriting his theory.

7.   I am reminded of a clinical anecdote shared in Lacanian circles. A patient complained of a sexual encounter with a man whose urethral opening was on the underside of his penis (a condition known as hypospadias). The analyst said, "So, something was not where it should be?" "Yes," the patient replied, "the hole was in the wrong place."

8.   For a brilliant Lacanian interpretation of David's struggle to inhabit his sexed embodiment, see Elliot (2010: 135–46).

9.   I thank the anonymous reviewer of this article for suggesting this formulation.

References

Bolin, Anne. 1998. *In Search of Eve: Transsexual Rites of Passage.* New York: Bergin and Garvey.

Brennan, Teresa. 1989. Introduction to *Between Feminism and Psychoanalysis*, edited by Teresa Brennan, 1–24. London: Routledge.

Butler, Judith. 1993. "The Lesbian Phallus and Morphological Anatomy." In *Bodies That Matter: On the Discursive Limits of "Sex,"* 28–57. New York: Routledge.

———. 2004. "Doing Justice to Someone." In *Undoing Gender*, 57–74. New York: Routledge.

Carlisle, G. Corey. 2016. "The Experience of Foreskin Restoration: A Case Study." *Journal of Psychology and Christianity* 35, no. 1: 83–88.

Carlson, Shanna. 2010. "Transgender Subjectivity and the Logic of Sexual Difference." *differences* 21, no. 2: 46–72.

———. 2014. "Psychoanalytic." *TSQ* 1, nos. 1–2: 169–71.

Cavanagh, Sheila. 2015. "Transsexuality and Lacanian Psychoanalysis." *CNPC 1: The Freudian Legacy Today.* cnpcrcpccom.files.wordpress.com/2015/12/6-cavanagh-transsexuality-and -lacanian-psychoanalysis.pdf.

———. 2016. "Transsexuality as Sinthome: Bracha L. Ettinger and the Other (Feminine) Sexual Difference." *Studies in Gender and Sexuality* 17, no. 1: 27–44.

Chapin, Georganne. 2012. "Honoring David Reimer." *Intact America* (blog), May 5. intactamerica .wordpress.com/2012/05/05/honoring-david-reimer/.

Chiesa, Lorenzo. 2007. *Subjectivity and Otherness: A Philosophical Reading of Lacan.* Cambridge, MA: MIT Press.

CIRP (Circumcision Information and Resource Pages). 2008. "Normal Development of the Prepuce: Birth through Age 18." November 14. www.cirp.org/library/normal/.

Colapinto, John. 2000. *As Nature Made Him: The Boy Who Was Raised as a Girl.* New York: Harper Collins.

Dean, Tim. 2000. *Beyond Sexuality.* Chicago: University of Chicago Press.

Downing, Lisa, Iain Morland, and Nikki Sullivan. 2014. *Fuckology: Critical Essays on John Money's Diagnostic Concepts.* Chicago: University of Chicago Press.

Elliot, Patricia. 1991. *From Mastery to Analysis: Theories of Gender in Psychoanalytic Feminism*. Ithaca, NY: Cornell University Press.

———. 1998. "Some Critical Reflections on the Transgender Theory of Kate Bornstein." *Atlantis: Critical Studies in Gender, Culture, and Social Justice* 23, no. 1: 13–19.

———. 2001. "A Psychoanalytic Reading of Transsexual Embodiment." *Studies in Gender and Sexuality* 2, no. 4: 295–325.

———. 2010. *Debates in Transgender, Queer, and Feminist Theory: Contested Sites*. Surrey, UK: Ashgate.

Fausto-Sterling, Anne. 2000. *Sexing the Body: Gender Politics and the Construction of Sexuality*. New York: Basic Books.

Fink, Bruce. 1997. *The Lacanian Subject: Between Language and Jouissance*. Princeton, NJ: Princeton University Press.

———. 2004. *Lacan to the Letter: Reading Ecrits Closely*. Minneapolis: University of Minnesota Press.

Gallop, Jane. 1987. *Reading Lacan*. Ithaca, NY: Cornell University Press.

Gherovici, Patricia. 2010. *Please Select Your Gender: From the Invention of Hysteria to the Democratizing of Transgenderism*. New York: Routledge.

Gozlan, Oren. 2014. *Transsexuality and the Art of Transitioning: A Lacanian Approach*. New York: Routledge.

Gualtieri, Tom. 2012. "Our Bodies, Our Choices—Part One." Weeklings, August 31. theweeklings.com/tgualtieri/2012/08/31/our-bodies-our-choices-part-i/.

Hook, Derek. 2006. "Lacan, the Meaning of the Phallus, and the 'Sexed' Subject." In *The Gender of Psychology*, edited by Tamara Shefer, Floretta Boonzaier, and Peace Kiguwa, 60–84. Lansdowne, South Africa: Juta Academic.

Kennedy, Amanda. 2015. "Masculinity and Embodiment in the Practice of Foreskin Restoration." *International Journal of Men's Health* 14, no. 1: 38–54.

Lacan, Jacques. 1997. *The Psychoses, 1955–56*. Book 4 of *The Seminar of Jacques Lacan*, translated by Russell Grigg. New York: Norton.

———. 1998. *La relation d'objet, 1956–1957 (The Object Relation)*. Book 4 of *Le séminaire (The Seminar)*. Paris: Seuil.

———. 1999. *On Feminine Sexuality: The Limits of Love and Knowledge (1972–1973)*. Book 20 of *The Seminar of Jacques Lacan*, translated by Bruce Fink. New York: Norton.

———. 2006a. *Écrits: The First Complete Edition in English*. Translated by Bruce Fink. New York: Norton.

———. 2006b. "Subversion of the Subject." In Lacan 2006a: 671–702.

———. 2014. *Anxiety, 1962–63*. Book 10 of *The Seminar of Jacques Lacan*, translated by A. R. Price. Cambridge: Polity.

Leader, Darian. 2011. *What Is Madness?* London: Penguin.

Lemma, Alessandra. 2013. "The Body One Has and the Body One Is: Understanding the Transsexual's Need to Be Seen." *International Journal of Psychoanalysis* 94, no. 2: 277–92.

Lemoine-Luccioni, Eugénie. 1982. *Partage des femmes (The Sharing of Women)*. Paris: Seuil.

Millot, Catherine. 1990. *Horsexe: Essay on Transsexuality*. New York: Autonomedia.

Mohl, Paul C., et al. 1981. "Prepuce Restoration Seekers: Psychiatric Aspects." *Archives of Sexual Behavior* 10, no. 4: 383–93.

Money, John. 1991. "Sexology, Body Image, Foreskin Restoration, and Bisexual Status." *Journal of Sex Research* 28, no. 1: 145–56.

Morel, Geneviève. 2000. "Psychoanalytical Anatomy." In *Sexuation*, edited by Renata Salecl, 28–38. Durham, NC: Duke University Press.

Namaste, Viviane. 2000. *Invisible Lives*. Chicago: University of Chicago Press.

NORM (National Organization of Restoring Men). 2017. "I'm Not Missing Anything by Being Circumcised; Why Should I Restore?" www.norm.org/whyrestore.html (accessed March 8).

Osserman, Jordan. 2016. "On the Foreskin Question." *Blunderbuss Magazine*, May 10. www .blunderbussmag.com/on-the-foreskin-question/.

Prosser, Jay. 1998. *Second Skins: The Body Narratives of Transsexuality*. New York: Columbia University Press.

Ragland-Sullivan, Ellie. 1982. "Jacques Lacan: Feminism and the Problem of Gender Identity." *SubStance* 11, no. 36: 6–20.

Rees, Mark. 1996. *Dear Sir or Madam: The Autobiography of a Female-to-Male Transsexual*. London: Cassell.

Rose, Jacqueline. 2016. "Who Do You Think You Are?" *London Review of Books*, May 5.

Salamon, Gayle. 2010. *Assuming a Body: Transgender and Rhetorics of Materiality*. New York: Columbia University Press.

Shepherdson, Charles. 2000. *Vital Signs: Nature, Culture, Psychoanalysis*. New York: Routledge.

Soler, Colette. 1995. "The Body in the Teaching of Jacques Lacan." *Journal of the Centre for Freudian Analysis and Research*, no. 6: 6–38.

Stoller, Robert. 1974. *Splitting: A Case of Female Masculinity*. London: Hogarth.

Suchet, Melanie. 2011. "Crossing Over." *Psychoanalytic Dialogues* 21, no. 2: 172–91.

Swanson, Jess. 2015. "Uncut: A Look at the Wacky, Wrinkly World of Foreskin Restoration." *Village Voice*, October 6. www.villagevoice.com/news/uncut-a-look-at-the-wacky -wrinkly-world-of-foreskin-restoration-7747950.

Van Haute, Philippe. 2001. *Against Adaptation: Lacan's Subversion of the Subject*. New York: Other Press.

Van Haute, Philippe, and Tomas Geyskens. 2012. *A Non-Oedipal Psychoanalysis? A Clinical Anthropology of Hysteria in the Works of Freud and Lacan*. Leuven, Belgium: Leuven University Press.

Žižek, Slavoj. 2005. *The Metastases of Enjoyment: Six Essays on Women and Causality*. London: Verso.

Zupančič, Alenka. 2008. *The Odd One In*. Cambridge, MA: MIT Press.

Queeranalyst

KATE FOORD

Abstract How do we work, and write of, the resistance of psychoanalysis to queer, to trans, at the same time as we work and write the contribution that psychoanalysis makes to these same fields? In addressing this question, this article focuses on the Lacanian clinic as a failure *and* as the site of a singular and powerful contribution to working with gender. In doing this, it resists the impulse to identify all Lacanian psychoanalysts as the same and instead engages with particular Lacanian analysts whose writing makes a contribution to the clinic of gender.
Keywords psychoanalysis, Jacques Lacan, queer, clinic

P sychoanalysis is not one. Freudian, neo-Freudian, Kleinian, Lacanian, others. There are, within each of these psychoanalyses, not one but many "saids" and "sayings" of gender.[1] As many as there are analysts, perhaps?

This proposition produces an immediate tension: between a theoretical approach that looks to the theoretical edifice for answers, and another way, which might be called that of the transmission of psychoanalysis. Jacques Lacan invited his audience, at the beginning of the fifth session of his seminar *Ou pire* . . . (*Or Worse* . . .): "I ask you to refuse what I am offering you because it's not that" (Lacan 1971–72). This invites us to consider the position we take up in relation to our desire to find answers in his work. If this gives us an idea of what not to do, it also raises the question of how this invitation can be taken up, and how in particular it can be applied to the question of how Lacanian psychoanalysis and queer theory speak to each other, intersect, work together, collide, encounter.

The transmission of psychoanalysis is what allows the formation of other analysts: transmission is not a teaching but a speaking from a particular position. An analyst is one who speaks, and one of the forms of that speech is testifying to crucial problems in psychoanalysis.[2] Discussions of formation tend to focus on the passage from analysand to analyst: how an analyst is formed. What happens to psychoanalysis in the process of the formation of an analyst? Nothing less than the reinvention of psychoanalysis, according to David Pereira (1998a: 6).

TSQ: Transgender Studies Quarterly ∗ Volume 4, Numbers 3–4 ∗ November 2017 **518**
DOI 10.1215/23289252-4189947 © 2017 Duke University Press

Does this reinvention necessarily entail the deconstruction of one's gender? Is this a necessary event in the formation of an analyst, in the passage from analysand to analyst? My proposition in this article is that this is the case. As someone who locates herself and her work within a school of psychoanalysis, I locate my thinking on these questions in and through the clinic. In this article, I will pursue the idea of the necessary deconstruction of gender through discussion of the queer clinic and with particular emphasis on three clinical events of an analysis: the preliminary sessions, the transference, and Lacan's notion of the semblant, as terms that orient us as practitioners to what is happening in the room with each analysand.

But we cannot go straight to that question because it isn't possible to discuss a queer psychoanalytic clinic without first acknowledging that there is considerable and justifiable distrust of psychoanalysis and of psychoanalysts from the queer community. So first, I will turn to the differences between these forms of distrust: of psychoanalysis itself, and of psychoanalysts.

Worst

First, to psychoanalysts. Jean Allouch has very powerfully and movingly recounted the shameful history, and shameful instances, of psychoanalysts' "contributions" to the often violent business of making a body fit into the assumed binaries of anatomical difference.[3] Here I will cite just one example from a chapter entitled, simply, "Shameful," from *Lacan Love*. Allouch was given a copy of Pat Califia's book *Sex Changes* from a member of the audience of a seminar he gave in Argentina. This audience member told Allouch of his experience: that, as an adolescent, his body could not be read unambiguously as male or female, and into that uncertain space medical practitioner and psychoanalyst alike made interventions that did not refer to their patient's own knowledge of his gender:

> When this person was an adolescent, the father had consulted medical specialists, who asked the advice of a psychoanalyst, who, from the lofty heights of his knowledge, declared: "She's a girl, it must be said." Except that this person knew that he was a boy—which counted for nothing in what followed: a terrible ordeal of painful surgical operations. . . .
>
> This expert, let me tell you know, was Lacanian. His bias compromises everyone who belongs to the same community. He is proof that Lacanian Psychoanalysis has not known where to stand as far as transsexuality is concerned. Where to stand? That is, to remain radically outside the medical and the pastoral. (Allouch 2007: 202–3)

Can psychoanalysts themselves remain radically outside these medical and pastoral domains, as Allouch indicates here is imperative—not simply distinct or different, but radically outside? It isn't possible to ask this question without also asking its corollary: does the theory itself take up the proper position outside the medical and pastoral?[4] My emphasis in this article, however, is not on the theory itself as a body of answers but, rather, on how the analyst takes this up in her function as analyst.

In her excellent article on the possibilities of a more fruitful encounter between gender theory and psychoanalysis, Shanna T. Carlson asks why Lacan's assertion that "there's no such thing as a sexual relationship"—and that there is a feminine way to respond to that failure and a masculine way to respond to it—does not offer proof that psychoanalysis is impoverished in the field of sexuality and sexual difference, compared with the approaches of Judith Butler or Jacques Derrida, for example. For Carlson, the answer is that psychoanalysis is far from impoverished in this field; however, "where psychoanalysis may appear limited resides in part in what I interpret as the too easy capitulation of the terms feminine and masculine to 'gendered' readings" (2010: 63). For Carlson, this capitulation is on the part of both gender theorists reading (and sometimes writing) psychoanalytic texts and psychoanalytic theorists reading and writing psychoanalytic texts. Given my emphasis in this article on the clinic and of the formation of analysts, I will take up this question of the capitulation to gendered readings from that perspective, the perspective of the clinic and of the formation of analysts.

In his eleventh seminar, Lacan had already defied, "perhaps for the first time in history," the myth of the complementarity of the sexes:

> Aristophanes' myth pictures the pursuit of the complement for us in a moving, and misleading, way, by articulating that it is the other, one's sexual other half, that the living being seeks in love. To this mythical representation of the mystery of love, analytic experience substitutes the search by the subject, not of the sexual complement, but of the part of himself, lost forever, that is constituted by the fact that he is only a sexed living being, and that he is no longer immortal. (1981: 205)

As this makes clear, the subject of psychoanalysis is not a subject who finds but, rather, is a subject who lacks. As an effect of the signifier, the subject lacks in two ways: in being, as the living being cannot be wholly represented by a signifier (as the signifier is by its nature differential and finds its identity only in being different from, thereby by definition it is not-all); and for whom the Other is lacking, in that there is no signifier in the Other that tells the subject who or what they are. The subject is doubly divided as an effect of the signifier: divided from being by meaning and from meaning by being; and divided by discourse, as the discourse of the Other is full of holes and therefore raises doubt for the subject about who or what s/he is there. This double division cuts the subject between being and meaning, and between the subject and the Other. Nowhere can the subject be fully represented, or said. This makes clear how it is that the desire of the subject is the desire of the Other, but not in any positive sense: it is engendered by what is lacking in the Other, by these intervals in the discourse of the Other.

This is why Lacan can say that "sexuality is represented in the psyche by a relation of the subject that is deduced from something other than sexuality itself. Sexuality is established in the field of the subject by a way that is that of lack" (1981: 204). Some nine years later, in his twentieth seminar, *Encore*, Lacan elaborates his theory of sexuation, which David Pereira takes up in an important contribution to both the writing of and the practice of the clinic of the intersex. In writing of Gina, a person who has a medical diagnosis of "partial androgen insensitivity syndrome," Pereira quotes the surgeon who is "presiding over" the course of surgery: "I can make a girl" (1998a: 214). This is the same grammatical stance of the "analyst" Allouch refers to earlier: "She's a girl, it must be said." In both cases—Allouch's analyst and Pereira's surgeon—the girl is already said, before s/he can say.

Pereira takes up a different position, a listening, which allows for a saying. The analyst attends to the dilemma articulated in the speech of the analysand. Gina says, "A real girl is a human and a pretend girl is not a human" (213). While the surgeon plants his flag in her body to stake his territorial claim to the unification of sex and gender, the real making, the making of a pathway for Gina with her gender is what the analysis does with what she says. What she arrived at, notes Pereira, was

> the point of realizing that the Symbolic universe is not bound by the parameters: real girl/pretend girl; that this opposition, proposing a certain contradiction, does not constitute ALL. Therefore, her assertion [a real girl is human, a pretend girl is not human] constitutes a naming which functions as a contingent inconsistency. For Gina, in the face of an impossibility, which leaves no room for an exception, she forges a function of exclusion, of inconsistency, which supports her existence. How does she do this? Through the assumption of this assertion as a naming function. Through that designation, . . . which she uttered in the moment in her analysis in which something began to change, which carries with it a NOT ALL. (220–21)

The signifier *girl* offers the analysand an opening into the contingent inconsistency of language. Through its capacity to be coupled with both *real* and *pretend*, it shows its instability; it shows the impossibility of language to say it all. We might say then that the name the analysand uses for herself is not simply *girl* but is held in the grammar of her whole utterance, expressed thus: "A-real-girl-is-human-a-pretend-girl-is-not-human." This naming function is the capacity to take up a subjective position in relation to the holes in discourse and to be animated by the enigma of desire the subject thereby encounters (of the Other and of the subject). It therefore marks the possibility of living, of not being petrified by the signifier in its imaginary consistency, of *girl*.

Pereira is elucidating here the making of a name through the knotting of the three registers, a knotting that hears the symptom that the analysand brings to the analysis and reworks it into a creation of the analysis itself. This creation, which provides the support of her existence as a desiring subject, occurs through "that naming which allows for a co-existence of the Imaginary, the Symbolic and the Real of her sex" (222). *Sex*, here, refers neither to biology nor to a cultural construction of gender but, rather, to a logic of subjectivity produced by the fact that subjectivity is an effect of the signifier.

Who is to say, prior to an analysis, what it is that has to be reworked? This is where the danger of the capitulation to gendered readings arises: the analyst who is deaf to Gina's saying is the one who will read not according to a logic but according to the body or the culture. This is the one who will say, with the surgeon, "I can make a girl," or with Allouch's uncastrated analyst, "She's a girl, it must be said." As Allouch has made clear, an analyst does not, ever, enter this domain—if she or he does, there is no hope of functioning as an analyst. If one enters the medical or the pastoral there is no hope of hearing the analysand, who is the only one to say the name from which to live. Who is to hear this and speak with the analysand in such a way as to provide the conditions under which the analysand can make such a name for herself?

This question—who is to hear?—takes us back to the question with which I began: if we take one of those who has this capacity to hear to be an analyst, is it necessary that the analyst has deconstructed—or now we can say reknotted—gender such that it is possible to hear the particular saying of the analysand with respect to that question?

The push to imaginary consistency is very strong in the field of gender: everywhere we hear versions of "I can make a girl, it must be said." This push to resolution reveals a particular mode of suturing of what we might call "the symptom of gender," the one that is brought to the clinic in the form of the suffering of the analysand. Psychoanalysis is as critical as queer theory is of the resolution of gender questions—indeed of any questions of identity and difference—into such an imaginary prison. At the same time, psychoanalytic theory does something other than critique such a resolution. Lacan, particularly in his later seminars, invented and elucidated the theory of the knotting, the necessary knotting, of the imaginary with the symbolic and the real. In this theory, Lacan both elucidates and performs the knotting of the three registers—in the descriptors "male" and "female" for the two different ways in relation to castration, in the use of "phallus" as the index of the grammar of castration, psychoanalysis is performative of gender in Butler's sense (Butler 1990): in psychoanalytic terms, it repeats this imaginary function of gender (at the same time as it does not suppose that this is all).

Psychoanalytic theory doesn't merely lend itself to gendered readings, while remaining pure or purely logical. It is mired in the language of this imaginary—the "masculine" and "feminine"—while elucidating the necessity of the function of the not-all. Psychoanalysis needs a sex change, then, in the same way that the culture does: it needs a divesting, a hanging up of the terms upon which these gendered readings are hung, a reknotting that takes place through the function of naming. And who is to do this divesting, given that we cannot look to Lacan for this?

It seems clear that this gendered language is a major barrier to many people who might otherwise be interested in entering psychoanalysis. Yet there is a certain imperviousness of psychoanalysis to the critiques of this language from outside its own theories and practices. No doubt there are many reasons for this, some of them compelling reasons regarding the necessity to theorize and show the knotting of the three registers, or the importance of maintaining psychoanalysis in its distinct contribution to theorizing sexuality and sexual difference. But this is not the entire explanation. It also may point to psychoanalysts' inability to renounce some ideas, ideas that are not psychoanalytic at all and that precede Sigmund Freud, including that the (so-called) anatomical distinction between the sexes determines gender identity.

How then, might we read the following argument, in David Pereira's article on Gina and sexuation, that the anatomical distinction between the sexes "supports" a logical distinction? He writes, "The impasse of the Real of sex . . . is the concern of psychoanalysis, whereby 'sexual identity' always returns to a Real and the enigma of sex is organized in reference to that division of speaking beings whose anatomical distinction supports a logical distinction" (1998a: 213). What does "supports" refer to here? First, the anatomical distinction at the level of the body is not equivalent to the logical distinction created by the signifier: it is not *the* difference but an imaginary consistency that underpins, in an architectural sense, a differentiating structure that is an effect of language and that makes the body as lived. Anatomical distinction supports—as the imaginary supports. We cannot do without the imaginary; nor can we do with the imaginary only. This would be to usher in the nightmare scenario of a world that is utterly consistent, with no holes, no gaps within which to desire. This nightmare scenario is one where an anatomical distinction is the difference between men and women (where there are only two). This would truly be the petrification of gender categories. It is precisely this collapse into imaginarized difference that Pereira "treats" in his work with Gina.

How is it that, in contrast to this case of Pereira's, sometimes psychoanalysts get the clinic of gender so wrong? I will return to Allouch's conclusion that the transphobes, those Lacanian pastorals he speaks of in his article, are "not castrated," where castration, he says, is something that transsexuals know all about. This is a stunning reversal of the position he is so stringently critiquing, of the accusation "get real, you're castrated," so often made to the transsexual using the authority of Lacan. Here, Allouch says to the so-called analyst: look to your transgender clients for those who know something about castration. Allouch's damning criticism here is that this "Lacanian" is no analyst at all, for to have gone through an analysis to its end is to find a way with castration, which means one must have submitted to it. And what is castration but the effects of being a subject of language, which necessitates taking up a position (a forced choice) in relation to the cut of language or the logic of difference?

And from this discussion, a question arises for Allouch: "Is a psychoanalyst qualified to decree someone's *gender*? To signify to this someone, and to those close to him, his position in the erotic? To play the expert? The answer is *no*, and it applies to anyone and everyone. Psychoanalysis does not identify itself with a gender. If it does, it is not psychoanalysis. In other words, the object-cause-of-desire [*l'objet cause du désir*] does not lend itself to being represented" (2007: 203). Cold comfort, then, for those seeking an analyst to work with on questions of gender, to say that not every person who designates themselves a psychoanalyst functions as one. How, then, does one find an analyst with whom one can work, if one wants to? And that raises two questions: Why would anyone who is questioning gender want to undertake an analysis? Why would they address that question to an analyst rather than anyone else?

Queeranalysis

I divide my clinical work between private practice and a queer LGBTIQ mental health service located in a nongovernment organization. This is more than a division between private and public. The queer team comprises a group of mental health clinicians who work in many different modalities (mostly not psychoanalytic). Whatever your gender identity or sexuality, if you work in this team, you are "queer" (where that is always itself a contingent inconsistency). This is assumed, both by colleagues within and outside the service, as well as by clients and referrers. What that "queer" is, however, is not reducible to sexuality (i.e., it is not a synonym for *lesbian* or *gay*, even though some of these colleagues or some clients might think of it that way), and nor is it reducible to transgender. The queerness of the team is an instance of how "queer" functions in the world. If

"I am queer" is an identity statement in contemporary life, it is also not possible to hear it or utter it as only that, as if it were prior to Judith Butler's *Gender Trouble*. Although queer can't be reduced to an identity or a sexuality, at the same time it is always under pressure to limit itself to that, both within the queer community and outside it. Queer as a deconstruction of the very notion of identity and as a critique of identity as a stabilizer of the body resists the idea of such a stable and noncontradictory identity.

Most people on the team do fall within the category of "lived experience" clinicians, which might be defined as those people who have had direct experience of suffering from the difference between queer and straight, cis and trans, polyamorous or monogamous. Ensuring that the team is one rich in lived experience is a response—and a very effective response—to the well-documented problems that our community faces in seeking mental health services from mainstream providers: discrimination, lack of understanding, abuse, and sometimes refusal of any service altogether.

Is lived experience, then, an answer to the problem of how to hear what is addressed to you as a clinician? There are ways in which it is not, but at the same time, it is vital that the team is made up in the way that it is, of people who can and do testify to this experience. What can we suppose about what that lived experience produces as a position from which to respond? *Lived experience* can be a synonym for *identity*, where "I am queer like you" closes over and even refuses difference. Then there is the possibility that we, those with lived experience, question and deconstruct from that position. This would be lived experience as the breaking down, deconstruction of binaries—sexuality and gender—which comes through finding oneself abridged of mainstream or "normal" definitions of gender and/or sexuality. Lived experience, then, like queer, is not a statement of identity; it is, rather, a position or a possibility of hearing. In this way, lived experience could be defined as the name of that gap between identification and difference. Another word for this is *psychoanalyst*—not *psychoanalysis* but *psychoanalyst*. Would a psychoanalyst belong in this team of queer clinicians simply by virtue of being an analyst? In this definition, yes.

I'd like to pursue the question I asked earlier—how to find an analyst with whom one can work—by speaking of the preliminary sessions of an analysis. What difference does it make when the body of the analyst is read as queer?

The Preliminary Interviews

The preliminary sessions of an analysis are those sessions that either prepare the ground and open onto an analysis or terminate in a punctuation in which no analysis will take place. This does not necessarily mean that no further sessions will take place but, rather, that the process will not be a psychoanalysis.

Of these preliminary interviews, Lacan says:

> When someone comes to see me in my office for the first time and I punctuate our getting down to business with some preliminary conversations, what is important is that it is the confrontation of bodies. It is precisely because it is from this that it starts, this encounter of bodies, that from the moment when one enters into the analytic discourse, there will no longer be any question of it. But the fact remains that at the level at which discourse functions which is not analytic discourse, the question is posed of how this discourse has succeeded in catching hold of bodies. (1971–72, session of June 21, 1972)

In the queer clinic, before I enter the room in which there is this confrontation, this encounter between bodies, I am read as queer in a way that is not determinable. What difference does it make, when the body of the analyst is read as queer, to this encounter of bodies that Lacan speaks of here? It is precisely because bodies are involved that he refers to the necessity of the prohibition of sexual contact. The analyst is open to this confrontation as that which is made possible by the absolute impossibility of a sexual encounter. For this impossibility there must also be a possibility, the one that is negated. This prohibition makes possible the transformation of the rapport of these fecund preliminary sessions into a different kind of rapport: that is, the negation is important here precisely because the encounter of bodies carries an intensity that the analyst cultivates and directs. This bodily encounter might be called the "support of speech." And surely the queer clinic has possibilities (to be negated) that are particular to it. What are they?

Lacan elaborates, in the next paragraph of *Ou pire* . . . , on the question of how the discourse that is not analytic discourse catches hold of bodies: "At the level of the discourse of the master, from which you are as a body, moulded, don't pretend otherwise, however you gambol about, this is what I will call feelings and very precisely good feelings. . . . It is jurisprudence and nothing else that grounds good feelings" (1971–72, session of June 6, 1972). You are as a body created by the discourse of the master—not somehow ontologically intact prior to the law, but created by it. Those whom he addresses in this seminar "gambol about," presumably trying to avoid knowing anything of the source of these good feelings. There is a system at work that molds, recognizes, and confers legitimacy on existence, and it is thereby productive of these good feelings. A jurisprudence applies to all within it: some find themselves against the law in some instances, but all are recognized as subjects of it. Their existence is affirmed by it. Is the clinic Lacan refers to here one that applies to all within it?

Many people have written, using Giorgio Agamben's (1998) work, on the homosexual as *homo sacer* (see Mills 2001). The homosexual is one of those who, subject to the sovereign power that decides what is within and what is outside the juridical order, is rendered *homo sacer*, outside the sphere of law, the exception. The homosexual is one—and of course not the only one—who can be killed with impunity. I can't hear the word *homosexual* without that definition implied, and I don't think I'm alone in that. It is the history of the homosexual body in the master's discourse, a history that presents itself in the clinic. I can't hear the word *transsexual* without that definition implied. And both these words are difficult to hear—as they are heard within psychoanalysis—as anything other than an indication of the failure of generations of analysts to hear particular analysands. The homosexual body, the transsexual body, is grounded not in the good feelings of legal recognition but brought to ground in the abjection of *homo sacer*. This is one way of defining the lived experience that queer clinicians bring to our work with LGBTIQ people. This is not to argue that we all have the same lived experience, either as individuals or as groups. There is a very particular and intense suffering of the trans community in this regard, and an undoubted shift— elevation?—of the *L* and the *G* in the LGBTIQ quilt bag. And yet, in Australia at the moment, we are listening, yet again, to the next wave of homophobic and transphobic hatred in relation to a postal survey on marriage equality.[5]

In a recent interview, Judith Butler was asked, "What kind of questions, concerns, interests, directions would for you be the ones that would keep Queer Studies alive as a project?" She responded by elaborating on a few of these questions and concerns, including, finally, this one: "What kind of life do I want to live with others, if the life that we are seeking to live is not regarded as a life at all?" (Ahmed 2016).

If the transsexual and homosexual is *homo sacer*, then perhaps queer is that which works to establish a possible jurisprudence, in the sense that Judith Butler names it: that one's existence is regarded as a life. That's all. It says nothing of truth within that system but simply establishes the possibility of being included within it, the legality of one's existence rather than the lethality of it. These are, I think, the discursive conditions that produced the impetus for the creation of the queer clinic where I work, and these are also part of the context in which a person seeks out a queer clinic. This queer jurisprudence is enacted in the smallest details: someone can tell us, for example, what their name is and what pronoun they use; this name is the name that we will call them by for all purposes other than legal ones; and their legal name is registered but unused and, more importantly, unusable except to identify them for legal purposes.

This is not to advocate a jurisprudence as a model for the analytic encounter, for the work in the clinic. It is, rather, to do two things. One is to acknowledge what Lacan points to in his discussion of the preliminary sessions: that the encounter of bodies *is* an encounter of the material effects of the master's discourse. One of these material effects, I am arguing, is the abjection the transsexual and homosexual is cast into by this discourse, abjection that occupies the body. This is precisely the opposite of those "good feelings" that Lacan refers to in the initial encounters in what might be called the "clinic of the heterosexual matrix." The good feelings of the queer clinic, then, can be located here: in the openness of the body of the analyst to a participation in the confrontation—the encounter—of the preliminary sessions as something other than this abjection, this compulsory heterosexuality that is still the place psychoanalysis occupies in the master's discourse.

There are profound limits to the usefulness of these "good feelings" in the clinic, not least because the idea of a jurisprudence posits an idea of truth as said, and possible to say, rather than the half-said that is the truth possible in the psychoanalytic clinic. Any other definition of truth refuses both the constitution of the human subject through language and the ex-istence of the unconscious thereby created.

How do analysands address, read, and encounter the body in these first sessions? I haven't had anyone say to me, "I'm straight, and I'm wondering if you are or if you know anything about this." I am the subject of the transferential "supposed to know," such that the person can speak. Whether that means I am supposed as straight I don't know because I don't ask people what they think I am. I wait to find out, and to try to hear who I am, what I am, in the transference for each analysand.

But I think the other question, "I'm queer, and I'm wondering if I can address my speech to you," is implicit if not directly stated in (all?) preliminary sessions, occasionally excruciatingly so. It isn't absent from the queer clinic, despite all the queerness there. There are in the queer clinic too, notwithstanding that this word *queer* defines in some important way both clinician and client, where there is a sudden, isometric pressure in the room of a question: do you regard mine as a life? I feel this as a bodily tension, a nausea-inducing tension, contributing to the form of the preliminary conversations.

So in the clinic caught within the heterosexual matrix, people—queer people—are anxious about what will happen with this question of existence: of being returned immediately to a trashing of one's existence in the first encounter with a clinician, to being a "transsexual" or a "homosexual," or of not being able to work out, from those first encounters, whether such a trashing is in store. So the "good feelings" of the queer clinic get them through the door and into the building and into the room and into speech and, hopefully, into transference and into analysis. And that's quite a long way.

The Transference

I asked earlier, how does the analysand find an analyst to work with? These preliminary interviews are one possible pathway—they are two-way interviews. They are a forum in which to encounter an analyst or to find that there has been no encounter and therefore there can be no analysis. To know that there has been an encounter that opens onto an analysis is to be affected by a transference, an intensification that is a response to and directed toward a "subject supposed to know." The knowledge of the analyst at play in this transference is a knowledge of lack:

> Our function, our power, our duty is certain and all the difficulties are resumed in this: it is necessary to know how to occupy one's place in so far as the subject ought to be able to locate in it the missing signifier. And therefore through an antinomy, through a paradox which is that of our function, it is at the very place that we are supposed to know that we are called to be and to be nothing more, nothing other than the real presence and precisely in so far as it is unconscious. At the final term, I am saying at the final term of course, at the horizon of what our function is in analysis, we are there as that, that precisely which remains silent and remains silent in that he wants-to-be. We are at the final term in our presence our own subject at the point where it vanishes, where it is barred. (Lacan 1960–61, session of May 3, 1961)

For a transference to function accordingly, the analyst cannot believe that she or he knows the missing signifier, the one that says the analysand. Rather, the analyst must know how to function as the place of that missing signifier for long enough to enable the analysand to work through the defiles of the signifier to the fall of the analyst as the subject supposed to know. One can see how quickly, how violently, an analysis with a queer person could run aground on an analyst's belief that, for instance, he "really is" a man, or she "really is" a woman.

Jean Allouch, in the final chapter of *Lacan Love*, says, "As a psychoanalyst, do I need to identify the analysand as hysteric, or psychotic, or God knows what else—black or white, man or woman? No. Rather, I must utterly abstain from doing so if my intervention is going to reach its liberating final term; if I must become myself that erotic object that the analysand will reject in order to be able to attain some degree of ease in his life at last" (2007: 213–14). Perhaps it's not so controversial to say that an analyst doesn't need to identify the analysand as psychotic or neurotic, black or white, man or woman. It is less easy to abstain, to "utterly abstain," from doing so. How does one utterly abstain from identifying someone as man or woman, straight or gay, when the culture in general—and perhaps even the analysand—so forcefully and repeatedly insists that this is possible and even necessary? Our culture still works hard every day to keep this binary in place. How do we know when we are failing to abstain? This is a question that implicates all of us, queer included: we are all formed in the master's discourse and not necessarily in ways that we know. We all know of the lateral violence that this can produce: the assumptions made of the legitimacy of others' claims (witness the radical feminist refusal to give up the category "woman" for anyone other than the cis-gendered).

Isn't transference enabled not only when one doesn't label the analysand but when one doesn't label anyone, analyst included, so that they might be taken for the semblant that they may be transferentially? One has to be an actor as an analyst: to lend oneself to the transference is also to respond from one's position in the transference, not as oneself. It is much harder to find one's place in the transference and to respond from that place than it is to answer from the position of your identity: I wonder if it isn't harder when the question touches on gender (if you are cis-gendered) or sexuality (if you identify as straight). How to be a semblant when something with which you identify is so close to that which is naturalized by the culture? Queer speaks to the soft spot of psychoanalysts here, as it refuses the so-tempting imaginary consistency of "I am a man" or "I am a woman." Acting from the position that such statements are fictions is the only way that one can take up the position of analyst for each analysand, and not just for those with whom the "good feelings" of a heterosexual/cis-gendered jurisprudence apply.

This capacity to work with whoever presents to the clinic is not the only thing that matters in deconstructing gender in this way. What also matters in the failure to abstain from knowing the gender or sexuality of one's analysand is that it produces them as already known and thereby resists and perhaps makes impossible the invention of their own name in the analysis. It refuses difference: not only the difference of gender or sexuality but, more importantly, the unsayable difference that language makes.

Are not the contemporary descriptors of gender—*genderqueer, genderfluid, transgender, nonbinary, nonbinary trans, transmasculine, transfeminine*—assertions that there is no attribute that delineates between man and woman, that "man" and "woman" as predicates can be replaced with others—others that more accurately name both the necessity of identity at the same time as registering the impossibility of identity as a holder of difference? Many of these names undo the binary logic of "I am a man" or "I am a woman": they register the impossibility of the delineation *and* the limits of a name, any name, to say what you are. Perhaps they are a response to the general cultural disavowal that gender itself is a theater as well as to the insistence that it is only cross-dressers, transmen, and transwomen who are players in this theater, rather than all of us.

What is it that might make us deaf to hearing in this way—to hearing, not as a man or a woman, as straight or gay, as black or white but hearing in a nonpredicative way? This question, for an analyst, might be framed as, can you hear from your place in the transference as semblant of the object *a*? One thing that produces such deafness is the belief that there is an affinity between the object *a* and its envelope—for instance, a belief that because one is a queer clinician one is more easily taken for this object by someone similarly queer. In *Encore*, Lacan warns analysts to be suspicious of the idea of an affinity of object *a* to its envelope (1999: 93). Belief in such an affinity makes it impossible to function as an analyst.

> One must not make the mistake of believing that we are already at the level of semblance. Before the semblance, on which, in effect, everything is based and springs back in fantasy, a strict distinction must be made between the imaginary and the real. It must not be thought that we ourselves in any way serve as a basis for the semblance. We are not even semblance. We are, on occasion, that which can occupy that place, and allow what to reign there? Object *a*. (95)

As we heard earlier from Allouch, psychoanalysis "does not identify itself with a gender. If it does, it is not psychoanalysis. In other words, the object-cause-of-desire [*l'objet cause du désir*] does not lend itself to being represented" (2007: 203). This impossibility of representing the object *a* is an impasse in formalization, and this impasse is the only basis on which the real can be inscribed. We discussed an instance of this inscription in Gina's formulation, "A real girl is a human, and a pretend girl is not a human." The queer clinic runs as much risk of failing to provide the conditions under which this impasse can be produced as any clinic, or more accurately any clinician, who takes themselves as already the semblance of the object, stumbling and falling on the ground of identification and failing to establish the conditions for difference to emerge and find its name.

Queeranalyst

Queer offers something of great value to psychoanalysis because it invites a pollution of the categories. It actively works to acknowledge the cultural function of semblance and participates in cultivating a certain know-how with becoming semblant. In this, it is Lacanian. Or perhaps more to the point, the Lacanian analyst is queer—not as an identity but, rather, as an "identity crisis" (Pereira 1998b: 4).

The psychoanalyst is queer inasmuch as she or he has attained this position of the maximum possible distance between identification and desire, between the ideal and the object, such that it is not only difficult to say "I am a woman" but also "I am a psychoanalyst." No being is guaranteed.

Kate Foord is a member of the Freudian School of Melbourne, School of Lacanian Psychoanalysis, and is the general manager of Queerspace at Drummond Street Services, which comprises an AOD (alcohol and other drug) service, an intimate partner violence service, and mental health services, as well as group programs, community events, and peer workforce development for LGBTIQ+ people and their families in Melbourne, Australia.

Acknowledgment

A version of this article was given at a seminar of the Freudian School of Melbourne, School of Lacanian Psychoanalysis, in August 2016. I would like to thank my colleagues in the school for their comments and questions on that day, which have informed some of the reworking of the article into its current form.

Note

1.   There is a considerable body of published work on the topic of queer theory and psychoanalysis. In particular, over the last two decades, see Braidotti and Butler 1994; Butler 2004, 2000, 1990; Copjec 1995; Dean 2000; Edelman 2004; Grosz 1994; Layton 2004; Stryker and Whittle 2006.
2.   In "The Proposition of the School of 1967," Lacan names three ways in which the passage from analysand to analyst is the passage to speech: the enunciation of the analyst, the testimony of the pass, and testifying to crucial problems in psychoanalysis (Lacan 1995).
3.   Jean Allouch was a student and analysand of Lacan's and a member of the École freudienne de Paris until its dissolution, and he contributed to the founding of the magazine *Littoral*. He is currently a member of the École lacanienne de psychanalyse and is director of Éditions Epel's series the Great Classics of Modern Erotology, which is working to make known, in France, North American feminist, gay and lesbian studies, and queer theory. (His website, jeanallouch.com, contains details of his writings, his publishing projects, and audio and video of presentations.) *Lacan Love* was an outcome of Allouch's engagement with the Freudian School of Melbourne, School of Lacanian Psychoanalysis, during a recent visit. Jean Allouch practices psychoanalysis in Paris.
4.   I understand Allouch's use of the term *pastoral* here to refer to the caring professions or the caring attitudes taken up within the medical. This is to be distinguished from a Lacanian ethic, in which the analyst cares less (about cure and normalization, for example) and therefore enables a different form of "treatment," one in which a subject is enabled to invent a position (and a gender if that is what emerges). Such an invention is not an effect of the pastoral but of the radical difference aimed at in analysis, and this is what the article goes on to show.
5.   There have been pamphlets distributed in Australia recently that assert that marriage equality will produce the next stolen generation. This refers to the genocidal policy of successive Australian federal governments, which resulted in the forcible removal of Aboriginal children from their parents and of Aboriginal people from their land over many generations.

References

Agamben, Giorgio. 1998. *Homo Sacer: Sovereign Power and Bare Life*. Translated by Daniel Heller-Roazen. Stanford, CA: Stanford University Press.

Ahmed, Sara. 2016. "Interview with Judith Butler." *Sexualities* 19, no. 4: 482–92.

Allouch, Jean. 2007. *Lacan Love: Melbourne Seminars and Other Works*. Edited and with a foreword by María-Inés Rotmiler de Zentner and Oscar Zentner, translated by Carolyn Henshaw. Lituraterre. Ourimbah, Australia: Bookbound.

Braidotti, Rosi, and Judith Butler. 1994. "Feminism by Any Other Name." *differences* 6, nos. 1–2: 27–61.

Butler, Judith. 1990. *Gender Trouble: Feminism and the Subversion of Identity*. New York: Routledge.

————. 2000. *Antigone's Claim*. New York: Columbia University Press.

————. 2004. *Undoing Gender*. New York: Routledge

Carlson, Shanna T. 2010. "Transgender Subjectivity and the Logic of Sexual Difference." *differences* 21, no. 2: 46–72.

Copjec, Joan. 1995. "Sex and the Euthanasia of Reason." In *Read My Desire: Lacan against the Historicists*, 201–36. Cambridge, MA: MIT Press.

Dean, Tim. 2000. *Beyond Sexuality*. Chicago: University of Chicago Press.

Edelman, Lee. 2004. *No Future: Queer Theory and the Death Drive*. Durham, NC: Duke University Press.

Grosz, Elizabeth. 1994, "Experimental Desire: Rethinking Queer Subjectivity." In *Supposing the Subject*, edited by Joan Copjec, 133–58. London: Verso.

Lacan, Jacques. 1960–61. "Transference: Seminar VIII." Unpublished translation by Cormac Gallagher.

————. 1971–72. *Ou Pire . . . : Seminar 19 (Or Worse . . .)*. Unpublished translation by Cormac Gallagher.

————. 1981. *The Four Fundamental Concepts of Psychoanalysis*. Book 11 of *The Seminar of Jacques Lacan*, edited by Jacques-Alain Miller, translated by Alan Sheridan. New York: Norton.

————. 1995. "Proposition of 9 October 1967 on the Psychoanalyst of the School." *Analysis*, no. 6: 1–13.

————. 1999. *Encore: On Feminine Sexuality, the Limits of Love, and Knowledge, 1972–1973*. Book 20 of *The Seminar of Jacques Lacan*, edited by Jacques-Alain Miller, translated by Bruce Fink. New York: Norton.

Layton, Lynne. 2004. *Who's That Girl? Who's That Boy? Clinical Practice Meets Postmodern Gender Theory*. New York: Analytic.

Mills, Catherine. 2001. "The Homosexual Advance Defence: The Law of Abandonment." Paper presented at the Third Annual Conference of the International Association for the Study of Sex, Culture, and Society, Melbourne, October 1–3.

Pereira, David. 1998a. "The Impossible Feminine and the Clinic of the Intersex." *Papers of the Freudian School of Melbourne* 19: 213–22.

————. 1998b. "Logos: Twenty Years of Training in the Freudian School of Melbourne." *Papers of the Freudian School of Melbourne* 19: 1–8.

Stryker, Susan, and Stephen Whittle, eds. 2006. *The Transgender Studies Reader*. New York: Routledge.

Depathologizing Trans

From Symptom to Sinthome

PATRICIA GHEROVICI

Abstract Pushing further the analyses of *Please Select Your Gender: From the Invention of Hysteria to the Democratizing of Transgenderism*, the author projects a new light on transgender manifestations. Drawing on her clinical experience as a psychoanalyst working with gender-variant analysands, she argues that those compelled to change gender often do it because they are facing the most crucial issues of life and death. What is at stake is less gender fluidity than a way of being. Challenging the pathologization of transgenderism historically enforced by psychoanalysis, the author makes use of Lacan's notion of the sinthome to propose an embodied ethics of desire capable of fundamentally rethinking sexuality by taking seriously the issue of mortality inscribed in sexuality.
Keywords psychoanalysis, death, transgender, gender, sexuality, phallus, *sinthome*

Psychoanalysis has a sex problem in more than one sense. Historically, psychoanalysts have taken a normative position by reading transsexuality as a sign of pathology. Nothing could be further from what one learns in the clinical practice as a psychoanalyst. There is no doubt that the transgender moment is changing our notions of gender, sex, and sexual identity. This evolution can reorient psychoanalytic practice. Psychoanalysis needs a major realignment, and the time is now.

We are living a "transgender moment" (CNN, the *New York Times*), a "trans revolution" (*Self* magazine, *Out* magazine), and a "transgender tipping point" (*Time* magazine), as headlines in the United States have called it.[1] It is the United States' "new civil rights frontier," and psychoanalysts might have a role to play in it. Despite the increasing media presence of transgender people, the transgender community continues to be a misrepresented and understudied population. This situation is more pronounced in the psychoanalytic field. In 2011, inspired by my clinical practice, I published an article ironically titled "Psychoanalysis Needs a Sex Change" (Gherovici 2011) wherein I addressed the fraught relation between psychoanalysis and transgender discourses that I initially

TSQ: Transgender Studies Quarterly ★ Volume 4, Numbers 3–4 ★ November 2017
DOI 10.1215/23289252-4189956 © 2017 Duke University Press

discussed in *Please Select Your Gender* (Gherovici 2010). When I began working on transgender issues, I had not foreseen then that I would be riding a wave that has eroded the heterosexist divide between genders in pop culture's imagination and also engulfed most psychiatric and psychoanalytic practices; psychoanalysts finally began reexamining their notions of gender and sexuality. But let's not be too optimistic. Let me backtrack a little.

As Susan Stryker (2006; quoted in Elliot 2010) notes, the varied transgender experiences of embodiment offer a critique of heterosexuality and gender binarism that puts forward new forms of legibility for trans identities. This reconceptualization has the potential to enlighten the psychoanalyst about the complex relationship of the body to the psyche; the precariousness of gender; the instability of the male/female opposition; the construction of identity at the sexual, social, and racial levels; the uncertainties about sexual choice—in short, the conundrum of sexual difference that, if taken into account, can help psychoanalysis remain current and relevant.

Since 2010, I have continued arguing for the depathologization of transgenderism. Almost twenty years ago, Patricia Elliot (2001) warned psychoanalysts against pathologizing the complex process of sexed embodiment and argued that it was much more productive to analyze it, concluding that "psychoanalysis is a potentially useful tool for theorizing transsexual subjectivity when it manages to raise questions about processes of embodiment without normalizing or pathologizing" (321). Ten years later, Shanna T. Carlson (2010) proposed that Lacanian psychoanalysis, in particular, could offer "a richly malleable framework for thinking through matters of sex, subjectivity, desire, and sexuality" and that "integration of the two domains can only ever be a scene of fruitful contestation" (69). At that time, I too argued for a productive confrontation between psychoanalysis and transgender discourses. I have shown how transgender people are actually changing the clinical praxis, advancing new ideas for the clinic that can be expanded to social and intellectual contexts (Gherovici 2011). Gayle Salamon (2010), Oren Gozlan (2011, 2015), Sheila Cavanagh (2016), and Damien W. Riggs (2016) have eloquently called for a reassessment of the usefulness of psychoanalysis when it comes to transgender issues. I could say that this group of authors, including me, agrees on one main point: the wish to replace the classical idea that trans people tend toward psychosis with other concepts derived from Sigmund Freud, Jacques Lacan, Judith Butler, or Luce Irigaray.

Breaking away from the medical model, Hervé Hubert (2006) proposed to address transgender phenomena while moving away from the notion of "transsexual syndrome" and using Lacan's original, nonpathological notion of the *sinthome*. Whereas Catherine Millot (1981, [1983] 1990) was the first to argue that a sex change could function like a *sinthome* operating as a supplement with a similar function to that which Lacan ascribed to writing for James Joyce, this claim also led to many Lacanian and post-Lacanian psychoanalysts to assume that transgender manifestations were inevitably a sign of psychosis. Taking his distance from this reductive position, Pierre-Henri Castel (2003) further investigated the notion of *sinthome* in regard to transgender embodiment. Castel employed Lacan's notion of *sinthome* as a restorative construction when the Oedipal metaphor fails. Geneviève Morel (2008) applied it to what she called "the sexual *sinthome*," testing the limits of the phallic function and the constraints of the binary model proposed in Lacan's sexuation formulae. The notion was taken up systematically by Rafael Kalaf Kossi (2011) to propose a "transsexual *sinthome*" that could be found in pathological and nonpathological psychic structures. The notion of *sinthome* in transgender embodiment has been found useful to avoid the trap of pathologization by Oren Gozlan (2011, 2014) and Sheila Cavanagh (2016).

As I proposed in 2010, I find that Jacques Lacan's theory of the *sinthome* offers an innovative framework for rethinking sexual difference—trans and cis. Since a *sinthome* can be found in both structures (neurosis and psychosis), with the help of this theory, one can challenge the pathological approach too often adopted by psychoanalysis when confronted with nonnormative expressions of sexuality and sexual identity. This approach calls for a more fruitful dialogue between Lacanian psychoanalysis and transgender discourses.

"I had no choice. I would be dead if I hadn't transitioned—I would have killed myself." My thoughts in this article derive from what I hear in my clinical practice from analysands like Jay whose trans desire was not just a wish to go beyond the gender binary but also a desire to overcome the limits of mortal existence. Pushing further the analyses of *Please Select Your Gender*, I look at transgenderism differently today by taking into account issues of life and death. I challenge the pathologization historically enforced by psychoanalysis while proposing an ethics of desire capable of fundamentally rethinking sexuality and of taking seriously the issue of death.

The present time offers a unique opportunity for psychoanalysis because the psychoanalyst—at least in the Lacanian definition—is in a privileged position to offer an ethics of choice and subjective responsibility. There is a growing interest in the works of Lacan among clinicians of other theoretical persuasions. His contributions are no longer seen as doctrinaire—pure speculation divorced from the practice—but begin to appear as helpful when working with patients. Could it be that today's psychoanalysts are no longer as afraid of Lacan as they were yesterday? Are they not more afraid of sexual and gender nonconformity?

"Why are you interested in transgender people?" I am often asked. The answer is simple: the analytic couch is a window. Through it we can see new things happening in society. If one maintains analytically alert ears, there is a lot to hear and discover. In my clinical practice as a psychoanalyst, I let my patients guide me, and through them, I learn. I have been hearing the comments of my patients shift from an emphasis on questions of sexual choice ("Who do I like? Men or women?") to questions of sexual identity ("Am I straight or bisexual?"). In contrast, I have noted that for patients whose bodies and sense of self did not align, the question was not about the certainty of their identity. Instead, they asked, "Why can't I be loved for who I am?"

"So, are you a specialist in LGBTQ+ patients?" I have to confess that at times I am bothered by this question. As a psychoanalyst, one is never a specialist, in the sense that one should keep an open mind and refrain from limiting one's scope. The key lies in analysis's fundamental rule of free association. This refers to the invitation to say whatever comes to mind disregarding whether it is inconvenient, offensive, or inappropriate. It not only helps the analysand talk freely but also implies that the analyst is ready to listen without being judgmental or pushing a hidden agenda. One might say that the fundamental rule makes the analysand the only specialist in the consulting room. Expressing themselves unrestricted, analysands may say whatever they intend to say, but also more than they want to say, more than they think they know. In other words, this rule assumes that the analysands are the experts, possessing knowledge that is unknown to them because it lies in their unconscious but that can emerge during the cure. So, when I am asked whether I am an LGBTQ+ specialist, I answer, "I am not—my analysands are." Despite—or perhaps because of—that attitude, I see in my practice a lot of gender-nonconforming people.

For psychoanalysis to "work," analysts position themselves not as "specialists" (or Masters who have the last word) but as enablers for exploration and subversion of received knowledge.[2] Often, someone who consults a psychoanalyst has a question in mind, for example: Why am I depressed? What is happening with my sexuality? Will I be loved for who I am? Even though quite often the analysand has a few ideas of what the answers might be, the question addressed to the psychoanalyst raises them to the position of Other: the Master of a knowledge they are supposed to have about this question. This question constitutes a demand that dislodges need and opens up the dimension of desire. Whoever accepts the challenge by trying to articulate an answer will become this Other and thus be raised to the position of Master. The Lacanian analytic relationship overcomes the temptation of domination by offering a different mode of social link—analytic discourse. The Lacanian analyst's work progresses because it assumes that the symptom is something uncontrolled by the subject and to which certain knowledge is attributed. These two factors, which are at the basis for the establishment of any transferential relationship, allow the treatment to start. The knowledge that the analysand will attribute to the analyst dissolves if the analyst operates with the "wise ignorance" systematized by German Renaissance philosopher Nicholas Cusanus—for the analyst knows that if there is a knowledge, it resides in the analysand's unconscious. Thus, the analysand's initial idealization of the analyst due to transference to the analyst, which is a precondition to the progress of the treatment, will eventually let the analyst fall from the position of subject-supposed-to-know. Then the knowledge contained in the symptom will emerge not from the analyst's expertise or knowledge but from the analysand's unconscious. This shift requires that the analysand should direct the cure toward the supersession of illusions, including the illusion of the analyst's knowledge, which will be given up too. This experience has transformative effects that induce a new social link. This social link, rather than regulated by a Master's model to which one is supposed to adapt or subject oneself, is regulated by the desire for pure difference. This social link acknowledges and accepts difference, meanwhile offering not only a new relation to one's unconscious but also a restitution of knowledge from which the analysand had been alienated. In the process, what is provided is the experience of a new model of social link that is of particular importance for minorities oppressed by race, class, or gender.

Phallus or Not Phallus

Since we are discussing psychoanalysis's sex problems, let us explore a little further one of its most controversial and contested notions—the phallus. While Lacan debiologizes the phallus (in Freud's writings one might be misled to think that the phallus is an organ), he gives this concept a centrality, a "phallocentricism" that has been rejected by feminist criticism. It is true that Lacan attributes to the phallus a central role in psychic life but as a symbol of what compensates for a certain lack; it is an attribute that nobody can have, while everyone aspires to have it or embody it. Lacan's most radical political intervention is his theory of sexuality, which introduced a separation of the phallus, as an instrument, from the penis, as an organ, clarifying the distinction between sexuality (he called it "sexual difference" or "sexuation"), anatomical sex, and symbolically constructed gender.

The phallus works as a signifier and may or may not be a body part. It might be an appendage to the body (as could be the case in the exhibitionistic pleasure of a man parading his pretty girlfriend as arm candy, showing off the proverbial trophy wife, or driving a red convertible sports car) or it might extend to the whole body. How does this happen? Only because the phallus functions as an exchange ratio; as a signifier it can be ascribed with various meanings, as illustrated in a case of a cross-dresser discussed by the important psychoanalyst Otto Fenichel (1949; see also Lewin 1933.) Fenichel's analysand loved his penis so much that he had invented a pet name for it. When he cross-dressed, fantasizing that he was a girl, it happened that "the girl's name which he wanted to have as a girl bore a striking resemblance to the pet name for his penis" (Fenichel 1949: 304.) Fenichel observed an equivalence derived from a "symbolic equation" that had been proposed very early by Freud, who had observed that a young girl's desire for a penis would be replaced by a desire for a baby. Fenichel's analysis of the case concluded that an unconscious series of substitutions was at work; the thought of "I am a girl" and "My whole body is a penis" would be condensed in one single idea: "I = my whole body = a girl = the little one = the penis" (304.) In his treatment, Fenichel appealed to an organ that was not physical but imaginary. He identified something that was more than any anatomical organ, pointing to an excess that might be illustrated by the phallus as represented in ancient Greek comedy, mostly in Aristophanes. That impossibly gigantic prop was so huge and absurd that its mere appearance onstage would make the audience roar with laughter. Lacan would develop the concept of this phallus, a phallus presented by Fenichel as a token with a representative function. The phallus is a token that enters into a relationship of equivalence or interchangeability and promotes a movement from object to object. It acquires value only insofar as it enters into a symbolic exchange.

The same "phallus" is still present in contemporary life. If I walk in the street with a friend who owns an adorable little dog, everyone will turn and shriek in delight, "Oh my God, such a cutie." They have recognized that my friend has her phallus with her and can take it for a walk; they are then seized by the wish to do the same. In another example, an analysand was describing how her new male lover had undressed for the first time in front of her; he displayed something that she was embarrassed to name because it was "so hard and so big." It was not what you think: she expressed her awe facing his toned six-pack abs.

The controversial phallus seems also to make an appearance in the statements of some trans people, like the protagonist of the film *The Danish Girl* (dir. Tom Hooper, 2015). In the movie, just before Lili Elbe is about to undergo a sex-change surgery never attempted before, she responds to warnings about the dangers involved by telling the surgeon, "This is not my body. I have to let it go." What Lili wants to let go of is her penis. She imagines that the removal of this organ will make her whole body go. Genitals and body appear conflated. Here, an "organ" becomes the *organon*, an instrument, a means of reasoning, a system of logic. This is an example of how someone assumes a sexual position (as man, woman, and anything else) relying on the phallus (albeit imaginary). Lili fully abides by phallic premise while others might not, an alternative explored by Lacan when he introduced the notion of sexuation as a strategy to move beyond the limitations of the model of the Oedipus complex. Lacan sees sexuality not in terms of gender but in terms of modes of enjoyment (*jouissance*). Even though Lacan proposes a "male side" and "female side," these are not determined by biology but by the logic of unconscious investments. The proposed division is based on two forms of being, masculine and feminine, corresponding to two forms of *jouissance*: phallic and Other. *Man* and *woman* are therefore signifiers of imprecise meaning, creations of discourse, mere symptomatic solutions that stand for sexed positions relative to a phallic premise. The potential of Lacan's formulae of sexuation to think transgender subjectivities has been highlighted by Shanna Carlson (2013), who observed that "'transsexuality' is not in and of itself any more extreme a type of symptom than is 'man' or 'woman'" (311). Damien W. Riggs (2016) sees the lens of sexuation as a useful alternative to "sexual difference" and "gender" because the latter propose "a politics of choice within constraints" (128).

Let us note that Freud introduced the notion of the phallus within the Oedipus complex. Recall that the phallus is not the penis but a "universal premise": it is the impossible infantile theory according to which sexual difference is denied under the absurd belief that everyone, and even everything, is equipped with a penis. The phallus, far from being an organ, is a theoretical speculation applied to both women and men. Moreover, the phallus, since no one can be or have it, most importantly introduces the dimension of the lack that defines human sexuality. This lack has a theoretical function in psychoanalysis.

In a 1971 seminar, Lacan remarked that transsexuals have trouble with the phallus because they dispense with lack and therefore confuse the actual organ with the signifier, a term that has to be understood as the material and linguistic side of language (1971). I will return to this passage and only note here that Lacan was aware that the transsexual demand for the surgical removal of attributes like the breasts or the penis might derive from an inability to use metaphors for those organs. A transsexual would literalize the old Freudian mechanism of castration. As I noted earlier, Lacanian psychoanalysts in France led by Catherine Millot started a tradition of pathologizing transgender manifestations.

Lacan retains the notion of castration and makes an important move toward overcoming the limitations of the Oedipal model one year later, contradicting the previous assertion still founded on the central role of the phallic organ, when he proposes the sexuation formulas in which women are positioned outside the phallic realm as "not-all," which gives them a different relation to the phallus (see Lacan 1998: 7, 35, 78–81, 102–3). The sexuation grid formalizes modalities of sexual realizations for men and women by using a model derived from logic and not determined by anatomical contours. Lacan separates the positions according to types of enjoyment and places a masculine modality of enjoyment or phallic *jouissance* on one side, and a feminine modality of enjoyment on the other, or Other *jouissance*, not completely subjected to the phallic premise. According to the formulae, for the male side, we read that all are subject to the law of castration. On the female side, we read that no X exists which is not determined by the phallic function. In other words, castration is an absolute that functions for all—men and women. On the lower line, a negation bars the universal quantifier, to be read as "not-whole," which entails that the woman's side is not wholly subjected to the phallus.

Lacan's innovations from 1972 reopen the question of femininity as neither sex nor gender because difference is seen from the pole of *jouissance*. Whereas for Freud there is only one libido, Lacan proposed a division based on two modes of being, masculine and feminine, that correspond to two forms of *jouissance*: phallic and Other. Lacan located phallic *jouissance* on the male side and gave it the force of necessity (all men), which relies on the exclusion of one man—the unlawful or impossible *jouissance* of the primal father. In this model of sexual division, we encounter two positions: one, that of the phallic one (man) who is limited by the father exempted from castration (the exception to the phallic rule that provides its support), and on the other side the unlimited *jouissance* of a woman who is "not all" subjected to the phallic constraints.

Unlike the Lacanian unconscious, the Freudian unconscious is unable to recognize the elaborate system of difference that we call "gender." From the point of view of the Freudian unconscious, there is an impasse on sexual difference; the sexual binary is the symptom of this impasse. As Ian Parker (2007) observes, what we call "gender" is "a signifier that operates as an imaginary effect of a real difference." The "imaginary effect" we call "gender" is also an attribution assigned from outside the subject and without the subject's consent, as it is often inscribed in the birth certificate of the newborn long before the child acquires the ability to speak.

Lacan's sexuation formulas offer a way of thinking about trans because they are free from the shackles of anatomical constraints. The model of sexual difference still recognizes that there is only one logical operator that is the phallus, but it acknowledges that some individuals are placed in a position in which the phallus is not operative. We are seeing more and more patients who do not think that they are in the wrong body but feel that the gender binary does not fit them. Their identity is nonbinary or agender—they do not identify as either male or female. They are careful about using language—instead of the pronouns *he* and *she*, these analysands refer to themselves using the pronoun *they*, which already exists in the dictionary, or employ new gender-neutral pronouns like *ze*, *hir*, *xe*, *ou*, and *ey*. And even when they may not want to change genders, they may take hormones to redistribute muscle and change how their voice sounds, precisely to inhabit the space between genders. Most importantly, they seem to be able to deal with sexual difference without fully relying on the phallus.

One of the truths the transgender phenomenon illustrates is that body and gender consistency is a fiction. They are both constituted in a process of identification that can be undone and is never fully stable, as Gayle Salamon (2010) has eloquently argued. Embodiment is always precarious and evolving. It is absurd to ascribe to anatomy the role of normalizer in a type of sexuality by focusing on the genitals or on a single prescribed act, as classical psychoanalysis has traditionally done. This normalizing role has been effectively challenged by transsexual discourse and practices.

Sexual identity issues all revolve around a particular body, a body that one is not born into but becomes. Today we see analysands in our practices who tell us that the sex they were assigned at birth does not align with the gender with which they identify. They prove that, in matters of gender, anatomy is not destiny, and that some may experience their body as one that does not match one's inner sense of self. In their testimonies, we confirm that having a body entails a complex process of embodiment—that of becoming a body. As Leo Bersani has observed, "the frequently presumed 'gender trouble' of transgender people is in fact a universal condition: the impossibility of representing sexuality, an impossibility that implicitly subverts the fixity of all identitarian claims" (cover blurb for Gherovici 2017). Far from being deviant, the trans experience opens to what Alain Badiou calls the "generic," that is what is relevant for all human subjects.[3]

Lacan's Way

Today's practitioners may not know that Lacan was the first psychoanalyst in France to work with a gender-variant patient in a manner that expressed an ethics of sexual difference. Lacan set an example of an analyst willing to learn from his analysands; his ethical stance should have put an end to psychoanalytic gender-identity narrow-mindedness. At the time when Christine Jorgensen was becoming an international media sensation and the first global trans woman celebrity, responsible for making the word *transsexual* a household term, every week between 1952 and 1954, Lacan treated a patient who was requesting "a castration with amputation of the penis, plastic surgery of the scrotum to make it into a vulva, creation of an artificial vagina, and treatment with feminizing hormones" (Delay et al. 1956: 52).

Forgive me for returning to a case discussed in *Please Select Your Gender* (Gherovici 2010: 154–66.) I will revisit Lacan's treatment of a gender-variant person to highlight his clinical stance when dealing with a subject requesting a sex-realignment surgery who also might have been intersex. This patient, as it has been my experience with many analysands with gender trouble, had a history that included a failed suicidal attempt and was often navigating the treacherous liminal space between life and death. Henri, as the patient was known, was hospitalized at the prestigious Sainte-Anne Psychiatric Hospital in Paris in the ward of eminent psychiatrist Jean Delay, who had been a pioneer in France in the psychiatric treatment of patients identified as transsexual. Lacan approached this case not only with remarkable prudence but also with great zeal. Even though Lacan did not write about this case, Delay, also known for his excellent psychobiography of André Gide, published a detailed description of Henri's case in which he drew conclusions about the clinical management of transsexual patients. Delay et al. sum up Lacan's work: Henri "found in him an 'unrivaled understanding'" (1956: 53).[4]

Henri's case is complex.[5] Henri was forty years old when he began a two-year hospitalization to determine whether he was a suitable candidate for gender realignment. Henri identified as a man and had been living as such since age sixteen. At birth, he had been declared a girl. He had been born with undescended testicles (cryptorchidism) and presented as a full-term newborn with the characteristics of a premature baby. The family initially thought that the baby would die. Despite the somber medical prediction, the child survived and was named Anne-Henriette, assigned as female in the birth certificate, and raised as a girl until her adolescence.

Following the birth of a half-sister whose gender was also not easily determined, just when Anne-Henriette was entering late puberty and starting to show romantic interest in a man, all of a sudden, the father, who had been distant and uninvolved, made a sudden, forceful demand: "You can't help but make a choice" (Delay et al. 1956: 45). Thus Anne-Henriette was forced to give up dresses, cut her hair, and wear only male clothing to assume a male persona. The teenager acquiesced without any protestation. According to Delay et al., Henri "welcomed that transformation with obvious indifference and a lack of surprise that still astonishes him today. He was already aware that he was not like other people" (45).

This change, which Henri referred to as "the catastrophe" (50), marked the beginning of a period of intense emotional suffering, which led to a suicide attempt at age thirty-one (ingestion of barbiturates followed by a brief hospitalization), and of many practical challenges, since he presented as a male but his legal gender was female. Henri concocted false documents and often impersonated his brother. This precarious arrangement put him in danger when he attracted the attention of the Gestapo during France's occupation.

In terms of his gender identity, Henri said that he had "a feminine soul. I'm morally like a woman" (50); yet he opposed the idea of wearing female outfits, finding such an option "ridiculous 'on account of his physical attributes'" (46). He strongly objected to homosexuality and had recurrent dreams of being a "normal" woman in a relationship with a heterosexual man, from which he awoke with intense anxiety (51).

In April 1952, Henri started an exhaustive multidisciplinary assessment— a two-year stay at Sainte-Anne Hospital. Besides his weekly treatment with Dr. Lacan,

Henri went through numerous tests by a team of endocrinologists. This thorough examination process led the team to deny Henri's request.

What happened then? Henri and Lacan quickly "agreed on the uselessness of pursuing an attempt at changing his condition, a change to which the patient apparently never subscribed" (53). The use of the word *subscribe* is quite puzzling. One might speculate that it meant that despite the length of the hospital observation procedure, Henri accepted the refusal without much protestation, a fact quoted by Delay's team to confirm that for Henri "the quest of his chimera was more important than its realization" (53). Did Henri feel not fully entitled to his own request? That Henri evinced no haste to realize his gender realignment is quite revealing; it teaches us something crucial about Lacan's direction of this treatment. For Henri, gender appeared as an injunction that was imposed by others, and had been done and undone in capricious and sudden ways. Sexual identity was a destiny in which one had no say and that had to be accepted without protestation. This dynamic was repeated during Henri's stay at Sainte-Anne, where he spent a long time waiting for the medical authorization and passively accepted a decision that perhaps contradicted his wishes. Did Lacan grant a little bit of freedom by sending the decision back to Henri?

Henri's female gender attribution was predicated on a phallic premise that was a "mistake." The "mistake" was abruptly "corrected" during puberty. As Anne-Henriette's sexuality was awakening, the testicles descended into the scrotum, and she suddenly was mandated to become Henri with the father's admonition, "You can't help but make a choice" (45). However, Henri was never given a chance to make a choice. Let me reiterate that, during the evaluation process at Sainte-Anne, Henri was all along expecting the medical team to decide for him, while he never seemed to have fully "subscribed" to the decision of a change in his condition. For Lacan, Henri needed to make a decision and subscribe to it. It would have to be Henri/Anne-Henriette's choice and not that of other people.

Organon

As we have seen, Lacan mentioned in a 1971 seminar that transsexuals "confuse the organ with the signifier" and argued that the penis (an organ) can be confused with the phallus (an instrument), that is, as a signifying tool that is operative only as an effect of language.[6] This is a common error that in some cases can lead to the surgical removal of physical attributes like the breasts or the penis. Those instances might derive from an inability to use metaphors for those organs, and castration is no longer symbolic but real, literalized in a removal of an actual bodily organ. As a result, Lacanian psychoanalysts led by Catherine Millot, who was dubbed by Kate Bornstein a "gender terrorist" ([1994] 2016: 91), started a tradition of systematic pathologization of transgender manifestations.

Millot's position has not changed since 1983. In her recent memoir *La vie avec Lacan* (*Life with Lacan*, 2016), Millot uses the case of a transsexual seen at the Sainte-Anne Hospital as an example of Lacan's ethical stance on clinical presentations. Millot praises Lacan because he does not capitulate in front of the delusional belief of a male patient who thinks that he is a woman, reminding him that he is a man and no surgical procedure will make him a woman. Millot observes that Lacan ends his interview by calling the patient "*mon pauvre vieux*" (my poor old man), using an almost friendly manner that she does not consider condescending but, rather, a gesture to remind the patient of his masculinity while pointing to the impossibilities and unhappiness marking the human condition (50–51).

In a transcription made available in an English translation more than thirty-five years ago (Schneiderman 1980), a very different picture emerges of how Lacan conducts this interview at a psychiatric hospital before a group of psychoanalysts and psychiatrists. "Primeau" stated that he was able to be "in love with a woman as I am with a man" (27) and had sexual relations with both men and women. While relating the story of a woman he had loved because she had a beauty that "radiated" (27), Primeau suddenly turned his attention to one of the female clinicians in the audience. He mentioned that she had a luminous beauty despite the fact that she wore makeup.

In an astute clinical move, Lacan immediately turned the question around and asked Primeau if he ever wore makeup, and he explained that indeed, he would occasionally put on makeup: "It has happened to me, yes." Smiling, he clarified that he would do this because he "had a lot of sexual complexes . . . because nature endowed me with a very small phallus" (30). Asked to elaborate further, Primeau continued, "I had the impression that my sex was shrinking, and I had the impression that I was going to become a woman. . . . I had the impression that I was going to become a transsexual" (31). "A transsexual?" inquired Lacan. "That is to say, a sexual mutant," responded Primeau. Lacan retorted, "That is what you mean. You had the feeling that you were going to become a woman." "Yes," confirmed Primeau, well aware that he still had a masculine organ and that he never felt what it was to be a woman; nevertheless, he had seen himself as a woman in a dream and thus hoped to become one. He experienced himself as a woman, "feeling it psychologically" (31).

Lacan wanted Primeau to explain what he meant when saying he was transsexual; this referred to a transformation without any medical intervention— he was not changing genders but, rather, undergoing a spontaneous transformation into a woman. He did not explicitly express any demand for sex realignment. Lacan asks him to further explain. Primeau elaborates, "Yes, I had certain habits, I used to put on makeup, I had this impression of shrinking of the sex and at the same time the will to know what a woman was, to try to enter the world of a woman, into the psychology of a woman, and into the psychological and intellectual formulation of a woman" (31). More exactly, Primeau had the impression that this spontaneous change into a woman resulted from the feeling of shrinkage of what was in place of the phallus.

Let us note that Lacan asked several times if Mr. Primeau felt he was a woman. Lacan had a clear purpose and asked, "Finally, you never felt yourself to be a woman?" Primeau answered, "No." Lacan insisted, "Yes or no?" Primeau responded, "No. Can you repeat the question?" Lacan obliged, "I asked if you felt yourself to be a woman." Again, Primeau talked about "feeling it psychologically" as an "intuition." Lacan made Primeau clarify by asking: "Yes, pardon me, of intuition. Since intuitions are images that pass through you. Did you ever *see* yourself as a woman?" To which Primeau answered, "No" (31).

Here we see Lacan carefully discerning a transsexual delusion from a demand for gender reassignment by testing Primeau's position. He never adopted the moralistic position of asserting that surgery would never make him a woman, as Millot claims. Millot reads their interaction as proof that Lacan rejects all transsexual desires as psychotic. In fact, what we see here is that Lacan is carefully distinguishing the case of a man that he sees as psychotic from a more legitimate demand for sex change, which was not Primeau's situation. In Stuart Schneiderman's translation, Lacan ends the interview by saying good-bye, shaking his hand, and calling Primeau "my friend" (41).

After Primeau is no longer in the room, Lacan briefly discusses the case with the audience. He shares his pessimism about the prognosis of this case, which he diagnoses as a marked instance of "'Lacanian' psychosis." He recommends further study of this type of clinical picture, which he feels has not been properly described in the literature. Primeau's presentation could be compared to Lacan's original reading of Judge Daniel Paul Schreber's case, a case of someone who cured himself with writing after he experienced what Lacan calls "transsexual *jouissance*." Schreber, like Primeau, thought that he was becoming a woman rather than expressing a demand for a sex change.

When Lacan asked Primeau if he *saw* himself as a woman, he was exploring whether his "intuition" was a visual hallucination while probing the imaginary of the body, which in psychosis is often fallen or missing. Primeau and Lacan close the interview with an exchange about writings (*écrits*), which refers to Primeau's awareness about Lacan's book (*Écrits*) and possibly indicates his transference to him, as well as reveals the function of writing in issues of embodiment, when what Ezra Pound calls the *ego scriptor* (the writing I) can make flesh and author become one.[7]

Lacan's intervention with Primeau was faithful to his clinical position on psychosis. He never challenged a delusion. As we know, the delusion is for Lacan an attempt at self-cure. It is a metaphor that functions as a supplement (*suppléance*) so as to make sense of chaos and help to frame *jouissance*. Lacan reminded Mr. Primeau "that nonetheless, you still have a masculine organ" (Schneiderman 1980: 31), not to question the delusion as such but to loosen a conviction coming to the patient as "imposed speech." The "imposed sentences" of the hallucinations were experienced by Primeau like a return of a foreclosed idea, an impossible (Real) idea that could not be integrated. Lacan's strategy was not to dispute the feminization experienced by Primeau, which is a feature often seen in psychosis,[8] but he was not complicit with a delusional conviction, either. Lacan mentioned Primeau's masculine organ in a skillful clinical maneuver that introduced something of the phallus so as to set a limit on the excessive *jouissance* that invaded Primeau.

Primeau was not the only case of a trans patient approached by Lacan, as we have seen with Henri/Anne-Henriette. Indeed, the same clinical finesse is visible in Lacan's reading of the case of Schreber, whose memoirs had been commented on by Freud. Lacan's theoretical elaboration about Schreber in his seminar differed markedly from that of Freud and was colored by what he had learned with his work with Henri/Anne-Henriette.

Freud's study of Schreber can be considered the first psychoanalytic inquiry on transsexualism. Schreber had spent six years in a private psychiatric clinic and, feeling sufficiently recovered, wrote a thorough account of his illness to argue in court for his discharge from the asylum. It succeeded in granting Schreber freedom. *Memoirs of My Nervous Illness* may be the autobiographical account of psychosis most often discussed in psychiatric literature; it is also one of the first sex-change memoirs.

The complex, delusional world of Schreber had a center—his body. Schreber's body was a body without teeth, larynx, eyes, stomach, and intestines; it was a body consuming itself, a body of miracles, a body of God's divine rays, a body of sacred fertility, but above all, it was the site of an astounding transformation:

> The month of November, 1895, marks an important time in the history of my life and in particular in my own ideas of the possible shaping of my future. . . . During that time the signs of a transformation into a woman became so marked on my body, that I could no longer ignore the imminent goal at which the whole development was aiming. In the immediately preceding nights my male sexual organ might actually have been retracted had I not resolutely set my will against it, still following the stirring of my sense of manly honor; so near completion was the miracle. Soul voluptuousness had become so strong that I myself received the impression of a female body, first in my arms and hands, later on my legs, bosom, buttocks and other parts of my body. (Schreber [1903] 2000: 163)

Schreber was certain that he was becoming a woman. He would become God's bride, a consenting prey to God's voluptuous pleasures. Freud interprets Schreber's paranoia as a defense against homosexuality, while Lacan centers his analysis in what he calls Schreber's transsexual drive and most importantly, his transsexual enjoyment. This should not surprise us. As we have seen with Henri, Lacan was well aware of the differences between transsexuality and homosexuality (see Castel 2003: 351).

In Schreber's delusional transformation into a woman, Lacan found new meaning to a recurring phenomenon in psychosis: feminization. This was the key element in Lacan's original reading of the case—he distanced himself from Freud's interpretation of Schreber's paranoia as being determined by the patient's rejection of homosexuality (for Freud, Schreber had to imagine that he was turning into a woman in order to accept the idea that he was going to have sex with a man or with a male father figure). For Lacan this transformation had other implications. In Schreber's transsexualist delusion, in his conviction that he was becoming a woman, Lacan found the lineaments for a new theory of sexual identity.

Lacan displaced the Freudian question of interpretation with a question of reading and writing—reading the symptom and writing the symptom. I will use the term he coined to describe this conjunction, that of *sinthome*. This coining in Lacan's works is quite useful in my clinical experience with analysands who identify as trans and for whom a process equivalent to writing takes center stage in their cure. The "curative" role of writing is more poignantly observed in the chronicles of people who changed sex, but it is somehow universal. The testimonies of gender transition express most clearly that there is a new writing on the body.

The Art of Having a Body

Indeed, the transgender experience brings to the fore the challenge of assuming a different or transformed body. This is similar to the experience of becoming a work of art. The body becomes an artistic endeavor, a body of work, a lifetime oeuvre. Thus, an art similar to that of actual artists is to be found in transsexual artificiality. As I have argued elsewhere, on occasion, such art is tantamount to a *sinthome*, which means that it occupies a structural function analogous to the role Lacan ascribed to writing, particularly that of James Joyce, who, Lacan argued, was able to use art as a supplement, as an artifice to create a body Joyce did not feel he had (see Gherovici 2014).

For Joyce, art played a central role, and his writings may have saved him from the psychosis that engulfed his daughter; he once blurted out that only a *trans*parent sheet of paper separated *Ulysses* from madness.[9] Lacan's year-long seminar of 1975–76 focused on Joyce, offering an extensive exploration of artistic activity. As Lacan unambiguously stated in the opening session, "This year will be my interrogation of art" (2005: 22). When Lacan turned his attention to Joyce's writings, he discovered a new understanding of art and creativity: from Joyce's "art," Lacan deduced a new and original definition of the symptom. Breaking away from the medical model by bringing the symptom closer to a mathematical function, Lacan developed a new theory of artistic creation from Joyce's unique though not unusual situation and found a new meaning for the term *symptom* that he rewrote as *sinthome*. This word, apparently an invention, is the ancient spelling of *symptom* in French; it is, moreover, pronounced identically to the contemporary word *symptom*. This subtle difference, inaudible in speech but patent in orthography, is a deliberate gesture hinting at the importance of the dimension of writing.

How productive was this neologism? The shift in terminology related the symptom to art, with *sinthome* defined as the creative knotting together of the registers of the Symbolic (language, speech), the Real (whose effect is the mixture of pain and pleasure Lacan calls *jouissance*, the distribution of pleasure in the body), and the Imaginary (images, meaning) whose interlocking sustain the subject's reality.

By the time he coined *sinthome*, Lacan was working on models taken from mathematics (set theory) and topology (knot theory) that defied intuitive grasp, borrowing a different syntax and a new vocabulary in an effort to offer a formalization of what he observed in the analytic experience. This shift from linguistics to topology engendered major consequences. Lacan no longer thought of the symptom simply as something to decode, a carrier of a repressed message (a signifier), which can be deciphered by reference to the unconscious "structured like a language," but as the trace of the unique way someone can come to be and enjoy one's unconscious. The symptom as *sinthome* is an invention that allows someone to live by providing an organization of *jouissance*. Identification with the *sinthome* occurs when one identifies with the particular form of their enjoyment, thereby deriving their selfhood. For Lacan, the aim of the cure was no longer to remove the patient's symptoms but to let the patients identify with their unique *sinthome* in order to enjoy it.

The *sinthome* is inscribed in Lacan's theory of the Borromean knot, made out of three intertwined rings that correspond to the tripartite structure Lacan called the Real, the Imaginary, and the Symbolic orders. Although heterogeneous, these registers intersect and are held together. Lacan chose the Borromean knot because of its main characteristic—the rings are so interdependent that if one ring is unknotted, the other three come loose. A fourth term intervenes to repair the failure in the knotting, relinking the rings and holding together again the rings that had disentangled. Lacan called *sinthome* the fourth ring capable of remedying the negative effects of unraveling the Borromean knot.

Inventing the *sinthome*, Lacan not only put forward a new technical term but also opened a revolutionary theoretical avenue. Let us not forget that the term was coined for a gifted artist like Joyce, whom Lacan claimed personified the *sinthome*. Lacan's theory of the *sinthome* applied above all to the singularities of Joyce's art but could be generalized. Joyce's case constructed a clinical example explaining how the art of the *sinthome* worked.

Lacan's idea was that Joyce's writing was a corrective device to repair a fault, a slip of the knot. According to Lacan, Joyce's enigmatic writing in *Finnegans Wake* would undermine or undo language by creating a verbal stream of polyglot polysemy, saturated with multiplying meanings, a cosmos of indeterminacies; this revolutionary practice became his *sinthome*. Lacan then adds that Joyce wanted to make a name for himself, and he produced a new ego through artifice. This turned into his signature, the mark of his singularity as an artist.

I connect here the peculiar meaning given to the concept of "art" by Lacan in his interpretation of Joyce's works with what I discovered in my clinical practice when treating patients who identify as trans. Joyce's art compensated for a defect in its author's subjective structure and saved Joyce from insanity. The *sinthome*-art granted him access to a new know-how that repaired a fault in the psyche; this produced a supplement that held together the registers of the Real, the Symbolic, and the Imaginary in such a way that it could fasten or reknot the subject. With the theory of the *sinthome*, Lacan reached a turning point. He created a new vocabulary in an effort to formalize what he observed in the analytic experience.

Making Life Livable

Let me now turn to a clinical example to see how Lacan's *sinthome* works in treatment as an invention to make life livable. Jay, a trans man, came to analysis to talk about his addiction rather than any "gender trouble," describing himself as a mild addict. The word *addict* gave him a place in the world with other addicts—it was his master signifier. Jay's girlfriend, a cis woman, fought with him a lot. Jay was gaining weight. Everything was oral—all food and screaming. The nickname Jay had adopted for his girlfriend then opened a way out of the cycle of repetitions. Jay would affectionately call Marty "Ma." He had a slip of the tongue; trying to say "Ma," he stuttered and said, "Ma . . . Ma." I repeated back to him, "Mama?" He seemed annoyed: "Not, Ma . . . not mama." Jay appeared utterly confused. We ended the session there. At the next session, Jay acknowledged that the fights provided an exhilarating sensation similar to that of his drunken high; this excitement related to the continuous disappointment he had experienced with his father, the parent who was "not mama." His absences made him feel that nothing existed beyond his mother's love. "Nothing" became an object he searched for in his alcohol- and drug-induced highs. Later, Jay noticed that while his nickname for Marty was "Ma," hers for Jay was "Dumpling." Jay stopped himself mid-sentence and repeated, "Dump." "Dump?" I asked. He replied, "Yes, this is what Ma is doing, treating me like shit." Jay broke up with Marty soon after.

This reckoning with the oral and anal object led the treatment to a final move that I would call a *sinthomatic* construction, by granting Jay a new name and a better way of inhabiting his body.

Jay never talked of transitioning as a destiny but, rather, as a survival strategy, as a necessary transformation that allowed him to live: "I had no choice. I would be dead if I didn't transition—I would have killed myself." He reflected on his mastectomy: "I had surgery, a serious surgery. It has been all worth it. It has had a kind of healing quality." He said that he avoided looking at himself in the mirror for fear of finding traces of a female body. "Whenever I am about to take a shower—other than sex, the only time I am naked—I am reminded that I was born with a female body. It doesn't feel right, especially with all this body fat I have now. I do not hate my body; I just do not like it. I was born female but now I am male. It still puzzles me."

Finally, it is at this point during the treatment that I was now able to learn about Jay's body, the pains and puzzles of his transition. He experienced a voice, a reproach against his body, that necessitated the transition . . . but something still ailed him. In a *sinthomatic* resolution, Jay sold his business, paid off a loan to his mother, and started a new career selling vinyl records, which proved quite successful. The voice still addressed him, but now the register of sound and acoustic materiality prevailed differently: "Not everyone listens to the music I like . . . but those who like it, love it. . . . I care about this, in ways I could not imagine before." He wanted to leave a mark, to make a singular contribution using his know-how—a signature. The new business brought him closer to his father, who up to then had been absent. The father had been for a while a DJ. This made Jay understand that the name he chose was a way of rewriting his father's most treasured activity. In his new business persona, he was known as "J-J." He even named the new company "J-Music" with the caption "the Joys of J-Music." He went from being called Jessica at birth to renaming himself Jay, and most lately to being known in the music business as J.J. Jay had never heard of James Joyce; however, his *sinthome* curiously rewrote a Joycean solution.

When we turn to the cure, we understand that when Lacan says that some transsexuals confuse the organ with the signifier, in fact he is saying that the confusion is between the body and the signifier. The body is not tied to the ego. When this happens, something might need to be invented to reknot body and ego.

Lacan highlights the clinical value of the symptom as a knot. We can observe the emergence of a new materiality in meaning, a language that seems to abandon the signifying chain. This chain will be replaced by the Borromean knot insofar as it pertains to writing. The letter is thus inscribed, allowing the signifier to imprint itself, not so much as scar or a stigmata of trauma but, rather, as a mark akin to a signature.

Is the cure a cure by *sinthome*? Psychoanalytic work uses a deliberate practice of equivocation and verbal punning, as well as the cutting and punctuation of session, so as to undo the set of fixed and univocal meanings initially presented by the analysand. Above all, it interferes with *jouissance*. The symptom then is no longer a deciphering of a hidden meaning but, rather, the creation of something new. This is an idea that I find extremely helpful in clinical work with the most varied analysands, cis and trans. In some cases of analysands who identify as trans, inventing a *sinthome*, a subject trapped in the "wrong" body can become somebody—what is lived as an error or lethal flaw can be repaired with a *sinthome* as a supplement that grants access to a new form of being. Then, the body goes from being a deadly enclosure to becoming embodied flesh, and life is livable.

One important lesson I learned from analysands who identify as trans is that more often than not the key issue is one of life and death. This is an important point that I had not perceived fully when I published *Please Select Your Gender*. As Griffin Hansbury (2005: 22) observes, "Transition itself is, in some way, a kind of death." Like many Lacanian psychoanalysts, I had focused on the conundrum of sex and gender, not seeing with the required clarity that the transgender request was directly aimed at the border between life and death.[10]

However, all the elements had been known to me. Key figures in trans research such as Eugen Steinach and Harry Benjamin developed an interest in sex hormones as part of their medical research to prolong human life. They performed great numbers of "rejuvenation" surgeries in a quest for immortality. When Freud had a "Steinach operation," his immediate concern was to slow down the progress of his cancer of the jaw, but as he said in *Beyond the Pleasure Principle*, Freud was aware that cancers are caused by pesky cells that stubbornly refuse to die. This complex knotting of then recently discovered hormones, undying cells, and the ancient wish for an immortal life, somehow reappears in the request of many of the analysands who identify as trans. The triumph experienced in numerous cases, following the at times grueling process of gender transition, can be condensed in a simple sentence: "I exist." This "existence" seems to have been given to them as supernumerary, an excess beyond the dichotomy of life and death, and then this excess ends up embodying the truth of their desire.

Patricia Gherovici is a psychoanalyst. Her publications include *The Puerto Rican Syndrome* (2003), *Please Select Your Gender: From the Invention of Hysteria to the Democratizing of Transgenderism* (2010), *Lacan, Psychoanalysis, and Comedy* (with Manya Steinkoler, 2016), and *Transgender Psychoanalysis: A Lacanian Perspective on Sexual Difference* (2017).

Acknowledgments

This chapter includes sections from several chapters of *Transgender Psychoanalysis: A Lacanian Perspective on Sexual Difference* (Gherovici 2017).

Notes

1. See Griggs 2015; Sontag 2015; Sandler 2015; Brathwaite 2015; and Steinmetz 2014.
2. In his invention of an algebra of the four discourses, Lacan identified four forms of social link or discourse: Discourse of the Master, Discourse of the University, Discourse of the Analyst, and Discourse of the Hysteric. Whoever tries to occupy the position of power, authority, and knowledge (Other) will be intervening as Master and not as psychoanalyst.
3. For Badiou's concept of the generic, see Frasser 2015.
4. Note that one of the coauthors of this text, Jean-Marc Alby, had completed a ground-breaking thesis on transsexualism in 1956. This article was both a case study of Henri and a review of the existing literature on transsexualism at the time.
5. For a more detailed analysis of Henri's case, see my *Please Select Your Gender* (2010: 154–66).
6. "Le transsexuel souhaite réaliser La femme en tant que toute, et comme il veut se libérer de l'erreur commune qui est de confondre l'organe avec le signifiant, il s'adresse au chirurgien pour forcer le passage du Réel" (Transsexuals wish to realize Woman as Whole, and because they want to free themselves from the common mistake that consists in taking an organ for a signifier, they go and see a surgeon in order to force a breakthrough to the Real) (Lacan 1971).
7. Pound (1975) calls himself "ego scriptor" four times in the *Cantos*: *ego scriptor*: Canto 76; *ego scriptor cantilenae*: Cantos 24, 62, and 64.
8. To describe this phenomenon, Lacan coined the phrase "push towards Woman" (*pousse-à-la-femme*). This tricky phrase could be rendered in English as "driving one to become a woman," if "drive" was not already a translation of Freud's technical term *Trieb*. For more on "push towards Woman," see Gherovici (2010: 174–82).
9. My italics. Joyce said, "In any event this book was terribly daring. A transparent sheet separates it from madness." Quoted in Jacques Derrida (1978: 36).
10. I am indebted to Geneviève Morel for highlighting this connection.

References

Bornstein, Kate. (1994) 2016. *Gender Outlaw: On Men, Women, and the Rest of Us*. New York: Vintage Books.

Brathwaite, Les Fabian. 2015. "Televised and Turning It: The Trans Revolution." *Out*, April 27. www.out.com/popnography/2015/4/27/bruce-jenner-televised-turning-it-trans-revolution.

Carlson, Shanna T. 2010. "Transgender Subjectivity and the Logic of Sexual Difference." *differences* 21, no. 2: 46–72.

———. 2013. "Transgender Subjectivity and the Logic of Sexual Difference." In *The Transgender Studies Reader 2*, edited by Susan Stryker and Aren Z. Aizura, 302–15. New York: Routledge.

Castel, Pierre-Henri. 2003. *La métamorphose impensable: Essai sur le transsexualisme et l'identité personnelle* (*The Unthinkable Metamorphosis: Essay on Transsexualism and Personal Identity*). Paris: Gallimard.

Cavanagh, Sheila L. 2016. "Transsexuality as Sinthome: Bracha L. Ettinger and the Other (Feminine) Sexual Difference." *Studies in Gender and Sexuality* 17, no. 1: 27–44.

Delay, Jean, et al. 1956. "Une demande de changement de sexe: Le trans-sexualisme" ("A Request for a Sex Change"). *L'encéphale: Journal de neurologie, de psychiatrie et de médicine psychosomatique* (*Encephalus: Journal of Neurology, Psychiatry, and Psychosomatic Medicine*) 45, no. 1: 41–80.

Derrida, Jacques. 1978. "Cogito and the History of Madness." In *Writing and Difference*, translated by Alan Bass, 31–63. London: Routledge.

Elliot, Patricia. 2001, "A Psychoanalytic Reading of Transsexual Embodiment." *Studies in Gender and Sexuality* 2, no. 4: 295–325.

———. 2010. *Debates in Transgender, Queer, and Feminist Theory: Contested Sites*. New York: Routledge.

Fenichel, Otto. 1949. "The Symbolic Equation: Girl = Phallus." *Psychoanalytic Quarterly* 18: 303–24.

Frasser, Olivia Lucca. 2015. "Generic." In *The Badiou Dictionary*, edited by Steven Corcoran, 140–42. Edinburgh: Edinburgh University Press.

Gherovici, Patricia. 2010. *Please Select Your Gender: From the Invention of Hysteria to the Democratizing of Transgenderism*. New York: Routledge.

———. 2011. "Psychoanalysis Needs a Sex Change." *Gay and Lesbian Issues and Psychology Review* 7, no. 1: 3–18.

———. 2014. "The Art of the Symptom: Body, Writing, and Sex-Change." In *A Concise Companion to Psychoanalysis, Literature, and Culture*, edited by Laura Marcus and Ankhi Mukherjee, 250–70. Oxford: Wiley Blackwell.

———. 2017. *Transgender Psychoanalysis: A Lacanian Perspective on Sexual Difference*. New York: Routledge.

Gozlan, Oren. 2011. "Transsexual Surgery: A Novel Reminder and a Navel Remainder." *International Forum of Psychoanalysis* 25, no. 1: 1–8.

———. 2015. *Transsexuality and the Art of Transitioning: A Lacanian Approach*. New York: Routledge.

Griggs, Brandon. 2015. "America's Transgender Moment." CNN.com, June 1. www.cnn.com/2015/04/23/living/transgender-moment-jenner-feat/index.html.

Hansbury, Griffin. 2005. "Mourning the Loss of the Idealized Self: A Transsexual Passage." *Psychoanalytic Social Work* 12, no. 1: 19–35.

Hooper, Tom, dir. 2015. *The Danish Girl*. DVD. Universal Sony Pictures Home Entertainment Nordic, 2017.

Hubert, Hervé. 2006. "Transsexualisme du syndrome au sinthome" ("Transsexualism from Syndrome to Sinthome"). PhD thesis, Université de Rennes 2, Rennes, France.

Kalaf Kossi, Rafael. 2011. *Corpo en obra: Contribuições para a clínica psicanalítica do transexualismo* (*Body in Progress: Contributions to a Psychoanalytic Clinic of Transexualism*). São Paulo: Enversos.

Lacan, Jacques. 1971. "Le séminaire XIX . . . Ou pire. Le savoir du psychanalyste" ("Seminar XIX . . . Or worse. The Knowledge of the Psychoanalyst"), session of December 8, 1971, unpublished papers, Gaogoa.free.fr. gaogoa.free.fr/Seminaires_HTML/19-OP/OP08121971.htm.

———. 1998. *On Feminine Sexuality, the Limits of Love, and Knowledge, 1972–1973 (Encore)*. Book 20 of *The Seminar of Jacques Lacan*, edited by Jacques-Alain Miller, translated by Bruce Fink. New York: W. W. Norton.

———. 2005. *Le sinthome* (*The Sinthome*). Book 23 of *Le séminaire de Jacques Lacan* (*The Seminar of Jacques Lacan*). Edited by Jacques-Alain Miller. Paris: Seuil.

Lewin, Bertram D. 1933. "The Body as Phallus." *Psychoanalytic Quarterly*, no. 2: 24–47.

Millot, Catherine. 1981. "Un cas de transsexualisme féminin" ("A Case of Female Transsexualism"). *Ornicar*, nos. 22–23: 167–76.

———. (1983) 1990. *Horsexe: Essay on Transsexualism*. Translated by Kenneth Hylton. New York: Autonomedia.

———. 2016. *La vie avec Lacan* (*Life with Lacan*). Paris: Editions Gallimard.

Morel, Geneviève. 2008. *La Loi de la mère: Essai sur le sinthome sexuel.* (*The Mother's Law: Essay on the Sexual Sinthome*). Paris: Anthropos Economica.

Parker, Ian. 2007. "The Phallus Is a Signifier." *Symptom*, no 8. www.lacan.com/symptom8_articles/parker8.html.

Pound, Ezra. 1975. *The Cantos of Ezra Pound*. London: Faber and Faber.

Riggs, Damien W. 2016. *Pink Herrings: Fantasy, Object Choice, and Sexuation*. London: Karnac.

Salamon, Gayle. 2010. *Assuming a Body: Transgender and Rhetorics of Materiality*. New York: Columbia University Press.

Sandler, Lauren. 2015. "America's Transgender Revolution." *Self*, July 15. www.self.com/story/americas-transgender-revolution.

Schneiderman, Stuart, ed. 1980. "Lacanian Psychosis: Interview by Jacques Lacan." In *Returning to Freud: Clinical Psychoanalysis in the School of Lacan*, 19–41. New Haven, CT: Yale University Press.

Schreber, Daniel P. (1903) 2000. *Memoirs of My Nervous Illness*. New York: New York Review of Books.

Sontag, Deborah. 2015. "'A While New Being': How Kricket Nimmons Seized the Transgender Moment." Photography by Todd Heisler, video by Kassie Bracken. *New York Times*, December 12. www.nytimes.com/2015/12/13/us/kricket-nimmons-transgender-surgery.html.

Steinmetz, Katy. 2014. "The Transgender Tipping Point." *Time*, May 29. time.com/135480/transgender-tipping-point/.

Stryker, Susan. 2006. "(De)Subjugated Knowledges: The Recent Emergence of Transgender Studies." Paper presented at the Trans/Forming Knowledge: The Implications of Transgender Studies for Women's, Gender, and Sexuality Studies symposium, Center for Gender Studies, University of Chicago, February 16–17.

Transessualità Italian-Style
or Mario Mieli's Practice of Love

ELENA DALLA TORRE

Abstract The radical theories of Italian thinker Mario Mieli are still unknown to Anglo-American audiences. Founder of the Italian homosexual movement, Mieli must be rediscovered for his theory and embodiment of *transessualità*, developed in *Elements of a Gay Critique*. This article explores *transessualità* as the product of "erotic communism," the countersexual discourse of the 1970s, which enables *transessualità*, simultaneous discovery of the woman within every man and the release of polymorphous desires, suppressed by a culture of educastration. Building on the mobile desires of De Lauretis's lesbian subjectivity via rereadings of Freud, Laplanche and Pontalis, and Bersani and Dutoit, this article claims that *transessualità* is a "practice of love" and an intersubjective knowledge that involves two interrelated material and libidinal practices: staging the "woman within" and anal intercourse. A mimetic reading of Mieli's erotic communism (anus) and Irigary's female homo-economy (lips) provides a theoretical model for reading trans-subjectivity and desire.

Keywords *transessualità*, educastration, erotic communism, mobile desires, anal *jouissance*

I believe that the overcoming of present antithetical sexual categories will be transsexual and that we will find in transsexuality the synthesis of the individual and multiple expressions of liberated Eros.

(Io credo che il superamento delle attuali categorie separate e antitetiche della sessualità sarà transessuale e che nella transessualità si coglierà la sintesi una e molteplice delle espressioni dell'Eros liberato.)

—Mario Mieli, *Elementi di critica omosessuale*

I believe that my erotic desire for women is deeply alive in me, it is deeply located in my desire to be woman. (my translation)

(Io credo che il desiderio erotico per le donne sia vivo nel mio profondo, stia in fondo al mio desiderio di essere donna.)

—Mario Mieli, *Elementi di critica omosessuale*

TSQ: Transgender Studies Quarterly ★ Volume 4, Numbers 3–4 ★ November 2017   **556**
DOI 10.1215/23289252-4189965   © 2017 Duke University Press

"Stop making love to men, make love to each other, let's make love among ourselves": it is through a witty image of lesbian lovemaking that late Italian theorist and activist Mario Mieli tried to seduce women and feminists out of a heterosexual practice of love and into "erotic communism" ([1977] 2002: 198).[1] Inspired by Herbert Marcuse's *Eros and Civilization* (1955), erotic communism is a Freudo-Marxist theory that circulated in 1970s gay movements and postulated the fluidity of bodies and desires beyond sexual difference. In France, Guy Hocquenghem, cofounder of FHAR (Front homosexuel d'action révolutionnaire), read erotic communism as a sociosexual revolution in Deleuzian fashion calling for a resexualization of society via the sexualization of the anus. Hocqueghem claimed the anus as a site of undifferentiated desires and of equal sexual liberation among men and women. At the same time, he quickly dismissed the queer feminist implications of his countereconomy of desires, focusing strictly on gay male sexuality. Mieli's erotic communism, instead, took a queer feminist and even trans bent that is still hardly ever acknowledged among his critics, and which will be the focus of my article.

Cofounder of the Italian homosexual movement FUORI (Fronte Unitario Omosessuale Rivoluzionario Italiano) in 1971, Mieli is considered in Italy one of the most original voices of the movement and the *trait d'union* between the national LGBTQ movement and the transnational one. His contribution to queer, feminist, and trans thought, which remains largely unknown to Anglo-American audiences, is being rediscovered in Italy and Europe, especially after the reissue of his theoretical work *Elementi di critica omosessuale* (*Elements of a Gay Critique* [1977] 2002), followed by essays by Teresa De Lauretis, Tim Dean, David Jacobson, Gianni Rossi Barilli, Christopher Lane, Simonetta Spinelli, and Claude Rabant. Contributors emphasize Mieli's theoretical (dis)continuities with contemporary thinkers such as Gilles Deleuze, Hocquenghem, and Michel Foucault as well as his affinities with 1990s queer and transgender theories. Although the main focus of some contributions is Mieli's proposal of liberation via a homosexualization of society, critics such as Christopher Lane remain skeptical toward a homosexualization shaping out of an erotic alliance with women. Lane considers it a mere rhetorical tactic that would leave dissatisfied both the gay men and the women in question (2002: 286). However, Lane's skepticism is built on a dismissal of Mieli's theoretical and personal engagement with femininity and feminism in favor of a focus on men, masculinity, and gay desire.

In a recent volume dedicated to Mieli's life, work, and correspondence, Maria M makes her appearance as Mieli's *donna in sé*, his woman within, embodied through theatrical performance, theorization in *Elements of a Gay Critique* ([1977] 2002),[2] and his posthumous novel, *Il risveglio dei faraoni* (*The Awakening of the Pharaohs*, 1994). Mieli's own words can be useful to understand the importance that his feminine identification had in shaping a potent queer feminist imaginary and how his feminine identification has been disavowed. French psychoanalyst Claude Rabant points us to the psychic connotations of Mieli's connection with his "woman within." Rabant uses Mieli's words to foreground Mieli's trans sensibility: "Feeling transsexual was at once one of the causes and the results of the progressive alteration of the perception of my body and my mind, of the 'external' world and that of others. Sometimes, I really felt like a woman, at times spiritually pregnant, at other times, like the reincarnation of a woman" (Rabant 2002: 299).[3] Mieli's inner femininity reemerges in his only novel, a "schizo-trip," which Marco Pustianaz qualifies of "antinovel," "part family saga, part mystical transcendental tale" (2004: 208–10).[4] Pustianaz discusses the notion of Mieli's transivity of gender and desire as both an application of radical theories and the subversion of a heteronormative plot through the feminine reincarnations of the gay male protagonist (i.e., Maria, Franca) (208–10). Like Lane, Pustianaz cautions readers about a feminist reading of Mieli's transivity, which claims that the novel rests on the deconstruction and the reaffirmation of gay male subjectivity to the detriment of femininity (210). However, when considering Mieli's theoretical actualization of his own gender transivity in *Elements*, I argue, it is possible to see the connections between his "woman within" and a queer feminist discourse, with which Mieli already entertained a rich dialogue.[5] In light of Mieli's trans-subjectivity, his gay proposal (*gaia proposta*) to make love with women acquires unforeseen implications from a standpoint of transfeminism. While Mieli incited women to a rediscovery of pleasure via a lesbian practice of love, he also inscribed himself within it as a trans subject embodying his deeply felt desire for femininity: "I believe that my erotic desire for women is deeply alive in me, it is deeply located in my desire to be woman" ([1977] 2002: 197).[6] It is within this transgender and queerly feminine erotic perspective that I would like to reread *Elements of a Gay Critique*.

Written as an undergraduate thesis, *Elements of a Gay Critique* is an unprecedented piece of cultural and theoretical production on the subject of homosexuality and is a main reference for the queer Italian community. Starting from the premise that homosexual desire is universal but repressed, Mieli delves into the history of repression, which he names "educastration." Educastration is the result of the imposition of a monosexual norm via the mutilation of an inherent transsexual component and of the multiple erotic tendencies held within one subject in childhood. As such, educastration is reminiscent of cultural clitoridectomy, a phenomenon that radical feminist Carla Lonzi (1971: 72) uses to describe the sociosymbolic erasure of female sexuality and pleasure in a masculinist culture that "maintains a taboo on the clitoris." It is therefore within the intersecting contexts of educastration and of cultural clitoridectomy that Mieli's theory of *transessualità* and his erotic communism must be situated.[7]

This article aims to reread erotic communism as a somato-political fiction and queer feminist practice of love that enables *transessualità*, via two material practices: (1) the staging of the "woman within"—a "scenario" that liberates sexuality from its hetero inscriptions, and (2) anal intercourse, which, by simultaneously touching the deeper self and unshaming the anus, becomes central to the possibility of an intrasubjective knowledge or the feminine other within. In what follows, I first introduce Mieli's critique of educastration and its queer feminist implications. I further discuss how this critique is carried out through a theorization of two different forms of disavowal, of the polymorphous nature of desire and of the "woman within." Theorization of the "woman within" will be read alongside Teresa De Lauretis's lesbian "practice of love" as a mobile desire and subjectivity decentered from the phallus; Mieli's theorizing of the anus will come into dialogue with Luce Irigaray's conceptualization of lips/labia. By showing the specularity of these two countereconomies of desire and bodies, I demonstrate how Mieli's transgender subject is mimetically produced via a process in which the "woman within" comes out speaking with and through Irigaray's lips, collapsing distinctions between interior (self) and exterior (matter).

Situating Mieli and the Subject of *Transessualità*

Mario Mieli was born into an upper-class Milanese family in 1952. Although his life was cut short by a suicide on March 12, 1983, he lived and experienced it intensely. Quoting Mieli's friend Franco Buffoni, in the preface of the anthology devoted to Mieli, Andrea Maccarrone (2014: 8) writes that Mieli seemed to have condensed an entire life experience in only three decades. What made Mieli special to his Italian contemporaries was not merely his charismatic and eccentric personality but his ability to surprise, shock, and repel audiences. It was also that "he made his theories visible to all" and "embodied them" (7), performing the theoretical in queer fashion. His nomadic spirit took him to London in the early 1970s, where he witnessed the birth of the Gay Liberation Front and lay the foundation for his later theory of "erotic communism." Back in Italy, he cofounded in 1971 the Italian gay liberation movement FUORI and later became part of a gay theatre company. By the time of his death in 1983, Mieli was already disillusioned with the gay movement because he disagreed with the movement's political revisionism and need for integration, an aspiration that he deemed divergent from his radical politics. The radicalism characterizing Mieli's thought and activism was deemphasized in the early eighties when the Italian gay movement transformed into the LGBT association Arcigay and became more interested in issues of political representation and the legalization of civil unions (Malagreca

2007: 108).[8] Mieli's literary production, which ran parallel to his theoretical one, has been only partially rediscovered. Aside from the above-mentioned novel, *Il risveglio dei faraoni*, published against the wishes of his family in 1994, Mieli also authored *Oro, eros e armmonia* (*Gold, Eros, and Harmony*), a collection of essays, interviews, and short stories (2002).[9] Mario Mieli's impact on LGBTQ Italian politics is appraised in several Italian publications, including *Antologaia* (2007) by trans sociologist Porpora Marcasciano; Cristian Loiacono's "La gaia scienza: La critica omosessuale" ("The Gay Science: The Homosexual Critique," 2007), which provides a historical approach; and *Mario Mieli: 30 anni dopo* (*Mario Mieli: Thirty Years Afterward*, 2014), edited by Dario Accolla et al. The last work, in particular, pays homage to Mieli's militancy and creative personality by gathering some unpublished material, namely, notes, letters, articles, and reflections from 1972 to 1983. Mieli's theoretical contributions help to retrace a history of sexual thought that connects feminist radical thought of the 1970s in Italy with the development of queer and trans studies in the 1990s. While some of Mieli's notions, such as "educastration," are historically and culturally specific, they are still capable of more broadly resonating with the current trans and queer studies debate, as is the case of the "woman within" or even "erotic communism." It suffices to think of *Whipping Girl*, the work of Julia Serano, whose notion of "effemimania" is closely linked to educastration (2007: 286). In this sense, Mieli anticipated not only the queer theorizations of the 1990s but also the theorizations of transness within transgender studies, a field of inquiry that came into being in the early nineties fueled by the postidentity politics stemming from the AIDS crisis (Stryker 2006: 4). As Susan Stryker explains, Europe was unlike the United States, as it saw little trans activism and theorization between the 1970s sex liberation movements and the early 1990s (5). Perhaps because she limits her observation to the United Kingdom, Stryker does not consider the trans activism, trans theorization, and performativity that found renewed expression in erotic communism in France and in Italy. One development was the birth in 1979 of Movimento Identitario Transessuale (Movement for Transsexual Identity). *Transessualità* is not Mieli's invention, as Cristian Loiacono recalls. Mieli inherits the term and concept from philosopher Luciano Parinetto (1934–2001) to refer to the anti-identitarian stances of 1970s sexual radical thought through which the very terms *man* and *woman* lost meaning (Loiacono 2007: 99). As a concept, *transessualità* cut across the boundaries of feminism and gay theory in the 1970s and therefore can be culturally reappropriated as a queer feminist production. New pharmacoporno-graphic techniques of reproduction engendered new desires, embodiments, and subjectivities.[10] Whereas transgender studies is nowadays "more attuned to questions of embodiment and identity than to those of desire and sexuality" (Stryker 2006: 7), Mieli's *transessualità* emerged as a "gay science" (*gaia scienza*) or a form of "desubjugated knowledge" (13) that stands at the intersection of embodiment, identity, desire, and sexuality, bringing them all together and into question.

Like some Italian radical feminists in the 1970s, Mieli was more animated by the desire to discover and articulate a suppressed subject than by the push to get rid of it. While Mieli defined *educastration* as the coercion of the subject into monosexuality and into the erasure of polyerotic tendencies, radical feminist Carla Lonzi theorized the erasure of female sexual autonomy and pleasure in terms of "cultural clitoridectomy."[11] With this controversial term, Lonzi described in *Sputiamo su Hegel* (*Let's Spit on Hegel*; 1972) the sexual taboo that denied women's access to an active and autonomous sexuality freed from the constraints of penetration or/and reproduction.[12] Lonzi's theory is partly reminiscent of the 1972 *Hite Report*, in which sociologist Shere Hite denounced and dispelled the myth surrounding female access to pleasure, and the phallic construction of sexuality ([1972] 2005). Lonzi uses *clitoridectomy* to refer to a symbolic and material experience of female sexuality; the symbolic and the material, however, are one and the same when one considers how psychiatrists in turn-of-the-century United States suggested that female masturbation should be discouraged by performing excision of the clitoris or burning part of the buttocks near the genitals, as Paul B. Preciado explains in *Manifiesto contrasexual* (*Contrasexual Manifesto*; 2002: 96). Mieli takes up this concept in *Elements of a Gay Critique* when he explains the functioning of educastration via a discursive link between "cultural clitoridectomy," the repression of gay desire, and the negation of differently sexed and gendered bodies: "Educastration consists, besides the concealment of the clitoris, of the repression of homosexual desire and of transsexuality, of women's whole erotic-existential dimension. Female transsexuality must be violently repressed so that women may appear feminine, suitable to men's subjugation and to the power abuses of the 'only true' sex. On the basis of the Norm, female sexuality must not exist but as submissive" ([1977] 2002: 221). When associated with clitoridectomy, educastration appears to be primarily a feminist modality for understanding the erasure of pleasure and femininity within a male-dominated society. But the discourse of sociosexual erasure was also of concern to gay groups in Italy.

Mieli may have started theorizing educastration following his own practice of "*autocoscienza*" (consciousness-raising), which Lonzi transplanted to Italy in the early 1970s, drawing from US women's practice of consciousness-raising. Mieli actively promoted consciousness-raising as a way of engaging the repressed sexual and gender component. In feminist and homosexual collectives, consciousness-raising was a talking cure and an instrument of self/collective analysis that deeply engaged the effects of educastration on individuals. It also facilitated the rediscovery of what had been kept private or disavowed out of shame—in other words, the "woman within." This feeling of shame over the woman within is the reason the figure of the transvestite can be deeply troubling, conjuring the deepest fear of crossing: "The encounter with the transvestite awakens distress that shakes to the core, in whoever sees it, the forcibly static nature of the rigidly dichotomous categories that crystallize the dualism of the sexes" (223).[13] Interestingly, Mieli likens the transsexual to a potentially "revolutionary consciousness." This consciousness amounts to the recognition that all individuals harbor the other gender within themselves (Mieli uses the word *sesso* in Italian, the only term then available to designate both sex and gender): "Throughout this book I will call transsexuality the erotic polymorphous and undifferentiated infantile disposition, which society represses and which, in adult life, every human being carries within herself/himself in a latent state or confined to the depths of the unconscious under the yoke of repression. *It seems to me that the term* transsexuality *most adequately expresses at once the plurality of the tendencies of Eros and the original and deep hermaphroditism of each individual"* (19).

From a theoretical standpoint, Mieili defines *transessualità* as both the manifestation of subjectivity and an erotic modality that opposes educastration. In an effort to signify *transessualità*, Mieli uses and perhaps confuses transsexuality and hermaphroditism. This confusion signals a resistance to a culture of educastration that "does not concede any *confusion* between sexes" (20). The coexistence of both genders/sexes within all individuals is, for Mieli, a phenomenon that cuts across the material, the biological, and the psychic and, as such, implies both an idea of erotic disposition and of gender identification. *Transessualità* is as much about subjectivity as it is about desire; in both cases, it is not about identifying or desiring the same but the other. *Transessualità* is the embodiment of an erotically polymorphous subject that returns via Mieli's rereading of the Freudian "polymorphous perverse": "Society acts in a repressive way upon children via educastration, with the purpose of constraining them to suppress their genetic sexual tendencies which it deems 'perverse.' . . . Educastration's goal is the transformation of the child, who is tendentially polymorphous and 'perverse,' into a heterosexual adult, erotically mutilated but conformed with the Norm" (17).[14] Mieli suggests that some psychological mechanisms govern the trans subject consciousness, in particular, a disavowal of an alterity within the subject. In terms of gender identification, Mieli distinguishes between those subjects who consciously embrace the(ir) other sex, physically and psychically, and those in which the other sex remains latent, or disavowed: "In general we call transsexual all those adults who consciously live their hermaphroditism and who recognize within themselves, their body, and their mind, the presence of the other sex" (20).[15] Contrary to the later experiences, educastration functions as a process of disavowal of a feminine subject inherent in every male individual. Mieli defines this disavowal in two different ways: the disavowal of the "woman per se"—intended as the biological woman ("misconoscimento della *donna in sé*")—and the rejection of the "woman within" every male ("misconoscimento della donna *in sé*"). Targets of disavowal are expressions of femininity within and outside biological female bodies. The two forms of disavowal that Mieli describes produce an estrangement vis-à-vis femininity that is responsible for the reproduction of sexism among feminists and gays. Anticipating Judith Butler's notion of gender melancholia, Mieli asserts that "'masculine' women can be decidedly heterosexual and very 'feminine' women gay" (23). However, as I argue below, Mieli's gender melancholia takes a different turn.

Butler's discussion of gender melancholia has been taken to task by transgender studies scholars, including Jay Prosser, who critiques it in his chapter "Judith Butler: Queer Feminism, Transgender, and the Transubstantiation of Sex" (in Prosser 1998). Prosser engages the (mis)use of the transgender figure on which queer theory has become dependent in order to reveal the constructedness of heterosexuality, a move that obscures at once "the transsexual desire for sex embodiment as telos" (33).[16] Butler constructs her theory through a rereading of Freud's essay "Mourning and Melancholia" in the chapter "Melancholy Gender/Refused Identification" of *The Psychic Life of Power* (1997). Unlike Freud, who insists on the incest taboo, Butler argues that it is a prohibition on homosexuality that structures both the heterosexual object-choice and a subject's gender identification. The latter is the product of an unmourned loss of a same-sex love object, which gets reinscribed on the body through a process of its incorporation. This is the reason, as long as this homosexual component is constantly disavowed, the more masculine one appears, the gayer one is, the more feminine, the more lesbian because "masculinity and femininity within the heterosexual matrix are strengthened through the repudiation that they perform" (Butler 1997: 140).

Disavowed Subjectivities: Mieli's Woman Within and De Lauretis's Lesbian

Mieli's approach to gender and sexual disavowal somewhat differs from Butler's reading of gender melancholia mainly because, in his view, the taboo is not merely over homosexuality but also and simultaneously over transsexuality. The notion of "disavowal" is also pivotal to De Lauretis's discussion of lesbian desire and subjectivity in *The Practice of Love* (1994). There, De Lauretis draws on Freud's argument that all sexuality is inherently perverse, in which *perverse* does not mean pathological but, rather, "non-heterosexual or non-normatively heterosexual" (De Lauretis 1994: xiii). De Lauretis sets out to articulate a formal model of lesbian sexuality based on Freud's negative theory of perversion. This model should be able to explain, in her view, different modalities of lesbian desire and "might be usefully considered in relation to male homosexuality or even to forms of sexuality that appear to be heterosexual but are not so in the normative or reproductive way" (xiii–xiv). While De Lauretis focuses on formalizing lesbian subjectivity and desire, she does not consider the diverse and perverse forms such desire may take, including *transessualità*. Moreover, in assuming that the trans subject does nothing but re-create the rigid boundaries of sexual difference, De Lauretis precludes the possibility that Mieli's trans may complicate sexual difference and the practice of love by means of his or her perverse desires and embodiments.[17] In a way, De Lauretis's own disavowal of Mieli's "woman within" may allow for a possible connection between lesbian subjectivity and *transessualità*. Disavowal, according to De Lauretis, is the very structuring process of lesbianism and lesbian desire. She signals Adrienne Rich's "lesbian continuum" as an example of how the specificity of the lesbian experience is obscured when lesbianism is taken to signify a whole feminist experience. Lesbianism gets articulated at the same time as its gets disavowed (De Lauretis 1994: 192).[18] What exactly is disavowed in lesbianism for De Lauretis? Lesbian desire and subjectivity are intertwined with castration and its very disavowal. In the chapter titled "The Lure of the Mannish Lesbian" (in De Lauretis 1994), De Lauretis draws on Freud's notion of the phallus and on Leo Bersani and Ulysses Dutoit's theory of the mobility of desire to explain the fetishistic and mobile nature of lesbian desire. The fetishist is someone who, having resigned themselves to castration, "can be cut off from its object, the mother, and move onto other objects thus reconceiving desire away from the phallus" (224). It is this modality of detachment that Bersani and Dutoit call "mobility of desire." Lesbian desire is mobile and fetishistic because it is postulated on the freedom from the phallus and on disavowal, that is, on the negation of castration. As a result, "what a lesbian desires in a woman," explains De Lauretis, "is indeed not a penis but a part or perhaps the whole of the female body, or something metonymically related to it, such as physical or emotional attributes" (228–29). In describing what attracts a woman to a woman, De Lauretis talks of a lesbian fetish as "any sign whatsoever that marks the difference and the desire, between the lovers: say 'the erotic signal of her hair at the nape of her neck, touching the shirt collar'" (228).

How is lesbian fetishism related at all to Mieli's "woman within"? I believe that we may claim Mieli's relation to the "woman within" as a queerly fetishist one in the way that De Lauretis describes such queer feminine fetishism in lesbian subjectivity. It seems to me that the notion of castration is an equally constitutive factor in De Lauretis and in Mieli—let's not forget that they both came from the same educastrated Italian culture of the 1970s. What differs is their use of the phallus. De Lauretis seems to maintain the Freudian distinction between two kinds of phalluses, a paternal and a maternal one, the former signifying presence, the second absence. De Lauretis holds that the presence/absence dualism is responsible for sexual difference (224n). Mieli instead shatters that dualism when he associates the paternal not so much with the phallus but with its very absence, which is at the root of the concept of trans:

> The father has, in fact, already been educastrated, nor can the son truly identify with the father if not through self-mutilation. Progressively, via this identification, the child, like his father *projects* onto the mother and onto the other women the "feminine" elements that exist in his psyche; these elements, as effect of an imposition, are not allowed to surface at the level of consciousness and force him to be ashamed of them, despite the fact that he is deeply attracted to them insofar as they are a fundamental component of his being. From this derives one of the greatest calamities of the species: the refusal, on the part of men, to recognize within themselves, "the woman," transsexuality. ([1977] 2002: 25)[19]

For Mieli, the masculine body and psyche bear the mark of an erotic mutilation. As a result of this mutilation and of the recognition of the father's castration, men are seduced into their feminine component. As a man is always already educastrated, he is a disavowed woman who remains bound up in shame, a product of erotic mutilation. Unlike in Butler's theory of gender melancholia, what is incorporated is not the lost love object of the same sex but a love object of the opposite sex, which gets buried under layers of consciousness. In a way, what happens to the masculine subject who uncovers his feminine component is germane to the lesbian seduction into the feminine explained by De Lauretis. In both, resigning oneself to castration means being seduced into the feminine. The structure of disavowal of femininity is therefore an integral part of educastration, and it is also a mechanism that governs both femininity and masculinity, a paradox that *transessualità* brings to the fore. This disavowal of femininity is responsible for the reproduction of a variety of forms of gender oppression, including (trans) misogyny or *effemimania*, a term used by Serano to explain the prejudice as well as "the obsession and the anxiety over male expressions of femininity" (2007: 286). Mieli's critique of educastration can be therefore inscribed within a queer feminist genealogy and trans genealogy that help us understand certain forms of trans-oppression, namely, "misogyny" without women, or the persistent degrading of femininity even when it leaves the spaces of the female body.

Desiring/Staging the Woman Within: Maria M, the Corrupted Norm, and the Lesbian Seduction

Mieli's theorizing of *transessualità* goes hand in hand with his staging of *transessualità*. Mieli created a stage persona named Maria M for a play of his own creation, *La traviata norma: vaffanculo, ebbene sì* (*The Corrupted Norm: Fuck Off,*

Yes Indeed), a play conceived within a theatrical group that was also part of a consciousness-raising collective. The theatre troupe was named Collettivo Teatrale Nostra Signora dei Fiori (Theater Collective Our Lady of the Flowers), with a clear reference to Jean Genet's novel *Notre dame des fleurs* (*Our Lady of the Flowers*, 1943), depicting an underground Paris crowded with *travestis* and feminine men. *The Corrupted Norm* consisted of a theatrical pastiche debunking antigay stereotypes through a satire of heterosexuality and an ironic deconstruction of straight masculinity. The show made its debut in March 1976 in Milan and was then presented in Florence and in Rome. Because of its success among popular audiences, this comic play became the first mass-audience theatrical experiment after 1968, and the first to receive a lot of positive media attention on the part of the national press (Del Re 2014: 68). The show was followed by a discussion between performers and spectators as a way to perform a reflection on questions of gender and sexuality and thus queer the audience. The play did become a space of queering, known in the Italian parlance of the 1970s as "a space of gayfication" (*uno spazio di frocializzazione*). The term *frocializzazione* (Del Re 2014: 71) was derived from *frocio* (faggot), which, like the English word *queer* had and still has a pejorative connotation, though it also has been reclaimed by many queer male activists. The staging and the reception of the play became a moment of collective liberation, a staging of erotic communism that emotionally and physically involved the audience in what was perceived as a collective release of consciousness. This release was also erotically charged because the performance included agreements made between performers and spectators for later, off-stage sexual encounters. Francesco Paolo Del Re explains that the theatrical Mieli was always already transvestite and militant. His urge to create or, so to speak, release Maria M must be understood in his attempt to show the deep feminine component of each and every male individual who was repressed in straight society (68).

The essential role of the stage in the emergence of Maria M is reminiscent of the constitutive role played by scenarios in the making of lesbian desire and subjectivity. De Lauretis bases her idea of scenario on Jean Laplanche and J. B. Pontalis's notion of fantasy and seduction in "Fantasy and the Origins of Sexuality" (1968). De Lauretis's use of Laplanche and Pontalis's theory can be fruitful to my rereading of the "woman within"—De Lauretis herself states that Mieli's theory would have benefited from a reading of Laplanche (2002: 265). De Lauretis explains that seduction is the common denominator of theories of psychoanalysis and feminism, as they share the very fact of lesbian seduction, and that feminism takes from psychoanalysis the figure of lesbianism as a phantasmatic place of seduction and pleasure: "To the extent that all women may have access to that place, female homosexuality—like hysteria, to which it is often linked and occasionally assimilated—guarantees women the status of sexed and desiring subjects, wherever their desire may be directed" (1994: 156). As the passage suggests, the seductive trait of lesbianism for feminists is that the lesbian represents "the possibility of female subjectivity and desire: she can seduce and be seduced, but without losing her status as subject" (156). Such a seductive scenario, clarifies De Lauretis, does not "need to be confined in a patriarchal frame of 'a heterosexual love story'" (157), an argument that opens up to multiple configurations of desire. It may seem that this same fantasy seduced Mieli into creating what I call a "lesbian figuration" for his erotic communism and his *transessualità*. For him there could be no true revolution without women embracing their erotic potential as subjects and bringing to the surface their own homoerotic desire for femininity. In this respect, similar to lesbian separatists, Mieli seems to depart from some strands of 1970s understanding of female homosexuality as a strictly political practice.[20] Mieli reinfuses the active desire for femininity, which was lost or else disavowed in political homosexuality. This loss seems to be occasioned precisely as the effect of what De Lauretis calls "the homosexual maternal metaphor" that constitutes the matrix of feminism (190).[21]

Toward New Erotic Encounters: The Anus Meets the Lips

Mieli's figuration of erotic communism and *transessualità* as queerly feminine lovemaking should not be taken as a mere reappropriation of a feminist trope or, worse, as a violation of boundaries as Janice Raymond would have it in "Sappho by Surgery" (2006). Rather, it situates Mieli within a sexual difference that, as Gayle Salamon understands it, is postulated on a place of encounter "between bodies and psyches who do not find easy home or place within [these] categories" (2010: 133). Mieli's erotically political fiction of *transessualità* illuminates the historical and culturally specific boundaries of feminism in light of queer and trans studies. It points us to the ways in which trans-subjectivity can creatively use feminist discursive tools while questioning them. In what follows, I propose to read Mieli's erotic communism next to Luce Irigaray's female homoerotic economy. Both economies are predicated on the activation of desires that run counter to the phallic economy and are therefore attached to and signified via nonreproductive organs, namely, the anus of erotic communism and the vaginal lips of female homoeroticism. In examining how these two countereconomies are specular, my aim is to show how Mieli's transgender subject is mimetically produced through a process in which the "woman within" comes out speaking with and through Irigaray's lips.

In Irigaray's now famous essay "When Our Lips Speak Together" (in Irigaray 1985), the vaginal lips evoke an all-feminine language of bodies and desires, in opposition to the masculine construction of female sexuality, in which women have no options to articulate their desire other than through masculine language.

Much has been written on this essay, and feminist scholars have pointed out, for instance, that Irigaray's rediscovery of the multiple libidinal dimensions rooted in the materiality of women's bodies is no less phallogocentric than the "ho(m) mosexual" exchange between men. Feminist critics have also differed with regard to how Irigaray's discursive strategies work toward essentializing femininity and sexual difference (Jagose 1994; Schor 1994; Braidotti 1991). Queer feminist scholar Lynn Huffer takes a diverging path that aims to rediscover the queerness within Irigaray's sexual difference. In "Are the Lips a Grave?" she debunks the presumed heterosexist construction of the lips, arguing that sexual difference advocated by Irigaray is "more than the difference between 'man' and 'woman,' it already describes a queer alterity within heterosexuality" (2011: 526). Conceptualizing the lips as a figure for a queer heterosexuality, Huffer opens it up to the reconceptualization of an ethics of alterity. By further reading the lips with Bersani's rectum, she sets out to show that this ethics of alterity lies on Bersani's and Irigaray's shared "commitment to the queer undoing of modern subjectivity" (522) and "with a Foucaultian erotic ethics of the other that links the act of loving and of knowing" (533). I find the pattern of associating queerness with the undoing of subjectivity and self-shattering quite troublesome. Irigary's lips, when read via Mieli's "erotic communism," perversely signified by the anus, get recast not as a queer undoing of modern subjectivity but as the very making of trans-subjectivity.

In Irigaray's essay, the vaginal lips oppose the construction of sexuality as always already masculine and as a sublimation of male homosexuality, a process that, as Hocquenghem explains in *Homosexual Desire* (1972), happens through the privatization of the anus. According to Hocquenghem, the anus, associated as it is to its excremental function, remains the most controlled body part in society. In phallic terms, the anus is the "site of a mysterious and private kind of production: that is the excremental production" (98). The anus is therefore a shamed body part to be kept hidden and private. Such "privatization" of the anus can be read both as the disavowal of a desiring zone for all individuals and as a refusal to recognize a deeper intrasubjective feminine component. This misrecognition has to do, as Lorenzo Bernini points out in his analysis of *Homosexual Desire*, with the refusal to associate homosexual desire with a certain understanding of the feminine as passive, penetrative, and masochistic (2013: 83). Hocquenghem goes as far as warning his readers not to confuse the anus with the vagina, rejecting both the idea of a reproductive sexuality and of the homosexual man as a "femme manquée," the failed woman of a heterosexist order. In it, continues Hocquenghem, "homosexuality is thus defined by its lack . . . and assumed to signify hatred of woman, who is the only sexual object" (1972: 77). In relation to women, homosexuals are devoid of an object and have no access to women, a supposed lack that leaves but "the transformation of the homosexual into a substitute woman," "an

artificial woman," and "the image of an image" (120). While I understand Hocquenghem's rejection of a link between femininity and passivity, it seems to
me that what is at stake here is also Hocquenghem's own dependence on a
subject/object scheme, a dominant model that Mieli's "woman within" breaks
through. Mieli's erotic communism, unlike Hocquenghem's, may be said to enact
a sort of Deleuzian "*devenir femme*" (becoming woman) as evoked by philosopher
René Schérer in his "Entretien chimérique" ("Chimeric Encounter") with Roland
Surzur and Paulette Kayser (2008: 152–53). Lover and mentor of Hocquenghem,
Schérer recalls the sexualization of the anus precisely via the queer trans figuration
of the "*devenir-femme*," which he explains as a sociosymbolic process through
which men relinquish dependence on a naturalizing link between masculinity and
domination.

     This shift to the queer masculine process of "becoming woman" is also
what Mieli envisions when articulating men's inner femininity around his anal
practice, and then around his call for a queer feminine lovemaking. Within his
erotic communism, the anus does go from being a discrete site of shameful
discharge to being a public site of free-flowing desire; however, in contrast with
Hocquenghem's, it also marks a return to a deep polyerotic self and to the femininity shamefully hidden within men. The liberation of the anus is a practice of
love that acquires at least three sociosexual meanings: it becomes the place of
release of repressed desires and pleasures, a place of libidinal circulation, and the
site of liberation of the "woman within," the direct product of a deep anal
jouissance. Although a surface organ, the anus evokes, in Mieli's use of language,
an idea of depth: "The point is that if you let yourself be taken from behind, if you
know how deep of an enjoyment you may get from anal intercourse, you are
bound to become different from the 'normal' people with a frigid ass. You know
yourself more deeply" (Mieli [1977] 2002: 148).[22] Deep *jouissance* through the anus
is here associated with access and knowledge of a deeper part of oneself, which
Mieli characterizes as transsexual.[23] In a way it is as if the "woman within," so
deeply embedded within the educastrated self, comes to the surface—the surface
of the body and of the psyche—by means of deep anal *jouissance*.[24] In fact,
according to Mieli, the fear of anal intercourse in men stems from a fear of
castration and a return to femininity, in other words, a fear of crossing. This fear
reads both as misogynistic and transphobic (148).

     As Mieli's practice of love is inextricably linked with men's encounter with
their inner femininity, Mieli's anus can be seen as being in perpetual contact with
the "woman within," a "becoming woman" that evokes Irigaray's "*parler-femme*"
(speaking woman). Irigaray's *parler-femme* is signified through the lips/labia, the
queer image of women's constant (being in) touch with their own bodies and each
other's bodies: "Kiss me. Two lips kissing two lips: openness is ours again. Our

'world.' And the passage from the inside out, from the outside in, the passage between us, is limitless. Without end. No knot or loop, no mouth ever stops our exchanges. Between us the house has not wall, the clearing no enclosure, language non circularity. When you kiss me, the world grows so large that the horizon itself disappears" (Irigaray 1985: 210).

That passage from the "inside out" and from the "outside in," which characterizes Mieli's anal desublimation, perversely mimics the labial language of Irigaray. Lips are no longer there to delimit a threshold and a dichotomy between inside and outside, between depth and surface; they simply make borders and dichotomies meaningless. When the anus and the lips meet, they mobilize desire away from the phallus, as in Bersani and Dutoit's predicament. If we think of Mieli's call for an all-feminine lovemaking, lips and anus stand in a discursive continuum, in which feminine bodies recognize each other as "speaking bodies," to adopt an expression used by Preciado in *Manifiesto contrasexual* (2002: 13).[25] They also describe a polymorphous desire that can take different shapes from trans desire for femininity to a desire between women, and a desire between trans women and cis-women. Making the anus speak through the lips is not a mere rhetorical tactic; it is a gesture that already characterized Mieli's theorizing and his own relationship with a radical feminist discourse. Mieli's erotic communism is a practice of knowing self and the other posited as an act of loving: "Between women and queens a new way of making love is invented, which, despite the historical and biological differences between the sexes and the contradictions inherent in the power tied to them, [this love] is posited tendentially and intentionally as a new form of pleasure and of intersubjective knowledge" (Mieli [1977] 2002: 194).[26] The "new way of making love" points to forms of friendship, complicities, alliances, and love that make for a sensual and political continuum that is conducive to a different way of knowing, an intersubjective knowledge. For Mieli, this intersubjective knowledge is represented through a process of double and reciprocal mimicking. In it, the trans subject is not the only one mimicking the feminine. All women (cis-women) are also ultimately mimicking the language of femininity that the trans subject reinvents: "Femininity will be a male transvestite. Afterward a woman can return as the double of a transvestite . . . who imitated femininity. A woman is still nonexistent" (27).[27] In this process of double mimicking, the category of sex is declared "nonexistent" in favor of performances of femininity or polymorphous femininities, or femininities engendered by polymorphous desires. If, as Mieli recalls in *Elements of a Gay Critique*, "the achievement of transsexuality can only follow from the work of the women's movement and the complete liberation of homoeroticism" (38), his call was multidirectional: it was a call for women to liberate themselves from an educastrating experience of bodies and sexualities; it reflected the emergence of a revolutionary consciousness that carried the potential to make manifest everybody's own deep transsexual being; and it released the "woman within" from the rediscovery of a queer desire for femininity. Only at that point does Mieli's practice of love become not so much a lesbian practice but something like a queer trans feminist practice of love.

Caressing the Woman Within

Mieli's transsexual consciousness powerfully echoes recent cinematic narratives such as *The Danish Girl* (dir. Tom Hooper, 2015), which centers on the making of trans-subjectivity and desire. In *The Danish Girl*, the female artist Gerda Wegener (Alicia Vikander) approves of her husband Einar Wegener's deep desire to "come out" as "Lili," a transition that is retold with painful bliss. In a crucial sequence of the movie, Einar (Eddie Redmayne) goes to a brothel and pays to watch a woman touch her own body in an act of autoeroticism. However, the autoerotic perspective of the woman's caress is completely transformed by the protagonist's gaze. His gaze is not voyeuristic, however, and it is not merely narcissistic either. We may say that it is trans-erotic. As he watches, he simultaneously caresses himself, mimicking the autoerotic gesture of the woman; he touches himself as if he were a woman. Or better said, he touches and looks at herself as the specular image of the other woman, and ultimately as a woman. Touch and gaze collapse within a visually tactile economy that produces the protagonist as subject and object at once, as a subject erotically and mimetically engaged with his own inner femininity. That auto/homo/allo-eroticism is fecund in the sense that it engenders a subject that lies deeply underneath a surface by making that subject manifest. The generative impetus of the caress evoked by Irigaray's "Fecundity of the Caress" is "prior to and following any positioning of the subject" (Irigaray 1993: 186). However, in the movie sequence, the caress and the subject positioning as a woman are actually taking place at the same time, facilitated by the mimetic and the specular act. The following is a quotation from Irigaray's text, in which I deliberately perform a change of subject and object pronouns, using brackets to signal the emergence of a trans-subject from the fecund caress, just as we see it portrayed in *The Danish Girl*: "As he caresses [herself], he bids [her] neither to disappear nor to forget but rather to remember the place where, for her, the most intimate life is held in reserve. Searching for what has not yet come into being for himself, he invites [her] to become what [she] have not yet become. To realize a birth that is still in the future . . . awakening [her] to another birth—as a loving woman" (187). Like the protagonist of *The Danish Girl*, whose plot is based on real-life diaries, Mario Mieli died prematurely, leaving us with the sense of a subject and a body in the making, something like a transsexual subject. Only by rereading Mieli's joyous struggle to embody a trans-subject through the very language of theory may we have a fuller understanding of the ways in which erotic communism has been crucially generative, in the shadow of Deleuze, Foucault, and the French feminists, anticipating the transformative impact of queer and trans studies in the early 1990s. Although erotic communism may appear as the forgotten theory of 1970s European sexual movements, its transsexual character forcefully reemerges in Preciado's somatic communism[28] and in the burgeoning trans narratives across many fields of knowledge and representation.

Elena Dalla Torre is non-tenure-track assistant professor of Italian and women's and gender studies at Saint Louis University. Her articles on masculinities, radical feminism, and European migration cinema have appeared in the *European Journal of Women's Studies*, *Italian Studies*, and *g/s/i: Gender/Sexuality/Italy*. She coedited a volume on the cinema of director Marco Tullio Giordana, *Il cinema di Marco Tullio Giordana. Interventi critici* (*The Cinema of Marco Tullio Giordana: Critical Interventions*; 2015).

Notes

1. "Non fate più all'amore con i maschi, fate all'amore tra donne, facciamo l'amore tra noi."
2. The Gay Men Press in 1980 issued an English translation of *Elementi di critica omosessuale* by David Fernbach (Mieli 1980).
3. "Il sentirmi transessuale fu una delle cause e insieme dei risultati del progressivo alterarsi della percezione del mio corpo e della mente, del mondo 'esterno' e degli altri. A volte mi sentivo proprio donna, a volte spirtitualmente incinta, altre come reincarnazione di una donna."
4. Editor Luigi Einaudi already had a draft of the novel when Mieli died in 1983. The novel was later published in 1994 against the will of Mieli's family and with the support of the Centro di iniziativa Luca Rossi in Milan.
5. Lesbian activist Simonetta Spinelli acknowledges in "Passioni a confronto: Mieli e le lesbiche femministe" ("Passions Compared: Mieli and Lesbian Feminists"): "Mieli knew feminist theorizations. He kept quoting the writings of the Milanese feminists that appeared in the journal *L'Erba voglio*. His analyses on the connections between female subordination, reproductive sexuality, women's objectification, and male impotence veiled as violent machismo and expression of a mutilated Eros followed many analyses of the Roman feminist collectives" (2002: 314; translation mine).
6. All translations from Mieli's work are mine.
7. My use of the Italian *transessualità* throughout this article is intended to stress both the cultural and historical specificity of the term and its divergence from current uses of the words *transsexual* and *transgender*.
8. Miguel Malagreca writes, "Some segments of Italian gay activism had given up the radical politics of the 1970s in favor of an identitarian frame imported from the United States" (2007: 106).
9. Mieli's legacy perseveres in the active work of promoting and supporting the Roman-based association named after him, the Circolo Mario Mieli. Since its inception, the Circle has been invested in the politics of care brought about by the outbreak of AIDS.

10. I am here adopting Paul B. Preciado's use of *pharmacopornographic* as he clarifies it in *Testo Junkie: Sex, Drugs, and Biopolitics in the Pharmacopornographic Era* (2013). Preciado defines *pharmacopornographic* as "the processes of a biomolecular (pharmaco) and semiotico technical (pornographic) government of sexual subjectivity" (33–34).

11. Educastration and cultural clitoridectomy are reminiscent of, respectively, the Freudian narratives of castration and Gayle Rubin's sex/gender system.

12. For further discussion of "cultural clitoridectomy" and feminine subjectivity in 1970s Italian radical feminism, see Dalla Torre 2014.

13. "L'incontro con il travestito risveglia angoscia poiché scuote dalle fondamenta, in chi lo vede, la forzata staticità delle categorie rigidamente dicotomiche che cristallizzano la dualità dei sessi."

14. "La società agisce repressivamente sui bambini, tramite l'*educastrazione,* allo scopo di costringerli a rimuovere le tendenze sessuali congenite che essa giudica 'perverse.' . . . L'educastrazione ha come obiettivo la trasformazione del bimbo, tendenzialmente polimorfo e 'perverso,' in adulto eterosessuale, eroticamente mutilato ma conforme alla Norma" (17).

15. "In genere, si chiamano transessuali tutti gli adulti che vivono coscientemente il proprio ermafroditismo e che riconoscono in sé, nel proprio corpo e nella mente, la presenza dell'altro sesso."

16. Among the consequences of this theoretical interdependence has been the entanglement between homosexuality and transgender identity and the deliteralization of sex as well as its displacement from materiality (interiority) to fantasy (surface).

17. De Lauretis thus aligns herself with a feminist trend that condemns "the discursivizing of sex and "the utopia of free-floating desire" (1994: 7) as mere forms of sexual indifference and women's desexualization. However, De Lauretis does deal with questions of bodily surface and depth, and trans-identification in other essays such as "Sintomatologia dei generi" ("Gender Symptoms"), included in De Lauretis 1999.

18. The importance of configuring lesbianism as a sociosymbolic form at a time when it was seen as psychosis or sexual aberration has been all but eclipsed by the popular version of the "'lesbian continuum.' . . . The continuum has been invoked less often to articulate further the conditions and the many other modes of the lesbian existence than to metaphorize lesbianism into the sign of an implicitly heterosexual female resistance and desire."

19. "Il padre, infatti, è già stato educastrato, né il figlio può identificarsi realmente col padre se non mutilandosi. Via via, tramite questa identificazione, il bambino, come il padre, *proietta* sulla madre e sulle altre donne gli elementi "femminili" esistenti nella propria psiche; elementi che gli si impone di non ammettere alla coscienza, costringendolo a vergognarsene, malgrado essi lo attraggano profondamente in quanto componente fondamentale del suo essere. Da ciò deriva una delle più grandi calamità che abbiano colpito la specie: il rifiuto, da parte dell'uomo, di riconoscere in sé 'la donna,' la transessualità."

20. In her book *Movimento a più voci* (*Multivocal Movement*) Italian feminist Maria Schiavo distinguishes between lesbianism as erotic practice and political homosexuality, "something more dynamic and nuanced, which Italian women inherited from the psychoanalytic practice of the French *Psych et Po*" (2002: 63).

21. For De Lauretis, the problem with that founding, albeit seductive, metaphor lies in the fact that "by joining the two terms of desire and identification with the mother" it negates

"both lesbianism and narcissism while at the same time installing them at the core of female subjectivity and of feminism" (1994: 190).

22. "Il punto è che se ti fai inculare, se sai quale profondissimo godimento dal coito anale puoi trarre, diventi per forza diverso dalla gente 'normale' col culo *frigido. Ti conosci più a fondo.*"

23. "Diremo che se né l'omosessualità né l'eterosessualità manifeste corrispondono necessariamente a caratteristiche psichiche, somatiche e ormonali specifiche, sia il desiderio gay che quello per l'altro sesso sono espressioni del nostro essere transessuale profondo, tendenzialmente polimorfo, costretto dalla repressione ad adattarsi a una monosessualità che lo mutila" (We will say that neither manifest homosexuality nor heterosexuality necessarily correspond to specifically psychic, somatic and hormonal features. Both gay desire and desire for the other sex are expressions of our deep transsexual being, tendentially polymorphous, constrained by repression to adapt to a monosexuality that mutilates it; Mieli [1977] 2002: 23).

24. The question of anal politics has been reactualized and reread in Paul B. Preciado's transfictions, namely, in *Testo Junkie* (2013). Preciado has also authored the preface to the Spanish translation of Hocquenghem's *Homosexual Desire*, with the title "Terror Anal." Preciado's reterritorialization of the anus from the point of view of transmasculinity is a fascinating theoretical turning point that deserves a separate and in-depth treatment.

25. "En el marco del contrato contrasexual, los cuerpos se reconocen a sí mismos no como hombres o mujeres sino como cuerpos hablantes, y reconocen a los otros como cuerpos hablantes."

26. "Fra donne e checche si inventa un altro modo di fare all'amore che, malgrado le differenze storico-bilogiche tra i sessi e le contraddizioni inerenti al potere legate ad esse si pone tendenzialmente, e intenzionalmente come nuova forma di piacere, e di conoscenze intersoggetive."

27. "I emphasized the importance of the liberation of homosexuality within the frame of human emancipation: as a matter of fact, for the creation of communism, one necessary condition among the others is the complete release of the homoerotic tendencies, that once liberated can guarantee that a totalizing communication among human beings can be achieved regardless of their sex" (Mieli [1977] 2002: 27). Once again the translation is mine because the English edition omitted Mieli's quotation of the Italian feminist journal. This part is also omitted from the notes.

28. It is worth mentioning that "erotic communism" is being revitalized through Preciado's call for somatic communism. In *Manifiesto contrasexual* and *Testo Junkie*, Preciado inscribes its transnarrative into two different queer and equally important queer traditions, the one traced by Deleuze, Foucault, and Hocquenghem, and the other traced by French lesbianism and radical feminism, in particular, Monique Wittig's.

References

Accolla, Dario, et al. 2014. *Mario Mieli: 30 anni dopo* (*Mario Mieli: Thirty Years Afterward*). Rome: Circolo Mario Mieli.

Bernini, Lorenzo. 2013. *Apocalissi queer: Elementi di teoria antisociale* (*Queer Apocalypses: Elements of Antisocial Theory*). Pisa: Edizioni ETS.

Braidotti, Rosi. 1991. *Patterns of Difference: A Study of Women in Contemporary Philosophy.* Translated by Elizabeth Guild. Oxford: Polity.

Butler, Judith. 1997. *The Psychic Life of Power*. Stanford, CA: Stanford University Press.

Dalla Torre, Elena. 2014. "The Clitoris Diaries: *La Donna Clitoridea*, Feminine Authenticity, and the Phallic Allegory of Carla Lonzi's Radical Feminism." *European Journal of Women's Studies* 21, no. 3: 219–32.

De Lauretis, Teresa. 1994. *The Practice of Love: Lesbian Sexuality and Perverse Desire*. Bloomington: Indiana University Press.

———. 1999. *Soggetti eccentrici* (*Eccentric Subjects*). Milan: Feltrinelli.

———. 2002. "La gaia scienza ovvero la traviata norma" ("The Gay Science or the Corrupted Norm"). In Mieli (1977) 2002: 261–68.

Del Re, Francesco Paolo. 2014. "La perfomance totale di Maria M" ("The Total Performance of Maria M"). In Accolla et al. 2014: 66–89.

Hite, Shere. (1972) 2005. *The Hite Report: A Nationwide Study of Female Sexuality*. New York: Seven Stories.

Hocquenghem, Guy. 1972. *Homosexual Desire*. Translated by Daniella Dangor. Durham, NC: Duke University Press.

Hooper, Tom, dir. 2015. *The Danish Girl*. DVD. Universal Sony Pictures Home Entertainment Nordic, 2017.

Huffer, Lynne. 2011. "Are the Lips a Grave?" *GLQ* 17, no. 4: 517–42.

Irigaray, Luce. 1985. *This Sex Which Is Not One*. Translated by Catherine Porter and Carolyn Burke. Ithaca, NY: Cornell University Press.

———. 1993. *An Ethics of Sexual Difference*. Translated by Catherine Porter and Carolyn Burke. Ithaca, NY: Cornell University Press.

Jagose, Annamarie. 1994. *Lesbian Utopics*. New York: Routledge.

Laplanche, Jean, and J. B. Pontalis. 1968. "Fantasy and the Origins of Sexuality." *International Journal of Psychoanalysis* 49, no. 1: 1–18.

Lane, Christopher. 2002. "L'estetica transessuale di Mieli" ("The Transsexual Aesthetics of Mieli"). In Mieli (1977) 2002: 279–90.

Loiacono, Cristian. 2007. "La gaia scienza: La critica omosessuale di Mario Mieli" ("The Gay Science: The Homosexual Critique"). *Zapruder*, May–August: 96–103.

Lonzi, Carla. 1971. *Sputiamo su Hegel* (*Let's Spit on Hegel*). Milan: Rivolta Femminile.

Maccarrone, Andrea. 2014. Preface to Accolla et al. 2014: 7–10.

Malagreca, Miguel. 2007. *Queer Italy. Contexts, Antedecents, and Representation*. New York: Peter Lang.

Marcasciano, Porpora. 2007. *Antologaia* (*Anthologay*). Milan: Il Dito e la Luna.

Mieli, Mario. 1980. *Homosexuality and Liberation: Elements of a Gay Critique*. Translated by David Fernbach. London: Gay Men's Press.

———. 1994. *Il risveglio dei faraoni* (*The Awakening of the Pharaohs*). Milan: Centro di iniziativa Luca Rossi.

———. (1977) 2002. *Elementi di critica omosessuale* (*Elements of a Gay Critique*). Milan: Feltrinelli.

———. 2002. *Oro, eros e armonia* (*Gold, Eros, and Harmony*). Milan: Edizioni Croce.

Preciado, Paul B. 2002. *Manifiesto contrasexual* (*Contrasexual Manifesto*). Barcelona: Anagrama.

———. 2009. "Terror Anal" ("Anal Terror"). In *Deseo Homosexual* (*Homosexual Desire*), by Guy Hocquenghem, 133–70. Santa Cruz de Tenerife, Spain: Melusina.

———. 2013. *Testo Junkie: Sex, Drugs, and Biopolitics in the Pharmacopornographic Era*. New York: Feminist.

Prosser, Jay. 1998. *Second Skins: The Body Narratives of Transsexuality*. New York: Columbia University Press.

Pustianaz, Marco. 2004. "Transitive Gender and Queer Performance in the Novels of Mario Mieli and Vittorio Pescatori." In *Queer Italia*, edited by Gary P. Cestaro, 207–35. New York: Palgrave.

Rabant, Claude. 2002. "Un clamore sospeso tra la vita e la morte" ("A Clamor between Life and Death"). In Mieli (1977) 2002: 291–302.

Raymond, Janice. 2006. "Sappho by Surgery." In *The Transgender Studies Reader*, edited by Susan Stryker and Stephen Whittle, 131–40. New York: Routledge.

Salamon, Gayle. 2010. *Assuming a Body: Transgender and Rhetorics of Materiality*. New York: Columbia University Press.

Schérer, René, R. Surzur, and P. Kayser. 2008. "Entretien chimérique" ("Chimerical Interview"). In "Désir Hocquenghem: Revue des schizoanalyses," special issue, *Chimères*, no. 69: 149–68.

Schiavo, Maria. 2002. *Movimento a più voci* (*A Multivocal Movement*). Milan: Fondazione Elvira Badaracco.

Schor, Naomi. 1994. "This Essentialism Which Is Not One: Coming to Grips with Irigaray." In *The Essential Difference*, edited by Naomi Schor and Elizabeth Weed, 40–61. Bloomington: Indiana University Press.

Serano, Julia. 2007. *Whipping Girl: A Transsexual Woman on Sexism and the Scapegoating of Femininity*. Berkeley, CA: Seal.

Spinelli, Simonetta. 2002. "Passioni a confronto: Mieli e le lesbiche femministe" ("Facing Passions: Mieli and the Lesbian Feminists"). In Mieli (1997) 2002: 313–20.

Stryker, Susan. 2006. "(De)Subjectivated Knowledges: An Introduction to Transgender Studies." In *The Transgender Studies Reader*, edited by Susan Stryker and Stephen Whittle, 1–17. New York: Routledge.

Transgender Subjectivity in Revolt

*Kristevan Psychoanalysis and the Intimate
Politics of Rebirth*

AMY RAY STEWART

Abstract This article engages with the psychoanalytic works of Julia Kristeva in order to demonstrate how trans and queer experiences are shaped and mobilized by a psychic life of revolt. Reorienting the question of resistance toward the threshold of psychical and social life, the author claims that "intimate revolt," as conceived in Kristeva's later writings, is what mobilizes trans and queer subjectivities in a movement of endless regeneration. The article begins with an overview of the theme of revolt in Kristeva's psychoanalytic thought and stresses three interrelated movements — return, rupture, and rebirth — that together shape and sustain psychical life. Uncovering the exchanges between psychical and social life, the author identifies how inner experiences of revolt mobilize not only a resuscitation of meaning and subjectivity but also a reframing of resistance within Kristeva's intimate politics. The author then illustrates how this internal logic of revolt unfolds within trans and queer experiences of identity and embodiment. In doing so, the author examines conditions of precarity that threaten the survivability of trans and queer populations, particularly with respect to the psychic life of revolt that makes possible our psychical and corporeal capacities for resistance and renewal. Transitioning from the landscape of precarity to the language of liminality, the author contends that the intimate evolutions of revolt constitute a passage of perpetual rebirth in which meaning and subjectivity may be infinitely refashioned.

Keywords Julia Kristeva, psychoanalysis, transgender, intimate revolt, precarity

> Psychical life knows that it will only be saved if it gives itself the time and space of revolt: to break off, remember, refashion.
>
> —Julia Kristeva, *Intimate Revolt*

We Laugh at Danger (And Break All the Rules)

On May 15, 2016, only months after the passage of North Carolina's House Bill 2 (HB2), Against Me! arrived in downtown Durham to play a sold-out show. The politically conscious punk band led by Laura Jane Grace, an unapologetic transgender woman, announced through social media that their presence would

TSQ: Transgender Studies Quarterly ★ Volume 4, Numbers 3–4 ★ November 2017 **577**
DOI 10.1215/23289252-4189974 © 2017 Duke University Press

double as a protest to the troubling piece of legislation also known as the state's "bathroom bill." As is widely known, HB2 targeted trans and queer communities by mandating that citizens use public restrooms in strict accordance with their sex as assigned at birth.[1] Unlike the many artists, organizations, and corporations that have protested this law by withdrawing their engagements with the state, Against Me! resolved to play their show as scheduled as well as collaborate with local trans and queer activists to voice resistance against the discriminatory legislation. Just before launching into their set, Grace marched onto the cramped stage with her guitar, pulled out a lighter, and set fire to her birth certificate, smiling and shouting defiantly into the microphone: "Goodbye, gender!" (Monroe 2016). As Grace's legal documentation of name and sex went up in flames, the crowd erupted in shouts of support and solidarity. Her symbolic obliteration of the sexed signifier that had long haunted her private life thus drew precise public attention to the precarious conditions that shape and affect experiences of trans identity and embodiment. Collapsing purposefully the private into the public, the intimate into the social, Grace's performative act of burning her birth certificate onstage therefore solicits an engagement with the tenuous threshold of psychical and social life.

Grace's protest is, of course, but one of countless instances in which trans or queer persons have underscored that our existence is indeed resistance. To be sure, the queer life of revolt that witnessed the Compton's Cafeteria and Stonewall riots, the rise of STAR House, and so many other shapes of trans resistance over time and space, including Jennicet Gutiérrez's dissent during a pride celebration at the White House, continues to drive our resilient movements for inclusive liberation. This wider theme of revolt was celebrated, or arguably capitalized upon, in the recent special issue of *National Geographic* (2017) that proclaimed "Gender Revolution" boldly across its cover and featured narratives of how concepts and experiences of sex and gender are being resisted and refashioned around the globe. I chose to begin with Grace's performative protest not only because the punk scene from which Against Me! surfaced helped shape my political consciousness as a youth and later encouraged me to embrace my trans and queer identity but also because Grace's artistic navigation of identity and embodiment reflect precisely the forms of revolt that I aim to examine here through the psychoanalytic work of Julia Kristeva. What we will discover over the course of our analysis, then, is that trans and queer forms of resistance are both mobilized and made possible by the intimate evolutions that Kristeva identifies in the psychic life of revolt. Indeed, the guiding claim of this article is that trans and queer subjectivities reveal a precarious mobilization of what Kristeva terms "intimate revolt," which she posits as neither a form of social upheaval nor political revolution but, rather, as a psychical experience of regeneration (2002a: 3). In this way, Grace's act of resistance uncovers an internal logic at the heart of her social protest, an inner life of revolt that makes possible not simply a transgressive political rebellion but, more precisely, what Kristeva describes as a transformative "psychical rebirth" (2010: 158).

If queer forms of revolt, such as Grace's decision to publicly destroy her birth certificate, arise as a transgressive or transformative mediation of the social and political conditions of precarity peculiar to trans and queer communities, then it is Kristevan psychoanalysis, I contend, that delivers a most exacting discourse through which this unsettled threshold of psychical and social life might be recognized and reimagined. To be sure, the clinical and cultural assemblages of psychoanalysis, psychiatry, and psychology have a fraught and well documented history of producing trans identities as psychopathologies and reducing queer bodies to medical anomalies, routinely diagnosing difference as resistant cases in need of treatment or cure (Meyerowitz 2002; Singer 2006; Stryker 2008). Amidst escalating health-care disparities, expansive biopolitical techniques, and the contested status of diagnoses that face trans and queer persons navigating an increasingly globalized medical industrial complex, reservations and resistances to psychoanalysis and psychiatry on the part of trans and queer communities, scholars, and activists remain and are assuredly justified (Butler 2004a; Foucault 2003; O'Brien 2013; Spade 2006). As this article demonstrates, however, Kristeva's psychoanalytic writings enable us to address and articulate those precarious experiences felt so acutely at the intersection and exchange of psychical and social life, particularly with respect to subjectivities that exist in-between or beyond established binaries. What we discover at the heart of trans and queer subjectivities, then, is a psychic life of revolt that drives our discursive forms of resistance. "By limiting herself to *intimate* revolts," S. K. Keltner explains, "Kristeva is able to examine larger social and historical formations insofar as the trials of individuals concretely expose, as well as critically and imaginatively negotiate, social and political problematics" (2011: 106). Not unlike the "tiny revolts" that Kristeva unearths and claims as pivotal in artwork and literature, mysticism and music, and of course psychoanalytic praxis, the above narrative of Grace's protest is meant to reorient our understanding of the social and political problematics facing trans and queer subjectivities toward the intimate realms in which these problematics are deeply embodied and indeed lived through (2002a: 5). Psychoanalysis thus facilitates our return to this inner realm of experience in and from which intimate revolt erupts, for "no other discourse, no other inquiry or therapy," Kristeva maintains, "is better able to recognize lack of being and to inscribe it in a project of continual rebirth, whether subtle or startling" (2010: 43).

This article, which is arguably the first to couch a sustained analysis of trans and queer subjectivities in and through Kristeva's psychoanalytic thought, therefore imagines the possibilities that her psychoanalytic oeuvre may cultivate for future meanings of trans and queer experience.[2] Although my aim is not to present an account of Kristeva's position on trans or queer subjectivity as such, her broader emphasis on meaning and subjectivity as tenuous and always incomplete processes, as well as her approach to the interstices of psychical and social life, are what distinguish her psychoanalytic thought and make her intellectual corpus so productive for my analysis of trans and queer forms of intimate revolt. "Kristeva's understanding of sexual difference," Keltner indicates, "is neither biologically essentialist nor simply socially constructivist," for her psychoanalytic approach to meaning and subjectivity instead claims that sexual difference "is articulated at the boundary of flesh and word" (2011: 99). To be sure, since her earliest work on semiotic functioning and subject formation, Kristeva has proven to be a theorist of boundaries and thresholds, of limits and liminality, stressing a "material process of differentiation and non-differentiation that refuses any unity of subjectivity and meaning and instead thrives on the transitive tensions and passions of concrete life" (3). Insofar as Kristeva posits neither the sexed body nor gender or sexual identity outside language, culture, and representation, her psychoanalytic approach to meaning and subjectivity (always mediated by a dialectical tension of the semiotic and the symbolic) reminds us that the body is resistant to rigid binaries and, instead, remains an intimate locus of heterogeneity and discursivity. Moreover, Kristeva's formulation of a "subject in process/on trial" that is "based on a relation of alterity within" posits, with and beyond Freudian and Lacanian psychoanalysis, that the subject is fundamentally split by language and the unconscious, thereby making any notion of a "stable or unified subject, truth, [or] meaning" quite impossible (1984: 37; Oliver 1993b: 7). It is on the basis of this splitting and by virtue of "*our* uncanny strangeness"—our own and proper unconscious, that is, "the foreigner [that] is within me"—that Kristeva famously declares that we are strangers to ourselves (1991: 192). Perhaps, then, Kristeva's expression of psychical life may be extended to corporeal life as well, for trans and queer experience often discloses how our bodies too are strangers, if not also sites of trauma or loss, that might be rediscovered and refashioned through our intimate capacities for revolt and representation. Indeed, might the trans and queer forms of revolt that we seek to cultivate here be nothing less than our intimate labors to recover, represent, and rebirth our uncanny bodies and styles of unsettled embodiment?

Moving through the interstices of psychical and social life, my aim is to show how trans and queer subjectivities are mobilized by psychical and corporeal forms of revolt with respect to sex and gender, thereby illuminating how the regenerative evolutions of revolt might shape an intimate politics of rebirth. My analysis will thus begin with an overview of the theme of revolt in Kristeva's later psychoanalytic writings, engaging specifically with three interrelated shapes of intimate revolt—return, rupture, and rebirth—that together secure a future of meaning for psychical life. By uncovering the psychic life of revolt and its exchanges with social and political crises, I identify how Kristeva's conception of revolt not only serves as a resuscitation of meaning and subjectivity but also lies at the heart of what Sarah K. Hansen and Rebecca Tuvel term her "intimate politics" (2017: 7). I will then turn closer toward the threshold of psychical and social life, demonstrating how the evolutions of intimate revolt shape and give meaning to the unfolding of trans and queer subjectivities whose futures depend precisely upon this capacity for and cultivation of "psychical rebirth" (Kristeva 2010: 158). In doing so, I consider the politically induced conditions of precarity that threaten not only the existential survivability of trans and queer populations but also the psychic life of revolt that helps make possible our psychical and corporeal capacities for representation and renewal. Transitioning from these conditions of precarity to the queer logic of liminality, I illustrate how this "inner experience" of revolt shapes the future itself as a precarious threshold in which sexed and gendered meanings may be infinitely refashioned (Kristeva 2014: 1). I therefore argue that a Kristevan psychoanalytic reading of trans and queer subjectivities reveals an intimate politics at the heart of psychical life through which new visions of trans resistance and rebirth are made possible.

The Psychic Life of Revolt: Kristeva's Intimate Politics

The theme of revolt traverses several volumes of Kristeva's psychoanalytic writings and is arguably the quintessential concept that binds together and drives forward her wider intellectual corpus. As an active participant of the uprisings in France during May 1968, an unsettled historical moment in which she identifies "the freedom to revolt," Kristeva shoulders an extensive, embodied, and indeed intimate relationship to themes of revolt and revolution (2002b: 12). The question of revolution is already central in Kristeva's 1974 *doctorat d'état*, published as *Revolution in Poetic Language*, in which she claims that the movements of meaning and subjectivity are constituted by and through a dialectical tension or oscillation of two heterogeneous modalities that she terms the "semiotic" and the "symbolic."[3] Threading together Husserlian phenomenology and Freudian psychoanalysis, Kristeva uncovers in the distinct realms of art, literature, and the unconscious a "semiotization of the symbolic," or a "trans-symbolic *jouissance*" through which "semiotic functioning" incites a veritable revolution in meaning and subjectivity (1984: 79–80). In doing so, Kristeva's semanalytic "search within the signifying phenomenon for the *crisis* or the *unsettling process* of meaning and subject[ivity] rather than for the coherence of identity" thus posits the speaking subject as a "subject in process/on trial," that is, a subject who is quite literally put in process "through a network of marks and semiotic facilitations" and who is produced by and through this material dialectic of semiotic and symbolic functioning (1980: 125; 1984: 37, 58). A psychoanalytic reading of trans and queer life through the lens of Kristeva's "subject in process/on trial" is undoubtedly at the heart of my project, though the present analysis will focus more strictly on a reading of trans and queer subjectivities as typifying what Kristeva terms the "subject in revolt" (1984: 37; 2002a: 237). This distinction therefore requires a movement from Kristeva's early revolutionary standpoint to her later preoccupation with revitalizing a "culture of revolt" (2000: 6). Indeed, the revolution that Kristeva envisions in her early work, however analogous to social transformation or political resistance, is discovered most concretely in the force of the unconscious as mediated in the analytic setting as well as in forms of artistic representation such as literature or poetic language through which, in either case, a "displacement of instinctual energies into speech is facilitated" (1987b: 4). Over the past two decades, however, Kristeva's engagement with the revolutionary capacities of artistic and literary representation, especially in and through the labors of writing, has come to emphasize the cultivation of intimate revolt conceived as a ceaseless return and rearticulation that makes possible the resuscitation of meaning and subjectivity.

Between *Revolution in Poetic Language* and her volumes on revolt in the late 1990s, Kristeva's engagement with themes of revolution and revolt undergoes a transition. For it is no longer a question of social or political revolution (a moment that had perhaps passed, if not failed, for her) but, rather, a cultivation of the psychical capacities for revolt that now animates Kristeva's philosophical thought. Sara Beardsworth offers an incisive reading of this transition, particularly with respect to Kristeva's "departure from the revolutionary standpoint" in her trilogy of the 1980s — *Powers of Horror*, *Tales of Love*, and *Black Sun* — through which she investigates "three phenomena [that] exhibit both permanent and historical crises of meaning and subjectivity," namely, abjection, love, and loss (2004: 55; Keltner 2011: 38). For Beardsworth, the unfolding of Kristeva's thought, particularly in her 1980s trilogy, may be interpreted as "a philosophy of modernity sensitive to the problem of modern nihilism," that is, a philosophy that responds to the "failings of modern institutions and discourses [that] have left the burden of connecting the semiotic and symbolic on the individual" (2004: 1, 14). To be sure, the "suffering of this burden" is often witnessed in the struggles of trans and queer communities; for, not unlike "the sufferings of Kristeva's 'borderline' subjectivity," the trans or queer subject is routinely a "subject sent to and abandoned at its borders, at the limit of the ties between the individual and society" (15). This suffering at and of the borders of private and public life is precisely the experience that we will later examine at the intersection of embodiment and precarity. Kristeva's former "emphasis on the modes of and resources for subversion" is therefore displaced by a "profound turn to psychoanalysis" as a praxis through which these crises of meaning and subjectivity are uncovered and acknowledged, and through which our psychical capacities for transformation and renewal are cultivated (Beardsworth 2005: 37). This is why Kristeva, beginning in *Black Sun* and repeatedly thereafter, stresses the "regenerative potential" of forgiveness in psychoanalysis and artistic representation as that which "raises the unconscious" and facilitates an encounter with "a loving other—an other who does not judge but bears my truth [and suffering] in the availability of love, and for that very reason allows me to be reborn" (1989: 205).

If Kristeva's diagnosis of these crises in meaning, subjectivity, and culture marks her transition from revolution to revolt, which is incidentally her transition from the realm of the political to the realm of the intimate, then it is because the psychic life of revolt, she insists, remains our lasting capacity for rebirth. Our psychical capacities for such revolutions in meaning and subjectivity are threatened, however, by an increasing cultural depression and the modern onslaught of "the spectacle," which, Kristeva reminds us in *New Maladies of the Soul*, renders "neither the time nor the space needed to create a soul for ourselves" (1995: 7–8). Kristeva's therapeutic claim that our "darkroom needs repair" and that the society of the spectacle has only intensified a situation in which "psychic life is blocked, inhibited, and destroyed" thus culminates in her 1990s trilogy—*The Sense and Non-Sense of Revolt, Intimate Revolt*, and *The Future of Revolt*—devoted to the rebellious and regenerative movements of intimate revolt (8). Although "faced with the invasion of the spectacle," Kristeva affirms at the outset of *Intimate Revolt* that "we can still contemplate the rebellious potentialities that the imaginary might resuscitate in our innermost depths" (2002a: 13). This is also to say that if and when social transformation or political resistance stumbles or even fails, there nevertheless remains a possibility for psychical or intimate revolt, "tiny revolts" that Kristeva discovers not only in the analytic setting but perhaps most profoundly in art, literature, and music, each of which she views as "sublimatory solutions to our crises" (2002a: 5; 1989: 23). As creative forms of revolt and representation, "art and literature are the recovery of 'the lost' insofar as they work as sublimations of the corporeal and affective aspects of subjectivity that correspond to a confrontation with limit situations in individual and cultural life," which is why I began with Grace's cathartic protest and also why Kristeva has turned to writing fiction of her own (Beardsworth 2009: 135). Inasmuch as Kristeva's most recent writings remain gripped by the exigent question of psychical and social resuscitation, she therefore stresses the psychic life of revolt and, more concretely, the potential for psychical rebirth as a "trajectory of survival"; for it is precisely our "inner experience" and evolutions of revolt that shape and make possible any vision for—or future of—an intimate politics (Kristeva 2016: 22; 2014: 1; Hansen and Tuvel 2017).

In her efforts to displace "the overly narrow political sense [revolt] has taken in our time," Kristeva returns to the roots of the word *revolt*, presenting an interpretive etymology of the term in the opening pages of *The Sense and Non-Sense of Revolt*, her first sustained treatment of the concept in question (2000: 3). "The Latin verb *volvere*, which is at the origin of 'revolt,' was initially far removed from politics," Kristeva explains, and instead produces a constellation of meanings, "such as 'curve,' 'entourage,' 'turn,' 'return,'" as well as "'curvature,' 'vault,' and even 'omelet,' 'to roll,'" that further signify "circular movement and, by extension, temporal return" (1–2). "Today we are barely aware of the intrinsic links between 'revolution' and 'helix,'" Kristeva acknowledges, yet there remains in the phrase "to revolt" etymological traces of "the Latin meanings of 'to return' and 'to exchange'" (2). To be sure, not only do these meanings of *revolt* reveal a rotational logic of perpetual re-turn, which Fanny Söderbäck links to an alternative temporal model that she terms "revolutionary time," but they also underscore the oscillating tensions of exchange between the psychical and the social dimensions of human experience (2012: 303). It is in this sense, then, that the psychic life of revolt both mediates and is mediated by an endless exchange between the limits of the personal and the social, which is discovered in the precarious forms of revolt mentioned at the outset, namely, those "tiny revolts" that are at once psychical and political (Kristeva 2002a: 5). This rotational logic of revolt is already evident in Kristeva's etymological lesson inasmuch as she traces how the term oscillates between usages either devoid of or riddled by political connotation. Kristeva's interpretation of revolt is further clarified in a collection of interviews entitled *Revolt, She Said*, in which she emphasizes revolt as an intimate movement of "returning, discovering, uncovering, and renovating" that reveals the "potential for making gaps, rupturing, [and] renewing" (2002b: 85). Mirroring the archaeological metaphors that may be unearthed throughout Sigmund Freud's own writings, Kristeva therefore excavates not the political but, rather, the psychical senses that the term *revolt* may illuminate for us. Although Kristeva's return to these evolutions of revolt may invoke images or senses reminiscent of political revolution, she maintains that her interest in the powers and limits of this "inner experience" of revolt, which asserts itself "below the surface of images, elements of language and tensions of identity," has little to do with politics or the realm of the political as such (2014: 1). Against its popular political meanings, "revolt is not simply about rejection and destruction," Kristeva argues, but "it is also about starting over. Unlike the word 'violence,' 'revolt' foregrounds an element of renewal and regeneration," a capacity for psychical and, in turn, social or cultural rebirth that is vital to the structure, meaning, and possible future of psychical life (2002b: 123).

The revolt of which Kristeva writes is unequivocally an intimate affair, but this nevertheless does not mean that the psychic life of revolt is exclusive to our inner experiences or without social and political import. On the contrary, our psychical capacities for intimate revolt are precisely what shape and make possible our wider capacities for social transformation and political resistance. Indeed, Kristeva's psychoanalytic conception of revolt "points to a challenge to authority and tradition, analogous to political revolt, that takes place within an individual and is essential to psychic development," which is why she routinely frames intimate revolt as an introspective process nevertheless tied to social, if not global, contexts and concerns (Oliver 2005: 77). That Kristeva qualifies revolt as intimate, then, should not be read as signaling a severance of intimacy from the social or political realm. Kristevan intimacy, Keltner explains, signifies "not what is most familiar to me, but the strangeness pervading what is most familiar," that is, the intimate experience of what Kristeva posits in *Strangers to Ourselves* as the "uncanny strangeness" of the unconscious (2011: 61; 1991: 183). Cecilia Sjöholm likewise affirms that, for Kristeva, intimacy or the intimate "is not a place or a space but rather a function of subjectivity that is known or unknown to ourselves, but that always appears to touch the truth of ourselves" (2009: 191). Just as Kristeva's "conception of and concern for psychic space cannot be reduced to the private individual in opposition to a public, social domain," Keltner argues, neither should her conception of and support for intimate revolt be decontextualized from social and political life (2011: 61; Oliver 2004). It is in this sense, then, that Kristeva's investment in our capacities and forms of revolt pushes us toward an intimate politics (Hansen and Tuvel 2017). Kristeva engages with this threshold of psychical and social life, for instance, in her long-standing diagnosis of national depression, or what Beardsworth terms "a melancholic culture" whose social resuscitation relies precisely upon a cultivation of intimate revolt (2009: 130; Miller 2014; Oliver 2005). This is why Kristeva stresses the "urgent need to develop the culture of revolt" through imaginative and sublimatory experiences such as those at work in artistic and literary representation, for "revolt may be the only thing that can save us from the automation of humanity that is threatening us" (2000: 7). If Kristeva's psychoanalytic engagement with revolt privileges the private over the public, regardless of how interconnected the private and the public remain for her, then it is because revolt shapes and indeed reveals an intimate politics at the heart of psychical life, for this internal logic of revolt makes possible the rebirth of our psyche as well as our social links between subjectivity and otherness (Keltner 2011; Oliver 2005; Sjöholm 2005).

It is perhaps unsurprising, then, that Kristeva champions the intimacy of the analytic setting as a privileged space and time for inviting revolt. For her, it is on the couch, though also in and through creative forms of representation such as art and literature, that we are encouraged "to break off, remember, [and] refashion" (2002a: 223). Kristeva's own psychoanalytic praxis defiantly resists any "normalization of the patient" or of meaning and subjectivity more generally, for the intimate and amorous exchange between analyst and analysand, which she likens to "an idiolect [or] a work of art," is nothing less than an embracing of and encouragement for revolt (1995: 36). In contrast to a troubling history in which psychoanalytic thought has been deployed as a normalizing discourse aimed at pathologizing, regulating, or curing difference (evidenced especially in cases of so-called conversion therapy), Kristeva argues that psychoanalysis should be mobilized as an intimate and antinormative praxis that serves to revitalize the psychic life of revolt. Indeed, the therapeutic setting in which Freud discovered so many resistances to analysis is, oddly enough, where Kristeva invites us to cultivate our varied capacities for revolt. "Analysis becomes a *space of revolt*," Kristeva maintains in *Hatred and Forgiveness*, "and, if it does not become that, psychical life cannot be reborn" (2010: 154). Evidenced in the transgressive dialectic of transference and countertransference, Kristeva's psychoanalytic praxis embraces the revolutionary movements of the subject in crisis, for "the telling moment in an individual's psychic life, as in the life of societies at large," she contends, "is when you call into question laws, norms and values" (2002b: 12). This is to say that psychoanalysis, not unlike artwork or literary writing, may cultivate a space and time of revolt in which meaning and subjectivity are reconstituted through the intimate evolutions of return, rupture, and rebirth. "Questioning, putting into question," Kristeva writes, "is the quintessential mode of speech in analysis," an "eternal return [that] places us in the timelessness of the time of the session" and "challenges identities and values but also temporarily restructures the subject in a new rebirth" (2002a: 236–37). What is thus imperative at the end of analysis is that "the analyzed subject is not a reconciled subject" but, rather, Kristeva declares, "a subject in revolt" (237). For Kristeva, the introspective labors of psychoanalysis, paralleled by the imaginative and sublimatory efforts of art, literature, or music, may therefore operate as a privileged route for not only revitalizing a "culture of revolt" but also securing the psychic life of revolt as our lasting "possibility of new beginnings" (2000: 7; Keltner 2011: 153).

What comprises the Kristevan "subject in revolt," and her psychoanalytic conception of revolt more generally, are the intimate evolutions of return, rupture, and rebirth through which a resuscitation of meaning and subjectivity is made possible, though not guaranteed (2002a: 237). Indeed, these three distinct albeit interrelated shapes or senses of intimate revolt—return, rupture, and rebirth—together serve as our surviving capacity for sustaining psychical life and, as I will later show, find unique expression in the psychical structuring and precarious unfolding of trans and queer embodiment. The movements of intimate revolt that I am stressing here, which should not be read as constituting a teleological narrative, are an interpretive modification of the "three figures of revolt" that Kristeva discovers in Freud: revolt conceived as "the transgression of a prohibition," as "repetition [and] working-through," and as "displacement" (2000: 16). As I have stressed above, these "logically independent" albeit psychically interdependent shapes of intimate revolt are "imbricated in the psychical apparatus as well as in artistic or literary works" through which there emerges a mediation of the limits and thresholds of our experience (17). In her recent essay "New Forms of Revolt," Kristeva identifies the pressing psychical and existential particularities of this subject of revolt:

> This new species of rebels [*revoltés*] are enraged, but they have not lost the decisive and specific meaning of revolt. Each and every one of them is involved in a difficult and often tiresome life and carries out a risky struggle. Yet, they do share something new, something that has perhaps been there all the while, but that can now be confessed to and even redeemed. They are discovering through their experiences that there is no answer to social, historic and political impasses without a radical inner experience; an inner experience that is demanding, unique, and able to appropriate the complexity of the past in order to approach the present and the future. (2014: 2)

My return to this "radical inner experience" and the pivotal shapes of return, rupture, and rebirth therefore illuminates this psychic life of revolt that not only serves as a response to our modern social, historical, and political impasses but also mobilizes the intimate and imaginative revolutions of trans and queer embodiment (2).

The first shape of intimate revolt is discoverable in and through what Kristeva describes as a "retrospective return," that is, the introspective questioning of meaning and subjectivity that returns us to the archaic and exposes us to "the pulse of being" (2002a: 7, 9). Advancing the psychoanalytic work of Freud, whom she terms "a revolutionary in search of lost time," Kristeva clarifies how revolt as retrospective return is central to the time and space of analysis and artistic creation: "The return, or access, to the archaic," she writes, constitutes "access to a timeless temporality," namely, the unconscious (2000: 16). For Kristeva, this intimate process of "turning back" upon ourselves and the buried meanings of our experience, which Sjöholm (2005) and Söderbäck (2012) each stress as a temporal movement of repetition and displacement, is indeed fundamental to our capacities for resuscitating psychical life (2002a: 5). This is, of course, evidenced in the anamnesis of which Freud writes and in the tenuous return to the repressed in the analytic setting, where there is an amorous invitation, Kristeva says, "to put excitation, distress, or trauma into words. To *represent them* . . . but, above all, to name them" (2016: 50). With respect to Kristeva's preoccupation with the depressive subject, for instance, Kelly Oliver maintains that "questioning reopens the realm of words or signification through a challenge to signification itself that operates as an invitation to the depressive to find things within words" (2005: 80). Retrospective return, which Kristeva describes as "simultaneously recollection, interrogation, and thought," is therefore a vital movement in the intimate reorientations of meaning and subjectivity, for "consciousness is not alive unless it allows itself to be questioned" (2002a: 6, 125).

If the initial shape of intimate revolt revolves around a retrospective return to and questioning of meaning and subjectivity, particularly with respect to the past, then the second shape advances these evolutions of inquiry toward "the centrifugal forces of dissolution and dispersion" that are found in the rebellious and rupturing activity of displacement (7). "A modification, a displacement of the past, occurs," Kristeva remarks, "and, by returning to painful places, especially if they are nerve centers, there is a reformulation of the psychological map" (2000: 50). According to Kristeva, psychical displacement—of the past or trauma, for instance—creates a gap in and through which a psychical reshaping is made possible, thereby positioning intimate revolt as a double movement of what Tina Chanter and Ewa Płonowska Ziarek describe as a "rupture and rearticulation" (2005a: 3). This is to say, then, that the repetition and working through that emerge as central to revolt as retrospective return make possible our psychical "reconstruction and displacement of the past" whose rupture opens up a time and space for renovation (Kristeva 2002a: 125). What is nevertheless necessary for this rebellious "rupture and rearticulation" to take root, according to Kristeva, is a confrontation and transgression of "an obstacle, prohibition, authority, or law that allows us to realize ourselves as autonomous and free" (Chanter and Ziarek 2005a: 3; Kristeva 2000: 7). This rebellious and rupturing movement of revolt is founded upon and indeed reveals a "conflict [that] gives rise to a *jouissance* that is not simply the narcissistic or egoistic caprice of [subjectivity] spoiled by consumer society or the society of the spectacle" but, rather, a *jouissance* that "proves indispensable to keeping the psyche alive [and] indispensable to the faculty of representation and questioning that specifies the human being" (Kristeva 2002a: 7). Rupture thus names the pivotal moment of revolt—perhaps the closest to its everyday connotations of upheaval—in which a transgression or displacement occurs and opens up the potential for psychical regeneration.

Kristeva maintains that, above all, the key import of intimate revolt lies in its transformative capacities for recovering and renewing psychical life, which is why rebirth constitutes the third shape of its movement. To be sure, "Freud founded psychoanalysis as an invitation to anamnesis in the goal of a rebirth, that is, a psychical restructuring," which, according to Kristeva, is indispensable for not only the future of psychical life but the future itself (8). Achieved through the aforementioned efforts of questioning and displacement, rebirth names the transformative "inner experience" of renewal that sustains psychical life, social links, and our capacity to imagine a future for ourselves, others, and our shared world (Kristeva 2014: 1). Kristeva writes that "revolt, as I understand it—psychical revolt, analytic revolt, artistic revolt—refers to a state of permanent questioning, of transformation, change, an endless probing of appearances" (2002b: 120). Influenced by her readings of philosophical figures as varied as Saint Augustine and Hannah Arendt, Kristeva refers to rebirth as our psychical capacities for creation, regeneration, and transformation that open up a future for the psychic life of revolt to flourish. In this way, it is precisely our "tiny revolts," which neither follow a teleological narrative nor arrive at a discernable destination, that emerge as the conditions for the possibility of another future, namely, a future of revolt and perpetual rebirth (Kristeva 2002a: 5). Keltner reminds us, moreover, that "intimate revolt is not the accomplishment of a solitary individual, but rather depends on relations with others" (2011: 105). Composed of the psychical evolutions of return, rupture, and rebirth, which Kristeva believes are cultivated most deeply in the realms of art and literature, Kristeva's conception of intimate revolt thus names our capacity for and experience of transformation at the threshold of psychical and social life.

The psychic life of revolt is therefore indispensable, for "without it," Kristeva argues, "neither the life of the mind nor life in society is possible" (2002b: 12). Revealed as a kind of quilting point between the private and the public, revolt names the passage of a renewal of thought and representation that is at the heart of Kristeva's intimate politics. Indeed, Kristeva remarks that revolt "appears as a continuous necessity for keeping alive the psyche, thought, and the social link" (2000: 144). Our psychical capacities for revolt are thus marked by an urgency that is at once ethical and political, for what is at risk in Kristeva's wager on revolt are precisely these possibilities for rebirth and renewing the bonds between subjectivity and otherness. In the opening reflections of *Intimate Revolt*, Kristeva identifies at the threshold of private and public life this indispensable logic of revolt, which we might frame as central to her intimate politics:

> We may have reached a point of no return, from which we will have to re-turn to the little things, tiny revolts, in order to preserve the life of the mind and of the species. Revolt, then, as return/turning back/displacement/change, constitutes the profound logic of a certain culture that I would like to revive here and whose acuity seems quite threatened these days. What makes sense today is not the future (as communism and providential religions claimed) but revolt: that is, the questioning and displacement of the past. The future, if it exists, depends on it. (2002a: 5)

Returning us to the realm of the intimate in which our "radical inner experience" may take root and be reborn, Kristeva affirms that our psychical capacities for revolt are inextricably linked to—and indeed shape—the survivability of social and political life (2014: 2). Kristeva's final suggestion, that "if there is still time, we should wager on the future of revolt," reminds us that revolt is nevertheless "what is most alive and promising about our culture" (2002a: 223–24, 7). Envisioning an intimate politics at the heart of psychical life, Kristeva thus points us toward those "concrete instances of intimate revolt as the seeds of hope for new beginnings" (Keltner 2011: 153–54). For it is precisely in and through the intimate evolutions of our "tiny revolts" that Kristeva imagines a refashioning of and possible future for psychical life and that, as I will now show, trans and queer subjectivities might cultivate "a state of perpetual rebirth" (2002a: 5, 233). The horizons of any possible future or politics to come are therefore dependent upon our psychical capacities for revolt and rebirth, for "while Kristeva insists on the suspension of a certain conception of the future, she ties the concrete possibilities of the future to the emergence of new modes of connection" that are cultivated, however precariously, by and through our intimate revolts (Keltner 2011: 105).

The Precarious Cultivation of Revolt: Trans Resistance and Renewal

If Kristevan psychoanalysis uncovers the psychic life of revolt as indispensable for the resuscitation and regeneration of meaning and subjectivity, then there is now fertile ground from which to grow my analysis of trans and queer forms of revolt. In doing so, I illuminate how the intimate evolutions of revolt detailed above both shape and give meaning to trans and queer subjectivities that depend upon their perpetual albeit precarious cultivation. Situating trans and queer embodiment within Kristeva's psychoanalytic framework of intimate revolt thus enables us to better grasp not only the psychical meaning and unfolding of trans and queer subjectivities but also the tenuous cultivation of resistance and renewal in the midst of social, historical, and political crises specific to trans and queer communities. At the very least, enveloping trans and queer subjectivities in the language of Kristevan revolt accomplishes the intimate labor that psychoanalytic praxis has long known and developed as an "amorous discourse," that is, an analytic situation in which we are encouraged, Kristeva says, to "search for possible new identities and new ways of talking about ourselves" (1987b: 3). Indeed, what we discover at the heart of trans and queer experience are "the intimate well-springs of revolt—in the deep sense of self-questioning and questioning tradition"—that make possible our veritable rebirth, or what Kristeva also describes as a "re-rooting of the self" (2002b: 85). Trans and queer subjectivities therefore typify the Kristevan "subject in revolt," for the intimate and imaginative evolutions of trans and queer embodiment are shaped precisely by the three aforementioned senses of revolt: return, rupture, and rebirth (Kristeva 2002a: 237). These shapes of revolt are thus revealed as central to the psychical meaning and corporeal unfolding of trans and queer subjectivities whose precarious cultivation of resistance at the threshold of psychical and social life gives rise to what I will finally articulate as an intimate politics of rebirth.

Recalling Kristeva's emphasis on "retrospective return" reveals how the "tiny revolts" of trans and queer embodiment are sparked by an introspective and endless questioning of the self with respect to sex and gender (7, 5). For these intimate movements of return, which I claim are fundamental to the psychic life of trans and queer subjectivities, signal not only a "turning back" toward the self but also a rebellious questioning of binary logics and biopolitical apparatuses that have constrained our psychical and social capacities for revolt and refashioning (5). "Revolt as *return* is essential," Keltner argues, "because it takes us back to the necessary moment of affectivity and through an active interrogation holds on, experiences, and undergoes it" (2009: 166). Indeed, this tenuous process of "turning back" and going over a potentially unsettled relationship to embodiment is enacted over and again on the analyst's couch, though these intimate experiences of return need not be reduced to the analytic setting that Kristeva privileges alongside the aesthetic labors of art, literature, or music (2002a: 5). We might consider, for instance, the processes of coming out—especially to oneself—as well as the continued efforts to question the limits of our bodies, identities, and desires as nothing less than queer forms of this "retrospective return" (7). To be sure, this theme of retrospective questioning is evident throughout numerous anthologies of writing devoted to articulating trans and queer experience, whether it is the introspective questioning of intersectional identities and embodiments, the social questioning of norms and institutions, or the political questioning of laws and rights (Bornstein and Bergman 2010; Conrad 2014; Coyote and Sharman 2012; Nestle, Howell, and Wilchins 2002; Quesada, Gomez, and Vidal-Ortiz 2015; Shultz 2015; Sycamore 2006; Warner 1993). Moreover, the continued presence of memoirs and novels on trans and queer experience further exhibit these unapologetic evolutions of return and reexamination that Kristeva discovers in the intimate revolts of literary writing more generally (Andrews 2014; Binnie 2013; Bornstein 1994; Feinberg 1993; Grace and Ozzi 2016; McCloskey 1999; Mock 2014; Valerio 2006). Not unlike Kristeva's suggestion that intimate revolt is founded upon "a permanent state of questioning," trans and queer embodiment is often characterized by, if not experienced as, "an endless probing of appearances" that aims at a disruption or reorientation of meaning and subjectivity, regardless of whether one exists within or beyond established binaries (2002b: 120; Ahmed 2006). "We become who we are through questioning," Oliver affirms, "and we remain open to meaning and creativity only by continuing to question, continuing with this infinite psychic revolt" through which meaning and subjectivity may be refashioned (2005: 79–80). These queer movements of retrospective questioning are echoed in Sara Ahmed's claim that "in looking back we also look a different way," which is to say that "looking back is what keeps open the possibility of going astray," of rupturing and thereby renewing our psychical and corporeal orientations in the world (2006: 178). The intimate evolutions of trans and queer resistance thus begin, if nowhere else, with this introspective interrogation of meaning and subjectivity, for it is precisely the questioning and reexamination of the self that shapes our subsequent capacities for revolt and renewal.

Inextricably linked to this retrospective questioning of sexed and gendered meaning are the rebellious movements of rupture and resistance that Kristeva identifies as central to the psychical life of revolt. Recognizing that "when we speak of revolt today we first understand a protest against already established norms, values, and powers," Kristeva maintains that the ruptures and displacements effected by rebellion are vital for the reshaping of psychical life and subjectivity more broadly, for "when we rupture the chain of values" we open up new pathways for renovation (2002a: 3, 25). These psychical displacements that Kristeva discovers as fundamental to the evolutions of intimate revolt are likewise pivotal to the internal logic of trans and queer subjectivities, for it is precisely these transformative movements of displacement that effect an uprooting and reshaping of the signifiers of sex and gender that attempt to inscribe or interpellate fixed meanings onto the body and psyche. "Sex is something that [legal] documents themselves enact," Gayle Salamon confirms, "and sex becomes performative in the sense that the *m* or the *f* on the document does not merely report on the sex of its bearer but becomes the truth of and bestows the bearer's sex" (2010: 183). To be sure, what trans and queer subjectivities disclose over and again are the psychical and social struggles to displace not only the signifier itself but also the supposed truth that these unsettled letters bestow. The intimate labors of "rupture and rearticulation" with respect to these sociolegal inscriptions of sex are indeed evident across a range of experiences familiar to trans and queer persons: from the rejection of these performative signifiers found on birth certificates to the reclassification of sex or gender on identity documents, and from the decision to rename ourselves and define our own pronouns to the refusal of binary signifiers or identifications of sex altogether (Chanter and Ziarek 2005a: 3). In this way, trans and queer subjectivities are fashioned by the psychical and social displacements through which we resist, rupture, and reshape our intimate relationship to the discursive meanings of sex or gender. This is not to say, however, that a specific displacement of meaning is a monolithic or compulsory experience for all trans persons. For, as Julia Serano succinctly reminds us, "there is no one right way to be trans" (2007: 29). Rather, what we discover is that trans and queer subjectivities are, in part, constituted by these psychical displacements of the past, whether that past is a signifier of sex, a birth name, a relation to social conditioning, and so on. These psychical displacements should not be read as a "retroactive cutting [or] severing from being in the wrong body" but, rather, as an intimate and endless modification of psychical and corporeal life (Puar 2015: 63). Not unlike the subject of psychoanalysis whose intimate returns to the drives and the unconscious provoke a displacement and working through of the past in an effort to invite a time and space for rebirth, trans and queer subjectivities labor to cultivate a meaningful relation to transgression and transformation that, in Kristeva's view, opens up a possible future for subsequent evolutions of resistance and renewal.

If our capacities for revolt are shaped by these intimate evolutions of return and rupture, then it is rebirth that names the transformative "inner experience" of renewal and regeneration through which meaning and subjectivity are given a time and space for breaking off and refashioning (Kristeva 2014: 1). The language of rebirth at once recalls themes perhaps familiar to trans and queer experience, especially for those who pursue varying forms of transition, inasmuch as the liberatory events of renaming oneself or redefining one's sex or gender may, for some, effect a kind of (second) birth. It is not uncommon, for instance, to come across autobiographical descriptions of undergoing sex-reassignment surgery or hormone-replacement therapy, or even securing reissued forms of identity documentation, as being or having been experiences of rebirth. There is, moreover, an element of agency in such forms of rebirth, for these experiences are often a deliberate return to and refashioning of those unsettled meanings that were assigned at birth. Of course, Kristeva's psychoanalytic conception of rebirth must be understood more precisely as our psychical capacity for renewal, that is, a transformative experience of "starting over" (2002b: 123). In this way, the "psychical rebirth" that makes possible the intimate evolutions of trans and queer embodiment may be viewed as the logically final, albeit never finalized, shape of the psychic life of revolt (Kristeva 2010: 158). For the transformative experience of rebirth that Kristeva views as central to intimate revolt stresses not a linear narrative with a clear beginning or end but, rather, an intricate, innovative, and always incomplete process that perpetually aims for renewal. Indeed, Kristeva remarks that intimate revolt is precisely that which "opens psychical life to infinite re-creation" (2002a: 6). This is to say, then, that the "tiny revolts" that shape trans and queer subjectivities are what make possible their endless reconstitution and rebirth at the threshold of psychical and social life (5). Regardless of whether pathways for gender transition are pursued, and regardless of how transitioning might be experienced from one person to another, the intimate revolts that shape our precarious being in the world as trans or queer persons nevertheless involve this reformative experience that Kristeva describes as rebirth. Although neither rebirth nor the psychic life of revolt is exclusive to any particular population, trans and queer subjectivities acutely express this intimate and transformative experience of "psychical rebirth" (Kristeva 2010: 158). For if there exists a quasi-universal experience across trans and queer subjectivities, then it is perhaps this psychical capacity for renewal and regeneration with respect to sexed and gendered meaning. Kristeva's psychoanalytic language of renewal and rebirth may therefore resonate with many trans and queer persons whose varied experiences reflect this precarious "rupture and rearticulation" of sexed and gendered meaning (Chanter and Ziarek 2005a: 3). For not only do these shapes of revolt—return, rupture, and rebirth—name the intimate evolutions through which trans and queer subjectivities cultivate the capacities for psychical and corporeal refashioning, but Kristeva's sharp focus on forms of "psychical rebirth" in particular underscores the urgency of my turn to the threshold of psychical and social life (2010: 158).

What impedes these "tiny revolts" and their intimate capacities for "psychical rebirth," then, are the intensified conditions of vulnerability and violence that constitute what we might describe as queer precarity (Kristeva 2002a: 5; 2010: 158). Indeed, precarity names the largely irreversible and inscapable effects of modern forms of socioeconomic, biopolitical, and psychical crises and unacknowledged suffering experienced by trans and queer communities, among so many other marginalized populations viewed as disposable. Over the past decade, Judith Butler has turned to the social and political consequences of precarity, asking what these violent conditions of instability and injurability might mean for a given life's survivability, grievability, and capacity for resistance (Butler 2004b, 2009, 2013, 2016). In *Frames of War*, Butler clarifies this concept that is at once a condition and experience of radical vulnerability:

> Precariousness and precarity are intersecting concepts. Lives are by definition precarious: they can be expunged at will or by accident; their persistence is in no sense guaranteed. In some sense, this is a feature of all life, and there is no thinking of life that is not precarious. . . . Precarity designates that politically induced condition in which certain populations suffer from failing social and economic networks of support and become differentially exposed to injury, violence, and death. (2009: 25)

Butler's attention to the problem of precarity thus exposes us to the pervasive, if not imposed, conditions of vulnerability and violence that frame the fragile subject "in relation to a field of objects, forces, and passions that impinge on or affect us in some way" (2016: 25). As the above passage demonstrates, precarity is at least a twofold phenomenon of human experience; for precariousness is an irreducible feature of the finite and indeed vulnerable human condition, while precarity is an induced condition that frames and exposes the subject in relation to intensified, if not intentional, forms of vulnerability and violence. To be sure, there is a "difference between precarity as an existential category that is presumed to be equally shared," which Butler tends to call "precariousness," "and precarity as a condition of induced inequality and destitution" (2013: 20). In either case, however, what is at stake is the survivability of both psychical and corporeal life under the weight of widespread suffering that nevertheless makes some populations more vulnerable than others. Most recently, Butler has returned to the question of precarity in relation to wider capacities for social and political resistance, arguing for a "mobilization of vulnerability" in which our irreducible conditions of vulnerability "can be a way of being exposed and agentic at the same time" (2016: 24). In her efforts to recognize and reorient vulnerability as a "potentially effective mobilizing force" in assembling for social or political resistance, Butler declares that "precarity cuts across identity categories as well as multicultural maps, thus forming the basis for an alliance focused on opposition to state violence and its capacity to produce, exploit, and distribute precarity" across populations that are considered disposable (2016: 14; 2009: 32).

These induced conditions of precarity are indeed apparent, though disproportionately experienced, among trans and queer populations for whom survivability is particularly fraught. As the targets of intersecting axes of oppression, trans and queer persons are often struggling to survive, let alone cultivate the psychical capacities for intimate revolt. A recent press release published by Transgender Europe, for instance, reveals that at least "2,016 reported killings of trans and gender diverse people" have been documented "in 65 countries worldwide" between 2008 and 2015 (TGEU 2016: 1). These losses of life underscore not only the everyday vulnerability felt by trans and queer communities across the globe but also the underexamined intersections of transphobia, racism, heterosexism, classism, ableism, and the systemic dehumanization of persons working and surviving in criminalized economies such as sex work that significantly shape and contextualize this violence (Saffin 2011). Complicating these immediate threats of injurability are institutional forms of administrative violence, which Dean Spade describes in *Normal Life* as "the enormous role of harmful administrative and legal apparatuses in trans people's lives" that disproportionately affects the survivability and "distribution of life chances" for trans and queer populations (2011: 39, 11). To be sure, Spade's attention to administrative violence highlights the assemblages of social barriers and legal regulations that control and criminalize trans and queer lives through discursive systems of gender misclassification, sex segregation, and identity surveillance, each of which habitually impacts issues of identity documentation, employment, housing, education, and health care, as well as the processes of detainment, incarceration, and deportation (Feinberg 1998; Spade 2011; Stanley and Smith 2011). Such widespread conditions of queer precarity, which administrative and state violences only perpetuate, solicit a paradoxical appeal (of recognition) to the state or administrative agency, for precarity routinely operates as an "induced condition of maximized precariousness for populations exposed to arbitrary state violence who often have no other option than to appeal to the very state from which they need protection" (Butler 2009: 26). The impossible problematic that Butler identifies here is indeed a common experience across trans and queer communities whose relation to administrative agencies as well as the state and police is nothing less than tenuous. That Irvin Gonzalez, an undocumented transgender woman fleeing domestic violence, was swiftly arrested and detained by Immigration and Customs Enforcement agents upon seeking a protective order in the El Paso County Courthouse illustrates not only the unstable conditions of precarity familiar to trans and queer populations but also the insufficient frameworks for strategizing a trans "politics of recognition" or appealing to a conception of "trans rights" (Schladen 2017; Juang 2006: 243; Spade 2011: 13).

The conditions of precarity mentioned above are frequently diagnosed via interpretations—or resisted through interventions—that frame and thereby limit the volatile reach of precarity to social and political life, evidenced especially in Amber Hollibaugh and Margot Weiss's economic analysis of the "rising *queer* precariat" (2015: 18). Although such articulations of the social, economic, and political impasses experienced under the weight of precarity are essential to an understanding of these queer forms of vulnerability, their strict focus on the social, economic, or political conditions and consequences of precarity elides the intimate shapes of precarity that affect not only psychical life but also the psychic life of revolt. On the contrary, my analysis seeks to unearth the affects that precarity produces both in and through psychical life, for the unstable conditions of vulnerability and survivability that Butler rightfully links to "bodily life" must also be linked to psychical life and our intimate capacities or incapacities for resistance and renewal (2004b: 29). If queer precarity names those politically induced conditions of vulnerability and violence that disproportionately threaten the survival of trans and queer populations, then it is imperative to remember that the effects of such crises and suffering are experienced and indeed have impact on both the corporeal and the psychical level of the human condition. For not only does precarity threaten our always already finite capacities for survivability, but its affective grasp on psychical life—manifested in a range of experiences such as disorientation and depression—might tighten and therefore impede our capacities for intimate revolt.

To be sure, the conditions of precarity that differentially expose trans and queer communities to vulnerability and violence induce a kind of disorientation at the threshold of psychical and social life and, more concretely, at the threshold of private and public spaces such as sex-segregated restrooms. In *Queer Phenomenology*, Ahmed describes disorientation as "a bodily feeling of losing one's place, and an effect of the loss of a place: it can be a violent feeling, and a feeling that is affected by violence, or shaped by violence directed toward the body" (2006: 160). Although Ahmed's phenomenological investigation into the modes of orientation and disorientation are concerned primarily with the affective relations and movements of bodies as situated in time and space, her remarks on queerness and the "politics of disorientation" deepen our account of how precarity affects—orients, disorients, or even dispossesses—trans and queer subjectivities (24). Indeed, the affective logic of disorientation reveals at once a breaking off and refashioning, for disorientation not only designates the psychical and corporeal affects that precarity produces but also elicits pathways through which we might reorient ourselves and cultivate forms of resistance and renewal. "The point is what we do with such moments of disorientation," Ahmed declares, "as well as what such moments can do—whether they can offer us the hope of new directions, and whether new directions are reason enough for hope" (158). Compounded by the disorientations and dispossessions it produces, precarity organizes a tenuous situation in which trans and queer persons may or may not succeed in cultivating the capacities for intimate revolt. Butler's reflections on precarity and subsequent rethinking of vulnerability as a "mobilizing force" thus enable us to envision what we might do in and with these experiences of disorientation and dispossession, that is, how we might nevertheless cultivate new forms of revolt in the face of queer forms of precarity (2016: 14). At the intersection of social precarity and political protest, Butler identifies in vulnerability—in our necessary conditions of "dependency and interdependency" with others—a mobilizing feature, affirming that "vulnerability, understood as a deliberate exposure to power, is part of the very meaning of political resistance as an embodied enactment" (2016: 21; 2013: 22). Indeed, the conditions of precarity that render us vulnerable not only disorient us in our exposures to power and violence but also potentially reorient us in new and discursive directions. This is to say, then, that intimate revolt mediates our psychical and social experiences of precarity and mobilizes our lasting albeit tenuous capacities for resistance and renewal.

If the induced and disorienting conditions of precarity are, in part, what threaten our psychical capacities for revolt, and if the intimate evolutions of revolt nevertheless remain our lasting hope for futures of resistance and renewal, then trans and queer subjectivities are caught in a peculiar struggle to cultivate forms of revolt at the threshold of psychical and social life. This cultivation of revolt is thus a tenuous process, for what impedes our psychical capacities for resistance and renewal, according to Kristeva, are the limited possibilities for "presenting oneself, representing oneself," and thereby making meaning for oneself through practices of self-definition (2002a: 63). The threat of losing these intimate capacities for self-representation and redefinition is perhaps nowhere more salient than in the everyday realm of sexed signification in which the unsettled letters—M and F—attempt to box in the infinite expressions and embodiments of sex and gender identity. "From birth to death," Spade explains, "the 'M' and 'F' boxes are present on nearly every form we fill out," thereby signaling not only the bifurcations but also the mundane interpellations of sexed and gendered meaning that are grafted onto psychical and corporeal life (2011: 142). Indeed, "it is legally mandated that all our lives must fit into one of those two tiny boxes," Leslie Feinberg acknowledges, stressing how these unstable signifiers of sex nonetheless threaten to strangle our most intimate sense of freedom and therefore undermine the truth that we are all works in progress (1998: 68). To be sure, this specter of sexed signification routinely haunts trans and queer persons long after death, whether at funerals conducted by families who refuse to properly name or gender their lost relative, or in sensationalized headlines that curate a purposeful contradiction in gendered language. What makes these signifiers and significations of sex so unsettling, of course, is that they attempt to limit, if not altogether foreclose, our psychical and social possibilities for representation, which we might also term "self-narration" or "self-definition." In *Assuming a Body*, Salamon eloquently identifies the laborious process of affirming and narrating the materiality of trans embodiment: "To affirm a materiality," Salamon writes, "to insist on the livability of one's own embodiment, particularly when that embodiment is culturally abject or socially despised—is to undertake a constant and always incomplete labor to reconfigure more than just the materiality of our own bodies. It is to strive to create and transform the lived meanings of those materialities" (2010: 42). Salamon's remarks on the persistent labors of reconfiguring and rearticulating trans embodiment may be extended to, if not also understood as, the psychical labors of representation and meaning making that are shaped and made possible by the intimate evolutions of revolt. The possibilities for rupturing and rearticulating our relation to sexed signification—for resignifying those unsettled letters that haunt trans and queer persons from birth to death—thus depend upon these intimate labors of resistance and renewal, for it is through this precarious cultivation of revolt that our psychical, social, and political capacities for rebirth might be realized.

Not unlike Kristeva's own wager on "the future of revolt," we may now grasp how the psychic life of revolt remains one of our lasting possibilities for transformative resistance and renewal in the midst of intensifying precarity (2002a: 223–24). Indeed, we too have perhaps "reached a point of no return" in which our psychical, social, and political capacities for revolt arise as our surviving route for a veritable rebirth. As John Lechte reminds us, "it is precisely through revolt that the subject/self is formed," which is to say that our psychical and corporeal possibilities are, in fact, made possible through the "twists and turns" of intimate revolt (2004: 138; Kristeva 2000: 4). It is in this sense that trans and queer embodiment is shaped and mobilized by the transformative movements of intimate revolt. As is well known, the etymological traces of the prefix *trans-* signify a movement of transcendence, with meanings such as "across," "over," "beyond," and even "on the other side of" that designate an infinite capacity to "break off" and "refashion" (Kristeva 2002a: 223). In their introduction to the special issue of *Women's Studies Quarterly* devoted to a rethinking of *trans*, Susan Stryker, Paisley Currah, and Lisa Jean Moore ask what significance we might discover "by regarding 'trans-,' rather than gender, as the stable location . . . where we—if we can or if we must—might begin to enact and materialize new social ontologies" (2008: 14). By returning to the interminable capacities for renewal that are impelled by the stabilizing and destabilizing logic of this Latin prefix, we uncover a queer time and space in which meaning and subjectivity might be refashioned by and through the intimate evolutions of revolt. My turn to the precarious cultivation of revolt is thus a response to what Stryker, Currah, and Moore conceptualize as the resistant and renewing movements of subjectivities always in process: "The movement between territorializing and deterritorializing 'trans-' and its suffixes," they suggest, "as well as the movements between temporalizing and spatializing them, is an improvisational, creative, and essentially poetic practice through which radically new possibilities for being in the world can start to emerge" (14). The precarious cultivation of revolt that structures and mobilizes trans and queer subjectivities is therefore made possible by the intimate evolutions of return, rupture, and rebirth, that is to say, by the tenuous and poetic movements of psychical and corporeal renewal through which we might envision an intimate politics of resistance and veritable rebirth.

An Intimate Politics of Rebirth: Voyaging in Liminality

The psychic life of revolt that we have discovered at the heart of trans and queer subjectivities discloses an intimate politics of rebirth, uncovering an internal logic of renewal that mobilizes psychical and corporeal life as an unfinished style of liminality. An intimate politics of rebirth thus identifies the precarious cultivation of revolt that takes place at the threshold of psychical and social life and, more concretely, finds expression in the psychical and corporeal shapes of "rupture and rearticulation" through which trans and queer subjectivities create both meaning and a possible future for infinite refashioning (Chanter and Ziarek 2005a: 3). My psychoanalytic gesture toward an intimate politics of rebirth finds conceptual support in Oliver's remarks on the transformative capacities for renewal at the threshold of the psyche and the social: "What is at stake in both political struggles and revolts of imagination is renewing a sense of agency that allows each person to create meaning for themselves. We need robust psychic space to be creative, to revolt against an authority that demands that we conform. Belonging to culture, or creating meaning for oneself, is an ongoing process that is always relational, always tenuous, and always incomplete" (2004: 173). Drawing connections between psychical and social struggles for rebirth, Oliver clarifies that our psychical capacities for revolt are intimately and inextricably linked to our wider capacities for imagination, thought, and representation, namely, those psychical and corporeal movements of meaning that are never complete but, rather, always in process. As I have shown, Kristeva's psychoanalytic thought offers a robust discourse for theorizing this psychic life of revolt, which we might also frame as an intimate politics that accounts for the precarious situation of trans and queer embodiment. Although Kristeva never posits a positive political theory as such, framing her thought on revolt as an intimate politics in relation to trans and queer life thus centers "the political significance of marginalized subjectivities [that Kristeva views] as essential to any rehabilitation of politics as such" (Keltner 2009: 174). As a psychoanalyst and philosopher who has envisioned passionately an "outlaw ethics," which she terms "herethics" in *Tales of Love*, there is perhaps no other psychoanalytic figure than Kristeva whose oeuvre is better equipped to frame trans and queer forms of revolt as an intimate politics of rebirth (Oliver 1993b: 5; Kristeva 1987a: 263). Indeed, "the culture of revolt" that Kristeva seeks to uncover and revitalize throughout her intellectual corpus "not only has to de-center but also to renew the psychic life and social bonds through symbolic rearticulation," tenuous movements that are quite familiar to trans and queer life (Chanter and Ziarek 2005a: 3). These intimate evolutions of return, rupture, and rebirth therefore constitute an internal, mobilizing logic at the heart of trans and queer subjectivities.

Returning to the narrative of resistance with which I began, we may consider how trans and queer forms of revolt mobilize an intimate politics at the precarious threshold of psychical and social life. Grace's "rupture and rearticulation" of sex by burning her birth certificate onstage thus serves as a response to the conditions of precarity that continue to haunt the private and public lives of trans and queer communities (3). Indeed, setting fire to her birth certificate signaled not only a defiant return to and displacement of the sexed signifier inscribed on her legal document (and perhaps her own psyche) but also a rebirth and rearticulation of sexed and gendered meaning, conveyed both semiotically and symbolically in the dysphoria-driven music that immediately followed. Grace's brief yet triumphant "Goodbye!" left the meanings of sex and gender purposefully suspended without an identifiable future, thus signaling an embrace of liminality. Moreover, Grace's public disruption of this sociolegal interpellation of sex invited a collective and performative witnessing, further underscoring Kristeva's claim that intimate revolt is not simply a singular or private affair but, rather, an "inner experience" that bears an acute and necessary relation to others and one's social, historical, and political milieu (2014: 1). What makes Grace's cultivation of revolt precarious, of course, is that her destruction of this legal document nevertheless could not and would not safeguard her from being assaulted in a public restroom, unnecessarily questioned at an airport, or insulted from across the street. In the weeks following their show, news of Grace's revolt circulated widely on social media and was often praised as a symbolic and particularly political act of queer resistance: against the legal definitions and political apparatuses of binary sex and gender, against state-sanctioned discriminatory legislation, and against the induced conditions of precarity more generally. On the contrary, what I have demonstrated throughout my analysis of revolts such as hers is that what shapes and makes possible our social or political acts of resistance—perhaps what mobilizes trans and queer life more broadly—are the psychical evolutions of intimate revolt through which meaning and subjectivity are reborn. Speaking psychoanalytically, then, Grace's public act of resistance is her own effort to "give meaning to suffering" at both the psychical and social level of human experience, for intimate "revolt is the counterbalance to trauma" (Kristeva 2002a: 24; Oliver 2002: 57). Bidding a brazen farewell to her dissolving sexed signifier, Grace accomplished a cultivation of what Kristeva describes as a "time and space of revolt" through which her own psychical and corporeal refashioning could be realized and, importantly, witnessed (2002a: 223). What ties Grace's performative act to the internal logic of revolt, then, is her passage of "rupture and rearticulation" (of sexed and gendered meaning) that highlights the threshold of psychical and social experience (Chanter and Ziarek 2005a: 3).

The psychic life of revolt that mobilizes trans and queer subjectivities therefore hinges not upon the future but, rather, upon the tenuous and unfinished landscape of liminality in which meaning and subjectivity may be infinitely refashioned. In this way, the intimate revolts of trans and queer life echo Jasbir K. Puar's recent attention to the "impossibility of linearity, permanence, and end points" with respect to trans experience (2015: 63). This always incomplete movement of meaning, which finds familiar though not exclusive or universal expression across trans and queer subjectivities, is powerfully captured by Morgan Haven-Tietze, whose poetic reflections on trans embodiment describe liminality as an experience in which

> you're on the verge of something. It's the moment in a voyage when you've left one continent and have just lost sight of shore. You turn to face the wind, toward your destination, but you're not there yet. You are here, on the moving sea. . . . It's strange, to be defined simply as "between." You are not x and you are not y. Not

female and not male. . . . Which can leave you feeling like nothing. Like you are nowhere. Nowhere sometimes means Utopia, though. Since you're nowhere, you get to make the rules. You get to decide. Order dissolves into fluidity. Land gives way to waves. (2013: 31)

Signaling both the anxiety and the anticipation of inhabiting a liminal time and space, Haven-Tietze's narration suggests that the psychical and corporeal inde-terminacy experienced by so many trans and queer persons is precisely where the imaginative possibilities of embodiment might be cultivated. To be sure, this experience of liminality uncovers a logic of instability not unlike the one wit-nessed in the unstable conditions of precarity, for these destabilizing movements of negativity carry the possibility of either disaster or renewal, slow death or rebirth. To embrace and perhaps embody liminality, as Haven-Tietze does, is therefore to cultivate a queer time and space for what we have discovered as the psychical and corporeal possibilities of intimate revolt. For the precarious liminality that defines Haven-Tietze's present is also the imaginative liminality that describes their future, that is, a future of revolt. Indeed, might the intimate evolutions of revolt be precisely that through which trans and queer subjectivities embark on this precarious voyage of liminality? Is not the psychic life of revolt experienced as a most intimate capacity for mediation between the instabilities of precarity and liminality? Traversing the threshold of psychical and corporeal life, Kristeva's conception of revolt—uncovered and mobilized here as an intimate politics aiming passionately "to restore *psychical life* and allow the *speaking body* optimal life"—emerges as an indispensable framework for articulating the pre-carious passages of rebirth journeyed over and again by trans and queer lives (2010: 158). To envision an intimate politics of rebirth with respect to trans and queer embodiment therefore returns our attention to those inner experiences of resistance and renewal that shape and give meaning to the precarious life of revolt. For it is precisely these "tiny revolts" that mobilize psychical life and situate sub-jectivity in a transitional, if not altogether transformative, movement of meaning (Kristeva 2002a: 5). Through the language and labors of Kristevan psychoanalysis, then, we might begin to cultivate this queer life of revolt as an intimate politics at the heart of trans and queer subjectivities, whose own futures, if they exist, are liminal and perpetually a project of revolt.

Amy Ray Stewart is a PhD candidate in philosophy at Southern Illinois University Carbondale and teaches women, gender, and sexuality studies. She specializes in Kristevan psychoanaly-sis, continental feminist philosophy, and transgender studies. Her writings appear in *Psycho-analysis, Culture, and Society*, *philoSOPHIA*, and the volume *New Forms of Revolt: Essays on Kristeva's Intimate Politics* (2017).

Acknowledgments

I wish to express my appreciation to the editors, reviewers, and staff of *TSQ: Transgender Studies Quarterly*, especially Sheila L. Cavanagh for her generous time and support as well as the two anonymous reviewers for their insightful suggestions. Fragmentary forms of this article were presented at the Kristeva Circle, the American Philosophical Association, the National Women's Studies Association, the Southeastern Women's Studies Association, and the New School for Social Research's conference on the Futures of Queer Theory, where questions from audience members pushed me to refine my thoughts. I am ever grateful to Sara Beardsworth, Sheldon George, and Stacy Keltner for their invaluable mentorship and encouragement. Special thanks to Laura Jane Grace for accepting and reading my copy of Leslie Feinberg's *Trans Liberation* and later taking the time to talk with me. As always, I am thankful to my spouse, Corinne, for giving me the time and space to write and revise my work. This intellectual labor is dedicated to my daughter, Freja, who reminds me over and again of the power and *jouissance* experienced in our tiny revolts.

Notes

1.   Emerging as a swift legislative blockage of Charlotte's Ordinance 7056, which had barred discrimination against LGBTQ persons and specifically granted transgender citizens the right to use public restrooms that correspond to their gender identity, House Bill 2 was passed by the North Carolina General Assembly and signed into law by Governor Pat McCrory on March 23, 2016. HB2—also known as the Public Facilities Privacy and Security Act—not only overturned Charlotte's ordinance but also prevented similar local measures by imposing statewide regulations on access to restrooms and changing facilities in government buildings, including libraries, airports, and public K–12 schools and universities. Targeting transgender communities, these regulations mandated that people could only use such restrooms and changing facilities that matched the "biological sex" recorded on one's birth certificate. Although habitually referred to as the state's "bathroom bill," HB2 also included provisions that obstructed local governments from enacting or amending ordinances that could effectively protect LGBTQ populations from discrimination in a wide range of situations such as employment practices and public accommodations. On March 30, 2017, after a full year of national controversy and increased (economic and political) pressure by opponents of HB2, a partial repeal in the form of House Bill 142 was passed and subsequently signed into law by Governor Roy Cooper, who acknowledged that the repeal was far from ideal. Indeed, the supposed compromise, which LGBTQ activists and civil rights advocates criticize as a mere repackaging of discrimination, amends only the controversial article on state regulations of access to public restrooms, leaving in place the legal precedent for statewide discrimination against LGBTQ populations. The partial repeal of HB2 therefore keeps trans and queer communities suspended in a state of precarity inasmuch as the new law mandates that local governments are, in fact, banned from enacting nondiscrimination ordinances regulating employment practices and public accommodations at least through December 1, 2020.

2.   My coupling of "trans" and "queer" throughout this article is not meant to collapse or homogenize the specificity of these terms but, rather, to stress an inclusive reading of nonconforming subjectivities in which an assemblage of gender and sexual identities is central. Although this article focuses primarily on the processural movements of gender identity, my wider philosophical reconstruction of unsettled embodiment aims to

demonstrate how the psychic life of revolt is a mobilizing element across a diverse range of nonconforming identities and modes of subjectivity.

3.   Kristeva's pioneering distinction between the semiotic and the symbolic, which is elaborated in *Revolution in Poetic Language* and remains fundamental to her subsequent thought, has been articulated thoroughly by a number of scholars (Beardsworth 2004; Keltner 2011; Lechte 1990; Margaroni 2004; Oliver 1993a). On the one hand, the semiotic designates "a psychosomatic modality of the signifying process" that encompasses pre- or translinguistic elements and energies, namely, affective and corporeal traces such as rhythm, sound, or gesture that are patterned prior to the acquisition of language and subject formation (Kristeva 1984: 28). It is in this sense that the semiotic functions as a precondition for language and subjectivity and that Kristeva reminds us of the etymological significance of the term *semiotic* as a "distinctive mark, trace, index, [or] precursory sign" (25). The semiotic might also be described, then, as "the heterogeneous, affective, [or] material dimension of language that contributes to meaning, but does not intend or signify in the way that symbols do" (Keltner 2011: 22). In other words, semiotic functioning is that which expresses the drives in and through language and subjectivity. The symbolic, on the other hand, refers to the social, historical, and linguistic "realm of signification, which is always that of a proposition or judgment, in other words, a realm of *positions*" (43). For Kristeva, the symbolic encompasses "any social, historical sign system of meaning constitutive of a community of speakers" and thus "organizes subjects, objects, and others into a coherent unity" (Keltner 2011: 19, 22). As that which organizes subjects and objects, discriminating between signifiers and signifieds, the symbolic thus attempts to regulate its borders by repressing the force of semiotic functioning. Yet it is precisely through these breaks, or semiotic ruptures in the symbolic "realm of signification," that the "subject in process/on trial" establishes an identification and position as a subject of the symbolic (Kristeva 1984: 43, 37). Kristeva's theoretical distinction between the semiotic and the symbolic need not be understood as a neat severance or opposition of two independent terms, for it is precisely the heterogeneous tension or oscillation of semiotic and symbolic functioning that constitutes the signifying process as such.

References

Ahmed, Sara. 2006. *Queer Phenomenology: Orientations, Objects, Others.* Durham, NC: Duke University Press.

Andrews, Arin. 2014. *Some Assembly Required: The Not-So-Secret Life of a Transgender Teen.* New York: Simon and Schuster Books for Young Readers.

Beardsworth, Sara. 2004. *Julia Kristeva: Psychoanalysis and Modernity.* Albany: State University of New York Press.

———. 2005. "From Revolution to Revolt Culture." In Chanter and Ziarek 2005b: 37–56.

———. 2009. "Love's Lost Labors: Subjectivity, Art, and Politics." In *Psychoanalysis, Aesthetics, and Politics in the Work of Julia Kristeva*, edited by Kelly Oliver and S. K. Keltner, 127–42. Albany: State University of New York Press.

Binnie, Imogen. 2013. *Nevada: A Novel.* New York: Topside.

Bornstein, Kate. 1994. *Gender Outlaw: On Men, Women, and the Rest of Us.* New York: Routledge.

Bornstein, Kate, and S. Bear Bergman, eds. 2010. *Gender Outlaws: The Next Generation.* Berkeley, CA: Seal.

Butler, Judith. 2004a. *Undoing Gender*. New York: Routledge.

———. 2004b. *Precarious Life: The Powers of Mourning and Violence*. New York: Verso.

———. 2009. *Frames of War: When Is Life Grievable?* New York: Verso.

———. 2013. "The Logic of Dispossession and the Matter of the Human (After the Critique of Metaphysics of Substance)." In *Dispossession: The Performative in the Political: Conversation with Athena Athanasiou*, 12–27. Durham, NC: Duke University Press.

———. 2016. "Rethinking Vulnerability and Resistance." In *Vulnerability in Resistance*, edited by Judith Butler, Zeynep Gambetti, and Leticia Sabsay, 12–27. Durham, NC: Duke University Press.

Chanter, Tina, and Ewa Płonowska Ziarek. 2005a. Introduction to Chanter and Ziarek 2005b: 1–17.

———, eds. 2005b. *Revolt, Affect, Collectivity: The Unstable Boundaries of Kristeva's Polis*. Albany: State University of New York Press.

Conrad, Ryan, ed. 2014. *Against Equality: Queer Revolution, Not Mere Inclusion*. Oakland, CA: AK.

Coyote, Ivan E., and Zena Sharman, eds. 2012. *Persistence: All Ways Butch and Femme*. Vancouver, BC: Arsenal Pulp.

Feinberg, Leslie. 1993. *Stone Butch Blues: A Novel*. Ann Arbor, MI: Firebrand Books.

———. 1998. *Trans Liberation: Beyond Pink or Blue*. Boston: Beacon.

Foucault, Michel. 2003. *Society Must Be Defended: Lectures at the Collège de France, 1975–76*. Translated by David Macey. New York: Picador.

Grace, Laura Jane, and Dan Ozzi. 2016. *Tranny: Confessions of Punk Rock's Most Infamous Anarchist Sellout*. New York: Hachette Books.

Hansen, Sarah K., and Rebecca Tuvel. 2017. "Introduction: Twenty Years of Revolt." In *New Forms of Revolt: Essays on Kristeva's Intimate Politics*, edited by Sarah K. Hansen and Rebecca Tuvel, 1–14. Albany: State University of New York Press.

Haven-Tietze, Morgan. 2013. "Liminality." In "The Gender Stories Issue," edited by The Bandit, special issue, *Bandit Zine*, no. 9: 31.

Hollibaugh, Amber, and Margot Weiss. 2015. "Queer Precarity and the Myth of Gay Affluence." *New Labor Forum* 24, no. 3: 18–27.

Juang, Richard M. 2006. "Transgendering the Politics of Recognition." In *Transgender Rights*, edited by Paisley Currah, Richard M. Juang, and Shannon Price Minter, 242–61. Minneapolis: University of Minnesota Press.

Keltner, S. K. 2009. "What Is Intimacy?" In *Psychoanalysis, Aesthetics, and Politics in the Work of Julia Kristeva*, edited by Kelly Oliver and S. K. Keltner, 163–77. Albany: State University of New York Press.

———. 2011. *Kristeva: Thresholds*. Cambridge: Polity.

Kristeva, Julia. 1980. *Desire in Language: A Semiotic Approach to Literature and Art*. Translated by Thomas Gora, Alice Jardine, and Leon S. Roudiez. New York: Columbia University Press.

———. 1984. *Revolution in Poetic Language*. Translated by Margaret Waller. New York: Columbia University Press.

———. 1987a. *Tales of Love*. Translated by Leon S. Roudiez. New York: Columbia University Press.

———. 1987b. *In the Beginning Was Love: Psychoanalysis and Faith*. Translated by Arthur Goldhammer. New York: Columbia University Press.

———. 1989. *Black Sun: Depression and Melancholia*. Translated by Leon S. Roudiez. New York: Columbia University Press.

———. 1991. *Strangers to Ourselves*. Translated by Leon S. Roudiez. New York: Columbia University Press.

———. 1995. *New Maladies of the Soul.* Translated by Ross Guberman. New York: Columbia University Press.

———. 2000. *The Sense and Non-Sense of Revolt.* Vol. 1 of *The Powers and Limits of Psychoanalysis,* translated by Jeanine Herman. New York: Columbia University Press.

———. 2002a. *Intimate Revolt.* Vol. 2 of *The Powers and Limits of Psychoanalysis,* translated by Jeanine Herman. New York: Columbia University Press.

———. 2002b. *Revolt, She Said.* Translated by Brian O'Keeffe. New York: Semiotext(e).

———. 2010. *Hatred and Forgiveness.* Vol. 3 of *The Powers and Limits of Psychoanalysis,* translated by Jeanine Herman. New York: Columbia University Press.

———. 2014. "New Forms of Revolt." *Journal of French and Francophone Philosophy—Revue de la philosophie française et de langue française* 22, no. 2: 1–19.

———. 2016. "Inner Experience against the Current." Interview with Philippe Sollers and Colette Fellous. In *Marriage as a Fine Art,* translated by Lorna Scott Fox, 15–60. New York: Columbia University Press.

Lechte, John. 1990. *Julia Kristeva.* New York: Routledge.

———. 2004. "The Imaginary and the Spectacle: Kristeva's View." In *Julia Kristeva: Live Theory,* edited by John Lechte and Maria Margaroni, 116–42. London: Continuum.

Margaroni, Maria. 2004. "The Semiotic Revolution: Lost Causes, Uncomfortable Remainders, Binding Futures." In *Julia Kristeva: Live Theory,* edited by John Lechte and Maria Margaroni, 6–33. London: Continuum.

McCloskey, Deirdre N. 1999. *Crossing: A Memoir.* Chicago: University of Chicago Press.

Meyerowitz, Joanne. 2002. *How Sex Changed: A History of Transsexuality in the United States.* Cambridge, MA: Harvard University Press.

Miller, Elaine P. 2014. *Head Cases: Julia Kristeva on Philosophy and Art in Depressed Times.* New York: Columbia University Press.

Mock, Janet. 2014. *Redefining Realness: My Path to Womanhood, Identity, Love, and So Much More.* New York: Atria Books.

Monroe, Jazz. 2016. "Against Me!'s Laura Jane Grace Burns Birth Certificate at North Carolina Show." *Pitchfork,* May 16. pitchfork.com/news/65501-against-mes-laura-jane-grace-burns -birth-certificate-at-north-carolina-show/.

National Geographic. 2017. "The Gender Issue: The Shifting Landscape of Gender." *National Geographic* 231, no. 1.

Nestle, Joan, Clare Howell, and Riki Wilchins, eds. 2002. *GenderQueer: Voices from Beyond the Sexual Binary.* Los Angeles: Alyson Books.

O'Brien, Michelle. 2013. "Tracing This Body: Transsexuality, Pharmaceuticals, and Capitalism." In *The Transgender Studies Reader 2,* edited by Susan Stryker and Aren Z. Aizura, 56–65. New York: Routledge.

Oliver, Kelly. 1993a. *Reading Kristeva: Unraveling the Double-Bind.* Bloomington: Indiana University Press.

———. 1993b. "Introduction: Julia Kristeva's Outlaw Ethics." In *Ethics, Politics, and Difference in Julia Kristeva's Writing,* edited by Kelly Oliver, 1–22. New York: Routledge.

———. 2002. "Psychic Space and Social Melancholy." In *Between the Psyche and the Social,* edited by Kelly Oliver and Steve Edwin, 49–65. Lanham, MD: Rowman and Littlefield.

———. 2004. *The Colonization of Psychic Space: A Psychoanalytic Social Theory of Oppression.* Minneapolis: University of Minnesota Press.

———. 2005. "Revolt and Forgiveness." In Chanter and Ziarek 2005b: 77–92.

Puar, Jasbir K. 2015. "Bodies with New Organs: Becoming Trans, Becoming Disabled." *Social Text*, no. 124: 45–73.

Quesada, Uriel, Letitia Gomez, and Salvador Vidal-Ortiz, eds. 2015. *Queer Brown Voices: Personal Narratives of Latina/o LGBT Activism*. Austin: University of Texas Press.

Saffin, Lori A. 2011. "Identities under Siege: Violence against Transpersons of Color." In Stanley and Smith 2011: 141–62.

Salamon, Gayle. 2010. *Assuming a Body: Transgender and Rhetorics of Materiality*. New York: Columbia University Press.

Schladen, Marty. 2017. "ICE Detains Alleged Domestic Violence Victim." *El Paso Times*, February 15. www.elpasotimes.com/story/news/2017/02/15/ice-detains-domestic-violence-victim -court/97965624.

Serano, Julia. 2007. *Whipping Girl: A Transsexual Woman on Sexism and the Scapegoating of Femininity*. Berkeley, CA: Seal.

Shultz, Jackson Wright. 2015. *Trans/Portraits: Voices from Transgender Communities*. Hanover, NH: Dartmouth College Press.

Singer, T. Benjamin. 2006. "From the Medical Gaze to *Sublime Mutations*: The Ethics of (Re)Viewing Non-normative Body Images." In *The Transgender Studies Reader*, edited by Susan Stryker and Stephen Whittle, 601–20. New York: Routledge.

Sjöholm, Cecilia. 2005. *Kristeva and the Political*. New York: Routledge.

———. 2009. "Fear of Intimacy? Psychoanalysis and the Resistance to Commodification." In *Psychoanalysis, Aesthetics, and Politics in the Work of Julia Kristeva*, edited by Kelly Oliver and S. K. Keltner, 179–94. Albany: State University of New York Press.

Söderbäck, Fanny. 2012. "Revolutionary Time: Revolt as Temporal Return." *Signs: Journal of Women in Culture and Society* 37, no. 2: 301–24.

Spade, Dean. 2006. "Mutilating Gender." In *The Transgender Studies Reader*, edited by Susan Stryker and Stephen Whittle, 315–32. New York: Routledge.

———. 2011. *Normal Life: Administrative Violence, Critical Trans Politics, and the Limits of Law*. Brooklyn: South End.

Stanley, Eric A., and Nat Smith. 2011. *Captive Genders: Trans Embodiment and the Prison Industrial Complex*. Oakland, CA: AK.

Stryker, Susan. 2008. *Transgender History*. Berkeley, CA: Seal.

Stryker, Susan, Paisley Currah, and Lisa Jean Moore. 2008. "Introduction: Trans-, Trans, or Transgender?" *WSQ* 36, nos. 3–4: 11–22.

Sycamore, Mattilda Bernstein, ed. 2006. *Nobody Passes: Rejecting the Rules of Gender and Conformity*. Berkeley, CA: Seal.

TGEU (Transgender Europe). 2016. "Transgender Day of Visibility 2016—Trans Murder Monitoring Update." TGEU, March 30. tgeu.org/transgender-day-of-visibility-2016-trans -murder-monitoring-update/.

Valerio, Max Wolf. 2006. *The Testosterone Files: My Hormonal and Social Transformation from Female to Male*. Emeryville, CA: Seal.

Warner, Michael, ed. 1993. *Fear of a Queer Planet: Queer Politics and Social Theory*. Minneapolis: University of Minnesota Press.

Mourning Moppa

Mourning without Loss in Jill Soloway's Transparent

SIMON VAN DER WEELE

Abstract The notion of mourning without loss describes a situation in which a subject feels the urge to grieve for a loss he or she cannot claim as one's own. In the US TV series *Transparent*, such a loss emerges when Maura Pfefferman comes out to her children as a trans woman. The author uses the narrative of *Transparent* as a springboard to consider how loss figures (and fails to figure) in the "event" of coming out as transgender. Maura "loses" Morton, and her children "lose" their father, yet faced with Maura's presence, their loss remains opaque. Maura's coming out thus hints at the subjectivity of loss: in one and the same situation, loss might occur for some, vaguely, and for others not at all. The author performs a close reading of a scene showing the grief of Maura's son Josh to query theories of mourning rooted in the Freudian tradition. These models frame loss as the severance of a significant attachment, but *Transparent* fails to dramatize any such rupture, owing to Maura's sustained presence. The author proposes an alternative by considering Bracha Ettinger's notion of metramorphosis. Because for Ettinger attachments are never fully realized nor fully abandoned, her notion of transsubjectivity can help us make sense of affectively felt losses that aren't quite losses. These affects are legitimate, even if their objects might reasonably object to them: Maura, after all, was never lost, never not Maura.
Keywords mourning, loss, gender transitioning, intersubjectivity, Bracha Ettinger

I speak of mourning without loss in situations in which a subject feels the urge to grieve a loss he or she is unable to claim unambiguously—situations in which loss manifests itself obliquely, untimely, or intangibly.[1] With the general understanding that loss is the severance of an intimate tie that unravels the subject in some way, I employ the concept of mourning without loss to grapple with scenes that fail to dramatize the occurrence of such a rupture—because the "lost" object is still there, lingering somewhere between present and absent, or never properly emerged in the first place.

The Amazon TV series *Transparent* (dir. Jill Soloway, 2014) chronicles the life of Maura Pfefferman, a transgender woman on the cusp of transitioning who has recently come out to her family. As I will argue in this article, the series

TSQ: Transgender Studies Quarterly ∗ Volume 4, Numbers 3–4 ∗ November 2017
DOI 10.1215/23289252-4189983 © 2017 Duke University Press

suggests that Maura's transitioning constitutes a scene of unclaimable loss: Maura "loses" Morton and her children "lose" their father, yet faced with Maura's presence, their loss remains opaque. Loss arises as a question in *Transparent* because Maura's coming out hints at the subjectivity of loss: in one and the same situation, loss might occur for some, vaguely, and for others not at all. In this scenario, loss ceases to be simply something that dies or disappears or is otherwise displaced. Loss could "happen" right in front of our eyes, with nothing missing. As a result, Maura's children struggle to find a mode of mourning to express their grief.

In the first section of this article, I will perform a close reading of a scene of the season 2 finale of *Transparent* that explicitly makes a claim about the occurrence of loss in the "event" of transitioning. The scene quite eloquently outlines the situation of mourning without loss I wish to articulate and examine in this article—the mourning without loss incited by gender transitioning. In the second section of this article, I will use the reading of this scene as a springboard to consider how loss figures (and fails to figure) in the "event" of transitioning. To frame the discussion on mourning and loss, I will initially draw on Sigmund Freud's insights in "Mourning and Melancholia" ([1917] 1955) and rereadings of his ideas in the work of Nicolas Abraham and Maria Torok ([1972] 1994), Jacques Derrida (1989), and Judith Butler (2004a). While these models frame loss as the severance of a significant attachment, *Transparent* refuses to stage any such break, owing to Maura's sustained presence. If we follow Freud's argument closely, mourning without loss will end up registering as the prototype of a melancholic attachment, which Freud pathologizes. This article sets out to wrest mourning without loss from its melancholic connotations and revalidate the complex affects that steer its particular mode of intersubjectivity.

To sketch out a mode of mourning otherwise, the third section of this article will attempt to move away from Freudian models of subjectivity rooted in loss found in much writing on the topic of mourning toward an understanding of mourning and loss following a trans-subjective model of (inter)subjective encounters. To achieve this, I will borrow some concepts from Bracha Ettinger, whose work on the matrixial borderspace outlines a model of trans-subjectivity that explicitly challenges and supplements the Freudian approach. Because for Ettinger attachments are neither fully realized nor fully abandoned, her notion of trans-subjectivity can help us make sense of affectively felt losses that aren't quite losses. I will argue that these affects are legitimate, even if their objects might reasonably object to them: Maura, after all, was never lost, never not Maura.

Speaking of "mourning without loss" in scenes of gender transitioning, we can identify at least two possible loci for the occurrence of loss: there is a potential loss felt by the transgender subject, and there is a potential loss felt by the subjects with whom the transgender subject holds intimate ties. My focus in this article lies in the mourning process of those who hold intimate ties with the transgender subject. I will spend the final section of this article deliberating this choice more carefully, considering the implications of framing transitioning as a moment of loss, both for the transgender subject and the subject with whom they might sustain intimate ties. Why is it necessary to theorize mourning without loss in cases of transitioning? What do we gain—or lose—when we frame the process of transitioning as a scene of loss? Again, the *Transparent* scene helpfully alludes to the fact that opting for the semantics of loss in scenes of transitioning is a political decision, even if it supposedly serves to define an interiorized process. This leads to the question of who benefits from an idiom that frames gender transitioning as a scene in which loss can occur—and who may object to such an idiom. I will end the article by making a cautious case for how the claiming of our losses, ambiguous or not, as working through grief can serve to realign and strengthen our attachments in surprising and productive ways.

"Joshua, Your Father Died": Death as Placeholder

To illustrate how *Transparent* thematizes loss and grief, I wish to discuss a pivotal scene from the season 2 finale between Maura's son Josh and his mother's partner Buzz. (By Josh's mother, I refer to Shelly, who gave birth to Josh.) If the first season of *Transparent* deals with the hardships and thrills of Maura exploring her newly asserted womanhood, the second season seeks to complicate this narrative by looking at some issues that take longer to surface: importantly, we find Maura dealing with the ways in which her trans identity intersects with her class, religion, and sexuality, as well as with her—according to some—previously enjoyed male privilege. The impact of her transitioning on the lives of her children, too, complicates and intensifies as season 2 progresses (Kornhaber 2015). This narrative arc finds a climax in the scenes between Josh and Buzz.

Midway through the episode, Josh and Buzz find an injured white duck. Buzz carefully wraps the duck in Josh's red hoodie and lets Josh carry it home in his arms, cradling the duck like a baby, its head snugly resting on his shoulder. This spontaneous gesture of care and empathy sets up a sphere of unexpected intimacy between Buzz and Josh, while also metaphorically alluding to the care work Buzz will perform in the subsequent scene between them. (It is important to note as well that Josh recently saw his relationship crumble, wrapped up with his partner Raquel in a drama of miscarriage—another scene of mourning in which loss is not entirely tangible.)

In their next scene, Buzz and Josh gather in the bathroom to tend to the duck's wounds. In a move quite uncharacteristic for him, Josh decides to open up to his mother's partner about his state of mind: "It's like . . . I thought stuff would add up by now, but it's like . . . everything's slipping through," he admits. Buzz encourages Josh to link his feelings to the changes in his family: "You're in shock . . . mostly I'd say, [about] the loss of your father . . . Joshua, your father died." Josh at first responds incredulously, "I mean . . . I see mom all the time . . . I . . . I did not like him . . . You think I still miss Mort?" He then adds one more reservation: "Well it's like, politically incorrect to say you miss someone who's transitioned."

In this exchange, for the first time, Buzz allows Josh to conceive of his mother's transitioning as a moment of loss. Notably, Buzz compares Maura's transitioning to death; apparently, he thinks that only the notion of passing away suffices to evoke the severity of the rupture that he claims has taken place the moment Maura started to transition. Death becomes a placeholder for something much more ambiguous and complex. Josh's resistance to this perspective is threefold: there is the fact of Maura's continued presence, despite an absence ("I see mom all the time"); there is the fact that Maura could have never surfaced as an object Josh would miss ("I did not like him"); and there is a social convention that keeps Josh's liberal, middle-class instincts from accessing the experience Buzz tries to open up for Josh (it's "politically incorrect"). Buzz retorts to Josh's final claim, "This isn't about correct. Joshua, this is . . . this is about grieving. Mourning. Have you grieved and mourned the loss of your father?" Perplexed, Josh confesses, "Him, like losing him? No, I don't know how to do that." At this, Buzz embraces Josh, and Josh starts to weep intensely.

"I Don't Know How to Do That": Mourning without Loss

Josh's words, "I don't know how to do that," reflect the issue that lies at the core of this article: can we and should we entertain the thought of a possible mode of mourning for transgender subjects who start their transitioning? And what will such a mode of mourning entail? Josh admits that he doesn't know how to mourn his father. He struggles to make sense of the loss he feels, or thinks he feels, or thinks he should feel. He has the sense of his world collapsing—"everything's slipping through"—but the notion of loss emerges only in dialogue with Buzz. Loss was a category inaccessible to Josh because loss never materialized in a form recognizable to him. This is why Buzz has to invent Mort's death: the fiction of Mort's passing away provides a metaphor by which Josh can concretize some of the dormant affects he previously had trouble articulating. Without death, Josh is incapable of finding a vocabulary by which to voice his experiences, a script by which to exteriorize his grief, because loss manifested itself obliquely. His is a mourning without loss.

Josh is thus riddled by the absence of a script by which to channel his particular affects. At the root of his problem lies a conception of loss as some radical, irrevocable rupture. His assertion, "I see mom all the time," illustrates that Maura's ongoing presence in his life means an object of mourning fails to crystallize, despite the sense of loss that pervades his experiences. Indeed, the notion of loss tends to rely on the presupposition of a structure of attachment, which somehow collapses through a moment of displacement—the obvious example being death. Josh's loss is not so clear-cut, though. When Maura announced her transitioning (an announcement that, significantly, reached Josh through his sister Ali, ensuring this loss was lost even further in mediation), she implicitly issued a demand to let go of any notion of Mort's sustained presence. This is a demand that proves to be difficult for Josh to live up to, as the presence of that body that Josh used to call "dad" or "Mort" continues to be precisely that: present.[2] Underscoring this ambiguity, Josh and his siblings tend to call Maura "Moppa," verbally keeping their father present while acknowledging a change that will not quite become a rupture. Josh's loss oscillates between there and not-there. He feels loss, but the ongoing presence of the seemingly lost object constantly delegitimizes this feeling.

In traditional psychoanalytic accounts of mourning, mourning without loss always threatens to slide into melancholia. In "Mourning and Melancholia" ([1917] 1955), Freud famously differentiates between mourning, which for him means the process of letting go of a lost object by redirecting libidinal desire to another, and melancholia, which he sees as a pathological mode of mourning that insists on maintaining the attachment to a lost object by incorporating it in one's interior world (244). In the first instance, which Freud refers to as "the normal affect of mourning" (243), the subject respects loss and moves on; in the second, the subject narcissistically remains in mourning indefinitely, without an object outside herself. The structure of Josh's attachment to his father resembles the melancholic relationship in that Josh finds himself mourning without a concrete object: there is a *sense* of loss, but this loss failed to sufficiently crystallize and, as a result, could never be mourned "properly," in Freud's sense.[3]

This unspecified sense of loss is precisely the type of loss that Freud considers emblematic for the melancholic attachment. For Freud, mourning can occur in a variety of instances: mourning is the reaction both to "the loss of a loved person," as well as to "the loss of some abstraction which has taken the place of one" (243). In effect, for the process of mourning to be successful, a loss need not literally materialize, by the way of disappearance in a physical, embodied way. However, Freud notes that "mourning . . . is for the most part occasioned only by a real loss of the object, by its death" (256). If Freud thus singles out death as the prototype for the occurrence of loss, it remains unclear how this conception of "real" loss translates to the sphere of abstractions, which, according to him, constitutes another category of potentially grievable losses. He opens the door to the possibility of mourning the loss of abstracted investments in concepts, fantasies, or ideas, but he does not spell out the terms under which such losses may transcend the melancholic attachment. Instead, "Mourning and Melancholia"

very specifically links the melancholic attachment to losses that are more ambiguous than the seemingly clear-cut severance of death. Freud writes:

> [In cases of melancholia] there is a *loss of a more ideal kind* [emphasis mine]. The
> object has not perhaps actually died, but has been lost as an object of love. . . . In yet
> other cases one feels justified in maintaining the belief that a loss of this kind has
> occurred, but one cannot see clearly what it is that has been lost, and it is all the
> more reasonable to suppose that the patient cannot consciously perceive what he
> has lost either. This, indeed, might be so even if the patient is aware of the loss
> which has given rise to his melancholia, but only in the sense that he knows *whom*
> he has lost but not *what* he has lost in him. (245)

The condition of melancholia thus appears to consist in the failure to consciously
register and subsequently deal with a variety of losses more ambiguous than
death. To linger with such losses amounts to a pathological attachment. In the
Transparent scene, Buzz provides Josh with the semantics of death to help classify
the latent affects he was previously unable to articulate. This is to say, Buzz
designated a lost object for Josh to mourn. He takes on the role of the analyst,
whose task is to bring the object of the melancholic attachment back from the
unconscious to potentiate the process of mourning and healing. Josh's reaction
seems to be telling: as he begins to weep, melancholia appears to slide into
mourning. Echoing Freud, Buzz's intervention required the invention of a death
event, as if only death makes loss palpable enough for it to be mourned properly.
In this way, *Transparent* does allow itself to be read along the lines of a Freudian
take on mourning and melancholia.

However, the loss suffered by Josh evidently falls under Freud's category of
"loss of a more ideal kind." Although Josh never gets specific, he seems to concur
with Buzz's conjecture that what he lost was something like the image of his father,
not just in terms of his looks, body language, or scent but also in a more abstract
sense: what Maura's transitioning challenged was Josh's investment in the notion
of a father figure. Such abstractions do not easily lend themselves to be mourned,
especially not if the perception of such losses is subjective—and subject to the
objections of others. What complicates mourning without loss in scenes of gender
transitioning is not just that the loss itself is abstract or immaterial, and that a
sustained embodied presence appears to invalidate feelings of loss; rather,
mourning without loss exposes the subjectivity of loss, as it may be felt by some
(i.e., Josh) and not by others (i.e., Maura). In scenes of mourning without loss, the
object of mourning is uncertain, and claiming it may lead to dispute. For this
reason, even if a subject is able to apprehend the loss, claiming and mourning it
remain far from self-evident. The conceptual division between mourning and

melancholia does not productively capture the formal ambiguity of such losses because it reads the hesitation and confusion of the melancholic subject as pathology, rather than as symptomatic for this particular affective experience.

In "The Ego and the Id" ([1923] 1961), Freud partly reconsiders his thoughts on mourning and melancholia, recognizing that they are more difficult to tell apart than he initially believed. If in "Mourning and Melancholia" he seemed to suggest that internalization is a characteristic exclusive to the pathological melancholic attachment, here he offers the thought that any work of mourning might have to involve a move of internalization, a letting in of the other, keeping what we lost with us in order not to fall apart ourselves (19). In "Mourning *or* Melancholia: Introjection *versus* Incorporation" ([1972] 1994), Nicholas Abraham and Maria Torok elaborate on this idea, introducing two psychic responses to loss that reflect Freud's initial normative distinction between mourning and melancholia: introjection and incorporation. The first, considered the "healthy" reaction, alludes to an ego-enlarging mode of mourning that has the grieving subject absorb certain valued qualities of the lost other.[4] The second, deemed pathological by Abraham and Torok, involves a move of internalization they call building a "crypt" for the other in one's psyche, fixing the other and fixating on a fantasy of sustaining the other's presence (130). Both responses to loss contain an element of hanging on to the other, but in the case of introjection, the other is appropriated and effectively disappears, dissolving in the ego, while in the case of incorporation, the other is entombed, left intact, yet remains irreducibly other. Although Abraham and Torok thus further trouble Freud's distinction between mourning and melancholia, their framework is equally normative. A true work of mourning will have to involve a process of introjection. Incorporation denotes a pathological *refusal* to mourn: it is a fantasy that defends the psyche against necessary readjustments in the face of loss, by keeping the other alive in oneself, as if "through magic" (126). "Incorporation denotes a fantasy, introjection a process" sums it up succinctly (125).

Unsurprisingly, if we closely follow Abraham and Torok's description of the symptoms of incorporation, we will see that it closely resembles Josh's predicament, which their account would inevitably pathologize. They write, "There can be no thought of speaking to someone else about our grief under these circumstances [of incorporation]. The words that cannot be uttered, the scenes that cannot be recalled, the tears that cannot be shed—everything will be swallowed along with the trauma that led to the loss. Swallowed and preserved. Inexpressible mourning erects a secret tomb inside the subject" (130). The process of incorporation follows unspeakable losses, which the psyche refuses to acknowledge. As a result, such loss incapacitates the subject in fundamental ways: the loss will be affectively inaccessible to the subject who suffers it and cannot be felt, spoken, or otherwise acknowledged. Abraham and Torok's description of the subject doing this work of "inexpressible mourning" uncannily resembles the grieving process of Josh, whose affective incapacity to grasp the loss of Mort left him exasperated. And even if we have moved away from the stigma of the melancholic attachment, Josh's response again gains the stamp of pathology. Yet how may Josh mourn such a complex loss otherwise? How can a subject mourn the loss ensuing from gender transitioning if said subject justifiably hesitates to fully claim the loss?

Even if Abraham and Torok uphold the idea of a pathological response to loss in terms of incorporation, what is useful in their articulation of the mourning process is the recognition that the bereaved subject feels compelled to preserve the other in some way. Many accounts of the mourning process state that loss reveals how subjectivity is predicated on exposure to the other, on a structure of attachment; and this relational foundation of the subject is put under threat when faced with the erasure of said attachment. In *Mémoires: For Paul de Man*, Jacques Derrida writes:

> The "me" or the "us" of which we speak then arise and are delimited in the way that they are only through this experience of the other, and of the other as other who can die, leaving in me or in us this memory of the other. This terrible solitude which is mine or ours at the death of the other is what constitutes that relationship to self we call "me," "us," "between us," "subjectivity," "intersubjectivity," "memory." (1989: 33)

In this scenario, loss becomes a crisis for the subject who experiences it. Building on Freud, Judith Butler speaks of loss as what causes the subject's "undoing" (2004a: 24): loss, the severance of this tie to an other, reveals attachment as what makes subjectivity possible, all the while threatening to undo this subjectivity in its very showing. To mourn is to realize that there was never a "me" without "you" in the first place; but what is now left of this "me" without "you" (22)? Derrida summarizes it thusly: "I mourn, therefore I am" (1995: 321). Preserving the other as part of oneself—either in a process of introjection or a fantasy of incorporation, to draw Abraham and Torok back in—is a way of coping with the self-effacing effects of losing someone. However, Josh's predicament raises questions about the efficacy of this model. What happens when loss fails to announce itself, when the subject cannot apprehend whatever is missing as loss as such? And how might we mourn such a nonloss, if there is nothing to internalize, no lost object to hang onto and keep with us because that object is still there confronting us with its presence in the present?

In *Ambiguous Loss: Learning to Live with Unresolved Grief* (1999), Pauline Boss attempts to create a space for contemplating losses that are not "clear-cut" (1999: 9).[5] Boss speaks of ambiguous loss in cases "in which the status of a loved one as 'there' or 'not there' remains indefinitely unclear" (6). She writes, "People can't start grieving because the loss is indeterminate. It feels like a loss but it is not *really* one" (10–11). Boss distinguishes between two kinds of ambiguous loss. The first comprises situations of "leaving without good-bye," in which people are physically absent yet psychologically present; she offers as examples missing soldiers and kidnapped children but also less dramatic ones such as losses in adoptive or divorced families (8). The second consists of situations of "good-bye without leaving," in which people are physically present yet psychologically absent; here, she has in mind such ambiguous losses as the loss of people with Alzheimer's disease and comatose persons but also workaholics (9). Boss's notion of ambiguous loss goes some way into interpreting the particular affective experience hinted at in the *Transparent* scene, carving out the psychic space for something that feels like loss but isn't quite that, although her conceptual distinctions begin to fray when considering the loss ensuing from gender transitioning. On the one hand, Mort can be said to be physically absent and present; as Maura started to transition, her appearance, body language, and voice all erased parts of Mort's physique, although the embodied presence Maura sustains throughout the transitioning also serves to cancel out the apparent loss elicited by these changes. On the other hand, Mort can be said to be psychologically absent and present, too; while Maura's transitioning slowly requires Josh to revisit the father figure image he maintains in connection to Mort, Maura continues to perform the role of authority that Josh previously linked to Mort's fatherhood. Maura's transitioning thus elicits a range of losses, some physical, some psychic, in and between different subjects. Still, the notion of ambiguous loss is useful here because it forms a welcome addition to the vocabulary of loss and mourning we have encountered so far.

Unfortunately, Boss does not theorize the psychic process of mourning in much detail, proposing no alternative conception of the mourning process based on her conceptual formulation of ambiguous loss. In fact, she is, like Freud and Abraham and Torok before her, clear about one thing: the work of mourning is not possible without apprehending and dealing with the lost object in a "proper" way. Without a "proper" lost object, any work of mourning is inherently compromised, if not rendered impossible—and hence, pathological. The subject cannot begin to mourn without a notion of what is lost and a willingness to relinquish it. Boss notes ambiguous loss can have traumatizing effects on the subjects that face it, since it often does not register with subjects as an experience. It is thus crucial to open up ambiguous loss as an experience that can be named and felt. In the *Transparent* scene, Buzz secures a vocabulary for Josh to appre-hend his loss, naming what Josh couldn't or wouldn't. Moments later, Josh is crying. Does his tearing up signal the start of a work of mourning? Or is he mourning his incapacity to do so? Even if Josh can now semantically access his experience, he still lacks a script to deal with this feeling. He is left with the task of finding resolution for something that will not or cannot resolve—the loss of Mort, who, in a sense, was never lost, never not Maura. Boss's concept of mourn-ing without loss offers no alternative script by which to express these affects and mourn without loss.

It would appear, then, that the semantics of death don't help Josh to make sense of his experiences of ambiguous loss much at all, let alone help him to begin a "proper" work of mourning. In fact, I argue that ambiguous loss forces us to come to terms with the fact that in scenes of mourning without loss, we might never get over these losses and mourn "properly." As Boss points out, ambiguous loss is not "*post* anything" (1999: 24). Its constantly looming, sustained presence outside ourselves is what defines it. In *Precarious Life* (2004a), Judith Butler encourages us to "tarry with grief" (30), to grieve exhaustively and indetermi-nately, willfully engaging in what the early Freud would have deemed a melan-cholic attachment. Yet in the case of ambiguous loss, to tarry with grief is no longer one possible orientation toward a lost object but the only one—precisely because the object is not quite lost. Grief will not resolve, which in no way needs to signal pathology.

The scene of mourning without loss narrated in *Transparent* presents a subjective loss that cannot be claimed unambiguously and cannot be mourned unequivocally along the lines of the psychoanalytic models I have outlined so far. If the work of mourning generally starts with a complete break or rupture that ends a particular intersubjective attachment, the *Transparent* scene reveals that the complexity of mourning without loss is rooted in a (partially) sustained moment of intersubjectivity, against all odds. The refusal of the attachment between Josh and Maura to truly sever, the sustained intersubjectivity despite the changes Maura announced, is what defines the ambiguous loss I am discussing here. If psychoanalytically inflected theories of mourning understand loss as a crisis of subjectivity, then ambiguous loss frames loss as a crisis of intersubjec-tivity: being agape with the possibility of encounter, despite its apparent impossi-bility. The psychoanalytic models of mourning I discussed above fail to capture the ambiguity of such encounters. Their only answer to this peculiar grief is the sphere of pathology.

What thus troubles a "standard" mourning process here is not just the fact that the loss presents itself ambiguously, unwilling to provide a "proper," coherent object of mourning, but that choosing to claim and mourn this loss also amounts to an ethical decision. The processes of introjection or incorporation rely on the presupposition that a subject must preserve the other in some way, for the other has ceased to exist outside the subject. However, in scenes of mourning without loss spurred on by gender transitioning, this other—the trans subject—persists and continues to issue what Emmanuel Levinas (1985) might call the demand for a response from the bereaved subject: these scenes stage an ethical moment, in which the bereaved subject must find a way to combine their ongoing recognition of the trans subject with a mode of mourning that deals with the changes this trans subject has ostensibly undergone.[6] In this scenario, there is no ready object to internalize for the subject, at least not an undisputed one. The trans subject who is unwillingly and possibly unwittingly turned into an object of mourning can no doubt reasonably object to such a process of internalization—especially if, as Jacques Derrida argues in a critique of Abraham and Torok, this internalization creates a structure of narcissism that appropriates the other, reducing otherness to self (1989: 6).[7] In scenes of mourning without loss, mourning may turn out to be an unethical orientation toward the other, at least if we continue to understand mourning as "normal mourning" along the lines of the psychoanalytic models I have discussed so far. In the case of gender transitioning, the stage of mourning without loss is set by an encounter: the "loss" of gender transitioning recasts subject relations and implores those involved to reconceptualize their attachment to one another. In *Transparent*, this change is reflected in the signifier *Moppa*, which shows how relations between father (Mort), mother (Maura), mother (Shelly), and children have shifted but not severed. In this scenario, "normal mourning" is not an option, not if it would mean to deaden and appropriate the presence of the other (trans) subject, who continues to issue a demand from us. To mourn would be to formulate an appropriate response. If choosing to mourn is a slight to the other, rather than a gesture of recognition—what then remains of the mourning process?

Mourning Otherwise: Mourning and Metramorphosis

The crisis of intersubjectivity I delineated above hints at the incapacity of the Freudian conception of loss as a subjectivating force to contain the particular form of troubled relationality that characterizes scenes of transitioning. Operating in the register of ambiguous loss, the transitioning subject realigns subject orientations to recast relations between them. The process of transitioning does not sever ties but stretches and tightens them as it adds pressure to them. Self and other don't collapse, but they morph in surprising ways, alongside one another. How can we conceive of a mode of mourning that can grieve what is a not-quite-lost there, a mode of mourning otherwise that won't erase or appropriate the sustained presence of the other?

To probe such a mode of mourning otherwise, I wish to take a few cues from Bracha L. Ettinger, whose work on the matrixial borderspace explicitly proposes an alternative to the Freudian model of subjectivation through loss.[8] For Freud, entering the symbolic realm and becoming a subject is always preceded by a traumatic experience of lack that comes to define relations between self and other (Rodriguez 2016: 29). Subjects form attachments to others driven by a desire to undo or restore this originary loss, but these attachments will remain imperfect, as their completion requires giving up on subjectivity itself. Ettinger supplements this paradigm by modeling subject relations after what she calls the "intrauterine encounter," taking the matrix or womb as a signifier of a subjectivating force that transcends the individual subject (2006b: 218).

Intrauterine existence, staged between mother and infant, for Freud represents the moment of presubjective unity for which subjects will continue to yearn after the separation event of birth. Ettinger, however, moves away from this conception of the womb as a "basic passive space" (2006a: 64). Her notion of the intrauterine encounter suggests instead that there is a "prenatal meeting" between infant and mother in "an unconscious borderspace woven from affective and mental strings that are reattunable" (2006b: 219). Unbeknownst to the infant, it is already bound up with the other before birth in a form of relationality that is not quite an attachment but also not quite a separation, either. Rather, it is a relation of trans-subjectivity between subjects that are not fully formed and connected through "borderlinking," which Ettinger explains as "differentiation in co-emergence" (218): a suspension of self-other distinction through the ambiguous space of the womb, in which infant and mother are not quite one, or quite apart from each other. Ettinger calls the psychic space she creates for such relations the "matrixial borderspace."

While borderlinking is in the first instance a prenatal experience, the psychic space that accommodates it persists after birth. It thus provides a model of subjectivity in which subjects aren't quite coherent, whole, or individuated—the matrixial borderspace is both "trans-subjective and sub-subjective even if and when it arises in the field of the separate individual self and even if and when it operates in the intersubjective relational field" (218). Ettinger describes this mode of subjectivity thusly:

> Subjectivity here is an encounter between I and un-cognized yet intimate non-I neither rejected nor assimilated. If we conceive of traces of links, trans-individual transmissions and transformational reattunements, rather than of relations to and communication with objects and subjects, in terms of a transgressive psychic position in which the co-emergence and co-fading is prior to the I versus others, a different passageway to others and to knowledge arises—suitable for transformative links that are not frozen into objects. (218)

In other words, her model of subjectivity circumscribes a different way of relating to others, approaching them not as possible objects of attachments but as other selves-in-formation to whom I am always already intrinsically linked: "partial subjects" who link and transform in tandem (2006a: 65). Ettinger calls this process of linking and transforming "metramorphosis."

As I have shown, mourning without loss troubles psychoanalytic theories of mourning and the model of Freudian subjectivation that undergirds them because the sustained embodied presence of the object of mourning halts attempts at incorporation that would solve the crisis of subjectivity loss tends to generate. Instead, the subject faces a crisis of intersubjectivity. Ettinger's alternative to Freud is more receptive to the experience of mourning without loss because her partial-subjects form relations that never crystallize as subject-object attachments—and as a result, are never quite lost, either. In this way, Ettinger writes, the matrixial borderspace "can serve as a model for a *shareable dimension of subjectivity* in which elements that discern one another as *non-I*, without knowing each other, co-emerge and co-inhabit a joint space, without fusion and without rejection" (65, emphasis Ettinger). Relations without fusion and without rejection: if for Ettinger, such attachments are never fully realized nor fully abandoned, the matrixial borderspace provides a way to make sense of affectively felt losses that aren't quite losses. But if there is no loss, how can or should we mourn?

I want to begin answering this question by noting that even if loss doesn't figure much in Ettinger's writing on the matrixial borderspace, this is not to say that there is no pain or risk at stake in metramorphosis. Borderlinking as a self-effacing process requires vulnerability, destabilizing subjects as their contours get warped or even redrawn (Dasgupta 2009: 2). Ettinger points out that "matrixial co-emergence has a healing power, but because of the transgression of individual boundaries that it initiates and entails, and because of the self-relinquishment and fragilization it appeals to, it is also potentially traumatizing" (2006b: 219). Her description of self-shattering trauma is similar to Derrida's and Butler's. However, it is not set off by a moment of loss, and trauma is not the only outcome. Metramorphosis can be therapeutic, staging an encounter in which transformation and continuity stand side by side (Rodriguez 2016: 30). This is what I take Ettinger to mean when she speaks of "*an-other kind of loss* or separation which is not attributed to rejection, 'castration' or abjection" (2006b: 218, emphasis mine): a loss without losing, the residue of a transformative trans-subjective coemergence that has subjects unravel and rewoven at once.

The not-quite-loss at the basis of scenes of transitioning I isolated in my analysis of *Transparent* quite resembles this "an-other kind of loss" of which Ettinger speaks. I thus suggest that borderlinking provides a way to understand how subject positions shift (or don't) in scenes of transitioning. In the process of transitioning, there is continuity alongside transformation; a crisis of intersubjectivity. The loss that emerges as a result is an affectively felt loss that consists in what has changed in the wake of a transformative event between subjects, even if a peculiar continuity—that of the sustained embodied presence of both subjects—prevents this loss from registering properly, or being cognizable at all. And importantly, according to Ettinger, this not-quite-loss is potentially traumatic, but it doesn't need to be.

Nonetheless, my original quandary stands. What happens to the notion of mourning through incorporation if we reframe loss as the unspeakable residue of a transformation with continuity? I locate in the process of metramorphosis also the space for a kind of work of mourning, one that recognizes the subjective integrity of the other, who is a partner of coemergence. As I have shown, the work of mourning in the Freudian model entails storing memory traces of the other in the self, either through appropriation and absorption (introjection) or through encryption (incorporation). In this way, mourning propels subjective transformation by way of retaining the other in some way in the self.

The process of metramorphosis is structured quite similarly, although it importantly allows for cotransformation: it is built on the idea that sub-subjects evolve together, alongside one another, and both emerge from this entanglement again as individual (partial) subjects. Ettinger writes, "Metramorphosis is a conaissance—a transformational knowledge of being born together with the other whereby each individual becomes sub-subject in subjectivity that surpasses her personal limits, and whereby an other might become for me not only a sign of my archaic m/Other but also an occasion for transformation' (2006b: 221–22). Metramorphosis thus holds a certain promise of relationality, of yielding to the presence of the other, who will also have to yield to mine. This moment of mutual submission suspends subjectivity and proffers the possibility of transformation alongside the other. This process will bring a sense of loss, perhaps, although subjects can't readily get access to it. Yet there is something else there, too: a reemergence alongside the other (conaissance), whose traces will stay with me, enriching me in ways yet inexplicable.

If there is something to be "mourned" in scenes of transitioning, it will require us to test the elasticity of what mourning can be and do. Mourning is first of all a recognition of the fact that others affect me and affected me. It also carries a certain transformative potential. The work of internalization is one way of acknowledging this relation and becoming porous to the other, transforming the self through the other's imprint. But internalization needs an object and implies a subject that is coherent and self-sustaining enough to let the other in. Mourning without loss doesn't offer such an object. Ettinger's notion of metramorphosis gives us a model of relationality without attachments and without separations. It also facilitates a transformation, but its subjects reemerge together, thus upholding the integrity of all partial subjects involved. In metramorphosis, there is no objectification. In scenes of transitioning, the work of mourning without loss will have to take up such a form: tending to a loss that won't quite become a separation by continuing to engage with the other, through the other, rejoicing in how I can continue to be moved and morphed by the other's sustained presence.

Looking once more at *Transparent*, I would say that the signifier *Moppa*, used by the Pfefferman family to refer to Maura, forms the residue of one such process of mourning through metramorphosis. As a signifier, *Moppa* manages to contain Maura, Mort, and also the various ways in which Maura and Mort relate or have related to other members of their family, while maintaining the ambiguity of Maura's subject position vis-à-vis the other Pfeffermans. *Moppa* doesn't tell us who Maura was for whom, and when exactly. In this way, *Moppa* doesn't refer to a person as such, but to a network of attachments, reflecting the complex ways in which the Pfeffermans have recast their relations in the wake of Maura's transitioning. *Moppa* commemorates Mort, but it is not a eulogy; *Moppa* reflects a possibility, openness and optimism, rather than resignation. *Moppa* doesn't fix a past, nor does it erase one. *Moppa* reckons with what happens when attachments bend without breaking, an attempt to negotiate those complex changes that may feel like losses but aren't quite, or not for everyone. Such is the work of mourning without loss.

"This Isn't about Correct": Who Can Claim Unclaimable Loss?

I spent most of the previous discussion attempting to theorize the possibility of a work of mourning without loss that can supplement the Freudian model of mourning (via Abraham and Torok, Derrida, and Butler), taking cues from Bracha Ettinger's rich vocabulary of trans-subjective encounters. I have focused so far on the experience of loss felt by subjects with whom the transgender subject holds intimate ties. In what follows, I wish to consider this choice more explicitly and question to what extent the vocabulary of loss should be welcomed in scenes of gender transitioning. That is, framing Maura's scenes of transitioning as loci of ambiguous loss is potentially not without controversy. For this reason, I want to make some remarks pertaining to an ethics of mourning without loss.

In the introduction, I described the work of mourning without loss as grieving a loss that is unclaimable. The subject to whom this unclaimability pertains is the subject who has lost an object owing to the tearing of a structure of attachment. However, as we have seen, the structure of mourning without loss in the present case implies one of sustained intersubjectivity: loss is ambiguous precisely because the attachment has not quite collapsed and the encounter fails to cede. This also means that it is no longer obvious who can and should lay claim to the loss. There could be a dispute over its occurrence, or there could be divergent perspectives that will redefine the structure of attachment itself.

The semantics of this definition thus acquire a particular poignancy in the case of trans-subjectivity and scenes of transitioning. Buzz gives Josh a vocabulary by which to mold his affects, which, as Josh points out, is a vocabulary that toys with political incorrectness. Indeed, it is a vocabulary Maura might object to. Ayden Parish notes that "the transition from one gender expression to another is sometimes narrated as *loss* or even *death*, and friends and family may find themselves *in mourning* and struggling to accept the *new person*" (2013, emphasis Parish). But these semantics do not necessarily reflect the experience of trans subjects and in fact could even invalidate them. According to trans psychotherapist S. J. Langer, "In the trans phenomenon, it is the loss of what one never had but should have had, that is mourned" (2014: 68); transitioning is one way of reckoning with this loss, of mobilizing grief to effectuate healing. Why should Josh be able to claim as a loss something that for Maura might represent an opening up, a resolution, self-determination, what Butler might call a "social promise" (2004b: 6)?

What this tension shows us is the subjectivity of loss itself. If loss is the subjective apprehension of the severance (or not-quite-severance) of an attachment a subject holds to another subject, it follows that one event can figure as a rupture for some, vaguely, yet for others not at all. This is one function of theorizing mourning without loss: to understand how one might feel grief without a loss being apparent, to others or to oneself. But if loss is not impartial, this also means it can become the locus of antagonism. Making a claim to a feeling of loss is both affectively and politically charged. Or rather, it is by molding one's affects to the semantics of loss that one draws in the political. This no doubt holds true for the discourse on trans subjects, not only because claiming the loss of a trans person's "previous self" and mourning their "death" risks silencing the voices of trans people themselves but also because trans people have suffered and continue to suffer from having their experiences be read in terms of bodily or psychic lack, shortcoming or loss.

Still, I want to end this article by probing the possibility of making the semantics of loss available for trans subjects and the subjects with whom they hold close-knit, intimate ties. Not everyone will want to make use of the idiom. Nor will everyone be compelled to do so, affectively. I will not doubt the importance of acknowledging how our inner life is bound up with social norms, how politics saturate our emotions. Yet I wonder what we lose if we let a political discourse envelop our feelings to the point of cancelling them out, ignoring them, or telling ourselves they are false. There must be ways in which the "crisis of intersubjectivity" I tentatively described above might restructure our attachments in desirable ways, tightening them, bringing subjects in even closer proximity. But this asks for the crisis to be worked through, for subjects to claim their losses, although this claim perhaps will not resonate with others.

Even if *Transparent* tends to present itself as a comedy, one narrative that propels it is a drama of representation, of failing to dramatize loss. In *Transparent*, loss fails to figure properly. But it nonetheless suggests loss figures: it figures to feel loss.

Simon van der Weele is a PhD candidate at the University of Humanistic Studies in Utrecht, the Netherlands. His research revolves around concepts of care, disability, and mourning. His current work critically assesses notions of dependency and autonomy by means of a qualitative study of care relations between intellectually disabled persons and their caregivers.

Notes

1.   I first wrote of mourning without loss in my MA thesis, "Mourning without Loss: The Affective Life of Grief" (2015), in which I theorized a way in which we might grieve for strangers, whose deaths cannot touch us personally because we had no intimate, affective investment in their lives. In the present article, I look to expand the reach of the concept to encompass different and equally complex scenes of oblique loss.

2.   This dynamic similarly evolves in the relationship between Maura and her ex-wife Shelly, whose romance is briefly rekindled as Shelly recognizes something very familiar and comfortable in Maura. It is clear that for Shelly, Mort is still very much present, even if she now has to call her Maura.

3.   In "Prohibition, Psychoanalysis, and the Production of the Heterosexual Matrix," chapter 2 of *Gender Trouble* (1990), Judith Butler considers gender as being structured much like a melancholic attachment in Freud's sense. In a close reading of Freud's "Mourning and Melancholia" and "The Ego and the Id," she argues that the incest taboo is preceded by a taboo on homosexuality. For example, the son can only direct an incestuous desire toward the mother once the father has become unavailable as a sexual object. Here emerges a fundamental loss for the subject—a loss that can never be mourned because the taboo renders it unspeakable. According to Butler, gender identifications stem from this primary loss. Gender is a melancholic structure, a mourning without loss; and this loss finds expression only on the body, in the manifestation of sex. Trans studies scholars such as Jay Prosser (1998) have provided critiques of Butler's reading of Freud and its implications for theorizing transgender. While beyond the scope of the present article, the idea of gender melancholia as a form of mourning without loss and its bearing on mourning trans "losses" is one direction I wish to explore more extensively in future work.

4.   Introjection is an essential concept in Abraham and Torok's psychoanalytic vocabulary— its uses go far beyond their theory of the psychic life of mourning. In an editor's note to "Mourning *or* Melancholia," Nicholas T. Rand gives this general definition: introjection

is "the principle of gradual self-transformation in the face of interior and exterior changes in the psychological, emotional, relational, political, professional landscape" (101).

5. Being a psychologist, Boss has geared her work toward "curing" modes of grieving she deems pathological. I share little affinity with this goal, as, following Judith Butler's plea to "tarry with grief" (2004a: 30), I think to view mourning as pathological is to miss something essential about the way in which it instills us with a sense of vulnerability and a will to care. Nonetheless, I find the conceptual framework Boss offers to be helpful, hence her inclusion in the present article.

6. Here, my inquiry into mourning without loss gains a clear Levinasian dimension, as the question of mourning the loss of gender transitioning turns out to be a question of what kind of response a trans subject may demand from those with whom the trans subject holds intimate ties. Levinas is helpful for formulating the question of mourning without loss because his ethics are derived from the presupposition of an initial exposure to the other that shapes subjects and leads to an intersubjective relationship—a relationship the ambiguous loss of gender transitioning contorts and complicates without cutting it altogether. For writers like Derrida and Butler, the Levinasian model of subjectivity (based on an ethical relationship to an other to whom the *I* is literally subjected) is as much of an influence on their theory of mourning as is Freud's. To fully tease out the Levinasian dimension in the arguments of Derrida and Butler is beyond the scope of this article. For some elaborations, see Critchley 2014 and McIver 2012.

7. In *Mémoires: For Paul de Man* (1989), Derrida implicitly refers to Abraham and Torok's concept of introjection as "the most deadly infidelity" to the deceased other, for in a move of introjection, the subject fails to preserve the integrity and alterity of the other, who dissolves in the subject's ego (6). He calls the process of incorporation "narcissistic" because the subject who incorporates "refuses to take or is unable to take the other within oneself" (6). For Derrida, both responses do a grave injustice to the other, although he eventually makes a case for the virtues of incorporation over introjection. Following Derrida's argument in much detail is beyond the scope of the present article; what matters is that the work of mourning bears the risk of erasing otherness and failing to respect the other's alterity. (Here, Levinas's influence on Derrida becomes very apparent.) For Derrida's critique of Abraham and Torok, see Derrida 2005.

8. My article draws on Ettinger's work to make sense of the experience of loss in scenes of transitioning. It will not consider the implications of her work for the psychoanalytic understanding of the experiences of transgender and transsexuality. For work in this direction, see Cavanagh 2016.

References

Abraham, Nicolas, and Maria Torok. (1972) 1994. "Mourning *or* Melancholia: Introjection *versus* Incorporation." In *The Shell and the Kernel: Renewals of Psychoanalysis*, translated by Nicholas T. Rand, 125–38. Chicago: University of Chicago Press.

Boss, Pauline. 1999. *Ambiguous Loss: Learning to Live with Unresolved Grief*. Cambridge, MA: Harvard University Press.

Butler, Judith. 1990. *Gender Trouble: Feminism and the Subversion of Identity*. New York: Routledge.

———. 2004a. *Precarious Life: The Powers of Mourning and Violence*. London: Verso.

———. 2004b. *Undoing Gender*. New York: Routledge.

Cavanagh, Sheila. 2016. "Transsexuality as Sinthome: Bracha L. Ettinger and the Other (Feminine) Sexual Difference." *Studies in Gender and Sexuality* 17, no. 1: 27–44.

Critchley, Simon. 2014. *The Ethics of Deconstruction: Derrida and Levinas*. Edinburgh: Edinburgh University Press.

Dasgupta, Sudeep. 2009. "Resonances and Disjunctions: Matrixial Subjectivity and Queer Theory." *Studies in the Maternal* 1, no. 2: 1–5.

Derrida, Jacques. 1989. *Mémoires: For Paul de Man*. Rev. ed. Translated by Cecile Lindsay et al. New York: Columbia University Press.

———. 1995. *Points . . . : 1974, 1994*. Stanford, CA: Stanford University Press.

———. 2005. Foreword to *The Wolf Man's Magic Word: A Cryptonomy*, by Nicolas Abraham and Maria Torok. Minneapolis: University of Minnesota Press.

Ettinger, Bracha L. 2006a. *The Matrixial Borderspace*. Minneapolis: University of Minnesota Press.

———. 2006b. "Matrixial Trans-subjectivity." *Theory, Culture, and Society* 23, nos. 2–3: 218–22.

Freud, Sigmund. (1917) 1955. "Mourning and Melancholia." In *On the History of the Psycho-Analytic Movement, Papers on Metapsychology and Other Works*, vol. 14 of *The Standard Edition of the Complete Psychological Works of Sigmund Freud*, edited by James Strachey, 243–58. London: Hogarth Press and the Institute of Psycho-Analysis.

———. (1923) 1961. "The Ego and the Id." In *The Ego and the Id and Other Works*, vol. 19 of *The Standard Edition of the Complete Psychological Works of Sigmund Freud*, edited by James Strachey, 12–66. London: Hogarth Press and the Institute of Psycho-Analysis.

Kornhaber, Spencer. 2015. "The Brilliant Challenge of *Transparent*." *Atlantic*, December 14. www.theatlantic.com/entertainment/archive/2015/12/transparent-season-two-review/419943/.

Langer, S. J. 2014. "Our Body Project: From Mourning to Creating the Transgender Body." *International Journal of Transgenderism* 15, no. 2: 66–75.

Levinas, Emmanuel. 1985. *Ethics and Infinity: Conversations with Philippe Nemo*. Translated by Richard A. Cohen. Pittsburgh, PA: Duquesne University Press.

McIver, David W. 2012. "Bringing Ourselves to Grief: Judith Butler and the Politics of Mourning." *Political Theory* 24, no. 4: 409–36.

Parish, Ayden. 2013. "Gendered Selves, Gendered Subjects: Transgender Identities and the Divided Person Metaphor." Paper presented at Metaphor: Discourse Applications, University of Alberta, June 24.

Prosser, Jay. 1998. *Second Skins: The Body Narratives of Transsexuality*. New York: Columbia University Press.

Rodriguez, Karen. 2016. "Someone Else Is Singing through Your Throat: Language, Trauma, and Bracha L. Ettinger's Wit(h)nessing." *Critical Multilingualism Studies* 4, no. 1: 25–43.

Soloway, Jill, dir. 2014. *Transparent*. Season 2. Amazon.

Van der Weele, Simon. 2015. "Mourning without Loss: The Affective Life of Grief." MA thesis, University of Amsterdam. dare.uva.nl/document/613191.

"Taking the Risk of a True Speech"
Transgender and the Lacanian Clinic

SHANNA T. CARLSON

Abstract This brief piece brings forward some of the differences between the scene of a Lacanian analysis and that of the social link.
Keywords clinic, psychoanalysis, Jacques Lacan, transgender

Trans* people and transgender studies will transform the Lacanian clinic. They will do so first and foremost because of the changes they have already brought about within the social link. The changing landscapes of the social link matter to a Lacanian analysis precisely because a Lacanian analysis is fundamentally concerned with what falls outside the social link: it is concerned with that which is not wanted by society and with that which never entered language as such (Apollon 2014). On this topic, analyst Willy Apollon is quite concrete: that which "has no way to represent itself in language," he argues, constitutes the unconscious, and it "goes on working in the organism, building the body and making symptoms." It is the unconscious that furnishes the material of an analysis, for, as Apollon indicates, "what you cannot say is eating you, building and rebuilding your body from your organism" (2014).

Frame

Because a Lacanian analysis is interested in the subject of the unconscious, it is not interested in the ego or social actor, which represses the subject of the unconscious. Indeed, Jacques Lacan teaches that the ego is not that interested in itself either: in an analysis, the primary effect of the ego's empty speech is a feeling of frustration on the part of the analysand, who knows on some level that the ego "is frustration in its very essence" and who thereby, Lacan argues, regards as suspect any response made by the analyst to the ego (2006: 208). If the analyst were to respond to the ego, she or he would participate in the repression of the subject,

TSQ: Transgender Studies Quarterly ∗ Volume 4, Numbers 3–4 ∗ November 2017 **627**
DOI 10.1215/23289252-4189992 © 2017 Duke University Press

and the stakes of this repression are high: empty speech, Lacan writes, is that "in which the subject seems to speak in vain about someone who—even if he were such a dead ringer for him that you might confuse them—will never join him in the assumption of his desire" (211).

The "someone" of whom the ego speaks will never join the subject in the assumption of desire: it's a sobering thought. Fortunately, the subject of the unconscious arrives, rupturing the ego's discourse by way of silences, gestures, slips of the tongue, and sudden emotion. As analyst Patricia Gherovici has said, it's "an interesting internal advocate" (2016).

Thus, the analyst listens. She listens and waits for these ruptures, and the mode in which she listens provides a key to the experience. In her book *Wrestling with the Angel: Experiments in Symbolic Life*, Tracy McNulty argues that the constraint of the transference "call[s] forth" the subject of the unconscious (2014: 259). Building from Lacan's definition of transference as "the enactment of the reality of the unconscious" (1998: 146), McNulty explains that transference in a Lacanian analysis does not simply restage an individual's interpersonal relations with key figures in his/her/hir life but is structural in its scope and effects, for it concerns a subject's relation to an Other who is absent (2014: 61–72). The analyst does not enter into a relation with the ego on the couch attempting to address her because that relation would crush the space needed for the subject. McNulty cites Lacan: "'Like any other situation involving speech,' he reasons, the analytic situation 'can only be crushed if one tries to inscribe it in a dyadic relation'" (66). By remaining largely silent, the analyst creates a space and, usually, quite a lot of anxiety on the part of the analysand. This anxiety—"*the* affect of an analysis," McNulty writes (96)—is productive. For the analyst creates a space, explains analyst Lucie Cantin, so that the analysand can create the words, words to "evoke what has never been said" (2015). The words, meanwhile, bring the body: "Speech," Lacan writes, "is in fact a gift of language, and language is not immaterial. It is a subtle body, but body it is. Words are caught up in all the body images that captivate the subject" (2006: 248).

Ultimately, it is the analysand who must do the analysis: activated by the analyst's desire to know, the unconscious will furnish the signifiers that will carve out the space that attests to the traumatism of the subject, as well as the symptoms that will incompletely script the fantasy that subtends that experience. These productions come about in the push to a freedom that will enable the subject to take responsibility in a new way. But first, there's work: free association is a kind of work. In Lacan's words, it is "the forced labor of a discourse that leaves one no way out" (2006: 207). No way out but through, we might say—hence the necessity of traversal, as well as the necessity of the analyst's work of support through this traversal.

I bring forward these observations on the frame of a Lacanian analysis in order to draw out some of the differences between that space and the space of the social link and to outline some of the reasons an analyst does not respond to an analysand's demands for love. As Apollon explains, "The analysand comes [to an analysis] with a narrative—the ego narrative. We are not interested in that narrative. But we do as if. We listen to the narrative, waiting for a hole in the logic of the narrative" (2016).

Sexual Difference

One would think that Lacanian analysts would be wonderfully equipped to encounter analysands who bring with them pieces of a life story having to do with the experience of transgender. As with any other analysand, the analyst would desire to know, what is wanted in what is said? What has been left unsaid? What difference does it make? Yet we know from the history of psychoanalytic theory that the clinic cannot have proven welcoming, and not only because the analyst, as Apollon has said, hates the ego. ("You cannot imagine the hate the analyst can have for the ego. Hate is true transference!" [2014].) It's a question for practitioners: What does it take to be an analyst? What does it take to listen in that way?

Along these lines, it is worth noting that the analyst is not the only one in an analysis who waits. "True analysand[s]," Apollon suggests, wait as well: they "await[] some guarantee" that they will be met with "no judgment, no evaluation, no answer, no knowing" (2014). Given that the experience of being met with no judgment, no evaluation, no answer, and no knowing is itself connected to the problem of castration, that bedrock of psychoanalysis, it would seem to be a necessary condition of the analysand's emergence as a subject of desire. It is also an experience connected to sexual difference: from which side of the sexual difference divide will the subject respond to the analyst's desire to know?

In the past, I have argued that sexual difference for Lacanian psychoanalysis cannot be reduced to the fields of biological sex, gender identity, or gender expression—that it is not a manifestation of either nature or nurture, neither human invention nor biological given, but a mode of being resulting from humans' status as subjects of language. Its cut is real: subject to language, we are sexed by its division and sexed differently by virtue of the positions we assume with respect to this division. The real at stake here, however, tells us nothing about a person's "sex" or "gender." It tells us something about how the subject, in a primordial "decision," survived the division of language. In other words, if psychoanalysis has taught us anything, is it not that one person's real is neither more nor less real than another's—and that it is nearly unbearable, for its truth is the Other's?

Full Speech

As Lacanian analysts continue to listen and to wait, they will learn from new generations of analysands what constitutes the social link today, and they will be changed.

For my part, I look forward to reading the articles assembled in this special issue, so that I might learn the intricacies of the work that is taking place at those strange and fragile sites where psychoanalysis and transgender studies are linking and falling apart. *Linking* and *falling apart* strike me as appropriate words for this labor, too, for they remind me of a moment in Lacan's seminar on the psychoses, wherein he takes a break from considerations of the clinic to address the topic of social change. He writes:

> The emergence of a new signifier, with all the consequences, down to one's most personal conduct and thoughts, that this may entail, the appearance of a register such as that of a new religion, for example, isn't something that is easily manipulated— experience proves it. Meanings shift, common sentiments and socially sanctioned relations change, but there are also all sorts of so-called revelatory phenomena that can appear in a sufficiently disturbing mode for the terms we use in the psychoses not to be entirely inappropriate for them. The appearance of a new structure in the relations between basic signifiers and the creation of a new term in the order of the signifier are devastating in character. (1997: 201)

I think we can safely say that trans* people and transgender studies are making appear new structures in the relations between basic signifiers and creating new terms in the order of the signifier. If these creations are devastating in character, they are also necessary and, in both these ways, not unlike full or true speech, which is a risk you take because, in Apollon's words, "it comes and it must be said" (2014).

Shanna Carlson received her PhD in romance studies from Cornell University. She is a student of social work at the University of Minnesota and of psychoanalysis with the Groupe interdisciplinaire freudien de recherche et d'intervention clinique et culturelle.

References

Apollon, Willy. 2014. "The Unconscious, the Censored, and the Social Link." Lecture presented at the annual Yearly Training Seminar in Lacanian Psychoanalysis, Groupe interdisciplinaire freudien de recherche et d'intervention clinique et culturelle (GIFRIC), La Bordée, Quebec City, June 2.

————. 2016. "Function of the Dream." Lecture presented at the annual Yearly Training Seminar in Lacanian Psychoanalysis, Groupe interdisciplinaire freudien de recherche et d'intervention clinique et culturelle (GIFRIC), La Bordée, Quebec City, June 6.

Cantin, Lucie. 2015. "The Future of the Thing in Femininity and in Psychosis." Lecture presented at the annual Clinical Days conference, Groupe interdisciplinaire freudien de recherche et d'intervention clinique et culturelle (GIFRIC), Kedzie Center, Chicago, October 8.

Gherovici, Patricia. 2016. "The Unconscious Is the Last Activist: Cassandra Seltman Interviews Patricia Gherovici." *Los Angeles Review of Books*, February 8.

Lacan, Jacques. 1997. *The Psychoses, 1955–1956*. Book 3 of *The Seminar of Jacques Lacan*, edited by Jacques-Alain Miller, translated by Russell Grigg. New York: Norton.

————. 1998. *The Four Fundamental Concepts of Psychoanalysis*. Book 11 of *The Seminar of Jacques Lacan*, edited by Jacques-Alain Miller, translated by Alan Sheridan. New York: Norton.

————. 2006. *Ecrits*. Translated by Bruce Fink. New York: Norton.

McNulty, Tracy. 2014. *Wrestling with the Angel: Experiments in Symbolic Life*. New York: Columbia University Press.

What Does Tiresias Want?

TRISH SALAH

Abstract In concert with recent attempts to move beyond long-standing psychoanalytic equations of transsexuality with psychoses, this article offers some possible ways to consider "the Tiresian" as a site of both cissexual and transsexual fantasy and analytic fictions. It is interested in both the utility of a nonpathologizing psychoanalysis for trans people and in the capacity of trans people's literary writing to offer alternative imaginaries, knowledges, and analytics through which to reread and revise psychoanalytic conceptions of identity (sexed, raced, gendered) in relation to desire, time, and the human.
Keywords psychoanalysis, trans literature, Tiresias, Daniel Paul Schreber

If one sticks to the classics, the answer seems to be, not a lot. Unless it is to be left alone, to not be badgered by those who, having solicited insight and gained it will likely proceed to rail against what they have learned and also ignore it, to their own peril and inevitable ruin. How is that for a wish?

An alternately celebrated and infamous figure of Greek and Roman myth, poetry, and theater, Tiresias was a seer who twice changed sex and who adjudicated a quarrel between the king and queen of the Olympian deities, Zeus and Hera. In Rome, they were known as Jove and Juno. Their quarrel was over whose was the greater share of sexual pleasure—they thought Tiresias, who had lived both as a man and as a woman, could settle it for them. Tiresias's answer to the gods (that of the ten shares of pleasure, one belonged to man and the rest to woman) angered Hera and pleased Zeus. The goddess blinded Tiresias, and Zeus, unable to undo her work, gifted Tiresias with prophesy, the "second sight" (Ovid 1955: 67–68).

Tiresias is not a transsexual, but there are some commonalities: a change of sex (or more than one), an insistence on women's pleasure, and a measure of alienation from—if not outright criminalization by—the state. Some would say, a career in sex work. And people are always asking her about the other sex. No, not that one—the *other* other sex. Ladies and gentleman, as Lacan pointed out, are a matter of perspective.

Drawing upon the work of Bracha L. Ettinger (2000), Sheila L. Cavanagh has recently (2016) offered us occasion to think about the Theban seer Tiresias, not only as a way of displacing the House Oedipus with all its heterosexual melodrama from its pride of place within the psychoanalytic edifice but also to afford new vantages on what Sigmund Freud understood as our primary bisexuality and to revise and extend insights offered by Hélène Cixous (1981) and Julia Kristeva (1984, 1985) under the rubrics of *écriture féminine* and the semiotic or archaic maternal, respectively. Cavanagh (2016) is particularly interested in mobilizing Ettinger's excavation of Tiresias, as a corrective to psychoanalysis's long-standing, broadly antipathetic stance toward transsexual subjects (as psychotic or near enough as to be assimilable to it), and forwards a Tiresian psychoanalysis capacious enough to nonpathologically understand transsexual and other gender-nonconforming subjects. For Ettinger and Cavanagh, the Tiresian indexes a feminine other beyond the feminine construed through and contained by the symbolic cut of sexual difference, one arising from the subject's being with/in/toward the maternal other (matrixial borderlinking) and confounding what is posited as a sexed relation to knowledge with uncertainty and relationality across time (Ettinger 2000, 2006; Cavanagh 2016). The matrixial, both repository and destiny of partial attachments made with an unknown yet contiguous other in the space of the womb, is bisexual in the Freudian sense and confounds subject-to-subject interdependency with copoesis (Ettinger 2006). If I understand Ettinger correctly, here she parts company from Freud, for whom such a relation obtains only after birth and as a vestigial "primitive ego-feeling" or "oceanic feeling" from infancy, one that might also be retrospectively reconstituted in fantasies of primordial union in the womb (Freud [1930] 1957: 3–4).[1] In this formulation, psychoanalysis's gross misapprehension of Oedipus as the sorting hat responsible for distributing sexed destinies and psychic life (a complex for every girl and/or boy) can be supplemented or, better, displaced by the Tiresian modes' more holistically perverse orientation toward an intrasubjectivity that is bisexual and more open to difference(s) coemergent within and across the self and (unknown) others.

Classical sources aside,[2] my route to thinking a Tiresian poetics of psychoanalysis is somewhat different, though not necessarily incompatible with the model initiated by Ettinger and elaborated by Cavanagh, particularly in regard to the clinical framing of transsexuality. I say "classical sources aside," but in fact that is where I begin, with Tiresias as a figure of myth, drama, and poetry. For example, "Hysteria of Origins" is a suite of poems that doubles the inversion of psychoanalytic preoccupations with etiology with a hysterical enactment of the imperative to "always historicize"; it does so by projecting the origins of contemporary sex/gender arrangements across time and trans-sexing literary and mythic figures, including Pandora, Orpheus, Eurydice, Sappho, Phaeon, and, of course, Tiresias (Salah 2002). But what could it mean, at the dawn of the twenty-first century, to give Tiresias a change of sex? Or conversely, one could read the poem as asking, have we ever been doing anything else? Or, again, how does an other sex beyond cisnormative inscription stand in for yet haunt what sex is imagined to be? The literary figure of Tiresias has enjoyed a long and quite checkered itinerary inscribed both with cisnormative (often feminist, often transphobic) fantasies of transsexuality and in the discourses of transsexual, transgender, and gender-nonconforming writers.[3] I will return to the implied contradiction here—between transphobic fantasy and transsexual self-representation—but here I want to stress their common share in the literary as a site for elaborating questions, apprehensions, fantasies, and insights into what it might be to be a person, to have a life or be a sex, to feel desire or to have history, to know and live among others.

Rethinking the relation of psychoanalysis to transsexuality involves a double gesture. On the one hand, I read the psychoanalytic archive, as one archive among others, for its rhetorical and affective investments in, and phantasmatic deployment of, figures for crossing, blurring, transforming, or transcending sex. On the other, I turn to the creative writing of crossing sexed subjects (trans identified and otherwise) to investigate what they and their writing have to say about psychic life, sexuation, and related matters. Among other things, I'm interested in how trans writers fantasize, figure, and analyze psychoanalysis, sexuality, identity, and origin not only as politicized counterdiscourse but also as analytic fictions, or poetic philosophy. This approach—triangulating psychoanalysis, genealogy, and literature[4]—owes something to Freud's own sentiment, that literature, specifically poetry, provides a rich resource for thinking through the contouring and dissonant dynamisms of psychic life.[5] Adam Phillips's liberatory premise, leaning on Franz Kafka, also suggests that "art breaks the sea that's frozen inside us. It reminds us of sensitivities that we might have lost at some cost" (2014).

My archival reading of transgender figures within psychoanalysis also owes a debt to Gilles Deleuze and Félix Guattari's (1972) literary reading of the Schreber case (Schreber [1903] 1955; Freud, 1963) in *Anti-Oedipus*—though my reading of Schreber is not their own. Rather, it emphasizes Schreber's rather Tiresian qualities and the extent to which, had Freud been less interested in producing a reading that distanced himself and, equally, his theory from the late judge's wish for feminization, and self-making metaphysical poiesis, we might have from him a rather less Oedipal account of sexual identity—one in which gender variance might be more than a cipher for repressed homosexuality and in which the psychic labor of ethno-racial identification and abjection might be more readily thought (Salah 2009, 2014, 2017). This question can be teased out in multiple ways; my own work draws upon Abraham and Torok's thinking around the transgenerational transmission of encrypted trauma (1986), Laplanchian approaches to "afterwardsness" (1999), and as well upon recent work on racial melancholy (Cheng 2000, Eng and Han 2000). It also owes much to the insights of Viviane Namaste, who first brought our attention to the figural ab/use of trans figures within queer theory, and who has persistently and trenchantly challenged constraints upon trans self-representation within feminist, leftist, and queer discourses (2000, 2005). Though Namaste draws conclusions (contra the value of the humanities, for instance) that are, again, not my own, her insistence that trans theory center and be accountable to trans subjects seems to me a necessary baseline for any inquiry in this area.

This seems to me the basic point, that one cannot meaningfully and ethically think about human sexuality without humans at the center of the thinking, and that one cannot imagine or think about transsexuality without transsexual people at the center of the thinking/imagining. Patricia Elliot (2011) gives a strong account of the consequences within psychoanalysis and within queer feminism of failing to do so while also maintaining a commitment to both. Of course, psychoanalysis has its specificity as a discipline, as a form of knowledge, but as a theory of both the otherness of us all (our opacity to ourselves, our nonidentity with our selves) and a theory haunted by the unknowability of the o/Other, it seems constitutively flawed to the extent that it fails to be composed by and with black and other racialized people, transsexual and transgender people, and women.[6]

To say so is not simply to fall into uncritical reification of ego as identity so much as to suggest that psychoanalytic preclusion of transsexuals from the realm of ordinary egos into a rigid phallic overidentification says more about the cisnormativity of the clinic and the archly defensive fantasies of psychoanalytic practitioners than about the quite varied psychic lives of gender-variant people. As an alternative to such arch defenses, Oren Gozlan's (2015) *Transsexuality and the Art of Transitioning* offers an account of transsexuality as a psychic space, one that is comprehensible in relation to experiences of aesthetic conflict; and here one finds much that resonates with Cavanagh's and Ettinger's thinking of the Tiresian. For example, "Kapoor's opaque structure, like the maternal body, brings us into contact with momentary archaic jouissance, where the threat of fragmentation is joined with the thrill of merging" (Gozlan 2015: 18–19). In another example, Gozlan writes of Louise Bourgeois's *Le regard*, "The sculpture is evocative in its erotic insinuations but sexually undifferentiated, inviting a visceral identification with a signifier that is both lacking and in excess" (19).

To return to my earlier point, on the contradiction between cisnormative (often feminist, often transphobic) fantasies of transsexuality and in the discourses of transsexual, transgender, and gender nonconforming writers, let me conclude by suggesting that it is on the terrain of creative writing by transsexual and transgender authors that we may encounter trans peoples' imaginary and analytic responses to psychoanalytic and other sexological discourses, and to the questions they purport to address (sexuation, gendered suffering and pleasure, desire, time and the unconscious, etc.). As the persistence of Tiresias as a trans, historical touchstone attests, trans writers contend with a tradition of writing that imagines gender transformation, largely from the vantage of those who do not change sex. To the extent that this entails a form of double consciousness (Du Bois 1994: 2–3), trans people may write "the feminine," such that the feminine has been both occluded and excavated as the psychotic, or transcendent, or pathologically fetishistic, for example. (We may also do something else.) This kind of trans genre writing offers a vantage on the cisnormativity of the clinic in its imaginary and its practices, troubles psychoanalysis's fantasies about transsexuality, and supplements them with a more complex reading of sexuation that also has implications for how we understand desire, racialization, and the human.

Trish Salah is assistant professor of gender studies at Queen's University in Kingston, Ontario. She is the author of *Wanting in Arabic* (2002, 2013) and *Lyric Sexology, Volume 1* (2014).

Notes

1. Likewise, as Diane Morgan points out, in Lacan's reading of the Daniel Schreber case, he is "absolutely resistant to . . . [the] . . . idea of Schreber's fantasmatic contact with the eternally mutable 'life-substance'" as anything other than an Oedipal and homosexual wish, "a son wanting to give a baby to daddy" (1999: 226).

2. See, for example, Ovid (1955: 67–68, 73–74) and Sophocles's plays *Oedipus the King* and *Antigone* (1912).

3. I explore this tradition in *Lyric Sexology* (2014) and in "Time Isn't after Us" (2017: esp. 23–27).

4. I discuss this at greater length in Salah 2009, 2014, 2017, and forthcoming.

5. "'The poets and philosophers before me discovered the unconscious,' Freud said on the occasion of his seventieth birthday, 'what I discovered was the scientific method by which the unconscious can be studied'" (Phillips 2001: 9).

6. In fact, "surprising numbers" of transsexual and transgender people have become conversant with psychoanalytic and sexological discourses on transgender, so much so that since the early seventies medical practitioners have evidenced a persistent dis-ease with transsexuals because we are apparently too conversant with their theoretical accounts to be trusted. Katherine Johnson (2007) gives an overview of these issues; see particularly pp. 449–50.

References

Abraham, Nicolas and Maria Torok. 1986. *The Wolfman's Magic Word: A Cryptonymy*. Translated by Nicholas Rand. Minneapolis: University of Minnesota Press.

Cavanagh, Sheila. 2016. "Tiresias and Psychoanalysis with/out Oedipus." *European Journal of Psychoanalysis*, no. 28, November.

Cheng, Ann Anlin. 2000. *The Melancholy of Race: Psychoanalysis, Assimilation, and Hidden Grief*. Oxford: Oxford University Press.

Cixous, Hélène. 1981. "The Laugh of the Medusa." In *New French Feminisms: An Anthology*, edited by Elaine Marks and Isobel de Courtivron, 245–64. New York: Schocken Books.

Deleuze, Gilles, and Félix Guattari. 1972. *Anti-Oedipus*. Translated by Robert Hurley, Mark Seem, and Helen R. Lane. London: Continuum.

Du Bois, W. E. B. 1994. *The Souls of Black Folk*. New York: Gramercy Books.

Elliot, Patricia. 2011. *Debates in Transgender, Queer, and Feminist Theory*. London: Ashgate.

Eng, David, and Shinhee Han. 2000. "A Dialogue on Racial Melancholia." *Psychoanalytic Dialogues: The International Journal of Relational Perspectives* 10, no. 4: 667–700.

Ettinger, Bracha. 2000. "Transgressing with-in-to the Feminine." In *Differential Aesthetics: Art Practices, Philosophy, and Feminist Understandings*, edited by Penny Florence and Nicola Foster, 185–209. London: Ashgate.

———. 2006. "Matrixial Trans-subjectivity." *Theory, Culture, and Society* 23, nos. 2–3: 218–22.

Freud, Sigmund. (1930) 1957. *Civilization and Its Discontents*. Vol. 21 of *The Standard Edition of the Complete Psychological Works of Sigmund Freud*, edited and translated by James Strachey. London: Hogarth Press and the Institute of Psycho-Analysis.

———. 1963. "Psycho-Analytic Notes on an Autobiographical Account of a Case of Paranoia (Dementia Paranoides)." In *Three Case Histories: The 'Wolf Man,' The 'Rat Man,' and the Psychotic Doctor Schreber*, edited by P. Rieff, translated by J. Riviere, 103–86. New York: Collier Books.

Gozlan, Oren. 2015. *Transsexuality and the Art of Transitioning: A Lacanian Approach*. New York: Routledge.

Johnson, Katherine. 2007. "Transsexualism: Diagnostic Dilemmas, Transgender Politics, and the Future of Transgender Care." In *Out in Psychology: Lesbian, Gay, Bisexual, Trans, and Queer Perspectives*, edited by Victoria Clarke and Elisabeth Peel, 445–64. Hoboken, NJ: John Wiley.

Kristeva, Julia. 1984. *Revolution in Poetic Language*. Translated by Margaret Waller. New York: Columbia University Press.

———. 1985. "Stabat Mater," translated by Arthur Goldhammer. *Poetics Today* 6, nos. 1–2: 133–52.

Laplanche, Jean. 1999. "Notes on Afterwardsness." In *Essays on Otherness*, edited by John Fletcher, 260–65. London: Routledge.

Morgan, Diane. 1999. "What Does a Transsexual Want? The Encounter between Psychoanalysis and Transsexualism." In *Reclaiming Genders: Transsexual Grammars at the Fin de Siècle*, edited by Kate More and Stephan Whittle, 219–39. London: Cassell.

Namaste, Viviane. 2000. *Invisible Lives: The Erasure of Transsexual and Transgendered People*. Chicago: University of Chicago Press.

———. 2005. *Sex Change, Social Change: Reflections on Identity, Institutions, and Imperialism*. Toronto: Women's Press.

Ovid. 1955. *Metamorphoses*. Translated by Rolfe Humphries. Bloomington: Indiana University Press.

Phillips, Adam. 2001. *Promises, Promises: Essays on Psychoanalysis and Literature.* London: Perseus Books.

———. 2014. "The Art of Nonfiction No. 7." Interview by Paul Holdengräber. *Paris Review,* no. 208.

Salah, Trish. 2002. *Wanting in Arabic: Poems.* Toronto: TSAR.

———. 2009. "Writing Trans Genre: An Inquiry into Transsexual and Transgender Rhetorics, Affects, and Politics." PhD diss., York University.

———. 2014. *Lyric Sexology, Volume 1.* New York: Roof Books.

———. 2017. "'Time Isn't after Us': Some Tiresian Durations." *Somatechnics* 7, no. 1: 16–33.

———. Forthcoming. "A Return to Schreber? Trans* Literatures as Psychoanalysis." In *International Handbook of Transsexuality and Mental Health: Current Critical Debates in the Field of Transsexual Studies,* edited by Oren Gozlan. London: Informa.

Schreber, Daniel Paul. (1903) 1955. *Memoirs of My Nervous Illness.* Edited and translated by Ida MacAlpine and Richard Hunter. Cambridge, MA: Harvard University Press.

Sophocles. 1912. *Oedipus the King. Oedipus at Colonus. Antigone.* Vol. 1 of *Sophocles,* translated by Frances Storr. New York: Harvard University Press.

Psychoanalysis and Trans*versality

ABRAHAM B. WEIL

Abstract Félix Guattari arrived at Château de la Borde in 1956 to collaborate in an experimental psychiatric clinic with Jean Oury, the founder and then director. During his time at La Borde, and in conversation with Gilles Deleuze, Guattari developed the concept of transversality as an ethical, political, and philosophical approach to maximizing linkages between previously unexplored singularities in a field, and to create connections in other conceptual topographies at different levels of discursivity. This statement examines the connections between the work of Guattari at La Borde and his relationship to Lacanian psychoanalysis to analyze his framework of transversality in the context of the possibilities and limits for psychoanalysis and transgender analyses.
Keywords transversality, Félix Guattari, Château de la Borde, Jacques Lacan

Félix Guattari arrived at Château de la Borde in 1956 to collaborate in an experimental psychiatric clinic with Jean Oury, the founder and then director.[1] Given the constraints of the clinic as an increasingly private enterprise, Guattari remarks that it was a fascinating time to participate in the formation of a medicalized space that had limited resources but great possibilities for inventive treatment (Guattari [1995] 2009: 176).[2] He suggested that comparable institutions of the time treated psychosis as a zoolike enterprise, quarantining subjects in confined spaces to, as Michel Foucault (1977) elaborates, defend society against them. Guattari concedes that prior to meeting Oury, he too positioned psychosis as a peculiar inversion of reality and the psychotic a symptom of such strangeness ([1995] 2009: 177). He attributes his refreshed understanding to the communal functions of La Borde. Guattari stepped away from his formal studies of philosophy to join the Patients' Club, which possessed a certain "activist" goal, drawn from the anterior experiences of the personnel assembled to develop La Borde's procedures, wherein both clinicians and patients took on material chores. The "intrahospital" system relied on shared responsibility and participation in cleaning, laundering, sports matches, newspaper printing, collective workshops, and so on. Unfortunately, as Guattari reports, this did not last. As tasks became more diffuse and personnel changed, supervisors were put into place to ensure

TSQ: Transgender Studies Quarterly * Volume 4, Numbers 3–4 * November 2017 **639**
DOI 10.1215/23289252-4190010 © 2017 Duke University Press

organization, and with supervisors emerged a more salient hierarchy between doctor and patient. In such an ordering, a shift occurred at La Borde, and it lost the central tenet of resituating the world in favor of projective equivalents that looked to, once again, reorient the body.

Despite Guattari's partial disenchantment with the techniques of management that emerged at La Borde, his time there is no less important to the development of his philosophical and clinical practices of schizoanalysis and transversality. Guattari would later come to advance these ideas alongside his coauthor Gilles Deleuze, first in *Anti-Oedipus: Capitalism and Schizophrenia* ([1972] 1983) and in their continued collaborations. The primary goal of La Borde was to develop an institutional critique alongside a modified psychoanalytic treatment. In other words, the important interface of his early years at the clinic rested in the understanding that mental illness, which had predominantly been criminalized, could instead be understood as an alternative relationship to the world. Through his daily work—serving approximately one hundred patients at a time—Guattari argues that they began to contextualize their work in larger political frameworks, taking on global health struggles, pedagogical practice, as well as prison conditions, minoritarian issues, and spatial thought ([1995] 2009: 183). Thus, Guattari and Oury posited a new kind of "institutional psychotherapy" that sought to treat psychosis and the work of institutions as interconnected in ways that reached beyond the personalization of the psychoanalytic unconscious and in ways that were always connected to political struggle (176).[3]

This statement explores the relations that Guattari began to elaborate at La Borde and examines his framework of transversality to consider the possibilities and limits for psychoanalysis and transgender analyses. Transversality, which appears throughout his works, offered Guattari an alternative to the psychoanalytic use of transference between patient and analyst, though it retained some of its principles (much like Deleuze and Guattari's collective work retains elements of Oedipus while still seeking alternative methods of becoming). Guattari's critique of psychoanalysis is only a part of the larger picture of transversality; the purpose of transversality should not be to merely untangle psychoanalysis but to deterritorialize hierarchies that easily manifest in institutions and ultimately bear striking resemblance to the functions of capitalism writ large. Transversality is a tool to interrupt hierarchies or, in Guattari's terms, to allow people to relate from an affective point of view (to auto-produce, to adapt, to traverse). Transversality seeks to interrupt those theories that claim any totalizing logics—all that is X, is Y—in search of reassurance, a world of repression.[4] The central purpose of transversality was to create linkages between previously unexplored singularities in a field, and then to create connections in other conceptual topographies at different levels of discursivity.[5] This varied from the later Deleuzoguattarian formulation of assemblages (*agencements*) that operate as an example of an infinite multitude of singularities that can function transversally, bringing intensities into contact at different levels (Guattari [1996] 2009: 11). The theories of assemblage, becoming, plateaus, and flight often attributed to the collective work of Guattari and Deleuze articulate this in a number of useful ways, but transversality in particular lends itself to a political imputation in considering the increasingly capacious use of *transgender*, and more precisely of *trans** when not attached to *gender* alone.

A more complete argument of Guattari's relationship to psychoanalysis and use of transversality would mean to exhaust the terrain of Freudian psychoanalysis as well as the possible philosophical origins of Louis Althusser or Jean-Paul Sarte (Genosko 2002; Bosteels [1998] 2001; Schrag [1994] 2001). However, in this brief statement, I examine how the perceived rift between Guattari and psychoanalysis might be put into relief by the affinity found between trans* theorizing and psychoanalysis. Despite his critique, or perhaps radicalization, of psychoanalysis, Guattari recognizes Sigmund Freud as a brilliant thinker.[6] Guattari both praised Freud's understanding of the unconscious and criticized the personalization of it.[7] Guattari's confrontation with Freud's working of Oedipus and the superego shook out in his deployment of schizophrenia, which he hastily suggested Freud did not understand ([1995] 2009: 145). Instead, Guattari places schizophrenia, and psychosis in general, alongside political revolution, wagering that the two have been misplaced as taboos.[8] Guattari posits that transversality expresses the capacity of institutions to refashion access points offered to the superego so that symptoms and inhibitions can be removed, accommodating the superego in ways that make radical alterations to topographies that are always already possible (146). Despite their differences, Guattari accepts Freudian psychoanalysis as a critical formulation of the unconscious and of subjectivity. As such, here my reading of Guattari is situated within the resistance he places on psychoanalysis that rests, or at least is more pronounced, upon his own analyst, Jacques Lacan.[9]

Guattari has a curious relationship to Lacan.[10] On the one hand, the tension that existed between them was not unlike any other kind of mentorship, and on the other, productive critiques and distancing tactics emerge. Thus, Guattari's relation to Lacanian psychoanalysis might best be understood as processual rather than a purely frictional break. At many points, Guattari's training emerges with important insights to his work with psychoanalysis, even if it is done with a prescription of criticism. Perhaps, it is precisely this mentorship and his education in Lacanian psychoanalysis that positions him against the extension and interpretation of psychoanalysis more broadly. What he calls the "cult" of Lacanian psychoanalytic thought leads him to wage a philosophical debate about the role of environmental ecology amidst political, ethical, social, and aesthetic domains

(Genosko 1996: 69).[11] These reservations become more salient as he begins to elaborate transversality as a broadening approach that must move away from the hegemonic power figure in attempts to break up the standard gaze. Guattari's use of transversality emerged in the field of psychoanalysis and psychiatry to imagine a therapeutic practice capable of addressing the limits of the institution itself and to examine how mental illness was linked to political struggle. As Gary Genosko outlines, transversality relies most centrally on mobility, creativity, and self-engendering (2002: 54). Guattari's early aim to undermine Lacan's (institutional) transference opts for transversality to oppose the kaleidoscope of verticality and horizontality in favor of pure potentiality; rather than tracing and interpreting psychosis, one can transversally map fresh orientations to the world (Guattari [1972] 2015: 113; Bosteels [1998] 2001: 893–94). Though over time transversality materializes as its own philosophical concept in ways that deserve attention, my interest in applying transversality to trans* theorizing is indexed by the medical, social, and political positionality of trans* subjects that may be too high, or too low, to be articulated even in the context of transgender studies. Thinking transversally, we can imagine ways of articulating trans* as a collective mode of expression rather than a solitary confinement.

This truncated sketch of Guattari's handlings of Lacan might inspire us not to completely abandon the principles of psychoanalysis as we approach transversality; however, it should be made clear that Guattari's perspective on the questions of desire, the subject, and the group was fundamentally different from that of Lacan. Indeed, this departure, in part, is what inspires Guattari to begin to think about transversality. Guattari's essay "Transversalité" (in Guattari [1972] 2015) offered initial insight into the concept that he would develop more completely apart from La Borde, opening it up to a mutable approach to the reorganization of institutions on a broader scale. Reading initially as a thought experiment, he mined his studies of psychiatry and psychoanalysis and, more particularly, what he detailed as the study of psychosis (which in many ways resists Lacan's and that of the antipsychiatry movement), wherein he imagined how transversality could function at different levels of the psychiatric institution, bringing them into contact through the group's collective desires (117).

In advancing transversality in the dimension of trans* theorizing, I follow Guattari's provocation that its purpose is not a representational maneuver. Though the connections between psychoanalysis, Freud, Lacan, and Guattari have not been fully satisfied here, my argument is that we cannot adequately make representational attachments between binary mechanisms. Charting Guattari, I argue that transversality highlights a maximizing of communication in which the unconscious is made up of not only "part objects" or Lacan's "a-object" but also sensations, curves, unexplored topographies, and incorporeities that cannot be placed in universal categories of analysis (Guattari [1995] 2009; [1972] 2015).

Further, I argue that by examining the transversal relations between the categories of trans* and gender, we can come to think of these categories in ways that through psychic processes become manageable but also contain ungovernable molecular possibilities. Trans*versality can be understood as a tool to explore hierarchies and logics of difference that have been, in many ways, foreclosed. Guattari's use of transversality is philosophical, but as is always the case in his work, there are important material (or everyday) functions that reconfigure institutions of power; this is a provocation that we must turn the symptom on itself.

In Guattari's case, the implications for the psychiatric hospital were of chief concern and were elaborated during his time at La Borde; however, beyond the psychiatric clinic, Guattari's early thoughts on the state of social ecology in relation to environmental disaster, child labor, HIV/AIDS, the failure of the education system, water contamination, and queer sexuality, among others, bolster his arguments about the codification of identity, the proliferation of capitalism, and the clogging of radical politics. In a curiously predictive example of the political bottlenecking of transversal relations, Guattari says, "In the field of social ecology, men like Donald Trump are permitted to proliferate freely, like another species of algae, taking over entire districts of New York and Atlantic City; he 'redevelops' by raising rents, thereby driving out tens of thousands of poor families, most of whom are condemned to homelessness, becoming the equivalent of the dead fish of environmental ecology" ([1989] 2008: 29). Guattari (among others) predicted this moment of ecological disequilibrium, in which human life deteriorates along with the environment, suggesting that a "cloak of silence" has been, and will continue to be, thrown over the struggles for liberation. These material, aesthetic, and philosophical concerns are essential in imagining the reach of trans* theorizing, questions of sexuality, and the mattering of race in the collective milieu. Indeed, human "progress" and ecological deterioration are symbiotic. It is from this eco-philosophical musing that transversality finds an important political relationality.

Mapping transversality across Guattari's work allows us to understand that it does not completely abandon its origins in the clinical context (Freud and Lacan), nor does it wholly uncouple from a phenomenological perspective (Martin Heidegger).[12] In the case of psychoanalysis, it is essential for the purposes of radical politics to consider the ways that identity can inform political mobilizations without being reducible to them. Guattari's transversality allows us to push against any binary logics that continue to govern trans* ecologies wherein even the Deleuzoguattarian *and* is left wanting in the search of "an nth term . . . the opening onto multiplicity" (Guattari [1992] 1995: 31). Thus, transversality can offer trans* theorizing a sensuous temporality from which to analyze the collective assemblage that indexes trans* bodies but also trans* becoming beyond any biological, sociological, or psychic conditioning with which it is enveloped.

In my extension of Guattari's theorization of transversality, I ask how the work of the prefix *trans** can itself become a methodology. While insights should certainly draw on embodied psycho-social experiences of people minoritized as trans*, the critical potential of trans* theorizing frequently exceeds the milieu in which it is often articulated.[13] It could be said that bringing the asterisk into trans*versality (as I wish to do) risks making an arbitrary attachment between or unfulfilled extension of the concept's utility for the sociopolitical field and the bodies of trans* subjects. My intention is not to overcode this relation; rather, I am interested in the possibility of making a sensuous connection between the prefix *trans** (as it draws on the body but also shines light on political connections that extend far beyond bodily capacity) and the plasticity of the suffix *versality* capable of a dexterous incomprehensibility. The asterisk does not cut up the concept but, rather, pollinates it, making multiple arrival points possible. The communicative maximizing of trans*versality allows us to think psychoanalysis and transgender together, but it also might, with careful attention, imagine what agitations and intensities exist in the curvy topographies and referents of both.

Abraham B. Weil is a PhD candidate in gender and women's studies at the University of Arizona whose research focuses on trans* theory, antiblackness, poststructuralism, and continental philosophy. His dissertation project, "Transmolecular Revolution: Trans*versality and the Mattering of Political Life," develops the concepts of transmolecular revolution and trans*versality, drawn from the conceptual vocabulary of cultural theorist Félix Guattari as well as recent work in transgender theory to advance an antiracist transfeminist critique and highlight possibilities for creativity and invention necessary for a successful revolutionary project.

Notes

1.   Château de la Borde, hereafter abbreviated to La Borde, was located near the town of Cour-Cheverny in France's Loire Valley, approximately one hour south of Paris. The clinic was founded by Jean Oury, who asked Guattari to join him at the clinic shortly after it was opened. Though the clinic is still in operation today, here I focus on the early years Guattari spent working at the clinic, beginning in 1955–56, though he was affiliated with La Borde until his death in 1992.

2.   There is a curious note from the translators in *Anti-Oedipus* that is important to foreground in this statement's discussion of Guattari and Jacques Lacan and that highlights some of the political problems of translation: "*Institutional analysis* is the more political tendency of institutional psychotherapy, begun in the late 1950s as an attempt to collectively deal with what psychoanalysis so hypocritically avoided, namely the psychoses. La Borde Clinic, established in 1955 by Jean Oury of the Ecole Freudienne de Paris, served as the locus for discussions on institutional psychotherapy, and Jacques Lacan's seminars served as the intellectual basis for these discussions 'in the beginning.' Felix

Guattari joined the clinic in 1956, as a militant interested in the notions of desire under discussion—a topic rarely dealt with by militants at that time. Preferring the term 'institutional analysis' over 'institutional psychotherapy,' Guattari sought to push the movement in a more political direction, toward what he later described as a political analysis of desire. In any case this injection of a psychoanalytical discourse (Lacan's version) into a custodial institution led to a collectivization of the analytical concepts. Transference came to be seen as institutional, and fantasies were seen to be collective: *desire was a problem of groups and for groups*" (Deleuze and Guattari [1972] 1983: 30, emphasis in original). While this context might be useful, it is an incomplete analysis of Guattari's relationship to Lacan and to psychoanalysis more broadly. Despite Guattari's relationship to militant politics, his relationship to mental illness (which he explores in many interviews) would by his own admission benefit from a more delicate analysis.

3. Guattari's analysis of comparable pilot programs or psychiatric wards in prisons suggests that the further away patients drift from social conventions, the closer they become to bestial figures in need of containment and control in which "their guardians, who at that time had no training at all, were forced to retreat behind a sort of armor of inhumanity if they wanted to avoid depression and despair themselves" ([1995] 2009: 177). Under these sorts of practices, imbued with capitalist and biopolitical protocols and animacy hierarchies, treatment practices become more salient: lock them up.

4. Gary Genosko creatively signposts Guattari's early work with Lacan and his work at La Borde to demonstrate how Guattari's object is *the* institution, rather than the practice of psychotherapy in the hospital or clinic. The practical and philosophical functions of transversality rely on transitional phenomena that occur in intermediate experience and spaces of potential (as drawn from Donald Winnicott), holding space for creative and capacious operations (2002: 71).

5. This commitment functioned in tandem with Guattari's work to differentiate the "subject group" from the "dependent group" or subjected group (Guattari [1972] 2015: 107).

6. Deleuze in conversation with Guattari compliments Freudian psychoanalysis as a becoming and an endless narrative (Guattari [1995] 2009: 57).

7. Guattari's concerns with the Freudian unconscious derives from its inseparable relationship to the past—with trauma in particular—and concern with phallocentric logics, positioning of desire, and variants that rely on particular subjective positions.

8. Here, we might also consider Jean Baudrillard's writing on schizophrenia, which is hauntingly absent from Guattari's discussion. Baudrillard wrote, "The schizophrenic is not, as generally claimed, characterized by his loss of touch with reality, but by the absolute proximity to and total instantaneousness with things, this overexposure to the transparency of the world" ([1988] 2002: 27). As Gary Genosko notes, Guattari is often placed in opposition to Baudrillard. However, Guattari never published a full analysis of Baudrillard, so any disagreements (for example, regarding postmodernism) should simply be understood as such.

9. It is worth noting, since Guattari places emphasis on the use of psychosis, that Lacan's ([1932] 2005) doctoral research centers on psychosis, placing it in relation to the unconscious. The function of desire in their respective bodies of work helps to put this into relief.

10. Jean Oury was also a student of, and highly influenced by, Lacanian psychoanalysis.

11. Guattari notes that he was not suggesting that the work at La Borde could easily be transposed to a larger societal model. Many of the concepts that emerge in his writings

with Deleuze were inspired by, rather than models of, the clinic. He says, "In no way did I suggest extending the experiment of La Borde to the whole of society, no single model being materially transposable in this way" ([1995] 2009: 182).

12. Gary Genosko (2002), Eric Alliez, and Andrew Goffey (Alliez and Goffey 2011; Goffey 2016) all provide valuable insights to the trajectories of Guattari's work. While their primary focus is not the troubling of trans*, per se, they each offer detailed understandings of Guattari's thought.

13. Elsewhere I discuss the relations between blackness and trans* that I believe help to question the political life of mattering as well as the ways that certain subjects are rendered disposable (Weil 2017).

References

Alliez, Eric, and Andrew Goffey, eds. 2011. *The Guattari Effect*. London: Bloomsbury.

Baudrillard, Jean. (1988) 2002. *Selected Writings*. Translated by Jacques Mourrain et al., edited by Mark Poster. Stanford, CA: Stanford University Press.

Bosteels, Bruno. (1998) 2001. "From Text to Territory: Felix Guattari's Cartographies of the Unconscious." In *Deleuze and Guattari*, vol. 2 of *Critical Assessments of Leading Philosophers*, edited by Gary Genosko, 881–910. London: Routledge.

Deleuze, Gilles, and Félix Guattari. (1972) 1983. *Anti-Oedipus: Capitalism and Schizophrenia*. Translated by Robert Hurley, Mark Seem, and Helen R. Lane. Minneapolis: University of Minnesota Press.

———. (1980) 1987. *A Thousand Plateaus: Capitalism and Schizophrenia*. Translated by Brian Massumi. Minneapolis: University of Minnesota Press.

Foucault, Michel. 1977. *"Society Must Be Defended": Lectures at the Collège de France, 1975–1976*. New York: Picador.

Genosko, Gary. 1996. *The Guattari Reader*. Oxford: Blackwell.

———. 2002. *Félix Guattari: An Aberrant Introduction*. London: Continuum.

Goffey, Andrew. 2016. "Guattari and Transversality: Institutions, Analysis and Experimentation." *Radical Philosophy*, no. 195: 38–47.

Guattari, Félix. (1972) 2015. *Psychoanalysis and Transversality: Texts and Interviews 1955–1971*. Translated by Ames Hodges. Los Angeles: Semiotext(e).

———. (1989) 2008. *The Three Ecologies*. Translated by Ian Pindar and Paul Sutton. London: Continuum.

———. (1992) 1995. *Chaosmosis: An Ethico-Aesthetic Paradigm*. Bloomington: Indiana University Press.

———. (1995) 2009. *Chaosophy: Texts and Interviews 1972–1977*. Translated by David L. Sweet, Jarred Becker, and Taylor Adkins; edited by Sylvère Lotringer. Los Angeles: Semiotext(e).

———. (1996) 2009. *Soft Subversions: Texts and Interviews 1977–1985*. Translated by Chet Wiener and Emily Wittman, edited by Sylvère Lotringer. Los Angeles: Semiotext(e).

Lacan, Jacques. (1932) 2005. *De la psychose paranoïaque dans ses rapports avec la personnalité (On Paranoid Psychosis in Its Relations with the Personality)*. Paris: Seuil.

Schrag, Calvin O. (1994) 2001. "Transversal Rationality." In *Deleuze and Guattari*, vol. 2 of *Critical Assessments of Leading Philosophers*, edited by Gary Genosko, 863–77. London: Routledge.

Weil, Abraham. 2017. "Trans*versal Animacies and the Mattering of Black Trans* Political Life." In "Tranimacies: Intimate Links between Animal and Trans* Studies," special issue, *Angelaki: Journal of Theoretical Humanities* 22, no. 2: 191–202.

Psychoanalysis and Psychoanalytic Theory as Tools to Increase Trans* Visibility

MARCO POSADAS

Abstract The following statement engages with the question, how can psychoanalytic discourse be relevant to transgender studies when it lacks trans representation? A Latinx psychoanalyst discusses his journey with transphobia and institutional psychoanalysis.
Keywords psychoanalysis, representation, trans studies

These are incredibly challenging times to be a transgender person. Between the months of January and March in 2017, seven black trans women were murdered in the United States. It is undeniable that trans people are targets of violence and systemic oppression at every level: intrapersonal, interpersonal, in their communities, and within institutions. From murdering them to denying them basic civil rights and human dignity, erasing trans people from public life is perpetuating violence toward trans communities; in psychoanalytic institutions, we have not been the exception.

Within institutionalized psychoanalysis and, more specifically, within training institutes affiliated with the International Psychoanalytical Association (IPA), there are only two candidates who are out and self-identify as trans*. Their journeys require that they develop creative ways to harness the motivation to tolerate the institutional challenges of training and treatment, given transphobic enactments led by training clinicians. There are, in other words, only two out trans candidates of over six thousand candidates worldwide. Moreover, I am not aware of any out self-identified trans* psychoanalysts among the almost thirteen thousand IPA members. Whether this number accurately reflects the existing trans* and gender-variant population of IPA psychoanalysts and candidates is

TSQ: Transgender Studies Quarterly ★ Volume 4, Numbers 3–4 ★ November 2017 **647**
DOI 10.1215/23289252-4190019 © 2017 Duke University Press

uncertain, but there is a critical lack of representation of trans* and gender-variant candidates and IPA members.

How can psychoanalytic discourse be relevant to transgender studies when it lacks trans representation? We need trans people to offer narratives of experiences that are transpositive and go beyond pathology. It is also important to be mindful of the reductive trend toward hetero- and trans normalization in the clinic. What are the steps that psychoanalytic institutions need to take in order to be a leading voice in transgender studies?

I must admit that it is hard to answer these questions without first acknowledging the tremendous harm suffered by many trans and other gender-creative patients at the hands of their clinicians. By acknowledging it and being able to talk about it, we are accountable. It is crucial to first acknowledge the transphobia, misogyny, and cis-heteronormativity—among many other forms of culturally influenced prejudices—embedded in psychoanalytic theories.[1] The problem with transphobia in the clinic is multifold. The question is not only about whether or not our theories can be transphobic but, also, about how the application of the theories themselves in the clinic can be transphobic. We must consider how transphobia is often enacted and perpetuated in the analytic situation. The clinician's internalized transphobia can affect even the most competent clinician and cause transphobic injuries. Gender-based enactments led by the clinician can be traumatic for trans patients and can derail otherwise useful clinical work. In this type of situation, "the transphobic analyst" unfortunately becomes a caricature—a caricature of the transphobic enactments evident in culture at large.

I began working with trans people when I was in my late teens and early twenties doing a clinical placement in an AIDS hospice in Mexico City. Before I was a psychology intern working with newly diagnosed HIV-positive people in the late 1990s, I volunteered in the hospice's buddy program. During those days, I met Alejandro (not his real name), one of their education staff from the agency/hospice. A few years later, he accessed the inpatient unit as a service user and died several months later of AIDS-related complications.

Alejandro wore makeup the night the education team took the new volunteer group to "Alquimia," a gender queer dive bar hidden behind the Monument to the Mexican Revolution. A table of trans men sent a drink to my cisgender sister, while a group of Alejandro's friends escorted me to the restroom, as this was my first time in a gender queer bar. They retouched their makeup and redid their eyebrows while sharing stories of how some of them had to hide their makeup at home from their families. They noticed how fascinated I was with their makeup and offered to apply some to my face if I had my own brush. I felt so intrigued and anxious at the same time; I felt seen in my own gender struggle.

I remember feeling like I was about to get in trouble for being there, conflicted about being so comfortable in their company.

I did not have the words to say it then, but now I understand how knowing Alejandro first as a colleague, and then during the last few months of his life in the shelter as a service user, enabled me to begin to depathologize gender variance. This close experience with gender variance and gender performance, in Judith Butler's terms (1990), stirred up a lot of complicated feelings of shame and embarrassment attached to my own gender identity and gender performance. Much of this was shaped by a well-socialized macho Mexicano self-concept. I felt deeply embarrassed about what I now understand to be my own internalized misogyny, machismo, and heteronormativity. This limited my own knowledge of transgender existence and affected my own personal experience. I had always sought to attain a masculine presentation to avoid unwanted attention. I notice this psychic maneuver, and the consequences of it, in my clinical practice with trans* and other gender-creative patients. I sometimes listen with envy to my clients' experiences, which stems from my conscious (and unconscious) subscription to a socially sanctioned gender binary. As a Mexican male, I struggle to express my identity outside the cis-normative scaffolding.

In the 1990s, with the medical advances in genital surgeries in Europe and the United States, trans narratives became very popular in Latinx cable television. Shows like *Cristina* (a Spanish-language talk show in Miami) portrayed trans people in a sensationalistic and exploitative yet culturally normalized fashion. In a perverse way, this style of show created a type of visibility needed for trans narratives to exist in public. Slowly, trans characters started to appear in mainstream Mexican, Latinx, and Spanish-language media in the United States, for instance, "La Agrado," a trans woman in Pedro Almodóvar's *All about My Mother* (1999). Her character enabled one of the first transpositive narratives to emerge in Latinx film. Although it portrayed trauma associated with Latinx communities, it was also the first image of a trans-affirming narrative. It won an Academy Award for best foreign film in 1999.

During that time, I used La Agrado to write my mid-term paper for a class I was taking with a Lacanian psychoanalyst. The only psychoanalytic literature available and accessible on the topic at that time, in Spanish, followed the line of Catherine Millot's *Horsexe* (1989). Millot, unfortunately, reduces trans experience to a psychotic structure. Although this model of Lacanian psychoanalysis made trans subjectivities more visible, it did so at the expense of pathologization. Fortunately, there have been new transpositive readings of Jacques Lacan that counter Millot's view that transsexuality is psychotic (Gherovici 2010; Gozlan 2014; Carlson 2010).

Although sexist and infused with patriarchal stereotypes, Lacanian psychoanalysis does give us a way to understand transsexuality outside psychosis and with respect to the "paternal metaphor." The paternal metaphor enables us to understand how a medically supported transsexual transition can enable the subject to symbolize sexual difference. It allows us to question the way we understand the psychoses, and it also helps us to rethink the direction of the cure (Lacan 2016; Saal 1998). Physical transitions and gender-confirming surgeries can have a metaphoric function; this helps to validate the transgender person's existence as a sexuated subject. It also enables psychoanalysts to understand trans* in terms of neurosis, as opposed to psychosis. Although statistically atypical, psychosis is a solution to the sexual impasse, a defense against psychic death. But let us remember that trans* people can occupy any one of the three psychic structures (neurotic, psychotic, and perverse) theorized by Lacan.

Unfortunately, my reading of trans in my early days as a psychoanalytic student in Mexico was greatly influenced by Millot's *Horsexe*. Needless to say, I wrote a pathologizing case formulation of La Agrado, got an A+, and was not required to write a final paper.

Over the course of my analytic formation and experience with clients, I was able to challenge my own learned transphobic readings. It is with Lacan, and perhaps before him with the Winnicottian notions of "transitional phenomena" and the "transitional space," that I was able to see another way to account for experiences of transness. Donald Winnicott (1953) coins the term *transitional phenomena* to describe "an intermediate area of *experiencing* to which inner reality and external life both contribute. . . . It shall exist as a resting place for the individual engaged in the perpetual human task of keeping inner and outer reality [I would have said realities] separate yet inter-related" (90). It is in this intermediate space where I believe psychoanalysts have the capacity to listen to trans* narratives in a transpositive way.

It is hard to unlearn a pathologizing view, and institutionally it can take years to be able to see the shifts in technique and clinical views in our practice. In the analytic situation, it is well known that internalized prejudices obstruct our listening and can collapse the therapeutic space. It is with Winnicott and Lacan where I see in psychoanalysis a beginning to listen to the unconscious experience of transness apart from prejudice. Their work enables me to support and perhaps even affirm trans* existence and experience. By listening to trans* clients, psychoanalysis as a theory and clinical practice can help to make trans* experiences audible. Trans* people have important things to say that can help the cis-clinician provide a more accessible treatment option for everyone.

Laverne Cox's words (2017) addressing antitrans policies condense the transphobic conundrum as I see it in my clinical practice: "This is not only about accessing public restrooms, but about public existence. It's about the right of trans people to exist in public spaces." In my view, an antioppressive psychoanalytic approach is not only about addressing barriers so that we may enable trans people to access psychoanalytic training and treatment. Nor is it only about the refusal to reduce trans* experience to psychosis. It is about the right of trans people, as people, to exist as viable subjects in the psychoanalytic clinic. This is where I believe psychoanalysis may be able to contribute to transgender studies in a significant way. It is within the context of the clinic that psychoanalysis can make important contributions to validating transgender experience. Psychoanalytic theories have contributed to queer studies, lesbian and gay studies, women's studies, and critical race theories, and we are now beginning to see emerging contributions to transgender studies.

In my view, psychoanalysis provides a unique place to listen to transgender discourse. Psychoanalysis was able to witness (without fully grasping) transgender existences even when pathologized as psychotic. Freud reminds us of the role of neutrality in the analyst. I do not mean neutrality in the racist conception of the "blank slate" or "opaque mirror." I am here referring to neutrality in terms of its original Latin roots: "not either" (no other) or, in clinical terms, as that which cautions the analyst against othering the patient's experience. The clinician must listen with evenly hovering attention (Freud [1912] 1958). To me, Freud's discovery of the usefulness of neutrality as a part of psychoanalytic technique, even when infused with Freud's own culturally appropriate claim to whiteness, is the foundation for a profound understanding of antioppressive practice and trans-affirming clinical practice.

We can now respond to my previous question about how psychoanalysis can be relevant to transgender studies. I believe we can begin by stimulating the creation of knowledge at the intersection of psychoanalysis, antioppression clinical practice, and gender diversity. We need to begin by incorporating trans narratives and experiences into the psychoanalytic training curriculum. Moreover, we need to listen to trans narratives from a transpositive perspective and actively address transphobic prejudice by challenging psychoanalytic practices that render trans experience invisible. For example, our thinking about Oedipal configurations must consider gender variance; formulations of envy in the family romance must include parental capacities for gender creativity and so much more.

Lastly, I find it important to clinically approach gender performance when working with trans* and other gender-creative people in the same ways we address dream material in a session—as an unconscious formation that opens the door to a profound understanding of the inner world of the person. Transgender studies and psychoanalysis can inform each other and provide the psychic space to think, fantasize, and talk about gendered existence. This approach makes nonconforming gender performance an area rich with meaning and symbolism. After all, it was Freud who advised us to listen carefully to dreams.

Marco Posadas, MSW, RSW, is a psychoanalyst, clinical social worker, licensed psychologist (in Mexico), and PhD candidate at Smith College School for Social Work. He currently operates a clinical practice in psychotherapy, psychoanalysis, clinical supervision, and consultation in Toronto. He trained at the Toronto Psychoanalytic Society and Institute and is a member of the Canadian Psychoanalytic Society, the Mexican Psychoanalytic Association, and the International Psychoanalytical Association. He is the chair of the Sexual and Gender Diversity Studies Committee of the IPA.

Note

1.   The psychoanalytic myth that trans people are psychotic follows the line of other historical prejudices in psychoanalysis such as the prejudice that "homosexuals are perverse structures" (Socarides 1978). Another example of prejudiced, in this case sexist, views embedded in theory is Sigmund Freud's ([1925] 1961) quote, "Castration complex inhibits and limits masculinity and encourages femininity" (256). Here he places masculine and feminine as opposite: a binary with no other possibility.

References

Almodóvar, Pedro, dir. 1999. *All about My Mother*. DVD. London: Pathé, 2004.

Butler, Judith. 1990. "Subjects of Sex/Gender/Desire." In *Gender Trouble: Feminism and the Subversion of Identity*, 1–34. New York: Routledge.

Carlson, Shanna T. 2010. "Transgender Subjectivity and the Logic of Sexual Difference." *differences* 21, no. 2: 46–72.

Cox, Laverne. 2017. "Laverne Cox on Gavin Grimm, 'Doubt,' and Meeting Beyoncé." *CBS This Morning*, February 14. www.cbsnews.com/videos/laverne-cox-on-gavin-grimm-doubt -and-meeting-beyonce/.

Freud, Sigmund. (1900) 1953. *The Interpretation of Dreams*. Vol. 4 of *The Standard Edition of the Complete Psychological Works of Sigmund Freud*. London: Hogarth Press and the Institute of Psycho-Analysis.

———. (1912) 1958. "Recommendations to Physicians Practising Psycho-Analysis." In *The Case of Schreber, Papers on Technique, and Other Works*, vol. 12 of *The Standard Edition of the Complete Psychological Works of Sigmund Freud*, 109–20. London: Hogarth Press and the Institute of Psycho-Analysis.

———. (1925) 1961. "Some Psychical Consequences of the Anatomical Distinction between the Sexes." In *The Ego and the Id and Other Works*, vol. 19 of *The Standard Edition of the Complete Psychological Works of Sigmund Freud*, 241–58. London: Hogarth Press and the Institute of Psycho-Analysis.

Gherovici, Patricia. 2010. *Please Select Your Gender: From the Invention of Hysteria to the Democratizing of Transgenderism*. New York: Routledge.

Gozlan, Oren. 2014. *Transsexuality and the Art of Transitioning: A Lacanian Approach.* New York: Routledge.

Lacan, Jacques. 2016. *The Sinthome.* Book 23 of *The Seminar of Jaques Lacan,* edited by Jacques Alain-Miller. Oxford: Polity.

Millot, Catherine. 1989. *Horsexe: Essay on Transsexuality.* New York: Autonomedia.

Saal, Frida. 1998. *Palabra de Analista (Word from the Analyst).* Mexico City: Siglo XXI.

Socarides, Charles W. 1978. *Homosexualty.* New York: Aronson.

Winnicott, D. W. 1953. "Transitional Objects and Transitional Phenomena—A Study of the First Not-Me Possession." *International Journal of Psycho-Analysis* 34: 89–97.

Scenes of Self-Conduct
Transnational Subjectivities from Tehran to Laplanche

DINA AL-KASSIM

Abstract Casting off from the deployment of sexuality under modern biopolitics, the emergent subjectivities knitted between same-sex players and transexuals in Iran reveal networks of affiliation and fantasy best disclosed by psychoanalytic listening. Jean Laplanche's reworking of sublimation allows us to read a fantasy of fatality as evidence of transsexual inspiration in the materials gathered by Afsaneh Najmabadi's *Professing Selves: Transsexuality and Same-Sex Desire in Contemporary Iran* (2014).
Keywords Jean Laplanche, sublimation, Afsaneh Najmabadi, transsexuality in Iran, psychoanalysis and gender

Afsaneh Najmabadi's *Professing Selves: Transsexuality and Same-Sex Desire in Contemporary Iran* (2014) narrates a fantasy reported by several candidates for sex-reassignment surgery (SRS), whose transitions happen in serial operations over an extended period for several reasons, among them the fact that the government pays only a small portion toward surgical reassigment, an expensive and arduous proposition. "Imagining death," Najmabadi writes, becomes the condition of a wish that expresses an ideal: "When my body is being washed for burial, I want the washer (wo)man to see a completely (fe)male body" (2014: 245). Although legally able to live as and to enjoy the rights of their reassigned gender, including marriage and adoption, many transitioners persist on the SRS path even after having earned their new certification. State recognition of gender reassignment is insufficient to appease a yearning that is again and again expressed in these terms of finitude, one that paradoxically promises new life.

Knitting the New Self

With the publication of Najmabadi's study of the history of transsexuality in law, medicine, popular culture, and transactivisim in Iran since the 1930s, scholars of Middle East, West Asia, and North Africa are newly able to test our speculative

TSQ: Transgender Studies Quarterly ∗ Volume 4, Numbers 3–4 ∗ November 2017 **654**
DOI 10.1215/23289252-4190028 © 2017 Duke University Press

theories of contemporary subjectivity and its entanglement with modern state power. Arguing that Iran's Islamicized modernity paradoxically elaborated new subjectivities through the regulation of sexual and gendered morality, habitus, and identity in law, medicine, and civil status, *Professing Selves* locates a crucial techne of state power multiplied in the proliferation of interview, questionnaire, affidavit, testimony, and case study that sediments official state discourse on trans habitus. Najmabadi's historical approach locates attitudes in popular media, psychiatry, and law in the prerevolutionary period the better to track the medicalization of transsexuality as coeval with that of Europe and North America at that time.

Contemporary medical notions of psychology, pharmacology, and cognitive therapies do not constitute a foreign or "western" scientific matrix, though their implantation has necessarily evolved in tandem with the currents of local culture and taken up vocabularies of self and other that reflect regional, sedimented, and linguistic as well as religious inflections of place and people. The medical view, one preceding the Islamic Republic yet surviving the transition of state, that transsexuality reflects a "gender identity dysphoria" dovetails with one traditional, religiously informed view that the trans person suffers a discrepancy between soul and body (rather than gender, for on this account there is no clear notion of gender) that can be corrected by acknowledging social reassignment. As early as 1964, Ayatollah Khomeini published the view that sex change is permitted in Islam, while his 1984 formal ruling or fatwa affirmed the piety of sex change in response to a transwoman's request. This laid the foundation for the refinement over the next twenty years of a bureaucratic and medical apparatus, resulting in the institutional approach to trans habitus today. Like immigration, education, or any of a host of other government functions that shape our citizen being, SRS is achievable, partially funded, and highly regulated. This is to say that gender reassignment is not a matter of sovereign choice but a form of agency highly mediated by a social process. And yet, the juridical change of status proceeds from and requires as foundation the personal perception of suffering and, key, of a suffering soul whose social appearance and physical body fail to reflect inner being.

Despite significant disagreement among Islamic jurists, the weight of Khomeini's fatwa is indisputable as the basis of law, while its authority is directly attributable not to religious authority but to "his unique position as the leader of the most massive revolution in the late 20th century. . . . Only Khomeini in fact had the combined religious and political authority that would translate his . . . ruling into law" (Najmabadi 2014: 174). Countering the legal obligation to enforce SRS in all found cases of transsexuality, the state covers the costs of hormones but not SRS; thus the legal obligation to pursue surgery is unenforceable, while enforcement itself would be unpopular with a number of conservative religious jurists.

Reassignment also highlights personal narratives and an informal register of social chatter and cultural production in the particular forms of self-narration that support the medical and legal assessment of bodies and subjects. A dialectical pair emerges in the surfeit of a new confessional apparatus: the same-sex player (*kuni*, which is only unevenly described as "gay" and never as "lesbian") and the transsexual (and in particular male-to-female [MtF] persons). Their mutual self-definition highlights the entanglement of two seemingly incompatible models of subjectivity: the psychological, deep subject of self-reflection and the contingent self-in-conduct, who finds themself in litanies of action and surface appearance. Intertwined by law, medicine, parties, and home, this couple poses fundamental questions for postcolonial critiques of psychoanalysis and transnational accounts of subjectivity.

Earning the state's certification that one is indeed in need of SRS opens the self and its narration to subjection via medicalization while also authorizing a spiritual actualization of self endorsed by the state. Spiritual, religious, and moral truth of one's gender and sexuality is laced through the impersonal materiality of a documentary archive required for certification, one that is to be *made* rather than found, for it is created in tandem with a casting away of any similarity with the morally despised role of *kuni*. This negative determination is produced only in close proximity and intimate knowledge of the refused role and the negative path of determination, for legal approval and state sponsorship of SRS must pass through the knotted relation to and distinction from "same-sex playing," even if at some level same-sex playing is a matter of one's transsexual everyday practice. This is to say that the state can and does permit the transsexual, in pursuit of trans certification and SRS approval, to practice a sexuality that is not otherwise so sanctioned. Thus, in the process of becoming—a becoming that may extend indefinitely—the transsexual in a male body may continue to live and be loved by her man, all under the watchful eye of institutional authority. This material reality, along with overlapping social cliques and public meeting places, draws same-sex players and transsexuals into close and continuous knots of becoming and self-definition. In short, the Revolutionary Islamic State creates spaces of emergent subjectivities, as Najmabadi puts it, "safe havens" for gays and lesbians because of the unusual state sanction of transsexuality.

By way of illustration, a vignette: In the office of the resident clinical psychologist at the Navvab Safavi Emergency Center of the Office for the Socially Harmed of the Welfare Organization, the weekly transsexual support meeting is underway.

The previous week, [the physician] had talked about the importance of "knowing oneself" (*khaudshinasi*—literally selfology), and had asked everyone to contemplate that topic for the following week's conversation. He opens the day by asking if the group members had engaged in "knowing oneself." He is dismayed to see that his proposition had not been taken seriously. Shahla, an MtF, blurts out that she had had no time for it. What was she doing then? "I was busy with my boyfriend, cooking, making sure I make myself up in the style he likes." [The physician] is clearly annoyed, "are you that dependent on him?" Shahla is not fazed, [saying,] "Of course, I am really in love with him." . . . Yasaman, also an MtF, who was there the previous week in a black chador but on this day has shown up in his/her army uniform, is expected by the group to explain [the change of dress as change of gender habit]. "Yes, I do consider myself MtF, I do want to go for SRS, but I am also prepared to take my time. Once I change sex, I won't be able to pursue some of my ambitions. In any case, when I am in masculine clothes, I enjoy doing manly things; when I am in feminine clothes, I like to do womanly things. (Najmabadi 2014: 280)

These avowals suggest a recoil from the depth model of self-reflection that frames the clinical setting and a dispersal, but also a holding, of the trans subject in the agency of conduct. Najmabadi calls this dispersed subject the "subject-of-conduct" (277, 297) and shows convincingly that both models of conduct and deep interiority are interlaced through the trans and same-sex playing community.

"Maryam, another MtF," challenges Yasaman's commitment to their shared identity as transsexual only to face a pile-up of other criticisms as Houri and Shahla expand on the topic of the necessity of flexible gender habit to accommodate changeable work opportunities and the ups and downs of romance: "Yes, if my current relationship doesn't work out and I have to go back to work, I'd switch clothes to be able to get better jobs" (281).

Yet none of these SRS potentials would consider themselves gay or same-sex players and this without necessarily sharing in a homophobia of aversion, although certainly, some do voice extreme discomfort or shame at being "mistaken" for *kuni* or even about sex had under the assumption that both partners were of the same sex or, in a more extreme case, when a husband and wife had sex, though the wife felt herself to be male and others, including both female intimates and male friends, saw her as male identified. Trans identity in becoming is neither forced into a single path nor frayed or worn thin by the necessity to present as the "wrong" gender habit. Each member of the support group capably calculates with that necessity and risk of disapproval while also refusing the judgment of others who so calculate. This flexible sensibility loops back upon itself to escape the exposure of gossip and shame by avowing and embracing the potential "realities" of unpredictable fates, including the surprising evidence of God's "creativity" in creating the transsexual, as one testimony puts it.

In the early pages of *Professing Selves*, Najmabadi presents us with her regretful realization that she could not in good conscience write an ethnography of the contemporary trans community in Tehran. This insight came early in the twelve-year project, as she began to frequent trans support groups, activist spaces, and clinic and court archives. She resolves her conundrum by steering between the patterning of ethnography and an impersonal history of law and institution, all the while narrating snippets and fragments of stories told to her in over a decade of conversation and careful listening. As fragments of an archive of encounter, they have the uncanny effect of unweaving the categorical order of the state and dissolving the analytic lexicon of medicine and academic studies, while religious themes are not uncommon in the dreams and fantasies that Najmabadi reports. Several of these bear out what still other trans individuals reveal, namely, that for many their motivation or inspiration for transitioning is best expressed in a vision of their own body in death.

The Corpse Washer

Paraphrasing several SRS aspirants, Najmabadi writes, "When my body is being washed for burial, I want the washer (wo)man to see a (fe)male body." Preferred as an explanation for pursuing SRS even after legal reassignment has been achieved, this imaginary scene attests to a desire in excess of state law, community norms, and religious dogma. Jean Laplanche and J. B. Pontalis's famous essay ([1964] 1968) on fantasy contains the oft-cited claim that the subject is dispersed in the scene setting of the fantasy rather than represented in a single element or character. The corpse washer fantasy may indeed offer such a syntax for the desire of the SRS aspirant, but another, later formation of fantasy enables a reading of the fantasy as a particular form of sublimation of what Laplanche calls the enigmatic message as it is carried and repeated in an ongoing address to and from the other, who presents the enigma of gendered embodiment and desire ([1999] 2014: 77–104).

In 1999, Laplanche returned to Sigmund Freud's metapsychology to argue that the seduction theory holds the kernel of "human sexuality" insofar as the infant is the recipient of nurturing care, suckling, and caresses, which communicate the sexual unconscious of the caregiver and inscribe this unconscious transmission as a mystery or enigmatic signifier ([1999] 2014). The mystery of the other's desire has many psychic destinies but includes sublimation, which Laplanche associates with symbolization. The enigmatic message marks the irreducible dimension of otherness for which the forms of translation (repression, sublimation, etc.) are "process(es) of closure to the other's address . . . an enigmatic . . . seductive . . . sexual address" in the service of a primary drive to "know" by resolving the enigmatic message in flattening sublimations that bind the drive or by opening up to otherness as traumatic enigma (91). Far from signaling a freedom we associate with creativity, symbolization contains mystery and shuts down unbound energy. As a counterpart to binding, inspiration is an orientation of openness to trauma that "drives" the subject to seek further expression or find new symbols.

Gender is part of the message and positioned prior to sexuality insofar as the sense made of the enigma (in touch, silence, gesture, and signs between adults) arrives as already gendered and to be translated, repressed, or foreclosed as the advent of sexuality through fantasy. Among the overwhelming priority of unconscious signifiers is the question of gender as a mysterious imposition of the other's desire and iterative closure to the other's address or as responses to a goad. Underlining the significance of Laplanche's intervention for gender theory, Judith Butler (2014: 126–27) writes, "Laplanche's view is that we rethink gender assignment as an unconsciously transmitted desire, a view with implications for current sociological and legal approaches to questions of gender assignment and reassignment." The corpse-washing fantasy, as an answer to the suggestion that surgery is not necessary, engages the enigmatic other by repeating the gestures of intimate care and implantation in a fantasy of last rites.

The Muslim burial rite makes few demands, but among them, the body must be washed and wrapped in a clean cloth to be buried within three days. Beyond that, simplicity is the rule and variation the reality. Even the prayers may be brief. Thus the extension and suspension of time in the fantasy—its time of fantasy—which imagines the preparation of remains for burial when the aspirant is still living, is itself both reflective of the character of Muslim rites and a violation of the simplicity and letting go that this simplicity serves. Practices vary; it is of interest to note that among the general rules, the eldest relative of the same gender washes the body, and so the corpse-washing fantasy carries the kernel of familial care and gender decorum in the scene of an after-death where the encounter between the caregiver and the self stages only serenity. The silent labor of the corpse washer, who looks but sees that there is nothing to see, affirms the symbolic recuperation of the subject in an imaginary form. As Laplanche puts it, contra "a certain Lacanianism," "the 'symbolic' as well as the 'imaginary' are both in the service of the ego—and thus caught up in the almost inescapable position of 'Ptolemaic' reclosure" (2014: 91). Here, in the corpse-washing fantasy, the symbolic reinscription and redemption of the body and its true, preferred, and perceived gender work in tandem with the imaginary by "binding through the narcissistic image" (91).

This fantasy is also legible as an imaginary address to the enigma of the other—Laplanche's primary other—who is not represented in the scene, neither washer nor the washed but who is dispersed throughout the fantasy. Fundamentally a dramatization of the awakening of the subject to "new life" and "new sexuality," the scene conveys an image of passive receptivity or originary helplessness. What awakens here is the body as the true body, appearing in the guise of ego ideal or that which I wish another to see in me; yet, it materializes without authority, for the agency of the scene lies with the washer's caring hands and neutral vision. As Laplanche puts it, "inspiration is conjugated via the other. Its subject is not 'the subject' but the other," and "in its resonance with the originary adult other, this other comes to re-open at privileged moments the wound of the unexpected, of the enigma" (99).

The fantasy of finitude, expressible as "death comes despite my life," is also a fantasy of fatality, "my death as condition and evidence of new life"; the fantasy can be understood as a radical exposure or, as Laplanche puts it, the reopening and unbinding of the wound of the primary other's incursion. This fantasy of one's own death, legible as an imaginary address to, in Laplanche's terms, the enigma of the primary other, inspires particular trans subjects to pursue a more sincere and authentic embodiment of themselves. Here, the bodily ego imagines a scene of its ideal body, the one seen by the corpse washer as only a body without surprises, as expected—indeed, a body mirroring their own.

The trans fantasy of the corpse washer evokes a religious rite and spiritual devotion as a symbolization of new life. To become the ideal body, the cis-gendered body must die. Does the fantasy imagine the self as newly cis or transsexual? Does the accomplishment of SRS serve the function of erasing the labor of living conduct to replace it with the calm repose of indisputable gendered bodily form in deathly matter? Has the difference between cis and transsexual become indistinct and immaterial before the materialization of the new body, now only imaginable as lacking the animating soul? If the meaning of the religious ritual is not otherworldly but fixed on the experience of the washer after the self-in-conduct has relinquished the self, does it also carry a trace of ambivalent mourning for that unwanted body, who had to die so that they might live? Along the lines proposed by Laplanche and Freud that we imagine our own death through the death of the person "close to us," I am suggesting that the transness of the fantasy depends upon this translation or trace of the unwanted and mistaken body, while the inspiration allows the other, here the corpse washer in the "right" body, to reappear, to reopen the wound of the traumatizing message. In Laplanchean terms, this is to read a fantasy of originary seduction and implantation of the enigmatic message (gender-sexuality) while also understanding it as a making oneself available to the "other, who comes to surprise me" (98). Serenity of the death rite is the language of this surprise.

The self-in-conduct continues its practice, as, paradoxically, commitment to SRS might also act as a goad to linger in the group therapy, a space where conduct is schooled and adjudicated and where the liberty to assert new forms of the self not following from the prescriptions of one's fellows is upheld through the very elastic and tangled course of conversation and cultural elaboration. But this self-in-conduct conflicts with the desire of the fantasy for the serenity of the true self committed to a *vita nuova* for our time.

Dina Al-Kassim is associate professor in the Institute for Social Justice and the English Department at the University of British Columbia, Vancouver. She is the author of *On Pain of Speech* (2010) and recent articles in *Samyukta, International Journal of Middle East Studies,* and *Cultural Critique.*

References

Butler, Judith. 2014. "Seduction, Gender, and the Drive." In *Seductions and Enigmas: Laplanche, Theory, Culture,* edited by John Fletcher and Nicholas Ray, 118–36. London: Lawrence and Wishart.

Laplanche, Jean. (1999) 2014. "Sublimation and/or Inspiration." In *Seductions and Enigmas: Laplanche, Theory, Culture,* edited by John Fletcher and Nicholas Ray, 77–106. London: Lawrence and Wishart.

Laplanche, Jean, and J. B. Pontalis. (1964) 1968. "Fantasy and the Origins of Sexuality." *International Journal of Psychoanalysis* 49, no. 1: 1–18.

Najmabadi, Afsaneh. 2014. *Professing Selves: Transsexuality and Same-Sex Desire in Contemporary Iran.* Durham, NC: Duke University Press.

Report of SITE Transgender, Gender, and Psychoanalysis Conference

JORDAN OSSERMAN

Abstract This article reviews the 2017 conference, "Transgender, Gender, and Psychoanalysis," organized by the SITE for Contemporary Psychoanalysis and held at the Freud Museum in London. The event brought together clinicians, scholars, activists, and artists interested in putting psychoanalytic ideas into conversation with transgender issues and experiences. This review highlights interesting presentations, controversies that occurred, and theoretical problems that were explored, especially surrounding the relationship between transgender studies and psychoanalytic theories of sexual difference.
Keywords transgender, sexual difference, psychoanalysis

O n March 11 and 12, 2017, the SITE for Contemporary Psychoanalysis, a psychoanalytic training institute based in the United Kingdom, held a conference at the Freud Museum in London entitled "Transgender, Gender, and Psychoanalysis," one of the first conferences of its kind. The event brought together clinicians, scholars, activists, and artists interested in putting psychoanalytic ideas into conversation with transgender issues and experiences, helping to bridge the divide between the psychoanalytic and trans communities and to generate non-pathologizing, trans-inclusive psychoanalytic theory and praxis. Several contributors to this special issue of *TSQ: Transgender Studies Quarterly* were present at the conference as attendees and speakers, including editor Sheila Cavanagh, Patricia Gherovici, Jacob Breslow, and myself.

The main organizers of the conference were three psychoanalysts affiliated with the SITE, Dorothée Bonigal-Katz, Andie Newman, and Barry Watt. All of them expressed the sentiment that the time was ripe for the progressive-minded and theoretically diverse psychoanalytic organization to host a conference on this theme, to question psychoanalytic orthodoxies and revisit ossified theorizations surrounding sexual difference, gender, and transness.

TSQ: Transgender Studies Quarterly ★ Volume 4, Numbers 3–4 ★ November 2017 **662**
DOI 10.1215/23289252-4190037 © 2017 Duke University Press

One of the inherent challenges to organizing a psychoanalytic conference on this theme is that the subject is not just a clinical phenomenon (like mourning or trauma) but a category of identity. Inevitably, questions of representation arose, including the lack of trans masculine presenters and the problem of cis gender practitioners theorizing about, and presenting sensitive clinical material on, trans patients. Some members of the audience expressed concerns around these issues. In my conversations with the organizers, they acknowledged these problems and expressed regret that a number of potential trans identified presenters declined invitations to participate, mainly for scheduling reasons. These issues are made more complex by the nature of the psychoanalytic profession, as psychoanalytic work involves listening to and attempting to intervene in the psychic suffering of others. When an analyst is asked to share their clinical perspective on trans issues, this will invariably include a focus on how trans patients experience and navigate psychic distress, a subject that can easily appear pathologizing despite the best efforts of the clinician.

On the theoretical front, one key theme that emerged across several presentations was the relationship (or antagonism) between the concept of "sexual difference" as it is theorized in psychoanalysis and the deconstruction of the gender binary championed by many trans and queer theorists. Julie Walsh, a sociology fellow at Warwick University, opened the conference with a paper that addressed this topic, "Drawing Some Lines through Trans-Gender-Feminisms." She began by pointing out the problematic "sovereignty" of psychoanalysis's technical vocabulary and the challenge this presents to combining psychoanalytic ideas with feminist and gender theory. It is particularly challenging to demonstrate the relevance of Sigmund Freud to undergraduates steeped in the deconstruction of gender, and though one might be tempted to emphasize those aspects of Freud's thought on the subject that appear constructionist, it is quite unlikely that Freud would himself have endorsed a social constructionist view of gender had the relevant terminology been available in his lifetime. Instead, Walsh proposed that the psychoanalytic theorization of femininity may be expanded to include trans and gender-nonconforming experience. Feminist psychoanalysis understands femininity not as a static subject position but as a "transitory" condition in which one's relation to the category "woman" is "flickering." Sheila Cavanagh further developed these ideas with her work drawing out the relevance of feminist psychoanalyst Bracha Ettinger to transgender studies. Ettinger's theorization of the "Other jouissance," the nonphallic enjoyment that Jacques Lacan links to feminine subjectivity, can be productively related to the various creative aspects of gender transition. Cavanagh focused on the neglected figure of Tiresias in Sophocles's tragedies; the blind prophet's experience living both as a man and as a woman, and his enigmatic comments on the pleasures of sex as a woman, may offer a better starting point than Oedipus for a psychoanalytic theorization of sexed subjectivity. Both presentations thus raised the possibility that the psychoanalytic category of "femininity" may in fact transcend or subvert the gender binary, as it speaks to an aspect of subjectivity, highly relevant to transgender experience, that undermines rather than shores up normative identity. I am reminded here of the Lacanian psychoanalyst Bice Benvenuto's argument (1994: 75), "We could say that the unconscious is feminine, that it is the negation, the un, the other, of phallic consciousness."

The conference benefited from a wide variety of clinical orientations. Domenico DiCeglie, director of the Gender Identity Development Service at the Tavistock clinic in London (part of the United Kingdom's National Health Service), gave an overview of the history of this unique service, which offers a psychoanalytically informed approach to the treatment of children and adolescents struggling with gender identity. The clinic has experienced an exponential increase in referrals since its founding, from twenty patients in 1989 to about fifteen hundred in 2016. DiCeglie discussed the challenges involved in striving to offer a holistic approach that helps patients explore and come to terms with their difficulties with gender and reach a decision about what kind of physical interventions, if any, are desired. He gave an interesting example of the value of psychoanalytic work in this arena, in which psychodynamic therapy with a young boy helped him to link his struggles with gender identity to his difficulty symbolizing and mourning the loss of his grandmother, significantly reducing the boy's experience of dysphoria.

Patricia Gherovici offered her usual fascinating Lacanian take on a wide variety of trans issues relevant to the psychoanalytic clinic, previewing her recently published book, *Transgender Psychoanalysis* (2017). Gherovici summarized a number of cases from the early days of psychoanalysis involving patients struggling with gender identity who were treated with creative and nonpathologizing approaches by analysts; this history, she argued, has been obscured by a later generation of analysts who sought to bring patients more into line with normative gender ideals. She distanced herself from the equation made by some Lacanians between transsexuality and psychosis. In her clinical experience, she has found that transgender identification is often more closely related to the structure of hysteria, which in the Lacanian clinic is not a pathology but, rather, a way of questioning one's relation to the Other and attempting to draw out the repressed truth behind pretensions of knowledge and mastery. She concluded with a discussion on the relevance of Lacan's notion of the *sinthome* in her work with a trans patient. The *sinthome* involves the creative transformation of one's symptom into a singular, more agential method of confronting lack and inscribing a place for oneself in the social. I was particularly amused when she recounted a session in which her patient, intending to refer to his girlfriend whose name began with the sound "Ma," instead uttered "Ma . . . Ma?" "The patient appeared extraordinarily confused, so I ended the session there," Gherovici remarked. The audience, perhaps not so familiar with Lacanian clinical technique, burst into laughter. It was an affecting demonstration of the way that the Lacanian variable-length session works with the subversive nature of the unconscious; these sessions helped the patient construct a "sinthomatic" identity that wove together the influence of his parents, with whom he had experienced a fraught relation that troubled his romantic life, with his own singular subjectivity.

The conference also included a clinical roundtable in which SITE psychoanalysts James Mann and Francesca Joseph presented vignettes and summaries of some of their clinical work with trans patients. Joseph discussed a particularly challenging case involving a trans woman who had been mandated to undergo therapy as a condition of employment, owing to her aggressive sexualized behavior toward her colleagues. Joseph noted the potential for the discussion of gender to "overorganize" psychoanalytic sessions, experienced in this case as a block against analytical work; gender, she suggested, can offer a deceptively totalizing narrative of suffering that obscures the particularity of a patient's unconscious life. Other presenters, as well as the audience, were invited to comment on these clinical presentations.

This aspect of the conference was in my opinion one that necessitates some ethical reflection. In more traditional psychoanalytic settings, these types of detailed clinical cases are presented to fellow clinicians and trainees. The interdisciplinary and topical nature of this conference attracted a much wider audience, including people not used to thinking in a clinical psychoanalytic framework as well as grappling with the issues of privacy and confidentiality involved therein. My concern is less with the danger of sharing confidential information about patients, as efforts were made to disguise identifying details, than with the "wild analysis" that occurs when a guiding set of clinical and theoretical coordinates are missing. I felt that some of the commentary offered on the clinical cases drew quite sweeping conclusions on patients that did not do justice to the precision of psychoanalytic work, a concern made more pressing given the great possibility for prejudicial and pathologizing thinking when dealing with trans issues.

One of the strongest presentations of the weekend was trans writer Juliet Jacques's reading of her short story, "The Woman in the Portrait." The story was borne out of an invitation Jacques received from the Tate Modern museum to comment on a piece of her choosing from their collection, as part of their event *Transpose*. Frustrated with the Tate's lack of work by any openly transgender artists, Jacques instead chose to write a fictional story inspired by a 1927 piece in the collection by the German artist Christian Schad, *Self-Portrait with Model*. The painting depicts Schad sitting in bed next to a naked, masculine-looking woman, his torso blocking the view of the lower half of her body. Schad was an important figure in the artistic life of Weimer Germany and frequently depicted its sexually transgressive subcultures. Jacques's story imagined the anonymous woman of Schad's portrait as an aspiring artist and patient of the early German sexologists, preparing to undergo sexual-reassignment surgery. Jacques reproduced key historical moments of the Weimer period through a fictional exchange of letters between these characters. I was particularly struck by the erotic encounter that she imagined as the setting for Schad's painting. In it, Schad battled between desire for the woman and transphobic disgust, which he made no effort to conceal, and his seductive promises to help the woman advance in her artistic career proved empty. In the discussion after her reading, Jacques said that she drew on her own experience of troubling sexual encounters to craft the scene. Jacques's powerful work might perhaps serve as a contribution to a trans-positive psychoanalytic theory of sublimation.

The final presentation by Dany Nobus, professor, psychoanalyst, and chair of the Freud Museum, occasioned a highly impassioned debate. Provocatively titled, "Choose Your Gender! Tyrannical Freedom and Trivial Selectivity in Twenty-First Century Sexual Identity Politics," Nobus argued that transgender causes have been appropriated by the neoliberal imperatives of self-government, happiness, and unrestrained choice. Increasingly, capitalists are happy for you to experiment with your identity, so long as they can extract economic value from the process. While, in reality, the decision to declare oneself transgender involves a complex navigation of conscious and unconscious desires and identifications, the late capitalist emphasis on voluntarist self-fashioning and customization has given rise to the transphobic idea that gender transition can be undergone "on a whim." As an example of how mainstream culture portrays trans experience as the paradigm of self-mastery, Nobus pointed to the LGBT magazine *Advocate*'s cover image of Caitlyn Jenner, which is accompanied by her declaration in large type, "I can handle anything." Drawing on the ideas of radical trans writers such as Kate Bornstein and Sandy Stone, Nobus underscored the danger of this conceptualization of trans as one that invites reactionary transphobic fantasies linking trans subjects to neoliberal ideology. Several presenters and members of the audience felt that despite Nobus's declared intentions, his bombastic presentation style and selected examples reinforced the very transphobic ideas he intended to undermine. One audience member pointed to his repeated use of "ladies and gentleman" as evidence of his presentation's reification of normative gender ideals. I would recommend Nobus follow the example of avant-garde London drag performer David Hoyle, who always refers to his audience as "Ladies, gentleman, and those who are clever enough to have transcended gender."

In the ensuing debate, Nobus referred to Jacqueline Rose's arguments, in her recent psychoanalytical exploration of trans (2016), on the inescapability of the "bar of sexual difference." Trans or cis, we are all subject to this bar, although as Rose writes, "that doesn't mean that those who believe they subscribe to its law have any more idea of what is going on beneath the surface than the one who submits less willingly. However clear you are in your own mind about being a man or a woman . . . the unconscious knows better." What is the nature, the ontological consistency, of this "bar"? Is it a sociological phenomenon, potentially eradicable if the utopian project of deconstructing the gender binary is achieved? Or does something essential to human subjectivity rest upon the existence of sexual division, however trans-positive we may conceive of it? The SITE conference brought psychoanalytic perspectives on this issue into live conversation with the world of trans. This special edition of *TSQ* carries that important work further.

Jordan Osserman is a PhD candidate in gender studies and psychoanalysis at University College London. His dissertation examines the significance of male circumcision from a psychoanalytic perspective. A summary of his research, titled "On the Foreskin Question," appeared in *Blunderbuss Magazine*.

References

Benvenuto, Bice. 1994. *Concerning the Rites of Psychoanalysis; or, The Villa of Mysteries*. Cambridge: Polity.

Gherovici, Patricia. 2017. *Transgender Psychoanalysis: A Lacanian Perspective on Sexual Difference*. New York: Routledge.

Rose, Jacqueline. 2016. "Who Do You Think You Are?" *London Review of Books*, May 5.

Encountering Inheritance in Vivek Shraya's *I want to kill myself*

TOBIAS B. D. WIGGINS

My mother told me that I would end up like my uncles—"This is your destiny." Years later, I discovered both of my uncles had killed themselves before I was born.

Can the desire to die be inherited?
—Vivek Shraya, *I want to kill myself*

To inherit, broadly defined, means that which is passed along. In one sense, it is whatever we receive from someone familiar (or someone who is at least meant to be familiar, anyway). And along with this familiarity comes close associations, abiding memory trails, a type of metonymic progression to a particular moment in this present time: I inherited this. "This" is what I am left with, so what do I make of it now? "This" is a confluence of received parts, wanted and unwanted, left behind both intentionality and by chance. Or circumstance. Presently, we meet its trace residues, that may exist ephemerally, nonmaterial, or in a solid form. Confronting the weight of its meanings and history, its contradictions and unnamabilities, we may wonder, what do I do with "this," now? We are all heirs to things that aren't ever fully ours. But somehow, also, they become ours as we make sense of them, retroactively, reinscribing them into the folds of self.

I find myself mulling over inheritance as one cogent way to think, psychoanalytically, with Vivek Shraya's tremendous oeuvre—an attempt to truly do justice to the intricate social, political, and psychical implications that run throughout the many threads of her work. Since 2002, the Toronto-based South Asian/trans/femme/bisexual–identified artist has been producing a vast assortment of transformative and challenging creative projects, mostly available online for free and by donation (with the majority of funds raised being sent to nonprofit

TSQ: Transgender Studies Quarterly ★ Volume 4, Numbers 3–4 ★ November 2017 **668**
DOI 10.1215/23289252-4190046 © 2017 Duke University Press

Figure 1. Still frame from Vivek Shraya's *I want to kill myself*

trans organizations). She has pursued countless musical endeavors, including a tender single, "Girl It's Your Time," released to commemorate her use of female pronouns; and the synthy soundings of "Too Attached," a cocreation with her sibling. Her poetry (*even this page is white*), novel (*She of the Mountains*), and children's books (*The Boy and the Bindi*) have all received scores of awards and honors. All the while, Shraya continues to maintain a substantive visual art prac- tice, her film and photography weaving personal narratives into the multifacets of queer and trans South Asian identity, desirability, femininity, racism, misogyny, mental health, and community.

A year after releasing "Girl It's Your Time," and following two visual pieces about her relationship to her mother (*Holy Moly My Mother* and *Trisha*), on her thirty-sixth birthday on February 15, 2017, Shraya shared a powerful short film and photo essay starkly titled *I want to kill myself*.[1] At a gentle, yet steady pace, this new work moves across 8.5 minutes of still frames that capture components of her overlaid poetic narrative, which begins, "I wanted to kill myself when I was eleven. I learned I had a body through your condemnation of my body. *Please god don't let me wake up.*"

As the film traverses several annual accounts of her personal meditations on suicide, three thematic visual elements mirror the emotional components of its ideation. The first collection of images captures the tenor of isolation, and the individual struggles that accompany this difficult contemplation. We are privy to

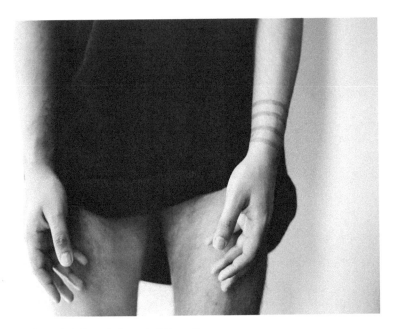

Figure 2. Still frame from Vivek Shraya's *I want to kill myself*

intimate close-up portraits of Shraya's body, of her bedroom and tangled bed-sheets, of her standing on an overpass, or alone in Toronto's long subway tunnels. These private affects are put in contrast with possible social supports—pictures of smiling family dinners, walks with friends, and being held by her sibling—which underscore suicide's everydayness and the complications of sharing these tabooed thoughts. The final thematic collection depicts a metropolitan architecture of gray apartment buildings, cable-stayed bridges, unremitting highway traffic, and lake water at the edge of the city. "Planning suicide comes down to metrics," Shraya explains, and the repetitious nature of the urban photos emphasizes the simultaneous comfort and despair in concrete, practical questions—"how high, how deep, how fast, how long, how many."

Fundamentally, Shraya's new work centers the importance of speaking about suicide, while also highlighting how acutely challenging this may be, especially for marginalized people: "I have long known the freedom and necessity of naming but until this year I had never said *I want to kill myself* aloud." In the context of disproportionately high suicide rates (Haas, Rodgers, and Herman 2014) and a profound lack of genuine representation, the value of art addressing trans mental health, especially made by trans women of color, cannot be overstated. It is in this context that many aspects of inheritance begin to emerge: the passing down of silence surrounding trans people's true lived experience, the impacts of prolonged and naturalized systemic violence, of trauma's persistent relics, intergenerational memory, and the inheritance of resistance and survival.

Psychoanalysis is particularly well suited to think through the concept of inheritance. In essence, it is a theory and clinical practice that pays closest attention to familial acquisitions, the legacies that are faithfully and unconsciously passed down, its impressions forming the bedrock of subjectivity (Freud [1925] 2006). The past's invisible force is secured in our psychic lives, expressing itself with an assortment of repetitions, symptoms,[2] or creative solutions to the problem of being in relation to other people (Freud [1914] 2006). Yet using psychoanalysis as a way to support trans resilience, and to think with Shraya's unprecedented art, perhaps feels comparable to commissioning quotes from the *DSM* as inspirational fodder. Both its clinical and theoretical components are notorious for transphobic content, in which gender variance has been essentialized as a symptom of pathology and trans people constructed as obsessive, narcissistic, borderline (Hansbury 2005), or even psychotic (see Millot 1989). Racist and colonial thought has been ingrained throughout psychoanalytic terminology since its inception, and it has largely gone unanalyzed (Frosh 2013).

Thus one cannot link psychoanalysis and inheritance to mental health without also connecting the sociopolitical heirlooms of Freud's conceptions, and the clinical repetitions of defensive splitting, required in the creation of certain types of otherness. In other words, as Karl Figlio (2012) and others have argued, social difference is shaped and maintained through the projection of unwanted internal parts of the self onto an outside source. This expulsion functions to make difficult aspects of the self more manageable, as they are no longer experienced as a threat to the subject's ego ideal. The implications of these projections, for trans people, people of color, and other marginalized groups, are not only material but also psychical. In the potential loyal internalization of these bad objects, a subsequent sense of inherent "wrongness" can be formed. For example, psychoanalysis has contributed the fantasy of the delusional, lying transsexual (see Ambrosio 2009) or the primitive, uncivilized racialized person (see Freud [1913] 2004).

Shraya's *I want to kill myself* therefore unmasks the oft-concealed potency of psychological inherent-ance, of how racism, transphobia, and misogyny can become enduringly fleshy and intangible ("I learned I had a body through your condemnation of my body"), a part of our composite identifications. Not only have these violent legacies been enacted from the outside (through colonial histories of institutional psychiatry, for example), but we also sometimes find their lingering presence housed quite intimately and corporeally. These tensions are well encapsulated in the film's movement between geometric representations of the city's formal, utilitarian architecture and Shraya's own form—the unin-hibited flow of her hair, the way she leans back against iridescent water, the vulnerability of her own hands pressing up against legs, arms, and neck. Meeting her suicidal calculations against this aesthetically variegated backdrop, we are reminded that inheritance is also about what is considered to be inherent, espe-cially in brown, queer, trans, and femme lives.

This is part of trauma's inheritance, or what Shraya so movingly calls "the gift of trauma—never having the ability to see ahead, build a future . . . the instinct to destroy to mirror my internal devastation." For marginalized people, internalized notions of "wrongness," even if they are amalgamated projections from an other, must also be managed and psychically negotiated. And in finding space for these internalizations on the "outside," they often wreak havoc. Shraya discloses, "I destroyed my home, my marriage . . . friendships. Especially the ones that told me 'When you are ready, you will fix it!'" Trauma, like any ambivalently precious birthright, is something we may have trouble giving up. Ann Cvetkovich (2003) has argued that the tenacity of traumatic experiences informs much of minoritarian life, giving it an everyday emotional quality. Echoing her claim, Shraya's chronological narration and urban imagery takes on characteristics of a standardized, daily routine, despite its unconventional substance.

A traumatic experience can be understood as any event that overwhelms the subject's capacity, leaving them without words to describe what has occurred. Freud's whimsical sci-fi account of the psyche's protective shell is a helpful personification. From its defensive membrane, the ego puts out "feelers that reach . . . tentatively towards the external world and then repeatedly draw back" ([1920] 2003: 67), guiding a personal hydraulics of how much we allow in. Therefore, any excitations that unexpectedly break this special barrier cause a "massive disturbance" (68) that could only be described as traumatic. Freud explains that once this defense has been breached (and especially if it is repeatedly breached), the subject is unconsciously driven to repeat aspects of the original disturbance and tailors their life accordingly ([1914] 2006).

These repetitions are a meaningful form of communication when lan-guage fails, and in this way art can also be a helpful medium for working through, or at least representing, the inexplicable. However, given Freud's description, one can also sense the veritable stickiness of trauma's legacy and surmise how its faithful reappearances may be passed intergenerationally. Thus in response to Shraya's somewhat rhetorical question, "Can the desire to die be inherited?" psychoanalysis can indeed affirm, with her, that this particular suffering is heri-table. But further, several essential additions have been imparted, found within the quotidian femme/queer/brown/trans wisdom of *I want to kill myself.*

First, these mental health inheritances are political, interacting with systemic oppression, and manifesting idiosyncratically as each subject or community takes them up. But further, and perhaps most importantly, so too can resistance, creativity, and strength be passed, bequeathed through that which is in some way familiar. Accordingly, it is the humble presence of Shraya's friends and family that both bear witness to and impart the knowledge of survival. This listening is perhaps the most important intersection between Shraya's work and psychoanalysis. We can only choose our relationship to the past once it loses its unconscious force, and for that to happen, we have to be able to somehow talk about it. Resilience can be found in the simplest and most challenging of acts—of speaking our truth but, also, of genuinely being heard. As Shraya shares in the final moments of her film, "saying *I want to kill myself* to the people who love me meant I was shown an immediate and specific kind of care that I desperately needed. Saying *I want to kill myself* kept me alive."

Tobias B. D. Wiggins is a PhD candidate at York University in Toronto. His dissertation investigates perversion and its relationship to transphobia through the lens of clinical psychoanalysis and trans studies. His forthcoming chapter, "Transsexual Chimeras and the Politics of Listening," will be published in *Slow Burn: Patients' Perspectives on the Political in Psychoanalytic Treatment*.

Notes

1.   Shraya intentionally keeps this title lowercase, rendering it more conversational, as if it were a personal letter.
2.   Psychoanalysis has a way of getting itself into trouble by assigning unique import to common words (*fantasy, phallus, woman*, etc). *Symptom* is not being used, here, as a set of particular medicalized characteristics that seek an expedited resolution. Rather, the symptom, like repetition, is a meaningful expression of personal experience—a vital (and nonpathological) form of communication.

References

Ambrosio, Giovanna, ed. 2009. *Transvestism, Transsexualism in the Psychoanalytic Dimension.* London: Karnac Books.

Cvetkovich, Ann. 2003. *An Archive of Feeling: Trauma, Sexuality, and Lesbian Public Cultures.* Durham, NC: Duke University Press.

Figlio, Karl. 2012. "The Dread of Sameness: Social Hatred and Freud's 'Narcissism of Minor Differences.'" In *Psychoanalysis and Politics: Exclusion and the Politics of Representation*, edited by Lene Auestad, 7–24. London: Karnac Books.

Freud, Sigmund. (1913) 2004. *Totem and Taboo: Some Points of Agreement between the Mental Lives of Savages and Neurotics*. Translated by James Strachey. London: Taylor and Francis e-Library.

———. (1914) 2006. "Remembering, Repeating, and Working Through." In *The Penguin Freud Reader*, edited by Adam Phillips, 391–401. London: Penguin Books.

———. (1920) 2003. *Beyond the Pleasure Principle: And Other Writings*. Translated by John Reddick. London: Penguin Books.

———. (1925) 2006. "Note on the 'Magic Notepad.'" In *The Penguin Freud Reader*, edited by Adam Phillips, 101–5. London: Penguin Books.

Frosh, Stephen. 2013. "Psychoanalysis, Colonialism, Racism." *Journal of Theoretical and Philosophical Psychology* 33, no. 3: 141–54. doi.org/10.1037/a0033398.

Haas, Ann P., Philip L. Rodgers, and Jody L. Herman. 2014. *Suicide Attempts among Transgender and Gender Non-conforming Adults*. American Foundation for Suicide Prevention and the Williams Institute.

Hansbury, Griffin. 2005. "Mourning the Loss of the Idealized Self: A Transsexual Passage." *Psychoanalytic Social Work* 12, no. 1: 19–35. doi.org/10.1300/J032v12n01_03.

Millot, Catherine. 1989. *Horsexe: Essay on Transsexuality*. Brooklyn: Autonomedia.

Shraya, Vivek, dir. 2017. *I want to kill myself.* vivekshraya.com/films/i-want-to-kill-myself/.

The Danish Girl's Death Drive

SHANNA T. CARLSON

Abstract This piece traces the significance of the workings of the death drive in creative expression in Tom Hooper's *The Danish Girl*.
Keywords death drive, Sigmund Freud, *The Danish Girl*

The sadness of a psychoanalytic reading of the film *The Danish Girl* (2015) gives one pause. It's a sad film, after all—what good could come, then, in offering said reading, a reading to make sadness grow? What purpose could this serve? These questions do give me pause. I notice, however, that they also participate in the very logic resisted by the death drive. The death drive, Sigmund Freud argues, is heedless to the good: its only purpose is its own. Moreover, wherever the death drive is, it will have its say. As Freud writes in *Beyond the Pleasure Principle*, "If we may assume as an experience admitting of no exception that everything living dies from causes within itself . . . , we can only say '*The goal of all life is death*'" (1922: 47).

Tom Hooper's *The Danish Girl* tells the story of Einar Wegener, a landscape artist who finds a woman named Lili Elbe living inside himself. Lili decides to undergo two surgeries, explaining at various points that she feels that she is a woman inside and at another that she is ill inside. As a man and a painter, Einar speaks of the landscape within. He paints the same thing over and over because, as he says, "I suppose I just haven't finished with it yet." As a woman, Lili can no longer find the landscape—"I can't remember the landscape," she tells her wife Gerda—and she does not paint. At the end of the film, Lili has a womb transplant that kills her. Her last words are to tell of the dream she had had the night before: "Last night I had the most beautiful dream. I dreamed that I was a baby in my mother's arms. And she looked down at me, and she called me Lili."

Numerous points of critique have been made concerning the film's depiction of Lili Elbe, critiques that importantly interrogate the film's position with respect to the multiple and lived experiences, histories, and political realities

TSQ: Transgender Studies Quarterly ★ Volume 4, Numbers 3–4 ★ November 2017 **675**
DOI 10.1215/23289252-4190055   © 2017 Duke University Press

of transgender people today. From a psychoanalytic perspective, the film could be said to perpetuate some of the social link's most trenchant norms and ideals by locating sexual difference in biology, conflating femininity and maternity, and figuring the doctor as the guarantor of a knowledge that will preserve the social link—and the woman—from the workings of the death drive. These critiques are worthwhile. For me it is nonetheless interesting that Einar is a painter and, more importantly, that Einar's landscapes bookend the film. Painting of course never really leaves the scene: Gerda's portraits along with her many paintings of Lili are central both to her art and to the film's narrative; and visually, the film has a painterly quality too—another point of contention for critics who have responded to the film's sumptuous images with questions about its substance.

It is Einar's unfinished landscape within, however, that most intrigues me. I would like to suggest that Einar's unfinished landscape could be read as a figure of the scene of the unconscious—more specifically, of that scene of subjective death that is also evoked in dreams. That the same landscapes reappear upon Lili's death, mere moments after she has recounted a dream of her own birth, provides an interesting point of contact between the scenes Einar painted and the woman Lili became, as well as a possible point of contact between psychoanalysis and trans studies. While the death drive serves no purpose but its own, might its figuration in this film provide some orientation for the creativity that is already practiced by and will continue to be required of trans studies today?

Einar's landscape drives a certain output, one his wife Gerda finds mystifying, even irritating, as she remarks, "I don't know how you paint the same thing over and over." In this exchange, Einar's success is at issue, as is Gerda's own artistry, for she seeks to make her signature untethered to her husband. At issue too, however, is repetition: How does Einar do it? And why?

According to Freud, what drives anyone to repeat is the death drive. By the time he wrote *Beyond the Pleasure Principle*, Freud had been led to question why it was that analysands' symptoms did not go away once they had been informed of their meaning. The death drive, therefore, was a discovery forged out of failure and experimentation in the clinic. Freud narrates the changes brought about because of this stubborn problem:

> At first the endeavors of the analytic physician were confined to divining the unconscious of which his patient was unaware, effecting a synthesis of its various components and communicating it at the right time. Psychoanalysis was above all an art of interpretation. Since the therapeutic task was not thereby accomplished, the next aim was to compel the patient to confirm the reconstruction through his own memory. In this endeavor the chief emphasis was on the resistances of the patient. . . . It then became increasingly clear, however, that the aim in view, the

bringing into consciousness of the unconscious, was not fully attainable by this method either. The patient cannot recall all of what lies repressed, perhaps not even the essential part of it, and so gains no conviction that the conclusion presented to him is correct. He is obliged rather to *repeat* as a current experience what is repressed, instead of, as the physician would prefer to see him do, *recollecting* it as a fragment of the past. (1922: 18)

They repeat, in other words, because they do not remember. What do they not remember? Freud suggests here that they do not remember experiences that were too traumatic to bear, but Lacanians since Freud have expanded the field to insist that they do not remember experiences that are not only repressed but those that have never entered language as such: repression necessitates a representation, but what has never entered language as such, according to analyst Willy Apollon, constitutes the unconscious (2014). These experiences may or may not correspond to anyone else's understanding of "reality," but they have made their mark on the subject and are, from a psychoanalytic point of view, the truest thing about her. They do not remember, thus, "the death at stake in the *jouissance* before which [they] recoil" (Apollon 2007: 37). *Jouissance*, recall, was Jacques Lacan's word for the death drive. Could we say, then, that they do not remember their own unfinished landscapes, that scene in which the subject is confronted with his/her/ hir own death—a scene whose construction constitutes the work of an analysis?

Lili tells Gerda that she cannot remember the landscape. It's near the middle of the film, and Gerda has asked Lili to sit for her, adding that she misses her, that she misses her working beside her. What if Gerda's longing in this moment is not for Einar, the person she had married, nor for Lili, the woman who used to sit for her, but for the painter who was her partner, who as she says used to work beside her? If this is the case, then Gerda is expressing in this moment that she has lost the person alongside whom she herself grapples with the work of the death drive within her. But Lili would appear to have lost something even greater: she has lost the form of the thing that used to drive her creative production. It's a moment in which both women could be said to express an acute loss.

Unfinished, unremembered: and when it is unexpressed? According to Apollon, all subjects experience "a surging up of free drives in the body," and "they have to take responsibility for it. . . . The only way they have is aesthetics or violence. There is no third way" (2017). The violence evoked here might take either internal or external form. It might, for instance, take the form of an illness. Is this sad? Or is this just human? Freud proposes that "the organism is resolved to die only in its own way" (1922: 48), and Apollon rephrases this notion by linking that which is beyond the pleasure principle to that which is specific to the human, suggesting that "we are not humans because we have reasons to live. We are humans because we have reasons to die" (2016).

At the end of *The Danish Girl*, the landscape reappears. Those scenes with which the film had opened, as the camera viewed Einar's paintings, now materialize for Gerda in reality: she leaps from the car in which she is traveling, recognizing from the road something familiar about these vistas—five trees evenly spaced, an island, and a sun-pierced mountain. Lili's death makes her art real—for Gerda. Has Lili finished with it? Did she remember? What had she borne, and what killed her? What had been her demand, and what was her desire? The film leaves these things in question.

Shanna Carlson received her PhD in romance studies from Cornell University. She is a student of social work at the University of Minnesota and of psychoanalysis with the Groupe interdisciplinaire freudien de recherche et d'intervention clinique et culturelle.

Acknowledgment
Many thanks to Kristine Klement and Eliza Steinbock, without whom I would have left this short piece unfinished.

References

Apollon, Willy. 2007. "The Dream in the Wake of the Freudian Rupture." In *The Dreams of Interpretation: A Century Down the Royal Road*, edited by Catherine Liu, et al., 23–38. Minneapolis: University of Minnesota Press.

———. 2014. "The Unconscious, the Censored, and the Social Link." Lecture presented at the annual Yearly Training Seminar in Lacanian Psychoanalysis, Groupe interdisciplinaire freudien de recherche et d'intervention clinique et culturelle (GIFRIC), La Bordée, Quebec City, June 2.

———. 2016. "Function of the Dream." Lecture presented at the annual Yearly Training Seminar in Lacanian Psychoanalysis, Groupe interdisciplinaire freudien de recherche et d'intervention clinique et culturelle (GIFRIC), La Bordée, Quebec City, June 6.

———. 2017. "Masculinity, Femininity, and Adolescence in Today's Psychoanalytic Clinic." Lecture presented at the annual Clinical Days conference, Groupe interdisciplinaire freudien de recherche et d'intervention clinique et culturelle (GIFRIC), New Center for Psychoanalysis, Los Angeles, March 10.

Freud, Sigmund. 1922. *Beyond the Pleasure Principle*. Translated by C. J. M. Hubback. London: International Psycho-Analytical.

Hooper, Tom, dir. 2015. *The Danish Girl*. DVD. Amsterdam: Universal, 2016.

Negligent Analogies

C. RAY BORCK

Trans: Gender and Race in an Age of Unsettled Identities
Rogers Brubaker
Princeton, NJ: Princeton University Press, 2016. 151 pp.

On June 11, 2015, National Association for the Advancement of Colored People chapter president Nkechi Amare Diallo became a brief but significant media sensation when a journalist outed her as a white woman who was secretly living as a black woman.[1] The Diallo story broke ten days after Olympian and reality television star Caitlyn Jenner appeared on the front cover of *Vanity Fair*, having recently come out as transgender. Hours into the Diallo affair, the Twitter hashtag *#transracial* emerged, provoking a cacophonous debate about whether Diallo had anything in common with transgender people. This debate emerged in social media, moved into the blogosphere, and was quickly taken up by more established news sources. The hype ended six days later when then twenty-one-year-old white supremacist Dylann Roof entered a black church in Charleston, South Carolina, to shoot and kill nine people in his self-described effort to start a race war.

Sociologist Rogers Brubaker takes the Diallo/Jenner affair as his point of departure in *Trans: Gender and Race in an Age of Unsettled Identities*, which seriously considers the question of similarities and differences between *transgender* and *transrace*. In two parts, five chapters, and 151 pages, Brubaker maps the terrain of the Diallo/Jenner comparisons, describing the range of arguments that emerged during the summer of 2015, a period he calls "the trans moment" (13). His primary theoretical intervention, "thinking with trans," describes a practice of applying concepts developed within the field of (trans)gender studies to an analysis of race and ethnicity in the United States, in order to draw comparisons between gender and race as identity categories.

TSQ: Transgender Studies Quarterly ∗ Volume 4, Numbers 3–4 ∗ November 2017   **679**
DOI 10.1215/23289252-4190064   © 2017 Duke University Press

Part 1 of the book includes the first two chapters, "Transgender, Transracial?" and "Categories in Flux." Chapter 1 chronicles the discursive proliferation generated by the Diallo/Jenner media frenzy. Brubaker distills the debates into two questions: "Can one legitimately change one's gender? Can one legitimately change one's race?" (9). He taxonomizes emergent perspectives, giving examples of various "essentialist" (viewing gender and/or race as given, fixed, unchangeable) and what he terms "voluntarist" (the perspective that one should be free to "voluntarily" change their race or gender) perspectives regarding both gender and racial identities. He uses these examples to show how gender and race are differently defined, operationalized, and deployed in order to rationalize, normalize, and legitimate various gender and racial identities, practices, and embodiments. He goes on to argue in the second chapter that gender identification, embodiment, and presentation have recently become more diverse, thus "throwing into question basic identity categories." Citing examples of gender nonnormativity (such as gender-transgressive adornment, third-gender designations, and increasing visibility of transgender people), he argues that identity itself is "unsettled" and "in flux" (40–41).

Part 2 of the book is devoted to developing Brubaker's primary intervention, "thinking with trans." For Brubaker, transgender identities, embodiments, and practices can map onto experiences of racialization and racial identity as forms of productive analogy. Brubaker distinguishes three modes of "thinking with trans" and dedicates a chapter to each, titled "The Trans of Migration," "The Trans of Between," and "The Trans of Beyond." Each mode uses a different type of trans identity (in short and correspondingly: transsexuals, androgynous people, and nonbinary people) as an analytical tool for understanding various racial situations. The "trans of migration" is exemplified by those who surgically and hormonally transform their bodies and formally change their legal identities (72). Brubaker conceptualizes this type of gender transition as "gender migration" and likens it to racialized experiences of geographic migration: "Immigrants may seek to be perceived as similar, to blend in and pass for native. In the same way, gender migrants can seek to pass as unmarked, cis men or women" (77). "The trans of between" is exemplified by androgyny (94). Brubaker compares cross-dressing, drag, and genderqueer presentations to "intermediate racial categories like 'mulatto,' 'quadroon,' and 'octoroon'" (104), arguing that just as people can identify as something "between" female and male, so too can biracial people identify "between" black and white. Finally, Brubaker turns to "the trans of beyond," typified by people who identify as simply trans (rather than cis), as nonbinary, or as genderless, to pose the possibility of a forthcoming postgender, postracial society, arguing that gender and race are weakening as categories of social organization and sources of subjectivity (129).

In his preface, Brubaker describes *Trans* as "an essay in trespassing," admitting that he is new to transgender studies and race studies: "My previous work has touched only glancingly on gender and not at all on transgender issues . . . [and] has not been centrally concerned with race per se" (xi). A professor of sociology at the University of California, Los Angeles, since 1994, his areas of specialization are described on his faculty webpage as "social theory, immigration, citizenship, nationalism, and ethnicity" (Brubaker 2017). In addition to *Trans*, Brubaker has published eight books, which address some combination of the themes of rationality, religion, nationalism, citizenship, immigration, and ethnicity. For *Trans*, he stepped out of his wheelhouse.

And it shows. In the remainder of this review, I address some of the conceptual, methodological, and analytic problems that arise when *transgender* and *transrace* are operationalized and juxtaposed as analogous identities. Brubaker is onto something with his claim that he is trespassing. His tolerance for and interest in the conceptual equation of *transgender* and *transrace* expose his neophyte status in critical gender and race studies. He acknowledges at the outset that his previous scholarship has not been centrally concerned with race, that he is an outsider to the field of gender studies, and that he has no personal experience with crossing gender or racial boundaries, saying that his analysis "is no doubt shaped and limited by my own identity as a white cisgender male" (xi).

But it is not because of Brubaker's identity that *Trans* falls short; it's because of his lack of familiarity with trans, queer, and critical race studies, which influences his research questions and methods. This lack of expertise is what allowed him to approach the Twitter-induced question of "transrace"—an Internet fantasy, not a lived identity—with a degree of genuine curiosity. Unfortunately, Brubaker's commitment to framing gender and race as analogous repeatedly leads him to their least common denominator. There are some base, rudimentary comparisons that can be made between gender and race—as between *any* two identity categories—but they don't take us very far in terms of understanding either. It is not useful to venture too far down the path of comparing concepts like gender and race as though they are apples and apples—ahistorical variables plucked from thin air. These concepts work differently as categories of analysis, systems of dominance and oppression, occasions for unequal distributions of power, locations of community and empowerment, and individual subjectivities. Their conceptual applications are so overdetermined that it is impossible to hold them in comparison without first producing a number of oversimplifications and erasures by operationalizing them so narrowly that a detrimental amount of conceptual, historical, and political weight is lost. Ultimately, therefore, Brubaker's analogies can't help but have a shallowing effect that conceals history, mutes difference, and ignores politics.[2]

Moreover, from a sociological point of view, Brubaker's approach lacks methodological rigor. Does *transgender* provide a useful conceptual lens through which to gaze at various racial identities? No. Sociologists typically go to great lengths to develop their research questions, which are informed by the literature, history, and data. There are countless ways to build thoughtful, responsible, careful studies and analyses of social identities, their meaning and import for individuals, their constructedness, evolution, and contingency as social categories within myriad contexts and milieus. But Brubaker hasn't done this. Rather, he has taken the application of Jenner's gender to Diallo's race that resulted in the fictional "transrace" and has conceptually tethered *transgender* and *transrace* throughout the text. Mainstream media outlets asked: if someone could legitimately change their gender, why couldn't someone legitimately change their race (see for example, Pérez-Peña 2015; Rich 2015)? Rather than expose the assumptions that such questions take for granted or the ideologies they reproduce, Brubaker takes up these questions as self-evidently worthwhile.

Media representations of individual experiences of identity are not good places to begin if the goal is to produce sociological analyses of the meanings, import, and significance of gender or race in the United States. There are as many personal stories of identity—any identity: gender identity and racial identity, but also sexual orientation, parental status, age, (dis)ability status, religion, ethnicity, and so on—as there are individuals. Any individual conceptualization of one's identity (in any category) will reveal itself to be inadequate when used to try to understand a larger population, and certainly when applied to questions about how classificatory schemes like gender or race work to stratify societies.

Anything that Nkechi Amare Diallo or Caitlyn Jenner (or anyone else for that matter) says about their subjective identity is "true" insofar as it is their individual experience and personal narrative. But this has little to no bearing on what is true about transgender people or black people or white people or any other population. That's not how sociological analysis works. Populations do not typically become populations because groups of people with common identities come together of their own volition. Populations become populations because they have been grouped, marginalized, or privileged by some set of discriminatory social processes.

Further, Brubaker's juxtaposition of *transgender* and *transrace* truly confuses more than it clarifies—a bit like explaining apples in terms of avocados. The most glaring problem with the pairing is the fact that there are no "transrace" people.[3] There is no "transrace" population. It might well be of sociological interest if white people began transitioning to black people (a concern for some, generated by Diallo's sometimes passing as black), but there are no documented cases of individuals attempting to "transition" their race in a manner analogous to how some trans people transition their genders. However, there *are* transgender people, with countless gender practices and expressions, and there is a transgender population, characterized by social, political, and economic vulnerability. Thus, Brubaker's book begins by comparing an imagined identity and population to a real identity and population, entirely avoiding the fact that conceptually operationalizing "transgender" as identity or as population will garner quite different questions, analyses, and conclusions.

Princeton University Press's webpage for the book showcases a review quote by Emma Green (2016) of the *Atlantic*: "The value in Brubaker's book is not in readjudicating old internet battles, but in laying out current conflicts of identity in a public, accessible way; academics have been thinking and talking about the fluidity and fixedness of gender and race for a long time, but their thinking hasn't always been part of mainstream conversations." Green interprets Brubaker's negligent lack of methodological rigor as accessibility. True, Brubaker's impulse is pedagogical—his main argument is that *trans* is useful for "thinking with," particularly when thinking about race—and his arguments are intelligible, if superficial. Further, his book is likely to travel far and wide, thanks to the imprint of such a reputable press and because its claims are simple and easy to digest. When Brubaker describes the ways that people cross gender boundaries as analogous to ways that others cross racial boundaries, many readers are likely to find the analogy reasonable. But it is worrisome that a reader new to thinking about gender or race would come away from the text believing that these two categories are essentially the same type of thing, just operating at different levels of embodiment or sociality. Accordingly, *Trans* ultimately fails to provide readers with the valuable opportunity to think about continuums, crossings, or culture that it promises them.

C. Ray Borck is assistant professor of sociology at Borough of Manhattan Community College, City University of New York. Avoiding specialization, he has published on social science methodology, educational inequality, horizontal pedagogy, and trans identity and politics. He lives in Brooklyn with his dog, Rudy Huxtable, and cat, Tuxedo Mustache.

Notes

1. At the time, Diallo's name was Rachel Dolezal, but news has emerged (at the time of writing) that she has recently changed her name to Nkechi Amare Diallo (Millner 2017). I am including her former name in this endnote for readers who may be aware of Rachel Dolezal but not of the name change.

2. A similar set of problems arise in philosopher Rebecca Tuvel's article "In Defense of Transracialism" (2017), which came to light as this review was turned in for publication.

Tuvel's article sparked widespread outrage in sectors of the feminist academic community, including an open letter signed by over six hundred scholars demanding that *Hypatia*, which published the article, rescind it (alongside other demands about language usage and peer review practices). A majority of *Hypatia's* board of associate editors distributed an open apology. Tuvel's account, which we might also characterize as "an essay in trespassing," is far less careful than Brubaker's (which, as I've been arguing, is itself far from careful). Where Brubaker juxtaposes *transgender* and *transrace* in a "productive analogy," Tuvel makes the argument that the two categories (and their attendant "ethics") operate according to the same logic. Tuvel argues that whatever logics are socially agreed upon to apply to *transgender* must also apply to *transrace*. The obvious problem is that they don't. Tuvel's analysis is screamingly tone-deaf to entire fields of scholarly endeavor, including transgender studies and critical race theory (to name only the two most striking omissions). In Tuvel's case as in Brubaker's, just because it is conceptually possible to cull a logic from the most banal of pop-cultural encounters with *transgender* and apply it to a sociologically nonexistent thing called *transrace* doesn't mean that doing so produces any kind of knowledge illuminating actual gendered or raced lives, histories, material realities, or political implications. Such is deeply saddening, if not enraging, for those feminist sociologists and feminist philosophers whose primary work is to apprehend, complicate, and/or politicize questions of identity.

3.   Since the original drafting of this essay, Nkechi Amare Diallo (who has also continued to use the name Rachel Dolezal) has self-identified as transrace. Thus, for those who accept Diallo/Dolezal's self-identification (of which there appear to be few), there is one transrace person that we know of so far: n = 1. Even if we are in a moment in which *transrace* is emerging as an identity category that individuals claim, I maintain that our best methods for understanding what it is or means will not be best produced by taking *transgender* as the point of departure or comparison.

References

Brubaker, Rogers. 2017. "Rogers Brubaker." www.sscnet.ucla.edu/soc/faculty/brubaker/ (accessed March 5, 2017).

Green, Emma. 2016. "If Americans Can Be Transgender, Can They Be Transracial?" *Atlantic*, October 2. www.theatlantic.com/politics/archive/2016/10/trans-brubaker-race-gender /502397/.

Millner, Denene. 2017. "Why Rachel Dolezal Can Never Be Black." *National Public Radio*, March 3. www.npr.org/sections/codeswitch/2017/03/03/518184030/why-rachel-dolezal-can-never -be-black.

Pérez-Peña, Richard. 2015. "Black or White? Woman's Story Stirs Up a Furor." *New York Times*, June 12. www.nytimes.com/2015/06/13/us/rachel-dolezal-naacp-president-accused-of-lying -about-her-race.html.

Rich, Camille Gear. 2015. "Rachel Dolezal Has a Right to Be Black." Cable News Network (CNN), June 16. www.cnn.com/2015/06/15/opinions/rich-rachel-dolezal/.

Tuvel, Rebecca. 2017. "In Defense of Transracialism." *Hypatia* 32, no. 2: 263–78.

JOURNAL OF THE

HISTORY

OF

SEXUALITY

Volume 26 Number 2
May 2017

UNIVERSITY OF TEXAS PRESS

Post Office Box 7819, Austin, Texas 78713-7819
P: 512.471.7233 | F: 512.232.7178 | journals@utpress.utexas.edu
UTPRESS.UTEXAS.EDU

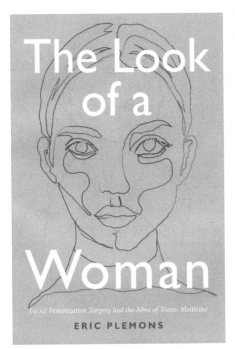